Field methods in ARCHAEOLOGY

6TH EDITION

Thomas R. Hester
Robert F. Heizer
John A. Graham

MAYFIELD PUBLISHING COMPANY

Library of Congress Catalog Card Number: 74-33732
International Standard Book Number: 0-87484-323-5

Manufactured in the United States of America

Mayfield Publishing Company
285 Hamilton Avenue, Palo Alto, California 94301

This book was set in Zenith and Elegante by Applied Typographic
Systems and was printed and bound by Banta West. Sponsoring editor
was C. Lansing Hays, Carole Norton supervised editing, and manu-
script editing was done by Autumn Stanley and Liselotte Hofmann.
Michelle Hogan supervised production, and the text and cover were
designed by Nancy Sears. Cover photograph by Roloff Beny from his
book *A Time of Gods*, published by Thames & Hudson, London.

CONTENTS

PREFACE

This volume bears little resemblance to its ancestor, which was first published in 1949 as a spiral-bound workbook of just under 40,000 words with a reference bibliography of 275 items. It has been revised five times and has grown, over the years, to its present size, roughly four times as large as the first edition.

The authors of the original chapters were a group of fifteen graduate and undergraduate students in the Department of Anthropology at Berkeley. It might be interesting to see what has happened to these original participants, many of them veterans of the recently concluded Second World War, in the intervening 25 years. Only one has died. Some went on to successful professional careers in archaeology; the rest have found positions as teachers or as appointees in state or federal agencies. All, so far as is known, have maintained their professional commitment to anthropology. We hope that each will approve of the present edition, which is, in a sense, their grandchild.

INTRODUCTION

1

Trace Science then, with Modesty thy guide;
First strip off all her equipage of Pride;
Deduct what is but Vanity, or Dress,
Or Learning's Luxury, or Idleness;
Or tricks to shew the stretch of human brain,
Mere curious pleasure, or ingenious pain;
Expunge the whole, or lop th'excrescent parts
Of all our Vices have created Arts;
Then see how little the remaining sum,
Which serv'd the past, and must the times to come.

      —ALEXANDER POPE, *An Essay on Man*

 This guide has had a long and, we believe, useful history. It has been both commended and criticized. For the praise we have been grateful, and from the criticism we have tried to learn and to improve our presentation. In the late 1940's, when a vigorous program of local archaeology was getting under way at Berkeley, something in the nature of a manual or guide was badly needed for instructional purposes, and a group of interested students cooperated to produce the draft of the first published edition, which ran to seventy-two pages. Subsequent editions and revisions by the original editor corrected errors, added useful information, and updated the references. A major revision was issued in 1967, and now the present revised edition is offered. For this latest edition of the *Guide,* specialists were invited to revise certain chapters: Lewis K. Napton, Chapter 4; Richard E. W. Adams, Chapter 7; Michael B. Collins, Chapter 8; and Alan C. Ziegler, Chapter 9. The other chapters in the book were revised or totally rewritten by us.

    There is nothing very exciting about techniques for recording data during an excavation—one simply has the obligation to record whatever information is there. Becoming aware of what to observe and what to record is, of course, another matter. We hope that students without much field experience will get some ideas about what to look for in an excavation from reading this

1

volume. Excavation can be exciting, sometimes because new and unexpected buried things come to light, more often because the activity of uncovering the past is a highly stimulating experience, and most often because such work constitutes intellectual inquiry of the most lively and challenging kind. Excavation can also be hard work (as it usually is to the hired workers on a dig), but for the real archaeologist, excavation is a challenge to think as hard as possible, see as much as possible, and recover as much meaningful information as possible. Time, weather, and vandals have eliminated so much evidence at many sites that perceptiveness, imagination, and ingenuity are all necessary to get the merest hints of things once obvious, to recognize the subtle residues of once-living cultures. When archaeology is called the re-creation of the past, this refers not to the way arrowpoints or pottery are classified, but to the prehistoric events and ancient situations that are evidenced in some fashion in each shovelful of earth the archaeologist examines.

This *Guide* presents some of the techniques of archaeology. But one cannot learn how to do archaeology by reading this or any other book. Archaeology is excavation, and excavation can be learned only by digging. Furthermore, no one should take the data-record forms presented here as anything more than a suggested minimum of the information that should be recorded. A file of such data sheets does provide a summary of certain basic information on the finds made in an archaeological site, but because each find is different and most finds are very complex, detailed written observations and additional data should be entered in a notebook.

This book, then, is a guide for reference and consultation and an introduction to basic principles. Out of the great mass of published literature, we have cited a wide selection of the relevant items known to us. Serious students are encouraged to look up the publications referred to and read what other workers have done. By reading carefully and critically, examining the evidence presented and the conclusions drawn from that evidence, they will be preparing themselves for their own actual experience in finding and studying archaeological materials. Obviously, we will have missed some things, but we hope we have neither misled the uninitiated nor betrayed to our peers too great an ignorance of published works that trainees should be acquainted with.

We repeat, however, that techniques of excavation, can only be learned by practicing them, and a year of reading about how the archaeologist works will teach a person less than a week at an archaeological site putting these techniques into practice. There now exist a large number of handbooks or guides to archaeological field methods, analysis, and interpretation. Some of these are general handbooks; others are limited to one area. We here cite, without evaluation, a selection of such guides: Albright (1957: 49–64), Atkinson (1953), Bernal (1952), Brennan (1973), Butler (1966), Colton (1953a), Copley (1958), Corcoran (1966), Dittert and Wendorf (1963), Goodwin (1953),

Gorenstein (1965), Hammond (1963), Hranicky (1973), Kenyon (1961), Laming-Emperaire (1963), Meighan (1961), Noël-Hume (1953), Parrot (1953), Pyddoke (1964), Robbins and Irving (1965), Swartz (n.d.), Webster (1963), Wheeler (1954), and Wilford (1954). In the 1958 edition of the present work the reader will find listed (pp. 121–125) a number of older, and for the most part outdated, handbooks.

It is obvious that there is more to archaeology than finding bones and tools once used by the former inhabitants of an area. If the collecting of artifacts, the thrill of discovery, and the satisfying of curiosity were the primary objectives of excavation, then the archaeologist would be no better than the "pot hunter" or vandal who collects for personal gain or private pleasure. The archaeologist digs in order to learn as much as possible about the culture and life style of prehistoric people. The way an excavation is conducted and the completeness with which the evidences of human activity are collected and recorded will be a measure of the archaeologist's high purpose as a student of the past. The excavator can never forget that every site, together with every object and feature contained in it, is unique and that a specimen once extracted can never be seen again in its original context. Photographic and notebook records of an excavation must, therefore, accompany the recovered specimens, and these records should be precise and complete enough so that future prehistorians will find them adequate for their specialized investigations. Like natural resources, archaeological sites are exhaustible, and it is the duty of all excavators to do well whatever they undertake in the way of primary field research.

From W. Taylor's *A Study of Archeology* (1948: 154–156) comes the following excellent statement on the responsibility and objectives of the archaeologist, which we quote at length:

> The archivist and the experimental scientist may with impunity select from their sources those facts which have for them a personal and immediate significance in terms of some special problem. Their libraries and experimental facilities may be expected to endure, so that in the future there may be access to the same or a similar body of data. If, however, it were certain that, after the archivist's first perusal, each document would be utterly and forever destroyed, it would undoubtedly be required of him that he transcribe the entire record rather than just that portion which at the moment interests him. He would have difficulty in justifying his research if, knowingly, he caused the destruction of a unique record for the sake of abstracting only a narrowly selected part.
>
> The gathering of data from archeological sites, in nearly every instance, involves the destruction of the original record. Only to the extent to which that record is transposed to the archeologist's notes is it preserved for study either by the collector himself or by other students. A good axiom for archeologists is that "it is not what you find, but how you find it," and it is superfluous to point out that "how you find it" can be told only from notes and not specimens. An archeological find is only as good as the notes upon it. Therefore only one objective can be sanctioned with regard to the actual excavation

of archeological sites: that of securing the most complete record possible, not only of those details which are of interest to the collector, but of the entire geographic and human environment. That which is not recorded is most often entirely lost. In such a situation, selection implies wanton waste. . . . Within his broadly given cultural and geographic universe, the archeologist is a technician concerned with the production of data, and, although he should be aware of the concepts and goals of many disciplines, he should not be restricted in his exploitation of the site by the dictates of any of them. Time will come in his study and analysis when these factors will again assume the major role, but when he puts spade to ground the archeologist should be dedicated to an exposition unconfined except by the broadest stretch of the cultural and geographic frame of reference. This is what makes archeology a technique and the archeologist, as archeologist, a technician. His particular problems are concerned with the production of data. When he makes use of these data to some purpose, he becomes affiliated with the discipline whose concepts he employs and whose aims he serves.

Likewise, the archeologist is obligated to preserve, whether in publication or some permanent repository, the full body of his empirical data and records. Since he has destroyed the original record, his transcript and the recovered specimens are the only substitute. The archeologist has no more justification in submerging part of the record than he would have had in destroying without record, a part of the original site. Practical considerations, such as space and money, have sometimes been blamed for the failure to preserve the record fully. However valid these factors may be, the extent of their victory over the ideal of full preservation is a measure of the defeat of the very excavations which have been accomplished.

Archaeology is more than that which is prehistoric, more than flint arrowpoints and broken pottery—it is, above all, *a method for the recovery, study, and reconstruction of the past of man*. The measure of any method is its results, and clearly archaeology is still far from its goal of full and accurate recovery of the past. It is incumbent upon every archaeologist to contribute to innovation in techniques of recovering and studying prehistoric cultural materials. To see the dead past in its once-living form is usually possible only within the frame of generalizations so broad as to be practically meaningless. Where the documentary historian can deal with individual persons, particular places, specific events, and finite points in time, and can have opinions, at least, as to the thoughts that impelled the actions of those individuals at one moment in a certain situation, the archaeologist must deal with the results of human actions in the form of anonymous palpable residues that embody human thinking and actions. Thus, the archaeologist thinks not in terms of persons (although he is aware that most items he recovers were made by once-living individuals), but rather of groups or societies who organized life according to patterns of behavior that insured survival by solving the problems of common purposes and needs (Rouse, 1965).

The inability of the archaeologist to reconstruct the past in detail is, of course, largely due to the perishable nature of the greater proportion of culture. Behavior, art, language, religion, objects of wood, leather, fur, and the like have usually completely disappeared (Childe, 1956: 10–13; Braidwood, 1946a), thus largely eliminating the possibility of learning anything of these aspects of the culture of prehistoric peoples. The archaeologist values objects and items not for their intrinsic worth, but as clues to human action—the bits that remain are the available evidence from which the mentality and activities of persons who made and used them must be inferred.

There is no one approved technique of excavation, but rather as many techniques as there are archaeological sites. But all excavations should have certain things in common—care, patience, routine, continual thinking about what is being found, trying to avoid reaching easy conclusions that all too often turn out to be incorrect, and anticipating the kinds of questions that readers of the report on an excavation will want to have answered. The variety of human action, as evidenced in the form of archaeological sites and their contents, is so great that no reasonable amount of space could be found to try to inform the student about how to excavate each of the kinds of sites which exist.

This book attempts only to introduce the inexperienced but interested student to some of the basic principles of securing archaeological data. It does not presume to set out any rigorous procedures for investigating such varied sites as a Maya ruin in the Peten jungle of Guatemala; an open camp-site in the Canadian prairie; a dry cave site in Nevada; a Southwestern cliff-house; a frozen refuse deposit on St. Lawrence Island, Alaska; a shell-mound village site in Tierra del Fuego; a Paleolithic camp-workshop in Rhodesia or southern France; a Bronze Age megalithic tomb (dolmen) in western France; or any of the literally hundreds of other kinds of sites.

This book takes for granted the fact of prehistory and the method for its study which is archaeology. But that fact and this method have not always been known, and any serious student should take the trouble to learn something about how people came to understand that they had a past and how they learned to recover the facts of prehistory. The student can begin with the following; Ceram (1958), Daniel (1943, 1950, 1962a, 1966), Eydoux (1968), Greene (1959), Griffin (1959), Heizer (1962), Laming-Emperaire (1964), Lynch and Lynch (1968), Oakley (1964b), Peake (1940), Rowe (1965), and Toulmin and Goodfield (1965). The references in these works will lead naturally into the details of the history of archaeology.

A word should perhaps be said here about the special problems of American archaeology, which is the focus of much of this book.

The great purpose of archaeology is to help create a sense of the unity of mankind, something that will come from general awareness of common origins. This in turn will come from the piecing together of the long and intricate history of human migration and the cultural changes in human groups from millenium to millenium. An aware and interested public has slowly been developing in the United States. This has been good from the standpoint of landowners' receptiveness to excavations, public funding for archaeology, preservation of certain sites, and the like. However, it has also meant that many untrained people have become interested, through the public press, in archaeology, and have decided to take it up as a recreational pursuit. The result is wholesale depredation and destruction of information by these untrained collectors. Curbing the public appetite to dig and collect for recreation is one of the greatest challenges facing American archaeology today. It is generally agreed that legal prohibitions against despoiling archaeological sites on public lands have been ineffectual. We need either better enforcement of existing laws or more effective public education.

American archaeology deals for the most part with aboriginal cultures, but there is no cultural communion or continuity between these and post-1492 Caucasian culture. Where European archaeology, for example, serves to illuminate the prehistory of the modern peoples, the detachment between prehistoric aboriginal and historic Caucasian cultures in the New World does not permit such identification. Further, for American archaeologists now being trained there can be little hope of achieving firsthand knowledge about American Indians. Forty years ago, North American Indian ethnology was still a fairly important field of investigation, but from now on, American archaeologists will be studying the prehistory of peoples known to them primarily through museum specimens and published historical and ethnographic accounts. All archaeologists should try to secure some firsthand acquaintance with a living primitive group since this will help them to visualize the American Indians' vanished way of life.

GOALS AND APPROACHES IN ARCHAEOLOGY

2

The trend of all knowledge at the present is to specialize, but archaeology has in it all the qualities that call for the wide view of the human race, of its growth from the savage to the civilized, which is seen in all stages of social and religious developments. Archaeology is the study of humanity itself, and unless that attitude toward the subject is kept in mind archaeology will be overwhelmed by impossible theories or a welter of flint chips.

—MARGARET MURRAY

 Although archaeology is a comparatively young discipline, the goals and approaches of its practitioners have undergone many changes. At the conclusion of Chapter 1, we listed several publications dealing with the history of archaeology; the volumes by Heizer (1962) and Daniel (1950, 1962a, 1966) are particularly instructive reviews of archaeology's early development. Additionally, several studies of the rise of archaeology in North America have been published in recent years, including the works of Ceram (1971), Fitting (1973b), Schuyler (1971), Willey (1974), and Willey and Sabloff (1974). The Willey and Sabloff book outlines the major periods and paradigms of archaeological research in the New World; similar surveys, on a regional basis, of changing research goals have been published by Hester (1973:3-5), and Longacre (1970b). Students may also find of interest several papers (Clewlow, 1970; Graham and Heizer, 1967; Wilmsen, 1965) dealing with the historical development of "Early Man" studies in the New World.

Five major periods can be distinguished in New World archaeology alone, each with its own set of goals (see Willey and Sabloff, 1974). First came the *Speculative Period* (1492–1840), so called for obvious reasons. The overwhelming concern in this era with the origins of the American Indians was expressed more in speculative attempts to fit these puzzling people into what was known of ancient history than in what we would now call fieldwork. Nevertheless, archaeological exploration began, and publications by Jefferson, Barton, Kingsborough, and others appeared.

Next came what Willey and Sabloff have called the *Classificatory-Descriptive Period* (1840–1914), marked by rudimentary description and classification of archaeological remains, the mound research of Squier and Davis in the 1840's, the rising influence of archaeologists at the United States National Museum (W. H. Holmes) and at the Peabody Museum (G. W. Putnam). The first systematic stratigraphic excavations were carried out in North America by Nels Nelson in New Mexico in 1914.

Third came the *Classificatory-Historical Period: Concern with Chronology* (1914–1940), characterized by further refinement of the stratigraphic method (especially in the American Southwest), and the use of this technique, along with seriation (see p. 272), typology (see p. 273), and the direct historical approach, in efforts to reconstruct culture history in chronological sequence. In the second *Classificatory-Historical Period: Concern with Context and Function* (1940–1960), although there was a continued attention to chronology and culture history, archaeologists began to explore certain anthropological aspects of archaeology, including the inference of behavioral data from artifactual associations, settlement patterns, and cultural ecology.

Fifth and thus far last is the *Explanatory Period* (1960–), a period that has seen the rise of the "new archaeology" (as contrasted with the "old" or "traditional" archaeology of the Classificatory-Historical periods) and of concern with cultural process, implementation of the systems approach to archaeological research, and a greater dependence on scientific method (i.e., the formulation and testing of hypotheses, the use of deductive reasoning, and so forth).

The last decade in American archaeology has been dominated by the "new archaeology," with its explicitly stated aim of altering the course—and thus obviously the goals and approaches—of archaeological research. This new archaeology is usually said to stem from the writings of L. Binford (1962, 1964, 1968), with theoretical underpinnings largely derived from W. W. Taylor's (1948) "conjunctive approach" (see Sabloff, Beale, and Kurland, 1973: 104), and echoes of the earlier writings of European archaeologists such as Grahame Clark and V. Gordon Childe.

Even its most ardent proponents have a hard time defining the new archaeology succinctly; but we can say that it is problem-oriented, emphasizes research design (systematically formulating research goals and methods of attacking them before undertaking an excavation), and seeks to explain cultural change by the scientific procedure of formulating hypotheses and then testing them. Thus, the new approach is concerned with "processual archaeology" rather than just "culture history," with "systemic" as opposed to "normative" views of culture, and with distinguishing clearly between "particularistic" and "nomothetic" (generalizing) approaches. Clearly, the new archaeology represents a drastic—even revolutionary—change in the goals of archaeology, although at least one writer has debated with himself as to whether this revolution is over (Leone, 1971) or just beginning (Leone, 1972b).

Of the impressive number of essays and books devoted to the new archaeology, we have selected only a few: Binford (1962, 1964, 1965, 1968), Binford and Binford (1968); Clarke (1973); Flannery (1967, 1973); Fritz and Plog (1970); Harriss (1971); Hill (1968); Hole and Heizer (1973:31–39), Kushner (1970), Leone (1972a, 1972b), Longacre (1964, 1970a), Martin (1971), Redman (1973b), Sabloff, Beale, and Kurland (1973), Struever (1968b, 1968c, 1971), Taylor (1972), Watson (1973), and Watson, LeBlanc, and Redman (1971).

There are, of course, other views as to what the present goals of archaeology should be, which often conflict with goals espoused by the new archaeology (Chang, 1967; Hawkes, 1968; Trigger, 1970), and there have been several studies and reviews that either heavily criticize the philosophical and theoretical approaches of the new archaeology or point out certain problems and shortcomings in its application (e.g., Bayard, 1969; Chenhall, 1971; Johnson, 1972; Morgan, 1973; Tuggle, 1972).

Although there are still many divergent viewpoints on the ultimate goals of archaeology, there seems to be fair agreement on three major aims: (1) *reconstruction of culture history;* (2) *reconstruction of past lifeways;* (3) *the study of cultural process* (Binford, 1968: 8–16; Leone, 1972b: 25; Thomas, 1974: 3–4). In many archaeological research designs, these three goals can be viewed as steps in a single process (Deetz, 1970: 116). The *building of a sound chronology* would probably be added as (4) here except that chronological frameworks had become an obsession in many earlier archaeological research projects, and this obsession has been attacked by some "new" archaeologists. In disrepute or not, chronology-building remains a prerequisite for attacking the more complex problems of prehistory (Hester, 1973; Lamberg-Karlovsky, 1970; Thomas, 1974).

The three major goals just mentioned are being pursued in a variety of ways. In fact, perhaps the best way to give some idea of the specific goals of contemporary archaeology is to sketch some of the different kinds of archaeological inquiry going forward at the present time. As Lamberg-Karlovsky (1970: 11) has written, "The aims of archeology are . . . equal to the sum of the aims of archeologists and prehistorians at any one time." And the aims of a fair number of archaeologists and prehistorians just now seem to be shaped by systems theory (cf. Clarke, 1968; Flannery, 1968; Hole and Heizer, 1973)—specifically, using the concepts of General System Theory to study adaptation and adaptive changes in prehistoric cultures (see Hole and Heizer, 1973: 439 ff.). Published studies of major cultural subsystems are very numerous presently, especially studies of settlement and subsistence. Analysis of settlement systems has borrowed heavily from the investigative methods of geographers ("locational analysis"); Chang (1972) has reviewed the status of settlement studies, listing many of the important publications in this line of investigation (see also the papers published in the volume edited by Ucko, Tringham, and Dimbleby, 1972). Subsistence systems—societies' means of feeding themselves—have been elucidated through studies of faunal remains, human fecal remains, and other dietary evidence.

Much emphasis has also been placed on reconstructing patterns in the exploitation of resources and learning whether sites were occupied seasonally or not (Chaplin, 1971; Freeman, 1973; Isaac, 1971; Uerpmann, 1973). Interest in prehistoric or early historic trade and other forms of intercultural contact has revived, stimulated in large part by the application of physicochemical analysis of artifacts. Such research has aided in reconstructing patterns of trade in the Near East and in Mesoamerica (Cobean et al., 1971; Dixon, Cann, and Renfrew, 1968; Hester, Heizer, and Jack, 1971).

Some archaeologists are trying to gather information on prehistoric social organization and systems of residence and descent. There are many problems in such research (cf. Allen and Richardson, 1971), and the best results have been obtained in areas like the American Southwest where archaeologists can benefit from ethnographic analogy (for some recent useful comments on the role of ethnographic analogy in archaeology, see Anderson, 1969). Realizing that many existing ethnographies lack certain information needed for their research, some archaeologists have initiated "ethnoarchaeological" studies of contemporary primitive cultures and technologies and even of modern communities* (some recent publications in ethnoarchaeology include Ascher, 1968; Bonnichsen, 1973a; J. D. Clark, 1969: Pls. 7, 8; Gould, 1968a, 1968b; Reid, Rathje, and Schiffer, 1974; Stanislawski, 1969; Thomas, 1974; White, 1967).

Replicative experiments—repeating or attempting to repeat the technical achievements of primitive peoples, using their tools and methods—have also assumed a new importance in providing data on which to base archaeological inferences (see Chapter 11, and the bibliography of experimental research published by Hester and Heizer, 1973b). Many of the replicative experiments have been done in the field of lithic (stoneworking) technology, the work of François Bordes and Don E. Crabtree with stone axes and other tools and weapons being the most widely known. Lithic research has also included analysis of debitage (debris from making stone tools or weapons), manufacturing technology, raw materials, microscopic wear patterns, and so on.

In conclusion, we merely mention several other kinds of research, such as ecosystem analysis (Zubrow, 1971), analysis of burial patterns (Brown,

---

*In 1972 the authors conducted ethnoarchaeological (or "ethnotechnological") studies of an Upper Egyptian workshop manufacturing alabaster vases. Techniques similar to those of Old Kingdom times are still used there, as Figure 2-1 shows.

2-1. *Ethnoarchaeological research. Photographs taken in 1972 during the study and documentation of a workshop manufacturing alabaster vases at Gurna (Thebes), Upper Egypt. Left: workshop scene. Below: using a brace-and-bit drill to bore the interior of a vase.*

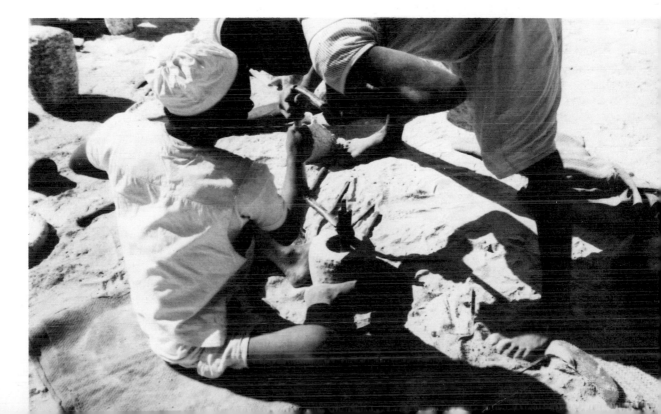

1971), demographic studies (Phillips, 1972), investigation into the collapse of Mayan civilization (Culbert, 1973), and astroarchaeology (Hatch, 1971; Aveni and Linsley, 1972; Baity, 1973).

We point out to the student beginning in archaeology that broad success in any one of the goals of this discipline may demand large, costly, interdisciplinary research programs like those mounted by R. S. MacNeish in the Tehuacan Valley of Mexico and the Ayacucho area of Peru. Statistical analysis and computers will almost certainly be needed for processing raw data (Chenhall, 1967; Longacre, 1970a: 132–135; Tite, 1972: 4–5; Tugby, 1965; Woodall, 1968).

The specific aims of archaeology may differ from one period to another, and a new archaeology will inevitably give way to a newer archaeology, but the student still must have certain basic knowledge about prehistoric research, and this includes the methods of field archaeology. The present book is intended to provide that basic knowledge. It cannot be used as a "cookbook," containing specific recipes for any given archaeological site. Rather, it is, as its title indicates, a general guide to field methods that must be adapted to specific sites.

SITE SURVEY

3

INTRODUCTION

An archaeological site is usually the scene of past human activity. It may be marked by the scanty remnants of a brief encampment, or by the abundant remains of a settled village. A site may consist of a quarry, a trail, a burial place, a shrine, or a station where game was killed and perhaps butchered. Or a site may be just a single boulder with petroglyphs or pictographs on it. Some archaeological sites are places where human remains or artifacts have been secondarily deposited, as by a river in the silts or fluvial gravels of a terrace. Even though human agency was not involved here, the find-spot is nevertheless most conveniently labeled as a site. If a site shows evidence of repeated occupation or use, it is still considered a single site, but various levels or periods of use may be distinguished within it. (For a discussion of various kinds of archaeological sites see Hole and Heizer 1973: 111–133.)

A systematic site survey is the logical way to begin investigating the archaeology of a given region. Such a survey should locate as many of the area's archaeological sites as possible, assess their nature and importance by surface examination and collection of associated artifacts, and leave behind an adequate record for future investigators. A properly executed survey will provide data for a preliminary characterization of the region's archaeology. Only from such data can an excavator plan and undertake a scientifically justifiable program of archaeological excavations within the region. Salvage excavations, of course, are an exception here.

The complexity of the archaeological remains and their vegetative covering, and the time and money available, are the principal factors determining the extent of surface recording to be done during a preliminary survey of this kind. In general, it may be said that except for very large ruins with several standing buildings or monuments, a general survey would be expected to record all of the observable data relevant to archaeological interests. When this is achieved, it may well be found that the survey in itself has provided information that will help to answer special problems in demography, cultural ecology, and similar fields. For example, there might result a study of the relationship between occupation sites and any one of such economically important features of the natural environment as streams, tillable land, oak groves, mussel rocks, oyster beds, and so forth. Such a study could not have been made before there was abundant and precise information on site locations and related features of the environment.

Aside from the reason just discussed, the commonest reasons for undertaking an archaeological survey are: (1) to locate sites as part of a salvage effort in a reservoir basin or in the right-of-ways of pipelines and highways; (2) to locate sites and obtain information relevant to specific problems previously formulated in a study of a region's prehistoric remains. See Ruppe (1966) for other reasons. Whatever the reason a survey is being conducted, those conducting it will usually try to (1) describe accurately the number and types of sites in the survey region; (2) analyze collected data as fully as possible and draw conclusions relevant to cultural process; and (3) delineate hypotheses to guide future research (Judge 1973: 319).

The literature on archaeological surveys is extensive, and thus the student should have little difficulty in learning what kinds of surveys have been done and in comparing the various approaches used in doing them. We provide a few selected references: *regional surveys:* Beals, Brainerd, and Smith (1945), Braidwood (1937), Clewlow (1968), Colton (1932), Drucker (1943a, 1953), Fisher (1930), Kelley, Campbell, and Lehmer (1940), Longacre (1962), MacNeish (1958), Shutler (1961), Steward (1941), Tuohy (1963); *state surveys:* Sayles (1935), Webb and Funkhouser (1932); *salvage and contract surveys of national parks, reservoir basins, and river drainages:* Petsche (1968) has prepared a comprehensive bibliography pertaining to such activities in the United States; other references that can profitably be consulted include Bennyhoff (1956), Dittert, Hester, and Eddy (1961), Graham and Davis (1958), Hayes (1964), Shafer (1971a), Taylor and Gonzales Rul (1961), Wendorf (1968); *settlement pattern surveys:* Anderson (1973), Bullard (1960), Gumerman (1971), Hester and Hobler (1969), Judge (1973), Willey (1953); *architectural surveys:* Pollock (1931–1940); *epigraphic survey:* Morley (1937–1938); *ceramic-seriational surveys* (aimed at establishing ceramic chronology in an area): Aten and Bollich (1969), Ford (1936), Ford and Willey (1949), Phillips, Ford, and Griffin (1951), Tolstoy (1958); *pictograph and petroglyph surveys:* Heizer and Baumhoff (1962), Jackson (1938), Roefer, English, and Lothson (1973), Schaafsma (1963). There is also a considerable body of literature specifically devoted to the *methods used in archaeological surveys:* Atkinson (1953), Colton (1953a), Crawford (1953), Dibble (1971), Dittert and Wendorf (1963), Gumerman (1971), Hayes (1964), Hester and Hobler (1969), Johnson (1963), Nunley and Hester (1966), Redman (1973a), Ruppe (1966), Sisson (1973), Stewart (1947a, 1947b), Struever (1968c), Swanson (1963), Wasley (1957), Wissler (1923).

It has been suggested that archaeological surveys will yield the most meaningful results if they are done on a regional basis and if other methods of locating sites are backed up by a system of probability sampling (cf. Binford, 1964; Thomas, 1969b, 1974; see also Chapter 15 below). The work of Judge (1973) provides an example of such an approach. For his survey of Paleo-Indian occupation in the central Rio Grande Valley of New Mexico, Judge developed a procedure he termed "site pattern recognition," whereby he analyzed topographic variables present at known sites in order to discover the criteria used by the local Paleo-Indian population in selecting their camp-sites. (A somewhat similar approach has been suggested by Butzer, 1971: 237–238.) Then he studied aerial photographs and topographic maps and, using his hypothetical criteria, pinpointed potentially suitable areas. These areas of the survey region were then intensively surveyed, with excellent results. To eliminate bias, additional areas were selected on the basis of probability sampling, and these areas, too, were thoroughly surveyed. In comparing the two techniques of survey, Judge (1973: 53) has commented:

> In retrospect, it is possible to check the effectiveness of the site pattern recognition technique based on the results of random sampling. In the 29 randomly selected grids, a total of 16 Paleoindian occupational loci were recorded. Since the 29 grids represent 20% of the population universe, one would expect to find a total of 80 occupational loci in the survey area. Actually a total of 59 were found by the site pattern recognition method. This is 74% of the presumed total and represents, I feel, a sample sufficient to permit reliable generalization.

CONDUCTING AN ARCHAEOLOGICAL SURVEY

Site survey was once considered a non-destructive activity, since no digging was usually done, and only surface materials were picked up during the course of the fieldwork. Thus, surveying sites was deemed a good way of keeping amateur archaeologists and students occupied. Surveys of this sort usually resulted in selective collecting of artifacts, most often projectile points and other finished tools. However, it has become increasingly apparent that selective, uncontrolled surface collecting can destroy meaningful patterning of surface materials. Site surveys, then, should not be a haphazard affair or busy-work for archaeological novices. Like excavation, survey necessitates advance planning, proper methods and controls, and discipline in its execution.

In preparing for a site survey of a given region, the archaeologist should first become familiar with all previous archaeological work in the area. (If no previous work has been done in the survey area, then the archaeological literature for neighboring regions must be consulted.) In addition to the published reports the archaeologist should also consult unpublished site records and field notes on file at local or state museums or college and university departments of anthropology. Both characteristic and uncharacteristic or unusual features and artifacts should be carefully noted so that the archaeologist may be alert to them in the course of the survey. In this way, he or she will become aware of site and culture classifications previously devised for the region, special problems or gaps in the archaeological picture, and the current status of archaeological knowledge about the region in general.

In addition to the archaeological literature, the archaeologist should also study the results of ethnographic work in the area. In many parts of the United States, local Indian groups have been the object of detailed study that provides good insight into the nature of the historic Indian culture of the area. These reports usually locate and identify Indian villages occupied within historic times, many of which are now archaeological sites. Local and county histories also often provide information on the location of Indian sites. Even place-names can sometimes provide important clues (Wainwright, 1962).

Another major source of preliminary information for archaeological survey is the local amateur historian or archaeologist. The local amateur archaeological society should also be contacted. Its members will know of sites in the area and will often be enthusiastic about fieldwork and the chance to get training in scientific survey methods. When such people can be enlisted they are invaluable, not only for what they can tell, but for their local contacts. An integral part of any archaeological survey is describing and illustrating local collections of archaeological materials that these people often have or know of (see Part E, about recording local collections). Such collections sometimes give a clue to the variety, type, and quantity of material to be expected when excavation begins. The county, school, or municipal museum, where isolated finds are often deposited, occasionally offers a useful sampling of local material.

Another important preparation for the projected survey is the acquisition and careful study of maps of the area. A good, detailed map of large scale is necessary for the accurate plotting of sites located during the survey. Unfortunately, there is no single series of adequate maps covering the entire United States. Perhaps the most useful series, where available, is the quadrangle topographic map series of the United States Geological Survey (USGS), varying in scale from 1:24,000 to 1:250,000. These maps are often available from engineering and surveying offices, sporting goods shops, and bookstores in the larger cities. Otherwise, they can be ordered from the Office of Map Information, U.S. Geological Survey, Washington, D.C., or, for states west of the Mississippi, from the U.S. Geological Survey, Denver, Colorado. State index maps and information on ordering maps can also be obtained from these two offices.

Maps of the World Aeronautical Chart Series (1:1,000,000) and the United States Air Force Pilotage Chart Series (1:500,000) are also useful although the scales are too small for detailed field use; an index of these maps is available from The Director, Coast and Geodetic Survey, U.S. Department of Commerce, Washington, D.C.

Other useful kinds of maps include the following: U.S. Forest Service maps (for areas within national forests); local and county highway maps, usually available from a state highway office in a county seat; U.S. Army Corps of Engineers and Bureau of Reclamation maps, prepared for local areas in advance of engineering and construction projects (for obvious reasons often used in salvage archaeology surveys); soil maps of the Bureau of Soils, U.S. Department of Agriculture, Washington, D.C.; and state geological maps (see Gray, 1961, for a complete listing).

Good aerial photographs of an area can be important adjuncts to topographic and other maps. Photographs show specific natural and other features, including, at times, archaeological sites. Dual photographs, viewed with a stereoscope, give best results. A series of aerial photographs covering much of the United States is available from the U.S. Soil Conservation Service, Department of Agriculture, Washington, D.C., or from district offices usually located in the county seat. The inexpensive photomaps of the Soil Conservation Services's soil-survey reports are sometimes useful (Saucier, 1966). The best source of general information on the various aerial map series is the Map Information Office, Federal Board of Surveys and Maps, North Interior Department Building, Washington, D.C. Miller (1957: 61) has provided a source list of aerial photographs.

Aerial photographs taken at different times of the year and with the sun low on the horizon can sometimes reveal important features of archaeological sites (Atkinson, 1953; Chevallier, 1964; Miller, 1957; Porter, 1965; St. Joseph, 1966; and, Solecki, 1957) or previously unknown phenomena (Strandberg and Tomlinson, 1969). For a historical review of the use of aerial photography in archaeology, see L. Deuel (1969). A more sophisticated application of aerial photography has come with the use of infrared photography (Atkins,

1972; Gumerman and Lyons, 1971; Gumerman and Neely, 1972; Hammond, 1971). Gumerman and Neely (1972) demonstrated the application of this technique in site survey work in the Tehuacan Valley of Mexico. Although their test of infrared aerial photography was not productive in terms of locating sites, it was valuable in delineating environmental features. Schaber and Gumerman (1969) discovered previously undetected prehistoric agricultural plots in north-central Arizona by using thermal infrared scanning imagery.

It should also be mentioned here that low-flying light aircraft (often available for hire by the hour) have sometimes been used for locating sites during archaeological surveys. The method can be especially valuable in areas of rough terrain, but its usefulness depends, naturally, on the plant cover and the visible characteristics of an area's sites.

The ultimate source of information for the archaeological site survey is the actual physical inspection of the terrain by the field worker or workers. Methods will vary with the nature of the terrain and vegetation, the resources of the survey, ease of access, population density, and other factors. Ideally, the archaeologist should explore on foot every bit of the area selected for survey. Obviously, this would be time-consuming, however, and the time allotted for the survey must bear a realistic relation to the extent and nature of the area chosen for exploration. Where it is not feasible to explore all sections of an area, the unexplored or briefly examined sectors should be carefully noted on the survey map and in the survey records.

Fieldwork can often best be done in teams of two. Larger numbers are often unnecessary and may actually be disadvantageous because of interference with stock and crops.

It is just as essential to maintain good local relations and to secure permission from property owners for the necessary entry during a site survey as it is during an excavation. This obligation to treat people's property with due care and to ask permission before entering it may seem burdensome at times, but scrupulously observing it will prove wisest in the end. When gates are left open so that livestock escape, if fences are damaged by careless climbing, or if crops are trampled by people taking short cuts—if the fieldworkers, in short, show an urban disregard for rural rights—the survey will get a bad local reputation and may be forbidden to continue.

If the landowners show any interest in the survey, the crew will usually find it time well spent to explain the reasons for the survey, what they hope to learn, and, later, what they have learned. More often than not, informed landowners will take steps to protect the archaeological resources on their property, whereas uninformed owners can scarcely be expected to care.

Parsons (1971) used a survey team normally consisting of three people during investigations in the Texcoco region of Mexico. One member of the team served as the mapper or recorder, carrying an aerial map of the area being surveyed, with which to orient the survey team and to plot all features and sites. The other members of the survey team walked parallel to the mapper at intervals varying from 15 to 100 meters according to changes in terrain, vegetation, and abundance of archaeological remains (see Sisson, 1973: 11 for a description of the work of survey teams on complex Mesoamerican sites).

As a further example of a survey team in action, we call attention to the monograph by Hayes (1964) on the archaeological survey of Wetherill Mesa:

> The ground was covered by a "line of skirmishers" with intervals of about 50 feet between men. The man at one end followed a recognizable feature, such as the crest of a small ridge or the course of a shallow draw, and the others guided on him. On reaching the edge of the mesa or the particular spot to be covered, the entire line would wheel, reverse direction with the outside man on the first sweep following close to his own tracks and becoming the guide. Keeping orientation and interval while at the same time looking for archaeological debris allowed no time for daydreaming. A crew of only four men was used. Contact and control was too difficult with a larger group (Hayes, 1964: 25).

As an aid to accurate plotting of sites located during this survey, a radio direction-finder was used (see also Hayes and Osborne, 1961). We again quote from Hayes (p. 25):

> This involved the use of two low-power, tripod-mounted, portable transmitters placed over known points . . . , and a small receiver which was carried to the site to be surveyed. Mounted on a compass rose and oriented to true north with the Brunton [compass], the receiver was then tuned to each transmitter in turn and the two azimuths plotted.

Various lists of equipment for site surveying have been compiled at one time or another. Obviously, the nature and amounts of equipment assembled for any given operation will depend upon local conditions and the types of sites anticipated as well as upon the amount of money available. The list on p. 20 includes only equipment useful under most surveying conditions; specialized sites and conditions will require appropriate additions and substitutions.

In some areas, snake-bite or anti-toxin kits (such as the Wyeth Laboratories Antivenin Crotalidae Polyvalent Kit) are advisable, and in arid areas, salt tablets might be added to the list.

One example of how field equipment has to be modified in response to local conditions is provided by Evans and Meggers (1959:6). Particularly important in the tropical environment of their Amazonian sites (where the climate made it impossible to use the usual paper sacks and other survey items that would be affected by moisture) were "specimen bags of unbleached muslin, linen tags, and duplicate sets of field notes."

When a site is found, it should be accurately and completely described, photographed, and located on a map. Then its surface should be examined for special features and exposed artifacts. Although excavation is not ordinarily part of a survey, if burials or other features are partially exposed by

Basic equipment carried by a two-person survey crew

Lightweight and easily usable camera, exposure meter, film

Cloth or paper sacks for collecting specimens

Large steel or wire-reinforced cloth measuring tape (100 feet; 30 meters)

Small steel pocket tape (6 feet or 2 meters)

Machete or brush knife for clearing undergrowth

Whisk broom and paint brush for clearing features

Pencils for writing notes and marking sacks

Army compass or Brunton pocket transit for map-making

Hand-level for rough contour-mapping

Small entrenching shovel for emergency excavation and clearing features

4- or 6-inch pointer's trowel for exposing features

Ruler and protractor for making sketch maps

Scale in inches or centimeters, to be used in photographs of site or features (scale may be in the form of a directional arrow, to indicate direction of photographs taken at site)

USGS topographic maps or other maps for site plotting

Notebook for holding record forms; graph paper, note paper

Knapsack for carrying equipment

erosion or plowing, and thus laid open to damage by weather or vandals or both, they should be examined. The tools necessary for such an emergency excavation (and for documenting it properly) are included in the basic survey equipment pack.

The way in which artifacts are collected from sites located during a survey depends, of course, on the survey's goals. "Selective" or "biased" sampling—picking up diagnostic sherds or chipped-stone implements that help to date a site—is the most common procedure. However, as mentioned earlier in this chapter, such collecting may destroy the spatial patterning present at the surface of a site (cf. Hayden, 1965). If a survey team has been directed to determine the chronology of the sites it finds, but does not wish to destroy possibly meaningful patterns in the placement of artifacts at the surface, it can do selective sampling without actually collecting. That is, it can sketch and record diagnostic artifacts, but leave them in place (cf. Skinner and Bousman, 1973: 6).

There are obvious drawbacks to such a procedure. For example, merely recording chipped-stone artifacts and leaving them in place will prevent future researchers from carrying out a variety of archaeological inquiries in the fields of lithic technology, microscopic wear-pattern analysis, and geologic-source analysis. Also, if a survey team can find the site, so can vandals and pot-hunters. In certain areas o' the world the artifacts might well have disappeared before the team was ready to excavate. Nunley, for example (1973), felt it necessary to collect exposed artifacts from sites in a reservoir area in north-central Texas, in order to "salvage" them from relic-hunters, even though the sites in question were on public lands and thus supposedly under the protection of federal antiquities laws.

The various methods of obtaining adequate artifact samples from sites are reviewed by Ragir in Chapter 15 below (see also Green, 1973: 59 ff.; Redman and Watson, 1970). Among the most common techniques (aside from "selective" collecting) are (1) *complete collection of all exposed materials* (often done on small sites; ideally done after the site has been subdivided in some manner); (2) *spot-collecting* (done within strips or transects across a site, or within areas chosen in another way—perhaps using the dog-leash technique suggested by Binford [1964] or some variant); (3) *combinations of systematic and random sampling* (a grid or other pattern can be superimposed on the site, and areas to be totally collected can be chosen at random, using a table of random numbers or a random number generator, as suggested by Rowlett, 1970; systematic and random sampling techniques are best used in later, more intensive investigations of a site, as they are too time-consuming for a general survey); (4) *collecting around specific features* (certain manifestations or structures on a site may be selected for sampling, such as house pits, mounds, or hearths [cf. Varner, 1968]; if these features are particularly numerous, they may be sampled by random methods).

Aside from the problems of sampling procedures the survey archaeologist has to make other decisions regarding artifacts found on a site. Large metates and grinding stones might be valuable pieces of preliminary evidence, but would burden the survey team too much if it tried to bring them in. These and other such cumbersome or heavy artifacts may be measured, photographed, and otherwise recorded and then left at the site. The survey team should also examine the site for noticeable concentrations or clusters of artifacts and debris, then measure, record and map them.

For the archaeologist who is not content merely to survey the surface of a site, techniques have been developed for detecting and exploring subsurface archaeological features. Although few fieldworkers will have occasion to use these techniques, they should perhaps be mentioned here. In resistivity surveying, an electrical current is directed through the ground while a meter measures resistance to the current's passage. Variations in this resistance provide clues to buried features. Atkinson (in Pyddoke, 1963: 1–30) describes the technique and equipment required; examples of its application can be found in Lerici (1962), Stirling, Rainey, and Stirling (1960), and Hesse (1966).

De Terra, Romero, and Stewart (1949) describe and illustrate another method of electrical surveying, magnetic surveying, in which variations in the intensity of the earth's gravitation field reflect various subsurface features. The use of magnetometers (including their application in underwater archaeology) has greatly increased over the past decade, as reflected in the following references: Aitken (1961, 1970b), Brothwell and Higgs (1963), Arnold (1974), Arnold and Kegley (1974), Belshé (1965), Breiner (1965), Black and Johnston (1962), Breiner and Coe (1972), Clausen (1966), Griffiths (1973), Hall (1966, 1970), A. Hammond (1971), Howell (1968), Hranicky (1972), Johnston (1965), Langan (1966), Linington (1970), Morrison (1971), Morrison et al. (1970), Morrison, Clewlow, and Heizer (1970), Rainey and Ralph (1966), Ralph (1969), Ralph, Morrison, and O'Brien (1968), and Scollar (1962, 1969, 1970).

Other sursurface detection techniques include the use of "induced polarization" (Aspinall, 1968), the sonic spectroscope (Carabelli, 1966), and a magnetic balance (Gramly, 1970). Tite (1972) has published a detailed review of the use of resistivity and magnetism in surveying.

Another form of subsurface detection or exploration is core drilling (Price, Hunter, and McMichael, 1964; Reed, Bennett, and Porter, 1968). At the Cahokia site, a solid-core drilling rig was used by Reed and his co-authors to investigate the internal structure of Monk's Mound, the largest earthen mound in the United States.

RECORDING THE SURVEY DATA

Most organizations engaged in archaeological research have devised record forms to facilitate and standardize the recording of data from site surveys. Most such forms contain a bare minimum of the categories of data that should be observed and recorded. Thus if a team were to adhere strictly to them and keep no other records, the survey would undoubtedly be inadequate. But the forms serve, and should be treated, as useful checklists.

On p. 24, we provide an example of a basic site-survey record form, and below we discuss briefly (by number) the items listed on it. With appropriate additions and modifications for local conditions and particular research goals (see Teotihuacan form on p. 25), this form can be used for virtually any specific region. Obviously, sites with complex features such as earthen monuments and standing architecture will require considerable adjustment, but the list still serves as a guide to the major types of information that should always be recorded.

We should also note that there is presently a trend toward computerizing site survey data, so that some insitutions have record forms (we have examined those of the Arkansas Archeological Survey and the University of Texas at El Paso) coded for key-punch operations.

1. *Site No.*   Any convenient and efficient designation for the site may be used in initial fieldwork. Most workers simply number the sites serially in the order in which they are found, assigning official designations when the survey records can be compared and correlated with master site files at the state university's department of anthropology, state archaeologist's office, museum, or other central clearinghouse.

Various systems of site designation have been established in different parts of the United States (Cole and Deuel, 1937: 22–23; Gladwin and Gladwin, 1928; L. Johnson, 1963, Hadleigh-West, 1967; Shaeffer, 1960; Solecki, 1949). Several systems employ a state number derived from the state's position in the alphabetical roll of the states, followed by a county abbreviation and then by a serial number corresponding to the numeration of sites within the county (this system is usually referred to as the Smithsonian Institution River Basin Surveys Trinomial Site Designation System, McKusick, 1969). Since the admission of new states to the Union has caused some disruption in this system (Alaska was assigned the number 49, and Hawaii, 50), Heizer (1968b) has suggested replacing the state numbers with the official United States Postal Service state abbreviations, a listing of which is provided herewith on page 26. In this system, United States dependencies are also included. Obvious advantages of this system are that it is easy to remember, and one need not know a state's alphabetical rank in order to recognize a designation. For discussions of site designation systems for the rest of the Americas, the reader is referred to Diehl (1970) and Rowe (1971).

Site designation systems derived from a uniform grid based on longitude and latitude, and thus usable anywhere in the world, have been recommended by some archaeologists as more useful for scientific purposes (Borden, 1952; Dills, 1970). The merits of this approach seem to be outweighed, in the United States, at least, by the difficulty of determining grid boundaries in the field as compared to county lines; grid numbers are also harder to remember than county abbreviations. For these reasons, Texas, which formerly used a grid system designation for sites, has adopted the county designation system (L. Johnson, 1963).

Edwards (1969) has proposed the use of the Universal Transverse Mercator Grid, a rectangular grid system found on all standard military maps. Use of the UTM could lead to standardization of site designations throughout the world; and, as Edwards points out, could "eliminate confusion by covering uniformly those areas not having any system of political boundaries or having various systems of political boundaries" (1969: 182). But because archaeologists, like other humans, are creatures of habit, it seems certain that this scheme will not come into general use.

ARCHAEOLOGICAL SITE SURVEY RECORD

1. Site No. _____ 2. Map _____ 3. County _____

4. Twp. _____ Range _____ 1/4 of _____ 1/4 of Sec. _____

5. Location _____

_____ 6. On contour elevation _____

7. Previous designations for site _____

8. Owner _____ 9. Address _____

10. Previous owners, dates _____

11. Present tenant _____

12. Tenant's attitude toward excavation _____

13. Description of site _____

13. Description of site _____

14. Area _____ 15. Depth of deposit _____ 16. Height _____

17. Vegetation _____ 18. Nearest water _____

19. Soil _____ 20. Surrounding soil type _____

21. Previous excavations _____

22. Cultivation _____ 23. Erosion _____

24. Buildings, roads, etc. _____

25. Possibility of destruction _____

26. House pits _____

27. Other features _____

28. Burials _____

29. Artifacts _____

_____

_____

30. Remarks _____

_____

31. Published references _____

32. Museum accession no. _____ Sketch map _____

34. Date _____ 35. Recorded by _____ 36. Photos _____

TEOTIHUACAN SITE SURVEY RECORD

1. SITE NUMBER _____ 2. Aerial photo _____ 3. Previous site designation _____

4. Municipio _____ 5. Village _____ _____

6. Type of holding: Ejido plot []; Pequeña propiedad []; Hacienda []; House plot []; Other _____
   Unknown []. 7. Type of cultivation: Humedad []; Temporal []; Riego []; Flood water [].

8. Setting _____

9. Location (in re other sites) _____

10. DESCRIPTION OF SITE (Streets, block?) _____

11. Area _____ 12. Height _____ 13. Depth _____

14. Vegetation: Milpa []; Barley []; Bean []; Cut alfalfa []
    Uncut alfalfa []; Nopal []; Fallow []; Uncultivated [];
    Other _____ Tepetate depth _____

15. Topography _____ 16. Soil _____

17. Amount of erosion _____ 18. Terracing _____

19. Modern buildings, roads, walls, etc. _____

20. STONE: a, Very abundant []; Abundant []; Moderate [];
            Sparse []; Very sparse []; Absent [].
         b. Relatively uniform distribution []; Localized [];
            Variable [].

21. OTHER EVIDENCES OF CONSTRUCTION: Cut stone []; Lajas []; Tepetate []; Adobe []; Other _____
    (X = Present, A = Abundant, M = Moderate; S = Sparse, N = None, Absent)

22. CONCRETE AND PLASTER FRAGMENTS: Concrete []; Plaster []; Painted plaster [].

23. FLOOR []; Wall []; Staircase []; Drain []; Wall fixture (in situ) []; Mural []; Almena []; Column [].
    Other _____ Comment _____

24. MANO []: Metate []; Mortar []; Pestle []; Plaster smoother []; "Plumb-bob" []; Wall fixture [];
    Other (Fire God, etc.) _____

25. OBSIDIAN: Blades []; Scrapers []; Points []; Cores []; Knife []; Waste []: Other _____

26. BASALT: Tools []; Cores []; Chips []; Other stone (Chert, Slate) _____

27. CERAMICS: a. Very abundant []; Abundant []; Moderate []; Sparse []; Very sparse []; None [].
    b. Figurines: Tzac []; Micc []; Tlam []; Xol []; Met []; Puppet []; Toltec []; Aztec []; Other
    pre-Cl []; Other or unknown _____ c. Candeleros: Common []; Other [].
    3 pronged burner [], Handled cover [], Censer []. e. Thin orange []; San Martin orange [];
    Red lipped olla []; Nubbins []; Wedge rims []; Stamped []; Plano-relief []; Stucco []; Talm.
    Incising []; Foreign _____
    Adorno []; Comal []; Miniatura []; _____ []; _____ []. f. Special Sample _____

28. PHASES: Tzac []; Micc []; Tlam []; Xol []; Met []; Oztotic []; Coyo []; Maz []; Azt []; Other pre-Cl [].

29. BURIALS _____

30. COMMENTS _____

31. SKETCH MAP []. PHOTOS []. CONTINUATION SHEET(S) []. 32. CODE _____ 33. RECORDER _____

34 SURFACE COLLECTION BAG NO. _____ 35. OTHER BAG NOS. _____ 36. DATE _____

United States Postal Service Official Abbreviations for States and Dependencies (see Heizer, 1968b)

Alabama	AL	Montana	MT
Alaska	AK	Nebraska	NB
Arizona	AZ	Nevada	NV
Arkansas	AR	New Hampshire	NH
California	CA	New Jersey	NJ
Canal Zone	CZ	New Mexico	NM
Colorado	CO	New York	NY
Connecticut	CT	North Carolina	NC
Delaware	DE	North Dakota	ND
District of Columbia	DC	Ohio	OH
Florida	FL	Oklahoma	OK
Georgia	GA	Oregon	OR
Guam	GU	Pennsylvania	PA
Hawaii	HI	Puerto Rico	PR
Idaho	ID	Rhode Island	RI
Illinois	IL	South Carolina	SC
Indiana	IN	South Dakota	SD
Iowa	IA	Tennessee	TN
Kansas	KS	Texas	TX
Kentucky	KY	Utah	UT
Louisiana	LA	Vermont	VT
Maine	ME	Virgin Islands	VI
Maryland	MD	Virginia	VA
Massachusetts	MA	Washington	WA
Michigan	MI	West Virginia	WV
Minnesota	MN	Wisconsin	WI
Mississippi	MS	Wyoming	WY
Missouri	MO		

2. *Map*   Enter the name of the map on which the site location is marked.

3. *County*   Record the full name of the county in which the site is located.

4. *Location in terms of the public land surveys.*   This entry can be used in areas where township and range grids have been drawn (major areas of the United States have no such grids). The township and section within which a site is located can be read from any recent, large-scale USGS map. In maps

of one inch to the mile and smaller scales, section numbers are not given. The sketch below illustrates the standard method of section designation. It is desirable to locate sites more specifically than to section. This can be achieved by quarter section and quarter-quarter section designation as illustrated in the accompanying figure:

6	5	4	3	2	1
7	8	9	10	11	12
18	17	16	15	14	13
19	20	21	22	23	24
30	29	28	27	26	25
31	32	33	34	35	36

NW		NE
NW	NE	SE
SW	SE	

Left: designations of sections within a township. Right: designations of quadrants of sections and quarter sections.

5. *Location*   When section designations cannot be secured, use this blank to pinpoint the location of the site.

6. *Contour elevation*   Distance above sea level can be read directly from any topographic map. Knowing the elevation of a site may be helpful in finding it again for further survey work or for excavation.

7. *Previous designations for the site*   It is important that any site name or number in previous use be recorded so that museum specimens collected by previous investigators may be correctly allocated to the particular site.

8 *Owner* and 9. *Address*   The archaeologist will need to write for the owner's permission to excavate. And if the owner lives at or near the site, his or her address may help in locating the site again.

10. *Previous owners, dates*   Previous owners may have information about the history of the site, how it was modified, if at all, during their ownership or within their memory, and what specimens may have been collected there.

11.   *Present tenant*   If someone other than the owner lives or works on the land, it is important to know that person's name in order to get his or her permission to excavate and in order to maintain good relations in general.

12. *Tenant's attitude toward excavation*   If this information can be secured in the field, extensive correspondence may be unnecessary. Any stipulations by the tenant as to excavation should be recorded in detail.

13. *Description of site*   Here the site should be described as to type and general physiographic setting. Particular attention should be given to the environmental situation; in fact, many current site survey forms devote considerable space to ecological data. A representative entry might read: "Rock shelter in bluff 15 meters above canyon floor; shelter faces east; Chihuahuan desert life zone."

14. *Area*   This should be accurately approximated by pacing off length and width or measuring them with a tape.

15. *Depth*   The thickness of a site deposit can often be estimated from erosional exposures, potholes, road cuts, test pits, etc. A soil-sample auger or a posthole-digger can be useful here (see Chapter 7).

16. *Height*   This measurement should be recorded whenever the deposit has a distinct mound form.

17. *Vegetation*   This entry calls for a description of vegetation and vegetational patterns on and around the site. Commonly occurring plants should be identified (and their frequencies estimated) and possible food plants commented upon.

18. *Nearest (fresh) water*   The direction and distance from the site as well as the precise location of the nearest supply should be recorded.

19. *Soil*   The nature of the soil at the site should be described in as great detail as possible. The word "midden," for example, should be modified by such characterizations as "loose" or "compact," "ashy," "shell-bearing," etc.

20. *Surrounding soil types*   These should be described, whenever possible, by reference to a local Soil Survey Report of the U.S. Department of Agriculture.

21. *Previous excavations*   Any evidence of or information on previous archaeological excavation at the site should be recorded.

22. *Cultivation*   Knowing how long a site has been cultivated, if at all, and for what specific crops is useful in estimating how extensively the surface of the site has been modified. For a site still under cultivation, knowing which crop is being grown will help determine when excavation will be feasible.

23. *Erosion*   Sites on the banks of degrading streams or on sea cliffs are exposed to erosion that will ultimately destroy them. Even gully wash can rapidly eat away at a site. In arid or semi-arid areas, wind erosion may be

active. The nature and extent of any such erosion should be described.

24. *Buildings, roads, etc.*   Any modern cultural features that may have modified the site or that may limit the area available for excavation should be described. Such features can be drawn on the sketch map on the reverse side of the site record sheet (see No. 33 below).

25. *Possibility of destruction*   This entry should describe any threats, either physiographic or cultural, to the site, so that priorities for excavation can be established among the sites of the region.

26. *House pits*   Since the number and size of the house pits or other traces of dwellings at an undisturbed site are obviously among the best clues to its population (Cook and Heizer, 1965a; Cook, 1972), any such pits should be counted, measured, and plotted on the sketch map on the reverse of the sheet. In a full site description, each separate indication of a dwelling should be fully described on a feature record form (see Chapter 6), and a reference to this record should be entered on the basic survey sheet.

27. *Other features*   Any surface features of aboriginal human origin should be described. These might include pictographs and petroglyphs, bedrock mortars, bedrock metates, quarries, rockshelters, etc. Feature record forms should be used to describe any of these and a cross reference to such a record should be made in this space.

28. *Burials*   Any evidence of the use of the site for burial should be noted. Such evidence might consist of surface finds of human bones, local traditions of burials having been found, etc.

29. *Artifacts*   Here record the disposition of any artifacts recovered from the site. Surface collections made during the site survey (and sampling methods used), local private collections, and specimens in museums should all be noted. When collections from the site are extensive, several continuation pages may be necessary. It is also useful to append sketches of artifacts, whether collected during the survey or found in local collections.

30. *Remarks*   This entry may be used for any pertinent data not called for elsewhere on the form. Recommendations for future investigations at a site, for instance, may be entered here.

31. *Published references*   Bibliographic reference should be made to any published account of the site, whether in ethnographic, historical, or archaeological publications.

32. *Museum accession No.*   Specimens deposited in museums are given an accession number. This number is a cross-file reference to all correspondence, technical reports, and publications describing the collection.

33. *Sketch map*   A sketch map showing the route of access to the sites, the relationship of the site to its physiographic environs, and major site features should be drawn on the back of the site record form. Be sure to indicate cardinal directions and scale. Item 33 should record the name of the individual who drew the map.

34. *Date*   Enter here the date of filling out the site record form.

35. *Recorded by*   Give the full name of the person recording the data.

36. *Photos*   Refer by field catalog number or by roll and file number to the photographs taken on the site. The final record should contain the permanent file catalog numbers of these negatives.

TYPES OF SITES AND ARCHAEOLOGICAL REMAINS

The variety of archaeological sites and remains is so great that a detailed descriptive list is beyond the scope of this book. Succinct descriptions of several major kinds of sites are presented by Hole and Heizer (1973: 111–119). We have found useful a list assembled by Nelson (1938: 146–148) in connection with a general survey of prehistoric archaeology:

I.   *Monumental or fixed antiquities, usually found on the surface of the ground*
1.   Refuse heaps, in caves by the seashore, near ruins, etc.
2.   Caches and storage pits for food, treasure, offerings, etc.
3.   Hearths, firepits, temporary camp sites
4.   House and village sites, tent rings, ruins, pile dwellings, etc.
5.   Trails, portages, and causeways connecting the settlements, etc.
6.   Workshops, smelters, foundries, etc.
7.   Graves and cemeteries
8.   Garden and field plots
9.   Excavations, such as pitfalls for game, reservoirs, irrigation systems, quarries, mines, burial chambers, subterranean dwellings, artificial dwellings cut into loess, pumice, and limestone
10.   Earthworks, including dams, ball courts, enclosures for field and for cattle, fortification walls, mounds, and pyramids
11.   Megalithic and other stone structures in the form of menhirs or monoliths, cromlechs or stone circles, alignments, cairns, dolmens and trilithons, stone chambered mounds or barrows, cist graves, pyramids, shrines, temples, fortification walls, forts, treasure chambers, enclosures for fields and for cattle, fish weirs, boulder effigies, and gravestones
12.   Petrogylphs and paintings on cave walls and exposed rock surfaces

II.   *Movable antiquities, ordinarily obtained only by excavation in either artificial refuse or natural earth deposits*
1.   Chipped stone work: tools, weapons, ornamental and ceremonial objects

2. Wood work: tools, weapons, boats and other means of transportation, ornamental and ceremonial objects
3. Bone work: tools, weapons, utensils, ornamental and ceremonial objects
4. Shell work: tools, weapons, utensils, ornamental and ceremonial objects
5. Skin, hair, and feather work: clothing, shelters, utensils, boats, and ornamental accessories
6. Wood fiber work: mats, baskets, boats, nets, clothing, hats, sandals, and ornamental accessories
7. Clay work: utilitarian, artistic, and ceremonial pottery, etc.
8. Ground stone work: tools, weapons, utensils, ornamental and ceremonial objects
9. Metal work: tools, weapons, utensils, ornamental and ceremonial objects

RECORDING LOCAL COLLECTIONS

As previously stressed, local private or civic collections can be important sources of information about the archaeology of an area, and the survey team should make every effort to record the contents of these collections fully and learn which areas and if possible which specific sites they came from. Each complete specimen and each fragment whose original form can be reconstructed should be described fully, indicating the kind or type of artifact, what it is made from, its dimensions, shape, weight, and general characteristics. Any unusual features such as incising, painting, or other decoration should also be noted. If the collection has been catalogued, the identifying numbers or symbols should be carefully recorded.

A checklist may be prepared and used as a guide during the documentation of collections, although it should not be adhered to so rigidly that pertinent data go unrecorded. A checklist should include, at the least, the following items: (1) the site name or number (if the site has not been previously recorded, a full description should accompany the notes); (2) the collector, the date, and the circumstances of collection; (3) the original catalog number (if any); (4) descriptions and sketches of the specimens; and (5) any available data on associated specimens. If any of this information is based entirely on memory (which it usually is), this fact should be carefully noted in the records. Although local collectors who rely upon their memory rather than notes are often "certain" where their specimens came from and about other details of their collections, the archaeologist cannot afford to be so unless backed up by records.

If the collection can be handled, outline drawings of specimens should be made where feasible. If specimens are mounted or kept in locked cases, scale drawing or photographs can be made instead. Each drawing and each photograph should be labeled to insure correlation with the proper written description.

It is always desirable to photograph as many specimens in a collection as possible. A portable light box may be included in the photographic equipment of the survey for this purpose (see Chapter 12D for references to artifact photography). For convenience in taking pictures, and for utility in later research, specimens can be grouped by site or by association within a site (as artifacts from a single burial). A clearly marked scale or rule must always be included in the photograph to indicate the size of the artifacts. A white celluloid ruler with every other inch (or centimeter) blacked in with India ink is well suited for this purpose. A description of each photograph taken should be recorded in the notes; alternatively, a written label can be placed alongside the specimens while they are being photographed.

It is advisable to make notes on local collections in duplicate or even triplicate. One copy may be given to the custodian or owner of the collection; the second copy should be deposited with the institution or agency primarily concerned with gathering archaeological information in the region. If extensive work is to be done in the area, the recording archaeologist will probably want to keep a file copy of the notes as well. It is, of course, wise to avoid depositing, in a place of ready access to anyone, information that could lead to destruction or vandalism of sites; and notes on a collection should never be used or deposited anywhere without the full approval of the collection's owner.

Personal relations established while a collection is being recorded can be valuable for both the collector and for archaeology in the region. The collector can get record sheets and instructions for obtaining full data on future specimens. The collector will often be interested in the methods of restoring and preserving specimens, and in the archaeologist's interpretation of them. Frequently, a collector will be open to suggestion concerning methods of collecting, cataloguing or excavation, and the archaeologist may be able to direct the collector into a local or state archaeological society in which he or she can learn about scientific approaches to archaeology. By maintaining a discreet and tactful manner at all times, the archaeologist may avoid giving offense while awakening the collector to the great amount of scientific knowledge that can be destroyed by improper collecting and excavation techniques or lost by a simple failure to record it.

Local archaeological societies seeking ways for their members to participate in archaeological activities can profitably be directed into the work of documenting collections. Most areas of the country have numerous relic collections, most of them unrecorded except in the collector's memory. Amateur archaeologists can make a valuable contribution by carefully documenting these collections and recording the collectors' recollections and observations. This activity is also a way of reaching collectors, making them aware of the scientific value of archaeological remains, and encouraging them to adopt proper methods of collecting and cataloguing.

ALTERATION OF ARCHAEOLOGICAL SITES AND MATERIALS

In the long run, geological forces are the main agents in the covering, uncovering, or alteration of archaeological deposits (Malde, 1964; Hole and Heizer, 1973: 120–127). However, people are also notoriously effective in changing the face of sites, removing objects from them or destroying sites altogether (Hole and Heizer, 1973; 100–104). Tombs are robbed for jewels and precious metals, for art objects of great beauty or interest—and even for simple beads or ornaments that have no particular resale value. Abandoned stone buildings become, in effect, quarries for new stone buildings. In Mexico many archaeological deposits have been used as a source of easily dug clay for adobe bricks. The Preclassic site of Tlatilco (Porter, 1953) was discovered in such a brick-earth pit, as was the site of Hoxne, Suffolk, where John Frere observed Paleolithic hand-axes and extinct animals in association in 1800 (Heizer, 1959:216–218).

This matter is worth mentioning because artifacts may be missing from any site. Yet unless made aware of such a possibility, the archaeologist, particularly the novice archaeologist, may never notice it. Let us take two hypothetical examples. During a surface survey of sites on the island of Malta, an archaeologist collects a sample of potsherds. The archaeologist is generally aware that unauthorized digging may have brought to the surface older materials that have now become associated with the later, surface materials. What she or he may not know (but could have learned from the published literature) is that on Malta the peasants grind up ancient pottery to form a much-prized ingredient of a cement called "deffun" used for roofing houses, and that the sherds are reduced to powder in a concavity worked into the tops of large stones in the same ruins where the sherds are gathered. At Memphis some disruption of the normal ceramic inventory as judged from surface sherds would have been caused by Major Bagnold in 1886 when he raised two colossal statues of Rameses II that were buried in the alluvial sediments, and used potsherds as packing of the pit he dug beneath the statues. Bagnold recounts the hiring of "a small army of village boys employed collecting potsherds from the ruins of Memphis," and that "some 500 cubic yards of this material, closely packed and rammed, formed a bed about 40 feet by 20 feet in plan" (Bagnold, 1888: 455).

Mention must also be made of the presence of "heirlooms" or "collector's items" of earlier date that may find their way into association with more recent material. There are many examples, and we add the record of

Southwestern Indians' collecting ancient turquoise (Bartlett, 1854: II, 247), and an ancient Oaxacan jade found in the ruins of the seventeenth-century church at Awatovi in Arizona (Woodbury, 1954: 164). There are also numerous examples of earlier materials being "collected" by later peoples and re-used, such as the ceremonial re-use of a fluted point by the Huichol Indians of Jalisco, Mexico (Weigand, 1970) and the possibility that Archaic Indians in central and southern Texas frequently re-used Paleo-Indian projectile points, sometimes chipping them into drills (Suhm, Krieger, and Jelks, 1954: 104–106; Hester, 1968: 159).

Archaeologists who fail to detect signs that deposits have been disturbed by earlier digging may draw mistaken conclusions about a site's history. A region's later inhabitants may have dug storage, cache, or burial pits at a site. Aikens (1970: 19) has observed that the ancient inhabitants of Hogup Cave, Utah, occasionally "leveled" the floor of the cave (see also Jennings, 1957: 1967–69). Relic-collector's pits (potholes) are also frequently encountered in sites. Some sites may even have been excavated by earlier archaeological expeditions, and may contain the spoil dumps of these earlier investigations. G. Loud, excavating at Khorsabad in the 1930's, for a time mistook Victor Place's century-old dump for a wall of the court of Sargon's Palace.

It is also appropriate to note here the "natural" introduction of materials into site deposits. Faunal materials can be carried into sites, particularly caves and rockshelters, by carnivores and owls; packrats can transport both faunal remains and artifacts (Heizer and Brooks, 1965; also, examination of packrat nests near southern Texas open campsites reveal that animal bones and flint chips from the sites have been carried into the rat nests); and artificial concentrations of land-snail shells and shellfish remains (which the archaeologist might interpret as specific-activity loci) can be created through the feeding habits of raccoons, roadrunners, and other animals. Furthermore, artifacts (such as projectile tips) embedded in migratory animals can be transported over considerable distances and subsequently introduced into the archaeological deposits of other regions (Heizer, 1968a).

The extraordinary amount of disturbance of the earth's surface that is being carried out today as a result of mechanized farming, drowning of river valleys with dams, the urban and suburban sprawl, and the voracious appetite for roads by the many millions of automobiles owned by American citizens are all destroying archaeological sites. As an example of the rate of site destruction from agricultural practices in only one state, Arkansas, see Ford, Rolingson, and Medford (1972).

The problem of site destruction has been further compounded by a public who, with increased leisure time, has begun to eagerly search for hobbies or avocations. While some spend their surplus time and monies on sports or travel, still others (unfortunately, too many) have taken up "hunting for

Indian relics." Many "archaeological societies" have thus been formed, some mere artifact-collecting clubs, but others composed of dedicated amateur archaeologists who frequently get a bad name because of the activities of the former groups (see Davis, 1971: 305).

The late 1960's and early 1970's have seen a tremendous rise in the rate of site destruction. Some of this is due to the growth in the numbers of relic-hunters (and their increased mobility), but most of the looting-and-pillaging has been done to satisfy the international art-collecting market.[*] There are, sadly, many published reports documenting the devastating effects of the illicit trade in antiquities, including Bruhns (1972), Coggins (1969), Reinhold (1973), Robertson (1972), Sheets (1973), Williams (1972), and a comprehensive book-length study published by Meyers (1973). Many major American museums have now passed resolutions affirming their intention not to purchase archaeological materials taken illegally from foreign countries.

SELECTING A SITE FOR EXCAVATION

Generally speaking, the less a site has been disturbed (by recent occupation, cultivation, vandalism), the more information it is likely to yield. Not only will more be preserved, but, equally important, less mixing of cultural materials will probably have occurred. Usually the larger and deeper a site is, the greater the chance of sequential occupation and therefore the greater the chance of significant cultural stratification. On the other hand, in such a site there will also be a greater chance of ancient mixing of cultural materials from the different periods of occupation. For this reason, an archaeologist may prefer to work with a series of briefly occupied sites where such mixing is less of a problem and where contemporary activities can more easily be ascertained.

Selecting a site for excavation is no problem for archaeologists engaged in emergency salvage work (for example, where sites are faced with destruction by highways, pipelines, urban expansion, or vandalism). Their responsibility is simply to save as much archaeological information as possible from sites destined to be destroyed. Even these endeavors will be limited by such practical considerations as the availability of time, funds, and technical resources.

---

[*]In countries like Egypt, archaeological sites have been pillaged for hundreds of years. G. Belzoni was one of the early agents for foreign collectors (Fagan, 1973). The citizens of Gurna at Thebes have long had a reputation for their skill at tomb robbing and other forms of archaeological thievery. Fahkry (1947) notes that between 1937 and 1942, the "thieves of Gurna" chiseled out large sections of the painted scenes in the Tombs of the Nobles. These thieves were so sophisticated that they filled the gaps they left in the tomb walls with material similar to that used by Antiquities Service restorers in earlier years. Thus, their deeds often went unnoticed, especially in tombs that had not yet been fully described in the archaeological literature.

Archaeologists not operating under the compulsion of salvage work, however, may face a complex problem of choice. In the past, sites were often chosen because they were easy to get to, because they dated from a period the excavator was interested in, because of the depth and richness of their deposits, and so forth (see Binford, 1964). Recently, however, as noted in Chapter 2, archaeologists have tended to select sites whose excavation will lead to at least partial answers for specific problems or will help to test previously formulated hypotheses. This "problem orientation" has begun to guide the selection of sites in all kinds of archaeology. The problem to be solved may be one of chronology or of culture history. Carefully conducted regional site surveys will often provide the evidence as to which site or sites will most likely help solve a particular problem.

Archaeological sites have often been used to train students in professional excavation techniques. Although the teaching of student archaeologists is of course necessary, we argue that no such undertaking be conducted without the intent for serious research on the part of the instructor. In May 1974 the Executive Committee of the Society for American Archaeology adopted a resolution addressed to this problem, which says in part that "the practice of excavating or collecting from archaeological sites solely or primarily for 'teaching' purposes is contrary to the provision against indiscriminate excavation of archaeological sites contained in . . . the by-laws of the Society for American Archaeology." The resolution adds: "Each archaeological site contains evidence of specific human activities . . . (and) no site can be written off in advance as unimportant or expendable. No site deserves less than professional excavation, analysis and publication."

SITE MAPPING AND LAYOUT

Lewis Kyle Napton*

4

In the name of the Most High, tell me, O Bey, what you are going to do with those stones. So many thousands of purses spent upon such things! Can it be, as you say, that your people learn wisdom from them; or is it, as his reverence, the Cadi, declares, that they are to go to the palace of your Queen, who, with the rest of the unbelievers, worships these idols? As for wisdom, these figures will not teach you to make any better knives, or scissors, or chintzes; and it is in the making of those things that the English show their wisdom. But God is great! God is great! Here are stones which have been buried even since the time of the holy Noah—peace be with him! Perhaps they were under ground before the deluge. I have lived on these lands for years. My father, and the father of my father, pitched their tents here before me, but they never heard of these figures. For twelve hundred years have the true believers (and, praise be to God! all true wisdom is with them alone) been settled in this country, and none of them ever heard of a palace underground. Neither did they who went before them. But lo! here comes a Frank from many days journey off, and he walks up to the very place, and he takes a stick and makes a line here, and makes a line there. Here, says he, is the palace; there, he says, is the gate; and he shows us what has been all our lives beneath our feet, without our having known anything about it. Wonderful! wonderful! Is it by books, is it by magic, is it by your prophets, that you have learnt these things? Speak, O Bey; tell me the secret of wisdom.

—An Arab sheikh speaking to A. Layard at Nineveh in 1845

 The increasing necessity for archaeologists to attain the highest professional standards in all aspects of their work makes it mandatory that field workers prepare detailed maps of archaeological sites that are to be sampled or tested as well as those that are to be excavated. Both planimetric and topographic maps are essential prior to sampling or excavating a site. The planimetric map shows the site in two dimensions only. Topographic maps depict the third dimension (depth or relief) often shown by contours.

*The author of this chapter wishes to thank Miss Elizabeth Greathouse for assistance in preparing this chapter.

37

The functions of archaeological maps are to graphically record the physical features of the site; to express the topographic contours that represent changes in elevation of the site surface; and to depict the surroundings of the site, encompassing an area sufficient to place the site in its environmental context. As excavation proceeds, the site map will show the location of test entries, trenches, etc., and will record the location and relationship of subsurface features revealed by excavation. For complex site features, several maps depicting features of the site at successive stages of excavation will probably be needed (Quimby, 1951: Figs. 5-8).

If a site is large and the surface is marked by complex irregularities, it is usually economical to secure the services of a professional topographic surveyor who has the necessary technical equipment and knowledge for making a map of the site. For most sites without complex architecture, archaeologists can prepare plats and contour maps of accuracy approaching professional standards. It is this type of mapping that will be described here. Topographic maps designed to show the relationship of an archaeological site to the local physiographic environment, such as have appeared in Heizer (1949: Map 5), Black (1944: Fig. 1). Cole (1951: Fig. 69), and Wedel (1941: Fig. 2), are desirable for archaeological reports.

Many of the urban sites in Mesoamerica are so large that an instrument survey on the ground may take years to complete. An example of this is the site of Tikal in the heavily forested Peten lowland of Guatemala. Most archaeologists will never be responsible for investigating such a large site, but Carr and Hazard (1961) describe how the Tikal ruins were mapped. Instructive also is the map of the site of Mayapan prepared by M. R. Jones, which plots 4,140 structures enclosed by one city wall (Pollock et al., 1962). The huge area covered by the ancient city of Teotihuacan, near Mexico City, was mapped by using airphotos (Millon, 1964).

Surveying methods similar to those described here are outlined in Cole et al. (1930), Cole and Deuel (1937: 24-27; Fig. 16), and Byers and Johnson (1939: 192-198). Methods employing more elaborate equipment are described in Atkinson (1953: Chap. 3) and Detweiler (1948). An excellent and easily available guide is that of Debenham (1955). Other useful reference works are by Gannett (1906), Greenhood (1964), Raisz (1962), Bouchard and Moffitt (1960), Brinker and Taylor (1955), Forbes (1955), and Wilson (1972).

USE OF EXISTING SURVEYS AND MAPS

An archaeologist who is planning an excavation or a survey will do well to become familiar with the system or systems used for surveying land in the region, as well as with any existing maps. Most maps will be somewhat outdated, but even the oldest ones may nevertheless contain valuable information such as old place names, routes of old roads, and the like.

Land survey systems The land survey system used throughout the United States began with the Jefferson-Williamson plan of land subdivision proposed in 1784. The Federal Congress in 1785 enacted a law providing for townships six miles square, each containing 36 sections one mile square. The same arrangement prevails today. As the land survey laws evolved, 35 initial control points were established. The latitude and longitude of these points were determined by astronomical observations. A principal meridian (north-south line) was then established as a true meridian through each initial point, perpendicular to which is the base (east-west) line.

In California, for example, the initial point is on Mount Diablo near San Francisco Bay. The Mount Diablo meridian extends north to Oregon, and the base line extends from Mount Diablo east through Nevada to the Utah border. In Montana, the principal meridian and the base line terminate at the state boundaries. In Oregon and Washington, land is surveyed in reference to the Willamette meridian, the initial point of which is near Portland. Along each meridian and base line, township corners and range lines (running through township corners) are placed at intervals of six miles (480 chains; a surveyor's chain is 66 ft. long). As already noted, therefore, the area enclosed by range lines—a township—encompasses 36 square miles. Townships are located by number with reference to the principal meridian: for example, Township 2 North, Range 18 East.

Permanent section corners (one mile apart) and quarter-section corners are established along meridians and base lines. Each square-mile section within the township is numbered, beginning at the upper right or northeast corner of the township and continuing west (1-6), then east (7-12), west again, etc. Each section contains 640 acres and can be subdivided into quarter-sections (160 acres), and further quartered into 40-acre tracts, etc. Section corners are located by placement of a "brass cap," which is a metal tablet 3¾ inches in diameter set in a rock or masonry pedestal. In national forests, section corners may be marked by steel or aluminum tags tacked to a tree. A corner tag might bear the data "T11S, R6W, S24"; meaning that the tree is located in Section 24, Township 11 South, Range 6 West. If the section corner is actually marked or witnessed on the ground, it is shown on USGS maps as a heavy red cross.

During areal site survey the legal location of all sites must be accurately recorded, at least to the quarter-section (160 acres) or quarter-quarter-section (40 acres), but preferably to the quarter-quarter-quarter section (10 acres), in view of the fact that one acre is approximately 209 feet on a side, and many sites cover less than one acre. Hence, the legal location of a site might read

"The SE quarter of the NW quarter of the SW quarter of Section 24, township 11 south, range 6 west, Mount Diablo Meridian." (SE ¼ NW ¼ SW ¼ S24, T11S, R6W.)

Another means of locating archaeological sites is by latitude and longitude. A few field workers are using the Universal Transverse Mercator (UTM) Grid given on military maps and marked by "tics" on the margins of USGS quadrangle maps. The use of the UTM grid by archaeologists is discussed by Edwards (1969: 180–182) and Dills (1970: 389–390).

Of great importance to the archaeologist are section-corner monuments, forest corner and quarter-corner location posters marked by tagged bearing-trees and often flagged with red tape, and USGS bench marks, which are brass tablets set in concrete. The location of each bench mark is given on the appropriate USGS quadrangle and is marked with the designation "BM," and the elevation of that point.

Section corners and other points of known legal location and elevation can be used as datum points if they happen to occur on or near a site, or the archaeological datum may be referenced to a nearby brass-cap monument by taping or instrument survey.

Topographic maps   Topographic maps depict the size, shape, and distribution of features on land surfaces. They provide several kinds of information: (1) *relief* or elevation, representing hills, valleys, lowlands; (2) *hydrology*, or water features, including springs, creeks, rivers, and lakes; (3) *vegetation,* indicated by forest or orchard patterns; (4) *culture*, or man-made features, such as buildings, towns, farms, roads, boundaries, and named features; and (5) the boundary lines of townships, ranges, sections, and land grants subdivided by public-land surveys. Conventionally, relief is shown in brown, hydrology in blue, culture in black, and vegetation in green. Culture features of recent origin may be shown in red-tint overprint.

There are five elements that must be part of any acceptable topographic map (Fig. 4-1). These are:

Legend   The significance of conventional signs employed by the cartographer is given at the lower righthand corner of all maps in a reference key or block called the legend. The signs are arranged in a column beginning with relief, followed by drainage and then by culture. Each symbol or line is customarily enclosed in a small rectangle of equal size, followed by the explanatory data. The legend also includes the map title, explanatory data, the cartographer's name, the date when the map was drawn, the scale, the contour interval, and any other necessary information.

Contours   Variations in elevation of the land surface, or relief, may be indicated on a topographic map in several conventional ways. Maps of large

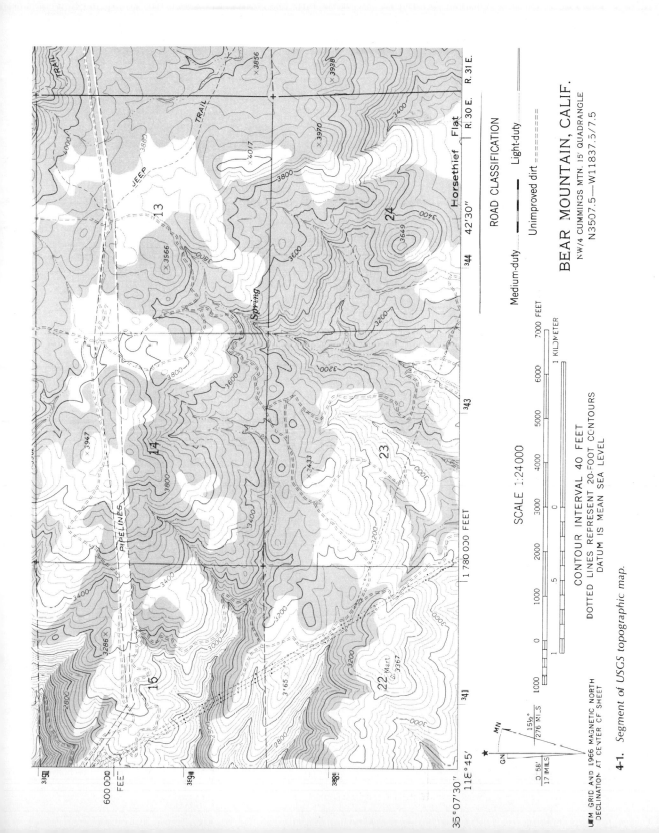

4-1. *Segment of USGS topographic map.*

areas, such as continents, use hypsometric coloring to represent changes in altitude. Hachure marks have also been used; in the Lehmann system of hachuring, the closer together the hachure marks the steeper the slope. The USGS has published shaded relief maps of certain areas.

Relief is customarily represented by contour lines. A contour is a line that connects points of the same elevation, the shore line at mean sea level being the contour of zero elevation. Beginning from that elevation, successive changes in elevation will be marked by contour lines. The map-maker determines a suitable contour interval, fifty feet being a common one. On USGS maps, 80-foot or 100-foot contour intervals are used. If a 20-foot contour interval is used, each 100-foot contour is represented by a heavier line than the other contours. These are *index contours*, which are labeled to denote elevation above sea level. Usually every fifth contour line is drawn in the field, with intervening contours completed in the laboratory.

Contour lines always close upon themselves eventually. They bend or loop upstream in valleys, lying close together to represent steep terrain and farther apart for level terrain.

Scale The scale of a topographic map appears in the legend or lower margin. It may be expressed verbally, as "one inch = one mile," or graphically, as a bar-scale or a measured straight line. It may also appear as a numerical scale or Representative Fraction. A scale of 1:125,000 means that the distance between any two points on the map is 1/125,000 of the actual ground distance between them. In a scale of 1:63,300, one inch equals one mile. Most USGS maps are either 1:62,500 (15-minute maps; one inch = about one mile); 1:125,000 (30-minute maps; one inch = about 2 miles); or 1:250,000 (one inch = 3.945 miles). Archaeologists may need to make large-scale maps having the ratio of 1:120 (one inch = 10 feet), 1:600 (one inch = 50 feet), or 1:1,200 (one inch = 100 feet). The graphic or bar scale is recommended in archaeological mapping.

Direction Compass directions are indicated on all maps. On large-scale maps, a full arrow is drawn pointing to true north, and a half-arrow, intersecting the full arrow at its center, shows magnetic north.

Date Since phenomena depicted by maps, culture features especially, are constantly changing in the United States, investigators should be certain to use the most up-to-date maps available. The entire United States is covered by the USGS in the scale 1:250,000, and there is detailed coverage in 15-minute and 7.5-minute quadrangles for many areas outside the western states and Alaska. In the 7.5-minute quadrangles, a given section (one square mile) may be sufficiently large to enable the archaeologist to pinpoint the exact position of the site under investigation.

PREPARING MAPS FOR AREAL SITE SURVEY

In most cases, existing maps will not be of sufficiently large scale to provide the data needed for recording of archaeological sites and features. Because of this, archaeologists must make their own maps.

Equipment   The two most essential pieces of equipment are the compass and the measuring tape. Also needed for map-making during an areal survey will be coordinate (gridded) drawing paper (sometimes a grid is printed on the reverse of the site survey form), a ruler or engineer's scale, a pencil (No. 3H), a protractor, and a drafting triangle.

All members of the archaeological field party should have a compass for finding their way and taking bearings to determine the location of sites. The compass may also may be included in photographs of site features. A frequently used low-priced compass is the military lensatic type with a movable glass bezel that can be used for observing direction and azimuth (Fig. 4-2,a). This compass usually retails for less than four dollars. Another compass recommended for student use is the Brunton Cadet pocket transit, an inexpensive version of the well-known Brunton compass or pocket transit. The Cadet combines the features of a compass, clinometer, hand level, and plumb. It is available for about $6.00 from the Brunton Company, Riverton, Wyoming 82501.

An intermediate-priced compass is the Silva Hand Compass. This model has the advantage of having a straight-edge paralleling the compass needle, useful in drawing the magnetic north line on maps. It retails for less than twenty dollars. One of the best-known compasses for geological and archaeological field survey is the Brunton pocket transit, which has been used by thousands of field workers. The pocket transit will last a lifetime if properly cared for. It retails for about $75.00 (Fig. 4-2g).

In addition to a good compass, the archaeological surveyor will need an accurate measuring tape. Before purchasing tapes, archaeologists must consider whether they will be recording data in the metric or English system. This is an important decision, because if the site is to be excavated, the control grid may be laid out in the English system. Grid units five by five feet are customary in this system, and depth measurements may be obtained with inexpensive and readily available carpenter's or household pocket steel-tapes. If the metric system is used, however, the grid will be laid out in one- or two-meter squares, and the pocket tapes used by the field crew must be graduated in centimeters. The surveyor will also need one or two 30-meter tapes. Tapes graduated in the metric system may not be locally available, but may be ordered from K & E, Lietz, Dietrich-Post, and other suppliers (Fig. 4-2,b,c).

A very useful and readily available tape is the 100-foot steel tape that is

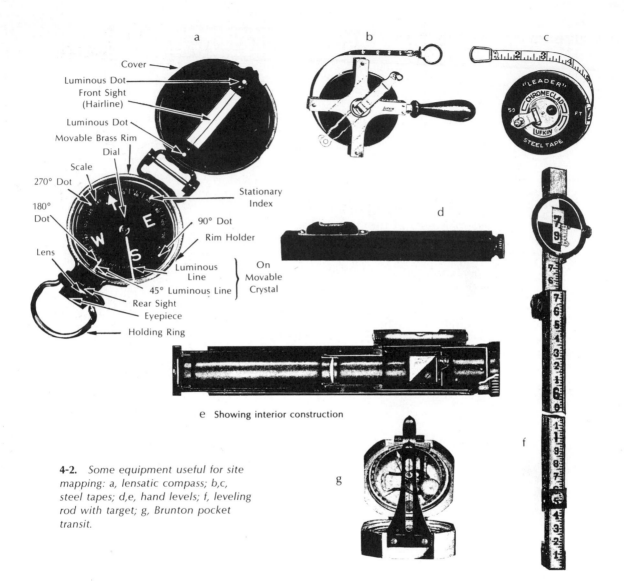

a

Cover
Luminous Dot
Front Sight
(Hairline)
Luminous Dot
Movable Brass Rim
Dial
Scale
270° Dot
180°
Dot
Lens
Stationary
Index
90° Dot
Rim Holder
Luminous
Line
45° Luminous Line
Rear Sight
Eyepiece
Holding Ring
On
Movable
Crystal

b c

d

e Showing interior construction

f

g

4-2. *Some equipment useful for site mapping: a, lensatic compass; b,c, steel tapes; d,e, hand levels; f, leveling rod with target; g, Brunton pocket transit.*

stocked in most hardware stores, usually retailing for less than $15.00. Civil-engineering suppliers manufacture a variety of tapes suitable for archaeological mapping. Two good tapes are Lietz *Symlon*, a glass-fiber 100-foot tape with feet graduated in tenths (1.2 inches), and the Keuffel Esser *Favorite Wyteface* 100-foot steel tape (KE 90-0015). The latter is excellent for archaeological applications, since it is graduated in feet and inches on one side and meters and centimeters on the other, to 30 meters. Both the Lietz and K & E tapes sell for under $20.00.

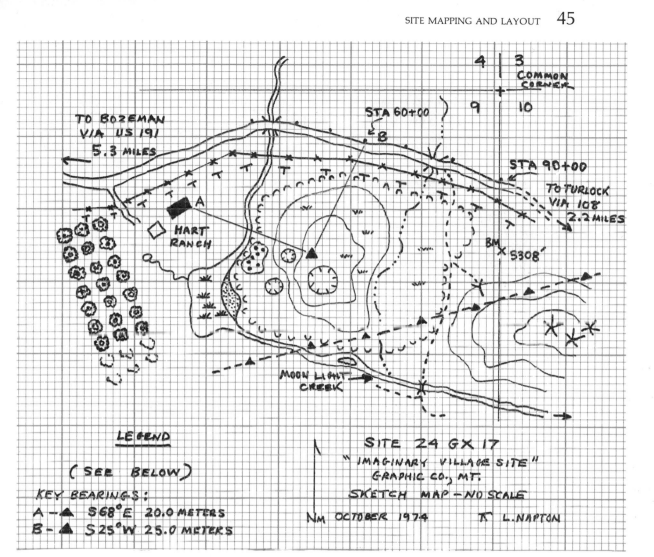

TO BOZEMAN
VIA US 191
5.3 MILES

STA 60+00
B

STA 90+00
TO TURLOCK
VIA 108
2.2 MILES

BM X 5308'

HART
RANCH

A

4 | 3
COMMON
CORNER
9 | 10

MOON LIGHT
CREEK

LEGEND
(SEE BELOW)

KEY BEARINGS:
A — ▲ S68°E 20.0 METERS
B — ▲ S25°W 25.0 METERS

SITE 24 GX 17
"IMAGINARY VILLAGE SITE"
GRAPHIC CO., MT.
SKETCH MAP — NO SCALE

N_M OCTOBER 1974   L. NAPTON

4-3. *Sketch map using standard cartographic symbols. This type of map is useful in locating archaeological sites, but would have to be redrawn for publication. (NB: This is a synthetic map locating an imaginary site.)*

Explanation of Symbols

Stream	
Intermittant stream	
Marsh	
Spring	
Sand	

Section corner (found)	
Survey station	
Bench mark	
Elevation	
Section number	

Road	
Dirt road	
Trail	
Bridge	

Housepit	
Bedrock mortar	
Cave entrance	
Areal extent of site	
Center of site	

Telephone line	
Power line	
Barbed wire fence	
House	
Shed, barn	

Orchard	
Pines	
Deciduous trees	
Meadow	

Sketch maps   A sketch map is necessary on all archaeological site-survey report forms, although it may show little more than the approximate locations of topographic, structural, and archaeological features. Sketch maps can be very useful and quite accurate if the people drawing them are skillful in visualizing the appearance of features in "plan" view, that is, as seen from the air. In any event, a sketch map is usually far superior to a written description of the relationships of various site features (Fig. 4-3). Sketch maps can be made more accurate by pacing or by taping, described below.

Compass traverse maps   A very good map can be made in the field by using compass and tape, or by pacing, or by combinations of these methods. A compass traverse map requires coordinate paper, a light-weight drawing board or clipboard, pencil, and protractor. The scale of the map should be adjusted so that the site can be plotted on a single sheet of coordinate or graph paper. With a known starting point established, hold the compass over the point, determine the bearing to another prominent object (turning point), such as a stake. Plot this bearing, and tape or pace the distance to this point.

    The surveyor should determine the length of his or her pace in advance, which is easily done by pacing a known distance between two points. (Pace the distance four times and determine the average number of paces.)

    If the distance along the bearing is to be taped, the tape must be horizontal and taut. If the terrain slopes, measurements must be taken by "breaking tape" into smaller horizontal measurements (Fig. 4-4). Slope correction to the horizontal may also be achieved by use of the Abney level. An Abney

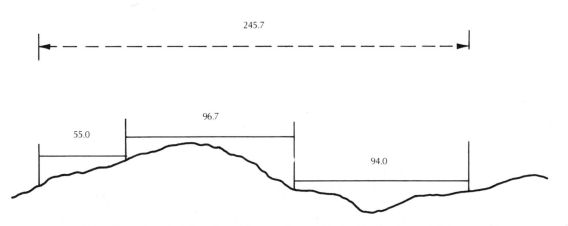

4-4. *"Breaking chain" or "breaking tape" to reduce measurements of distance to the horizontal plane. The cumulative total of the segments is 245.7 meters. The distance measured along the ground surface would be longer than the actual horizontal distance. This procedure is also used in setting stakes along grid control lines.*

level with topographic scale can be used with a special tape showing the difference between the sloping and horizontal distances at various Abney level readings. The use of this level and of the surveyor's chain is described by Forbes (1955: 30–31).

Other points may be located within the traverse area by intersection from two known points or by running a traverse line to the points. A bearing is taken by holding the Brunton compass or its equivalent waist high, with the sighting mirror to the rear. The instrument is correctly sighted on the object when one sees the black center sighting line in the mirror bisecting both the "V" of the reflected front sight and the object sighted. The north end of the needle indicates the bearing of the object sighted. Normally, determination by intersection of the bearings from two or more known points is the quickest and easiest method of locating objects such as trees, stakes, rock outcrops, and cultural features (see Kjellstrom, 1967).

In modern field practice, a sketch map or compass-traverse map should be prepared for all sites recorded in the field in order to make it possible for future investigators to find the sites again. The files of most American universities contain scores of site reports that lack adequate maps locating the sites described on the survey forms. It is essential that planimetric sketch or compass-traverse maps be prepared as part of any areal site survey (Fig. 4-5).

PREPARING MAPS FOR TESTING AND EXCAVATION

Two kinds of "maps" will be produced during testing or excavation of an archaeological site. These are (1) planimetric or topographic maps of the area under investigation, locating the site in relation to established reference points such as bench marks, section corners, highway survey points, buildings, roads, and other permanent natural and cultural features; and (2) a map of the systematic division of the site surface into sub-units for measuring and locating features and artifacts (datum and grid).

Equipment   Anyone doing mapping in the field will need a drawing board, or a plane-table with tripod (see below) if available, to which a sheet of coordinated paper is affixed, usually by drafting tape. Particularly suitable is paper gridded in light-blue, 16 x 22 inches in size, ruled 10 mm. to the inch. A ruler—or better, an engineer's triangular scale that has six scales ruled in 10 to 60 parts to the inch—and a protractor will prove useful. Equipment increases in cost as one progresses from simple pacing and sketch-map surveys to mapping with instruments. Basic equipment, in addition to drawing board or plane-table, paper, scale, pencils (No. 3H), protractor and triangle, includes a good compass and tapes of the types described in the preceding section.

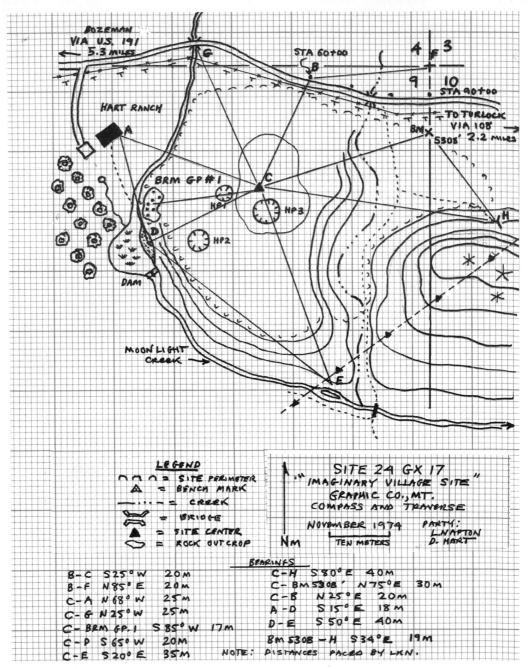

4-5. *Field map constructed to scale on coordinate paper by compass-traverse and intersection method. Compare with Figure 4-3, and note the more accurate placement of topographic features achieved by compass-traverse of the same site. This map requires contour intervals (cf. Figure 4-13), and will be re-drawn for publication (see Figure 4-14). Note the "key locator" bearings (C-A, C-G, C-B) taken from the center of the site (which will eventually become Datum A) to landmark features such as the Hart ranch house, a survey point on the main road, and a bridge abutment. The site can be recovered by reference to these bearings.*

If the site is to be sampled either by surface collection or by test-units, an accurate topographic map must be prepared, using instruments such as the plane-table and transit. In routine topographic mapping, the surveyor might complete the map and determine all necessary elevations in order to plot the contours. During archaeological projects, however, it usually will be necessary for the surveyor to establish the datum and construct the grid system on the site so that excavation can begin as soon as possible. In the following discussion, it is assumed that establishment of the datum point and grid system is the first task of the surveyor, followed by contour mapping as excavation proceeds.

Establishing the datum point   The datum point is the initial point, or control point, from which all measurements on the site are made. Also called the principal or *alpha datum*, this point should be located in a position central to the area of archaeological interest, and as close to the area to be gridded and mapped as practicable. Placing the alpha datum directly in the center of the site is not advisable of course, since excavation may destroy its location. The datum should be established off the site, and if the terrain permits, the writer prefers to set the alpha datum on the southwest periphery of the site, allowing the control grid to be laid out so that all measurements are taken north and east of the datum.

Ideally, the alpha datum should be located at the highest point on or near the site in order to provide a clear field of view for the surveyor. If there is an existing control point, such as a bench mark or section corner, it can serve as the datum, or the datum can be set in close proximity to a point of known legal location and elevation. Obviously, not every site will offer an ideal datum location, satisfying all of the specifications given above. The main function of the alpha datum is to establish the central reference point of the grid.

When a relatively permanent terrain feature (rock outcrop, solid foundation of a modern building, etc.) occupies a convenient location, a cross painted within a circle on this feature may be used as a datum point. When such a permanent location is not available, the alpha datum point should be marked by driving a metal rod into the ground, or, better still, setting a metal rod in a block of cement and burying the block in the ground so that only a short section of the rod protrudes above the surface. Segments of gas pipe or lengths of angle iron are often used. The metal datum rod should be painted with a brightly colored, weatherproof paint. If the datum point is to be used as a point from which magnetic bearings are taken, the rod must of course be made of nonmagnetic metal. The datum points should be located where they will not be disturbed by plowing. It must be remembered that the datum points will be used not only in the course of mapping and excavating the site, but to guide future workers in relocating excavated sections.

The field notes must contain a description of the datum points and explicit details as to their locations. Datum points should be marked on all maps (the conventional symbol is a cross within a circle). If the datum point lies beyond the limits of any of the maps made of the site, its location should be designated on the map by bearings and distance.

It may be desirable to establish secondary datum points. These should be designated sequentially, "Datum B," "Datum C," etc., and their precise locations must be defined relative to alpha datum. The notes (and preferably the map) should include all necessary information on elevation, distance, and direction of secondary datum points with reference to alpha datum.

The grid system   As an aid in mapping, and as a method of recording the location of artifacts and features found within the site, archaeologists construct a *Control Grid* originating at the alpha datum point. As mentioned earlier, it is necessary to decide whether one is going to use the metric or English system, because the site will be gridded either in meters or in feet. In practice, the writer recommends a metric grid laid out from alpha datum in reference to either true or magnetic north. An exception to this general rule could be a cave (see Fig. 4-9, for example) where the grid cannot be aligned on the north-south axis.

To construct the grid, a bearing is run north and south from the datum (initial point), and extended beyond the site. This north-south line is called the *Site Meridian*. Another control line is laid off from the datum at right angles to the meridian, and this is the east-west or *Site Base Line*. Auxiliary reference datums mentioned above may be set at the terminal points of the meridian and base lines.

It is important that the base line lies at a true ninety-degree angle to the meridian, for if it does not, the test units will be parallelograms, or at any rate will not be true squares, as they will appear on the map. It is possible to make the grid true by either of two methods. If one is using a plane-table or transit (described below), the ninety-degree angle can be turned with ease and the base line staked accordingly. If at least two tapes are available, the grid can be squared in the field by applying Pythagoras' theorem (Fig. 4-6). The tapes can be laid out in the proportions 3, 4, and 5, the last being the hypotenuse of the right-angled triangle (see Cole and King, 1968). For example, a tape is run along the site meridian from the initial point for 40 feet, at which point a reference stake is placed, and a small nail or *hub tack* is set in the top of the stake. Another tape is laid on the base line for a distance of 30 feet. A tape is laid from the stake at the 40-foot point on the meridian to the 30-foot point on the base line. The intervening diagonal must measure exactly 50 feet to achieve the right angle. The base line can be adjusted to establish the right angle.

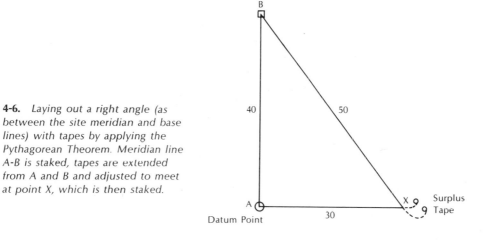

4-6. *Laying out a right angle (as between the site meridian and base lines) with tapes by applying the Pythagorean Theorem. Meridian line A-B is staked, tapes are extended from A and B and adjusted to meet at point X, which is then staked.*

The right-angled triangle can also be used in setting out 50-foot squares or ten-meter squares, when surface samples are to be taken from various areas of a site. The angle can be achieved with pocket tapes in the ratio of 3 feet–4 feet–5 feet to check the configuration of test units or test trenches. Test units can also be checked for true right angles by measuring across the diagonal of the unit. The diagonal of a test unit five feet square should measure 85½ inches. The diagonal of a two-meter square is 2.828 meters. The diagonal of a 10-meter square (often used in collection of controlled surface samples) is 14.14 meters.

A basic grid system is the *Finite* or limited grid (Fig. 4-7). If the site is small, it can be subsumed within the ninety-degree angle formed by the meridian segment running north from alpha datum, and by the base line segment extending east from alpha datum. This type of grid is useful for re-cording data on small sites or features such as house circles, "chipping stations," caves, and single burials. On large sites, for example occupation sites

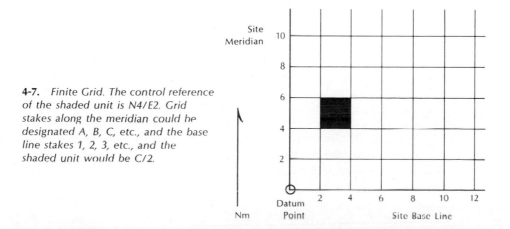

4-7. *Finite Grid. The control reference of the shaded unit is N4/E2. Grid stakes along the meridian could be designated A, B, C, etc., and the base line stakes 1, 2, 3, etc., and the shaded unit would be C/2.*

with subsurface components of unknown but probably extensive dimensions, the *Union Grid* is laid out (Fig. 4-8). The site meridian and base lines can be extended indefinitely, and ancillary datums placed at suitable points on the control lines. Black (1967) describes the carefully designed layout of an extensive grid at Angel Mounds, Indiana.

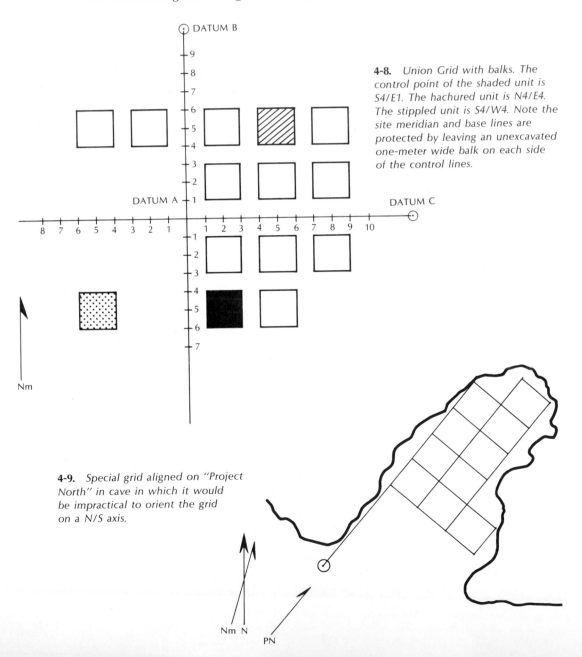

4-8. *Union Grid with balks. The control point of the shaded unit is S4/E1. The hachured unit is N4/E4. The stippled unit is S4/W4. Note the site meridian and base lines are protected by leaving an unexcavated one-meter wide balk on each side of the control lines.*

4-9. *Special grid aligned on "Project North" in cave in which it would be impractical to orient the grid on a N/S axis.*

All grids have in common the initial point (or alpha datum), and the right angle between the meridian ("y" or ordinate axis) and the base line ("x" or abscissa axis). Usually the grid is constructed on the site by driving surveyors' grade stakes at the intersections of the grid lines. Dowels, wooden stakes one-inch square, or rods of reinforcing iron cut to suitable lengths can be used. For temporary test units, chaining pins or even large spikes can be used to mark the grid units. The appearance of the site in photographs is greatly improved, and the units become more readily discernible, if the stakes all face the same way (flat side toward the alpha datum), and are painted red and white or some suitable color contrasting with the surrounding soil. A small hub tack or nail driven onto the top of the stake marks the exact intersection points of the grid.

Stakes may be set along the grid lines by use of a very taut string running from the datum along the control lines. However, two precautions should be observed if this method is used: first, the surveyor must bear in mind that on days when there is even a gentle breeze, the guide string may be carried out of alignment; and second, the guide string should be attached to the datum point and extended for the necessary distance along the meridian or base line, and the unit stakes set at appropriate intervals. The guide string should *not* be snubbed on the hub tack of each control stake, for this defeats the purpose of the guide string by breaking the control line into a series of short, non-aligned segments. Appropriate stake intervals are determined by measurement from the alpha datum point. The tape should be taut and horizontal, and not inclined along the slope gradient. Accurate units may be laid out on slopes by "breaking tape" as previously described.

The best way of designating control stakes marking grid intersections is in terms of the grid interval. For example, in a Finite Grid system laid out in two-meter increments, all stakes located north of the alpha datum would be labeled with an N for north and a number showing their distance northward from alpha datum: thus the row immediately north of the control point, two meters north, would be labeled N2, the next row N4, etc. All stakes located east of alpha datum would be labeled E (east), the row immediately eastward labeled E2; the next row E4, the next E6, etc. All stakes except those going due north along the meridian or due east along the base line would bear a double designation such as N4/E6, since each would lie both *n* distance north and *n* distance east of the control point. Thus, each stake is identified from the point of origin (alpha datum) of the grid system. The advantages of having the unit designation identify both the cardinal direction and the distance in meters from the alpha datum should be apparent.

In an alternative method of grid designation, stakes on either side of the site meridian are identified as left or right of the meridian, and the number of each stake denotes its distance from the alpha meridian; for example, 12L6, 16R6, etc.

A third method of labeling the Finite Grid is to designate the stakes along the meridian north of the alpha datum by letters and the stakes along the base line east of the datum by numbers, thus: unit A1, B2, C4, etc. This system should be applied only on very small sites, since it is limited to 26 rows of stakes. It is not good practice to extend this type of grid by resorting to designations such as AA, BB, or A', B', because doing sc increases the chance of human error in recording field data.

Whatever system is used, the surveyor uses a waterproof crayon or waterproof marking pen to write the unit control designation on both faces of each stake or on drafting tape affixed to the upper faces of the stake. The advantage of using tape is that it can be removed if the stakes are to be salvaged for work on another site.

The position of each specimen is measured from the unit control point, which is then measured from the alpha datum. Thus, the provenience of each specimen is determined exactly *n* meters or centimeters north and *n* meters or centimeters east of the alpha datum.

On the *Union Grid* system, the unit control stake is always the unit stake closest to the alpha datum (Fig. 4-8), and measurements within each unit are taken accordingly.

Examples of grid systems are discussed and illustrated in Byers and Johnson (1939: Fig. 20), Cole and Deuel (1937: Figs. 20, 27, 32), Hill and Kivett (1940: 151–153), Treganza and Cook (1948), Webb and Haag (1939), Mulloy (1942), Webb (1939: 7), Wedel (1941: Figs. 3, 8), Atkinson (1953: 41–43), Wheeler (1954: 66), Laplace-Jauretche (1954), and Lorenzo (1956).

Surveying instruments Two basic instruments are ordinarily used in constructing the control grid on archaeological sites. These are the *engineer's transit* and the *plane-table*. The plane-table is much to be preferred in archaeological mapping, but since transits are widely used in construction work and in general surveying, they are usually readily available.

The most significant difference between the transit and the plane-table for archaeological purposes is that when using a transit, the surveyor records distances, bearings, angles, directions, and other data in a notebook, and the site map is constructed later by reference to the field data. The transit is considerably more accurate than the plane-table. For example, grid stakes set with the plane-table *alidade* (see below) will not have the precise alignment obtained by transit, due to parallax. However, mapping is accomplished rapidly with the plane-table. One draws the site map in the field, detects and corrects mistakes, and plots detail during the progress of the survey. Most transit telescopes and plane-table alidades are equipped with *stadia* hairs to enable the surveyor to read the distance from the instrument to the *stadia rod* (Fig. 4-2,f). Distances can be measured as accurately as necessary for most purposes in archaeology by the stadia method. This method of determining distance is quicker than taping or chaining, and expedites plotting the position and configuration of site features.

Transits may be obtained from local equipment rental companies, or purchased from suppliers such as Sears. Transits can be used for measuring and laying off horizontal and vertical angles, directions, distances, differences in elevation, and control lines for archaeological grids. The principal features of a transit are the telescope, compass box, graduated circles and verniers, and various levels mounted on a rotating head attached to a tripod. Using the transit telescope and compass, surveyors can lay out a row of grid stakes aligned precisely on magnetic north or true north. The ninety-degree angle between the north-south meridian and the east-west base line can easily be turned using the graduated circle.

The *plane-table* is a drawing board mounted on a universal swivel head attached to a tripod. Used with the plane-table is the telescopic *alidade*, which is mounted on a pedestal attached to a flat base-plate (blade) that has a straight edge (Fig. 4-10). The alidade, plane-table, and tripod are referred to as the "plane-table outfit." The general principle of the plane-table is that one sights through the telescopic alidade, reads the stadia interval, and draws a line along the blade on gridded paper attached to the plane-table. Features along the line are drawn to scale.

4-10. *Plane-table and alidade in use. The surveyor is entering elevation notes in a field book. The top of the plane-table is free of objects, other than the alidade. (CSCS photograph by W Keener.)*

There are five basic steps in setting up the plane-table and getting ready to do mapping. (1) The plane-table is set up over the datum point, and a *plumb bob* is used to verify that the center of the table lies directly over the dead center of the datum point. (2) Next, the table is leveled, using either the level provided with the alidade or a short carpenter's level. (3) The table is oriented to magnetic or true north by means of the *barrel compass* that some manufacturers set into the edge of the plane-table, or by using a Brunton or Silva compass aligned on the gridded paper attached to the table. The line indicating magnetic north is drawn directly on the paper. (4) The surveyor must determine the *instrument height*. This is accomplished by placing the stadia rod immediately in front of the alidade telescope at the edge of the plane-table. The surveyor determines the distance from the center of the telescope barrel to the ground surface at the datum point and records this figure as the instrument height (Fig. 4-11). (5) The name of the site, map title, map scale, topographer's name, instrument height, and all other essential information should be entered in the *legend* block usually drawn in the lower right-hand corner of the map. This must be accomplished before any mapping is done.

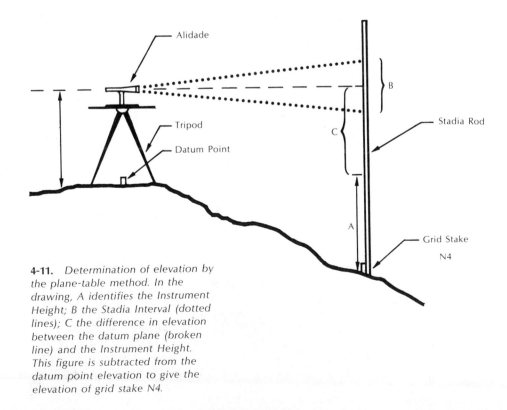

4-11. *Determination of elevation by the plane-table method. In the drawing, A identifies the Instrument Height; B the Stadia Interval (dotted lines); C the difference in elevation between the datum plane (broken line) and the Instrument Height. This figure is subtracted from the datum point elevation to give the elevation of grid stake N4.*

To use the plane-table, one sights through the telescope to the stadia rod held on a distant point, as mentioned above. The telescope is equipped with cross hairs. The surveyor aligns the vertical cross-hair on the stadia rod and draws a line (or "ray") directly on the gridded paper attached to the plane-table, using the edge of the alidade blade as a guide. Thus, the *direction* of the ray from the datum point to the distant point is determined and drawn on the map. The *distance* from the instrument to the distant point may be ascertained either by taping or by the stadia method. This method, using the oldest principles of surveying, consists simply of observing through the telescope the apparent locations of two horizontal stadia hairs, as they appear on the face of the stadia rod held on a distant point (Fig. 4-12). If the rod is held close to the instrument, only a small segment of it will be seen through the telescope. When the rod is moved farther away from the instrument, a larger segment of it is visible. This segment is called the *stadia interval*, and is a direct function of the distance between rod and instrument.

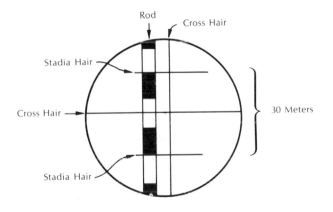

4-12. *Stadia rod marked in ten centimeter increments seen through the alidade telescope. The amount of the stadia rod that is visible between the stadia hairs shows that the rod is exactly 30 meters from the instrument.*

In addition to stadia hairs, the alidade is equipped with vertical and horizontal cross-hairs. Elevations of ground points may be taken with the alidade as described below. However, on steep gradients it may not be possible to see the rod when the telescope is level. The telescope must then be depressed to bring the rod into view. The distance and difference in elevation may then be read, and the slope gradient reduced to horizontal by use of the *Beaman Stadia Arc* with which most alidades are equipped. Using the Beaman arc in the field requires detailed instruction and a good deal of practice. Low (1952) has written one of the best manuals discussing this type of survey.

Another type of alidade, the microptic alidade, which features digital display of differences in elevation, is coming into use in the United States. A much less complex type of alidade that is often used in archaeology is the simple "peep-sight" alidade, which consists of a brass blade with peep-sight leaves hinged at each end. This instrument provides "open sights" useful in sighting direction, but will not give stadia distance or elevations. One can use a triangular engineer's scale to much the same effect, by placing it on an improvised plane-table and sighting along its edge. Other kinds of peep-sight alidades can be made for archaeological application.

Procedures and equipment for alidade and plane-table surveying are described by Compton (1962), Lahee (1952: 446ff.), and Spier (1970), as well as by Debenham (1955: Chaps. 8, 9), Cox, Dake, and Muilenburg (1921), Detweiler (1948), Spaulding (1951), Atkinson (1953: Chap. 3), and Kenyon (1961: 115–122).

Elevations and contours   The datum and grid system are references for recording two dimensions of the provenience of archaeological features. Elevation, the third dimension of archaeological provenience, is taken in reference to the *datum plane* that extends over the entire site. This plane can be conceived of as a "ceiling" above the entire site, clearing its highest point and level in all directions. The datum plane lies at the elevation of the surveying instrument above the alpha datum or highest point of the site (Fig. 4-11). For purposes of this discussion, we shall assume that alpha datum is located at the highest point of the site. If possible, it is desirable to establish the true elevation of the alpha datum. This can be done if there is a USGS bench mark or section corner nearby. Elevation can also be determined using an aneroid barometer or pocket barometer (altimeter) which responds to decreasing air pressure as elevation increases. However, elevations obtained with barometers are not always accurate.

The alpha datum or highest point on an archaeological site can be assigned an arbitrary elevation of 100.00 (meters or feet). In using surveying equipment, the hand level or sighting telescope will be perhaps a meter and a half higher than the datum point, depending on what the instrument operator considers a convenient working height. This "working height" or instrument height is the datum plane, which might be 101.50 meters. To determine elevations of all points on the archaeological site, instrument readings of all rod elevations are subtracted from this figure.

Elevation of topographic features can be determined with simple and quite inexpensive equipment. Minimal equipment for determining elevation is a hand level (Fig. 4-2, d,e) and a level rod of the self-reading type calibrated in the metric system or in feet. The hand level can be mounted on a photo tripod or the end of a straight 1" x 2" batten of suitable length, perhaps 1.5 meters or 5 feet long. The hand level and leveling rod can be purchased from

K & E, Lietz, or other suppliers. The "Philadelphia" or "Frisco" type rod is commonly used. Less expensive is the flexible rod ribbon that is graduated in the metric or English system and can be attached to any convenient batten or straight pole. A leveling rod may be made by painting alternate red and white divisions on a good-grade 1" x 3" batten and using black paint to mark the divisions in the metric or English system. A 30-meter (100 ft.) tape, plastic engineer's flagging tape, notebooks, etc. will be needed.

Survey of elevation is accomplished by a three-person team: an "instrument operator" who is stationed at the alpha datum or at the highest point on the area to be mapped, a "recorder" who works with the instrument operator and takes notes of all points recorded and their elevations, and a "rod carrier" who moves progressively from one leveling station (grid stake) to the next. The object of their cooperative effort is to establish and record the elevation of each grid stake or other point for which an elevation is needed, in relation to the datum plane of the site. The instrument operator rests the sighting level on the photo tripod or on the end of the prepared batten; the rod carrier places the base of the leveling rod alongside a grid stake, being careful to keep the rod perpendicular. This can be achieved by feeling the balance of the rod between the fingertips, or by attaching to the leveling rod an eyescrew, from which a plumb bob may be suspended.

The instrument operator sights through the hand level or instrument telescope, reads the mark on the leveling rod intercepted by the horizontal cross hair, and subtracts this figure from the datum plane elevation. The rod carrier marks the same figure on the grid stake and draws a horizontal line across the base of the stake, marking the elevation. The rod carrier moves to successive grid stakes until all necessary elevations are marked on the stakes and noted by the recorder.

To determine elevations using the transit or alidade and plane-table, a similar procedure is followed. (1) Set up the plane-table over the alpha datum level and orient the table and obtain the instrument height, as described in the preceding section. (2) Hold the stadia rod on a unit control stake while the surveyor sights through the alidade and observes which rod graduation is intercepted by the horizontal cross hair. The difference between the reading on the rod and the instrument height gives the ground elevation at the point where the rod is positioned. (3) The surveyor prints this elevation legibly on the map and the rod carrier writes it on the stake. The grid stake elevations and sightings on topographic points can be used to construct the contour map of the site.

Contour maps Contour maps of archaeological sites are usually drawn in 25 cm., 50 cm., or one-meter intervals. A rapid method for contouring a site is to determine the elevations of each grid stake along the site meridian and base lines. Other reference radii may be extended as tangents from the alpha

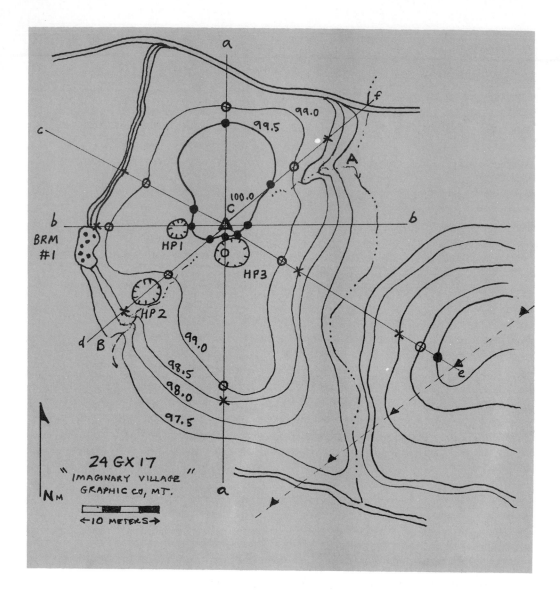

4-13. *Plan view of site: Contour map of mound made by connecting points of common elevation along the site meridian (a-a) and the base line (b-b). The total number of radii and their direction will depend on the terrain, the amount of time available for mapping, and the degree of topographic accuracy necessary for the situation. The elevation of alpha datum (c) is 100.00 meters. Assuming a contour interval of 0.5 meters, all solid black dots are −0.5 (99.5); all circles −1.0 meter (99.0); all x symbols are −1.5 meters (98.5). Note how the small drainages (A and B) between the reference radii are interpolated by the cartographer in the field.*

datum, and elevations are taken along these radii (Fig. 4-13). This is easily accomplished with the plane-table. The rod carrier progresses along a radius until the rod-reading changes an amount equal to the contour interval. This point on the ground, or any point where the leveling rod is set and a rod-reading taken, is called a *turning point*. The distance between the datum point and the turning point is then determined, either by stadia readings or by taping. All elevations are plotted on the site map and points of equal elevation are connected, forming contour lines. The production of a contour map that depicts the site topography reasonably well will depend on the experience and "topographic sense" of the map-maker.

In connecting points of common elevation, it is desirable to indicate undulations, stream channels, humps, etc., by the subtle forms of the contour lines. Study of USGS contour maps will of course aid the apprentice cartographer in understanding the relationship of contour lines to the actual terrain.

All archaeological maps should be copied in the field, since a single original may get damaged or lost. Transparent plastic "Mylar" film is excellent for tracing overlays of the grid system on the contour map, or *vice versa*.

PREPARING MAPS FOR PUBLICATION

Archaeological maps are redrawn from the field copies in the cartographic laboratory (Fig. 4-14). Drafting maps for publication is time-consuming and requires considerable skill and experience. Some persons are more gifted than others in draftsmanship, but the efficiency and neatness of both beginner and expert will be increased by careful preparation for map drawing. It is assumed that archaeologists are familiar with basic drafting equipment such as *Rapidograph*, ruling, speedball, and crowquill pens, T-squares, triangles, and gloss-top tracing tables. The apprentice map-maker should consult books on standard cartographic principles (Raisz, 1962; Robinson and Sale, 1969; Hodgkiss, 1970), and instructions from experienced colleagues (see Bryant and Holtz, 1965). One can profit by studying the modes of geographic depiction on USGS maps. Careful planning and preliminary working copies of maps will be useful in placing lettering, and will allow necessary detail to be shown without seriously affecting legibility.

In making maps for publication it is important to remember that certain conventions for representing topographic features have long been in use (Raisz, 1962) and should be followed so that the map is legible to all. There are conventional signs for various types of vegetation, instrument survey notations, ecological studies, forest resources, soil survey, etc. Lahee (1952: 615–690) and others give the symbols commonly used by geologists to represent rock formations and linear features such as dip and strike, faults, strata, joints, cleavage, etc.

METHODS
OF EXCAVATION

5

It is necessary that we [archaeologists] attempt to attain a measure of exactness in a study which deals so largely with the unknown and the shifting and the absent.

—J. A. WILSON, 1942:4

 Many books and articles have been written on excavation techniques. Although it is informative to read about these techniques, the only way to be an archaeologist is to do archaeology. We can scarcely improve on Robert Braidwood's epigram: "Archaeology is what archaeologists do."

TOOLS

The number and variety of implements used in archaeological excavation throughout the world are practically limitless. So many special or unusual conditions are likely to be met in the course of excavation that even a bare minimum of equipment must necessarily include an assortment of tools. Subject to the limitations imposed by money, convenience of transportation, and storage in the field, the more the better is a sound general rule.

Implements that have been found to be generally useful are mentioned below. Large or expensive tools and special equipment will usually be supplied by the institution sponsoring the dig, or by organizations that rent or lend them.

In the last analysis, excavation consists of moving earth; hence the shovel is the trademark of archaeology and perhaps its most indispensable tool. Long-handled, round-point standard No. 2 excavating shovels are recommended as basic. Square-point shovels are useful in excavating sandy deposits, and many archaeologists have found them valuable for cleaning excavation unit floors in the search for post-mold, rodent burrows, and other features. Scoops and spades are of little use in the excavating process, although scoops can come in handy for backfilling.

Ordinarily, enough shovels should be provided so that one may be issued to every member of the digging crew. Shovel handles should be sandpapered occasionally and treated with linseed oil. The conditions and methods for using shovels and other tools will be discussed in greater detail below.

Heavy, sharp, stout-handled "railroad" picks are often used, though lighter-weight miner's picks or short-handled army pick-mattocks are easier to handle and are preferred by some archaeologists. Since picks can cause considerable damage to artifacts, they are generally used only to loosen calcareous, highly compact, or stony deposits too hard for shovels to penetrate. They are nevertheless essential where such deposits do occur. A heavy pick swung with both hands represents considerable force, and workers should be cautioned not to strike themselves in the foot and not to hit other workers who may be nearby, particularly behind them. Where paid labor crews are used, workers usually specialize in the use of pick, shovel, wheelbarrow, and the like, often becoming very skillful and efficient with their particular tool.

Sifting excavated earth through screens enables the archaeologist to recover many materials that might otherwise be overlooked (leading to considerable bias in the sample obtained from a site). Each digging crew has a number of sizes and grades of screens for use under varying circumstances (two types of screens are shown in Fig. 5-1). Screens of 1/2" and 1/4" mesh have commonly been used, but these can often allow tiny flint flakes, animal bones, and other minute forms of archaeological evidence to be lost. Thus, fine-screening (with 1/8" or 1/16" mesh) has become a part of most modern excavations. Aten (1971: 15) has combined fine screening with "water screening" in processing deposits from coastal middens of mucky (or hard, when dry) clay, using a small gasoline-operated pump to wash deposits through 1/16"-mesh screen. This technique yielded "almost total specimen recovery," without destroying such materials as the bones of small animals as dry screening can (see also Sense, 1973; and Graham and Wray, 1962).

Screening has also been used to determine the quantitative composition of a deposit. Since 1946, for example, workers at the University of California have been screening large samples of refuse deposits, sorting the screenings into components (bone, shell, obsidian, rock, etc.), measuring the relative amounts of each, and using these quantitative data to attempt to gain some insight into the economy and industrial activities of the former inhabitants. For details of the method and results, see Cook (1950), Cook and Treganza (1947, 1950), Cook and Heizer (1951, 1962), Heizer and Cook (1956), Heizer and Squier (1953), and Heizer (1960: 95–96).

If a limited amount of screening is planned, small hand screens are most convenient (see Fig. 5-1). These may be made up in several sizes so they will

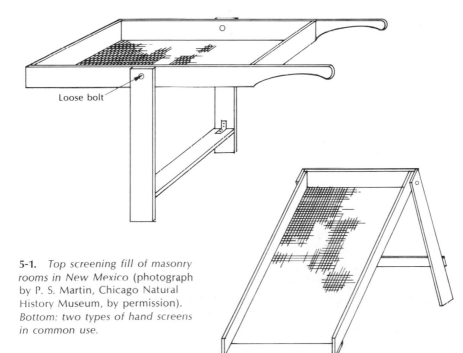

5-1. *Top screening fill of masonry rooms in New Mexico (photograph by P. S. Martin, Chicago Natural History Museum, by permission). Bottom: two types of hand screens in common use.*

Loose bolt

nest together for more convenient transportation (see Scholtz, 1962). Larger screens (often three by five feet) resting on sawhorses permit a greater volume of earth to be processed, yet are easy enough to move as excavation progresses. In some large-scale excavations, screens are mounted in frames supported by flexible steel bands that allow vigorous shaking. "Shaker screens" that are rocked by a motor on a carriage have been found to be useful (Bird and Ford, 1956), and other forms of mechanized screening have more recently been proposed (Bird, 1968; Guerreschi, 1973; Michie, 1969). The number and variety of screens provided for an excavation must depend on the character of the site and the goals of the research project, but two or three hand screens would probably be a minimum for any site.

It is often necessary to have water in the immediate vicinity of an excavation. Galvanized buckets are the most useful containers. Skeletons and artifacts are often washed in situ so that they can be seen and photographed clearly. In washing artifacts, care should always be taken not to remove, through inattention, some adhering fragments or flakes or fugitive material such as paint.

Soil samples from below and around the site at various depths may be important (see Chapter 6 for methods of taking soil samples). Such samples can be secured with an auger, preferably at least six feet in length. A two-inch-diameter worm auger and a four-inch barrel auger are often employed (Ford and Webb, 1956: 21). Augers can also be used to sample the depth and the extent of archaeological deposits at a site or to search for hidden construction or other buried features (Heizer *et al.*, 1973, used augers to search for 18th Dynasty docking facilities at Luxor in Upper Egypt). Fry (1972: 259–260) has suggested using post-hole diggers for similar kinds of exploration and sampling; in his case, locating dense occupation debris at Tikal in Guatemala.

A measuring tape at least 50 feet long is indispensable. A hundred-foot (or 30-meter) tape would be preferable, and a 300-foot reel tape is often useful. One should be sufficient. The measuring tape is essential in marking off the site according to the coordinate (grid) system, before excavation. Steel tapes are superior to cloth ones, though they are far more expensive and must be cared for by oiling and cleaning. Whitefaced tapes are the easiest to see and thus the least likely to be misread.

The following smaller implements are also considered essential. Every excavator may have to furnish himself or herself with one of each, since the sponsoring organization may not supply them.

Trowels are used for careful excavation, especially in uncovering and excavating in the immediate vicinity of burials or artifacts and wherever larger tools might damage or displace materials. A four- or six-inch "Marshalltown" or "Standard" brand pointing trowel (mason's trowel) is by far the best. Both brands are made of excellent steel, with the blade and stem of one piece. They are expensive, but worth the investment. Cheap trowels will bend and break, and more flexible mason's trowels and garden trowels are inconvenient.

A rigid, fine-point, wooden-handled ice pick is also a useful tool. It is used for exceptionally delicate excavation in exposing burials, recovering artifacts from hard deposit, dealing with fragile materials, etc.

Paint brushes two inches or less in width are very useful. Used dry, they are helpful in brushing away loose earth in delicate work such as exposing burials, and in preparing burials and stratigraphic profiles for photography. Dipped in water, they are a convenient aid in washing skeletal or cultural materials for in situ photographs.

A heavy brush and a metal dustpan can be used to collect dirt at intervals when careful exposure is being done. A six- or eight-foot (or 2-meter) rolled steel pocket tape or snap-rule is indispensable for measuring the location of materials recovered. Each excavator should carry one in his or her pocket. Again, a good rule will be found to last longer and will justify the added initial expense.

The U.S. Army Engineer's pocket compass (Fig. 4-2) is adequate for most archaeological purposes. Indispensable in site surveying, it is used once excavation begins for determining the orientation of burials and in recording the location of nonpermanent datum points.

Other useful items include enough blank forms to record all data likely to be obtained: artifact slips, feature and burial records, site survey sheets, photographic record sheets, and field catalog sheets. Graph paper will be needed for mapping. Large numbers of cloth bags or strong paper sacks are indispensable. Soft-metal or linen tags with copper-wire or string ties are handy for labeling or closing cloth bags, and for labeling catalogued objects. Felt-tipped pens are excellent for marking paper bags since the lettering is bold and permanent. Artifacts and other materials recovered are generally kept in small sacks during the actual course of excavation; large bags are used for burials and features. Matchboxes are useful for storing small artifacts. Whenever possible, cardboard cartons are used to store materials and to protect them during transport by automobile. Skeletons from burials should be placed in wooden boxes to prevent breakage, and all freight or express shipments must be in wooden boxes.

Stakes (or long iron spikes or bolts) will be needed for laying out the site before excavation and as local datum points in measuring thereafter. Wooden stakes can often be made at the site, but it is safer to take them along, if there is room. They should be at least a foot long, and stakes 1" × 2" × 24" (or even 30") are recommended. Cloth tags with tie-strings should be included for marking the stakes according to their coordinate location. Lastly, plenty of pencils should be on hand.

The items listed above should be considered a minimum equipment list; a number of additional implements will often be useful. With a little ingenuity, a great many other implements can be improvised in the field to meet special conditions. The list below, not by any means a maximum, comprises only tools used in the actual course of excavation. Additional equipment necessary in surveying, mapping, preservation of materials, etc., is discussed elsewhere.

A whisk broom may occasionally be more convenient than a paint brush for removing loose earth while exposing a burial, cleaning the dust off a vertical profile, etc.

A "scratcher" can easily be made by bending a file, awl, or large sailmaker's needle to a right angle at a spot between an inch and two inches from the point. Such a tool is sometimes handier than a straight ice pick for cleaning earth out of skeletal crevices and for other delicate work. Dental tools, toothbrushes, and scrubbing brushes are also useful for tedious clearing chores.

A pocket magnifying glass will be handy for examining small objects on the spot.

Before photographing a skeleton from a burial, a feature, or a stratigraphic profile, the archaeologist will want to remove any residual loose earth and dust. A bellows or a bicycle tire pump may be very useful for this purpose. The advantage of such instruments, if properly handled, is that they will not disturb fragile or lightweight objects.

A hand sprayer of the type commonly used to spread solutions on garden plants may be used to spray water on a wall or cleared flat surface to bring out color distinctions that are otherwise faint or invisible. Light spraying of this sort can be done immediately before photographs are taken in order to achieve greater contrast (Hole and Heizer, 1973: Fig. 45; Bruce-Mitford, 1956: 236).

Thin translucent plastic sheeting can be used to shelter an excavation from the rain (Borden, 1950).

APPROACHES TO EXCAVATION

Once a site has been mapped and laid out in a grid (see Chapter 4 above), the major problem confronting the archaeologist about to begin an excavation is precisely where to dig. In the past, this crucial question was often answered by intuition or by selecting an area that "looked rich." More recently, various random and systematic techniques have been devised for sampling a site to see which areas seem to merit further exploration (see Chapter 15; also Watson, LeBlanc, and Redman, 1971; 121–125). The particular technique used depends upon the research design of the excavation project. These techniques are not without their problems (such as "blank spots" not covered by random sampling; Watson, LeBlanc, and Redman, 1971; Johnson, 1972: 372), but they do undeniably eliminate subjective bias in deciding where to dig.

On the other hand, Dorwin (1971: 357ff.) has argued that random sampling techniques are a "waste of time" at small habitation sites such as the Bowen site in central Indiana. Dorwin drew up an excavation plan based on random sampling, and demonstrated that had he used this plan instead of excavating the site completely as he did, many facts would have been missed and the site and its contents misinterpreted as a result. A similar misreading of the Bowen site, says Dorwin, would have resulted from stratified cluster sampling.

It is obvious, as Dorwin states, that the only way to reduce sampling error to zero is to excavate sites completely. Unfortunately, in most research programs this is impossible.

Whatever sampling technique is to be used, after a site has been mapped (see Chapter 4) it is usually laid out according to one coordinate (grid) system or another. The center line, datum line, or base line, generally oriented in a specific direction (north-south or east-west), is marked off first by means of a compass and tape reading from the datum point. The intersections of future transverse lines are then marked at regular intervals (usually five or ten feet, or two or four meters) along it, and these lines can later be staked off from a compass reading at right angles to the datum line. It is then a simple matter to determine with a measuring tape and to mark at the appropriate points the corners of the remaining grid units. Stakes marking the intersections of grid lines should then be driven in wherever excavation is contemplated, and appropriately labeled with tags. These stakes will subsequently represent the corners of excavation units and will serve as local datum points in recording locations.

In his excavations at the Abri Pataud rockshelter (France), Movius (1974: 105ff) has used an elevated grid of 2-meter squares composed of north-south and east-west rows of pipe intersecting at 2-meter intervals, with plumbs suspended from the intersections.

Assuming, then, that the decision has been made not to excavate the entire site, archaeologists have various means at their disposal for locating within a site the area with the most potential for excavation, and thus deciding precisely where to concentrate their efforts. Unless sufficient advance information is already available about the contents of the site, exploratory or test excavations are usually carried out. These usually take the form of test pits (sondage; Struever, 1968b) or narrow trenches (Skinner, 1971: 167). Whether their location is chosen by a computer or by the excavator, at random, by intuition, by logical reasoning from survey evidence, or by a combination of the five, such preliminary excavations can provide information on the composition and stratification of a site, locate areas of activity or especially rich deposits within it, and thus serve as a guide for later, more extensive excavation.*

Sir Mortimer Wheeler (1954: 84–85) says of the test-pit (his "control-pit") system:

> This is the supervisor's own special charge, and upon it the accuracy of the general digging in large measure depends. . . . Its purpose is to enable the supervisor, with a minimum disturbance of the strata, to anticipate the nature and probable vertical extent of the layers which are being cleared by his main gang. It is a glimpse into the future.

Once an area of a site has been chosen for excavation, the archaeologist must choose the appropriate excavating method. The choice will depend on the type of site being investigated and on the specific goals of the expedition. Many methods of excavation are available, and can be used in combination as well as singly: trenching, the strip method, quartering, area and large-area or block excavation, and stripping, to name only some of the standard methods we discuss here.

Trenching has been used in obtaining cross sections of sites and is particularly important in stratigraphy in that it provides a single, long vertical profile (see Fig. 5-2). Excavation of trenches can be accomplished in a variety of ways. Most common is a linear interconnected series of pits, usually excavated in arbitrary or stratigraphic levels. The term "trench" can also be applied to variously shaped rectangular test pits dug in a site. Trenching can be done by power machinery if sterile overburden is being removed in order to expose buried cultural remains.

As indicated earlier, narrow trenching may be used as a sampling technique in the search for houses, cemeteries, or activity areas to be exposed by area excavation. At certain historic sites where only the approximate area occupied by a fort or mission building is known, the excavator may decide to run a series of narrow exploratory trial trenches in the hope of encountering foundations, bases of walls, a stockade line, or the like. Once something is known of the location of certain features (identifiable perhaps from illustrations of the original structures) and the extent of the site area, excavation of that area can begin.

In sites where extensive features such as structures are encountered, excavation by trench alone will not give a sufficiently extensive view of the situation. For example, Haury's sectioning of the great canal at Snaketown (Haury, 1937b) yielded the desired information on the size of the canal and its history of use over a long period of time. But in the large ballcourts at the

---

*Some archaeologists may be interested in learning more about the nature and depositional history of the soils in the site area. For such purposes, Deetz (1967: 13–14) has suggested digging a "control pit" in a spot away from the area containing cultural remains, although under some circumstances on- and off-site soil samples can be collected with an auger (Cook and Heizer, 1965b; 29 ff.).

5-2. *A trench through Mound A, Medora site, Louisiana. Note stakes forming a grid system of 5-foot squares. (After Quimby, 1951: Fig. 2; courtesy of the Field Museum of Natural History, Chicago.)*

same Snaketown site, a trench, though revealing a cross section of the court at one point, failed to provide all of the data needed on the structure.

In another excavation approach called the *strip method,* often used in mound and barrow excavation, digging begins at the edge of the area to be excavated, and work continues straight through the site in strips; i.e., the face of the deposit is exposed in successive parallel cuttings usually five feet wide (see Fig. 5-3). If a feature is encountered lying partly in one strip or section, and partly in the next, it is left on a pedestal while the one strip is excavated

5-3. *Right: excavation technique for Hiwassee Island burial mounds. The mound is investigated by working toward the center in cuts 5 feet wide. The approach trenches in this diagram have been dug to mound subsoil and when continued will permit examination of 5-foot slices of the mound. North-south and east-west standing profiles are left, and stratification is recorded at every 5-foot interval before excavation proceeds. (After Lewis and Kneberg, 1946: Fig. 1.) Below: dissection of small clay platform mound at the La Venta site, Mexico, illustrating retention of sections for stratigraphic control. Photograph by Robert F. Heizer, 1955.)*

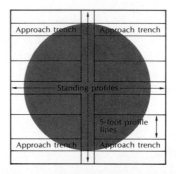

and not fully exposed until the excavation advances to the other strip. Then, as the feature is brought into full view, it is noted and removed and the pedestal of earth on which it rested is excavated (see Perino, 1968: Fig. 30). As each section of the mound is exposed, a stratigraphic profile is drawn so that the construction of the entire deposit can later be worked out. Illustrations of this excavation approach are presented by Cole (1951: 59, Pl. 5A), Perino (1968), Wheeler (1954: 94–95; Figs. 18, 19), and Atkinson (1953: Fig. 10, adapted below).

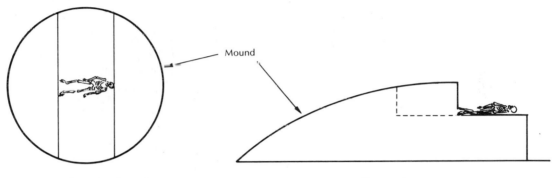

View from above showing strips   Cross-section

An alternative technique is *quartering* or the quadrant method, where the mound is laid out into four quadrants by balks three or more feet wide. Excavation of each quadrant proceeds systematically, and the coordinate balks preserve the contour and stratification of the deposit as shown in the following diagrams. (For further details see Atkinson, 1953: 59; Wheeler, 1954: 95; Grahame Clark, 1947: 97; Kenyon, 1961: Pl. 7.)

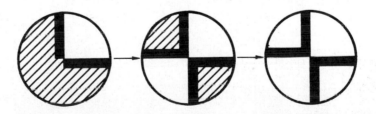

Jelks and Tunnell (1959: 8) describe the quadrant excavation of a mound in eastern Texas:

A stake was placed near the center of the mound and a grid of 5-foot squares was established which tied in with the centrally located stake. Then each quadrant of the mound was excavated separately. Beginning at the top of the mound, an entire quadrant was taken down by regular vertical intervals, usually of 0.5 feet each. The floor of the excavation was cleaned and examined after each level was removed, and measured drawings were prepared to record any zoning or occupational features that were observed in the excavation floor. The four profiles radiating in the cardinal directions from the central stake were always left intact until measured drawings had been prepared.

Easily observable architectural features such as house depressions, pit houses, or rooms in Southwestern American pueblo ruins (cf. Deetz, 1967: 17; Fitting, 1973b) may be used as excavation units. Even so, however, it is wise to establish systematic horizontal and vertical controls in excavating them. Also, if many rooms or other architectural features are present at a site, there must usually be some process for selecting the rooms to be excavated. Hill (1967) used probability sampling in such a situation at Broken K pueblo, Arizona.

Area excavation, by which is meant the orderly exploration of a sizable expanse of a site, allows the archaeologist to obtain a larger (and more meaningful) sample of artifacts, features, activity areas, and other buried remains than trenching or other less extensive methods. Area excavation is usually but not always done within a grid system. The grid system (see Chapter 4) allows each unit to be excavated so that a wall or balk is left between adjoining squares. The balk, often about two feet wide, preserves, until the very end of excavation, the stratigraphic profile on all sides of the excavation unit. The careful preservation of balks is shown in the excavations of Atkinson, 1953: 42–43; Cookson, 1954: Pl. 5; Bruce-Mitford, 1956: Pl. 8A; Goodwin, 1953: Fig. 8; Kenyon, 1961: Pl. 8; Ponce Sanginés, 1961 (see Fig. 4); and Wheeler, 1954; Pl. 5.

Although area excavation can use a grid system and still be conducted so as to expose buried features and structures (see Fagan, 1972: Fig. 4:6 for an

5-4. *Excavations at Tiahuanaco, Bolivia, showing balks.* (Photographs courtesy of Dr. Carlos Ponce Sanginés.)

5-5. *Area excavation, with balks preserved Chencherere II rockshelter, Malawi.* (Photograph courtesy of J. Desmond Clark.)

example), in North America it has usually been used to explore "vertical" problems (stratification, chronological sequence of artifacts, and general questions of culture history). In such an excavation, each unit is carried downward by arbitrary or natural levels (usually independently of what is going on in nearby or even adjacent units).

If one is seeking "horizontal" information, then one should work for broad exposure of buried cultural remains, using "large-area excavation," or as some have called it, "block excavation." Block excavation may be undertaken as one phase of an overall excavation plan (Binford, 1964; Redman, 1973a).

Large-area excavation may or may not involve a grid layout, and balks may or may not be preserved (see Fig. 5-5 for an example of such an excavation using a grid). For example, if living floors or architectural features are found in digging, the excavator might wish to follow these and expose them fully, ignoring the grid. The chief value of large-area or block excavation, according to Struever (1968b), is that it "provides a broad expanse of living surface enabling recovery of the total population of cultural items resulting from activities carried on in that particular precinct" (see also Hole and Heizer, 1973: 185).

Biddle and Kjølbye-Biddle (1969) report the use of what they call "open-area" horizontal excavation at Winchester, England, covering in detail the techniques and problems of this kind of excavation (p. 211–213). The advantage of this approach, according to the Biddles, is that "an overall view of the horizontal is always obtainable" (p. 212); the disadvantage is that it is difficult and "requires . . . great site discipline and well-trained workers" (p. 213). Another disadvantage of block, large-area or open-area excavations, especially if done within a grid system, is that they cost a lot of time and money (Fagan, 1972: 88). For additional examples of large-area excavation, see Binford *et al.*, 1970; Cole, 1951; J. G. D. Clark, 1954; Sankalia, 1969.

"Stripping" excavations have been used recently to remove large areas of overburden in order to expose stable land surfaces bearing living floors, houses, or other cultural features (cf. Binford *et al.*, 1970). This kind of excavation may be the third phase in the investigation of a site, the first phase being test-pitting, and the second phase "block" excavation (Binford, 1964). Stripping is costly as it usually involves power machinery. However, it is a most valuable excavation technique, permitting archaeologists to examine very large areas and to sample a greater number of phenomena within a site.

What we have provided here is but a brief review of certain major approaches to excavation. So many considerations can affect the plan of an excavation that archaeologists rarely use exactly the same system twice. The best approach to the excavation of a site will be flexible, allowing the excavator to take advantage of the techniques that will best elucidate the problems he is investigating. Adapting techniques to the site at hand is up to the individual in charge of the excavation. As an example of modifying excavation techniques to the situation at hand, we have assembled the series of four photographs in Fig. 5-6–5-9. These show excavations in Mound C, a large Caddoan burial mound at the George C. Davis site in eastern Texas. A huge trench had been cut into the mound early in this century by treasure-hunters. The excavator, Dee Ann Story (University of Texas at Austin), used power machinery to clear most of this trench, then a crew with shovels and trowels to locate the edges of the disturbed area. In the process of recording the stratigraphy exposed by the treasure-hunter's trench, she recognized and excavated large burial pits.

METHODS OF EXCAVATION

The process of actually digging units, like the process of deciding upon their location, varies according to the character and content of the site and the research objectives of the excavator. Here again a number of alternative systems are available.

Occasionally a unit or a connected series of units is dug entirely in a horizontal direction, a single *vertical face* from surface to site bottom being maintained at all times. This is equivalent to the "slicing" procedure often used for excavating in the Mississippi Valley and other parts of the Eastern United States (cf. Ford, 1963: 9; Pl. 1). One disadvantage with this method is that materials may fall out unseen, and if they do, their location is lost forever. Also this kind of excavation makes it exceedingly difficult, if not impossible, to trace horizontal relationships of artifacts and features.

Level-stripping is a widely used variation of the vertical-face system. It consists of excavation in a staggered series of vertical faces, from 6 to 12 inches or more in height, at successive depths, and looks in cross section like a flight of steps (Martin, Quimby, and Collier, 1947: Fig. 1; Lloyd, 1963: Pl. 2). The result is that levels, rather than coordinate squares, are excavated as discrete units by the workers assigned to them. This method, perhaps better termed *"step-trenching,"* is particularly useful in digging large mounds. For example, Lamberg-Karlovsky (1974) describes and illustrates step-trenching as used at Tepe Yahya (see also Lloyd, 1963: Pl. 2).

The *unit-level method* is undoubtedly the most common method of excavating sites showing little stratigraphic variation. Here the technique is to dig each section, defined by the lines of the grid system, vertically as a discrete unit, always completing one before another is begun. This is done in a succession of separate levels, each 6 or 12 inches (or 10 cm. or 20 cm.) deep, the excavation of each level also being completed before the next is begun. Deposits from each unit level are screened to recover chipped stone artifacts, potsherds, animal bones, mollusk shells, debitage, etc., that were not collected at the moment of discovery.

The unit-level technique is best employed in sites with no visible stratification and in projects emphasizing chronology or culture history. There are many such sites in North America. For example, in California shellmounds, there are lenses of mollusk shells interspersed with layers of earth, but these are usually very localized occurrences within the deposit that run for a span and then disappear. The nature of these small lenses in such sites is clearly shown in illustrations published by Schenck (1926: Pls. 36, 37), Uhle (1907: Pl. 4), Nelson (1910: Pl. 49) and Wedel (1941: Figs. 5, 10).

In North American sites like these shellmounds, workers have become accustomed to digging in arbitrary levels within the unit-level system. The British archaeologist Sir Mortimer Wheeler (1954: 53) bemoans the use of this "outworn system, with its mechanical unit levels" and Pallis (1956: 326) also objects to excavating by arbitrary levels or merely recording depth of finds from a datum-line as "substitutes for actual stratification."

No archaeologist will disagree with Wheeler's or Pallis' insistence on

5-6. *Mound C at the George C. Davis site (Texas), 1968, prior to systematic excavation. Trees fill depression left by 1904 treasure-hunter's trench. (Photograph courtesy of Dee Ann Story.)*

5-7. *Mound C, George C. Davis site (Texas), 1968. Treasure-hunter's trench has been cleared and undisturbed mound fill and burial pits exposed. (Photograph courtesy of Dee Ann Story.)*

5-8. *Mound C, George C. Davis site (Texas), 1970. Excavations enlarged to expose burial pits in southern part of mound. Crew is clearing floor of excavations so that pit outlines can be plotted. (Photograph courtesy of Dee Ann Story.)*

5-9. *Mound C, George C. Davis site (Texas), 1970. Excavation of large burial pits in progress. Tractor with backhoe and endloader attachments used in moving backdirt. (Photograph courtesy of Dee Ann Story.)*

visible stratification as the surest means of accurate and meaningful recovery (and subsequent interpretation) of data. The fact remains that there are many instances where the archaeologist finds himself dealing with a deposit that does not contain such stratification, and in this situation, the excavator turns to a mechanical method of stratigraphic collection that will at least yield chronological results.

For example, see the cave deposit in Iran illustrated in Hole and Heizer (1966: Fig. 10). Or note the remarks of MacNeish (1958: 33), who writes: "The deposits [of Nogales Cave, Mexico] contained no definable strata, and all the material from the surface to the bottom of the excavations was one stratum of grey powdery ash and refuse. Occasionally a short lens of white ash or charcoal could be discerned, but none was extensive enough to define as zones." Evans and Meggers (1959: 8) show why the Amazonian area sites lack evidence of clear-cut natural strata, this being mainly the result of heavy precipitation and leaching.

Indeed, not all of Wheeler's British colleagues decry the method of "metrical stratigraphy," as witness the statement of Burkitt (1956: 235): "Where there is no obvious stratigraphy but more than one industry is present . . . uniform layers 6 to 9 cm. thick [are] removed." No less an authority than V. Gordon Childe states in one of his last books, *Piecing Together the Past* (1956: 62), that such a method, while not preferable to "peeling" of natural strata, will "suffice to establish a sequence of ceramic styles . . ."

Excavation by arbitrary levels has become so ingrained in American archaeological tradition that the technique has often been used even in naturally stratified sites. Krieger (in Newell and Krieger, 1949: 65) has some valuable observations on the problems that arise when this happens. An example of a stratified site excavated by arbitrary levels is furnished by Strong and Corbett (1943). Although the derived sequence of pottery styles became clear at Strong and Corbett's site, a much sharper differentiation between styles would have undoubtedly been possible if natural strata had been used as excavation units. The same thing seems to be true at the Gallinazo site in the Viru Valley (Strong and Evans, 1952: Fig. 10 and Table 4, Fig. 28 and Table 11), at Cordova Cave, New Mexico (Martin *et al.,* 1952: Figs. 25, 26), and Graham Cave, Missouri (Logan, 1952: 17ff.). Willey (1939) describes the indecisive results of collecting potsherds from a Georgia site by 3-inch mechanical levels and the much clearer ceramic sequence obtained by collecting sherds from the natural strata. Willey and McGimsey (1954) present a careful account of using both techniques at a single site (see also Cole, 1951: 61).

As an example of the history of the controversy over the use of "metrical" versus "natural" stratigraphy, we reproduce here a quotation from Phillips' section in the *Archaeological Survey in the Lower Mississippi Alluvial Valley* (1951: 240–241) in which he calls attention to the problem of finding cultural differences in unstratified deposits and distinguishes between the two terms "stratigraphy" and "stratification":

> The use of stratigraphic methods in the eastern United States has not yet developed to an extent comparable with their use in other areas of American archaeology. This is mainly due to an earlier impression on the part of Eastern archaeologists that the method was not applicable, owing to the paucity of deep deposits yielding long cultural sequences. It is also partly due, perhaps, to a misconception regarding the stratigraphic method. To many archaeologists, stratigraphy necessarily involves a situation in which materials can be segregated on the basis of distinct and separable soil zones. Such is fortunately not the case. It frequently happens, as we shall show, that a homogeneous deposit, without observable soil stratification, may be made to yield a stratigraphic record of the utmost value. Obviously, such an unstratified deposit will have to be excavated by arbitrary levels, to which method the term "metrical stratigraphy" has sometimes been applied in derogation, as opposed to "natural stratigraphy" obtained by peeling stratified layers. If we were to regard "natural" stratigraphy as the only valid method, the discouraging outlook referred to above would be justified. On the other hand, unstratified or weakly stratified midden deposits of sufficient depth for excavation by "metrical" analysis are not rare. An example of successful exploitation of such deposits is to be seen in the excavations of Willey (1949) and Willey and Woodbury (1942) on the Gulf Coast of Florida in 1940.
>
> There is no need for injecting this terminology into the present discussion, since our stratigraphy—so far at least—is all of the metrical variety. The distinction, however, between "stratification," the description of the actual ground situation, and "stratigraphy," as applied to the chronological interpretation of the ground situation, whether by "natural" or "metrical" methods, is a useful one, and will be maintained here. Under the heading "stratification," we shall refer to soil zones as revealed by trench profiles; under "stratigraphy," the analysis of the excavated material and interpretation of the results. The one is what you find, the other is what you do with it. The separation will serve to bring out the fact that it is possible to have stratigraphy without stratification and vice versa. In line with this distinction, the terms "stratum," "zone," "deposit," etc., will be hereinafter used to refer to the ground stratification, the term "level" being reserved for the arbitrarily excavated unit of "metrical" stratigraphy.

In practicing metrical stratigraphy accurate depth recordings of finds are obviously essential. Where the occupation deposit is thin, very small differences in the depth at which objects lie may have meaning. Indeed, in a deposit without visible stratification, these minute distinctions may be the only means whereby the worker can recognize and separate successive occupations (see Bruce-Mitford, 1956: 273).

It is also important when excavating by arbitrary levels to watch for evidence of disturbance. For instance, intrusive pits will contain fill, ordinarily dating from a later time than the level into which they penetrate (see Phillips, Ford, and Griffin, 1951: 290-291; see also Bruce-Mitford, 1956: Fig. 43, for graphic illustration of much-disturbed stratification).

The excavator also has to think about what the surface of the site may have been like at any given point in time. Not every object found during excavation lies at the exact spot where it was dropped or thrown away. The surface of a living area at any given point in time may have been unstable, so that objects were thrust upward or downward. Such mixing could be intensified by later occupants digging pits, by rodents burrowing at the site, and the like. For further discussion, with examples, see Phillips, Ford, and Griffin (1951: 232–233) and Althin (1954: 271–275); see also Chapter 3 above.

Successful users of metrical stratigraphy in America have been Reichel-Dolmatoff and Reichel-Dolmatoff (1951: esp. p. 14), Kroeber (1925), Bennett (1946), Willey and Corbett (1954), Drucker (1943b, 1952), Phillips, Ford, and Griffin (1951: 243–290), Ford and Willey (1949: 44–52), Haury (1937a: Chap. 4), Nelson (1916), Willey (1949), and Kelly (1945a, 1947).

Excavation by "natural" stratigraphic levels involves peeling off the visible strata in a site deposit. We illustrate this technique by reference to several published reports. Keller (1973) began his excavations at Montagu Cave in the Republic of South Africa by making some preliminary cuts, the profiles of which indicated stratigraphy so complex that arbitrary levels would have been unsuitable. One 6-inch level in one of these test cuts yielded microliths from one side of the square, and much older hand-axes from the other. Obviously the strata dipped, so that the single level cut into different zones would have caused mixing of the artifacts of different occupations. Thus, the major excavations were done by "natural" units, but with one further provision, as Keller (1973: 8) states:

> However, within these "natural" units we encountered concentrations of artifacts that appeared to represent material deposited during a single occupation and so were called occupation horizons or surfaces. The occupation horizons were termed "cultural" units until it became apparent that the layer containing them was equally as cultural in its formation as the horizons themselves.

Keller (*ibid.*) also provides a useful discussion regarding the differentiation between "natural" and "cultural" depositions at a site. For further comments on natural stratigraphy, see Chapter 7.

Other examples of excavation by visible stratigraphic levels at cave and rockshelter sites can be found in monographs by Aikens (1970; Hogup Cave, Utah) and Alexander (1970; Parida Cave, Texas). At Parida Cave and similar sheltered sites along the Rio Grande in Texas, the cultural deposits are extremely complex, but if carefully excavated they can yield much anthropological information (see Collins, 1969: 2–4; Word and Douglas, 1970: 8; Fig. 5).

Many open sites are also amenable to excavation by natural stratigraphic layers. The *"isolated block" method* is sometimes used when stratigraphy is visible; the method entails digging a square trench to isolate a block or pillar of deposit. The stratification thus exposed on all four sides of the block is carefully recorded, and the block is then peeled layer by layer (see Fig. 5-10).

5-10. *Above: a test block isolated and ready for excavation at Punta Morado site, Taltal, Chile. Left: test block isolated and ready for stratigraphic dissection at Cerro Colorado site, Taltal, Chile.* (Photographs courtesy of Junius Bird.)

Examples of this technique are provided by Schmidt (1928: 258–259), R. E. Smith (1955: 13–14; Figs. 82–83), Bird (1943: 253–257), and Webb and De Jarnette (1942: 95ff.; Fig. 27; Pl. 142).

Although open camp sites in the southeastern United States have usually been excavated by arbitrary levels, Morse (1973) excavated the Brand site (a Dalton "butchering station" in Arkansas) by natural stratigraphic levels. By peeling off the visible stratigraphic layers, Morse was able to expose *in situ* working floors at the site (see Morse, 1973: 24; Fig. 2).

At the Belcher Mound in Louisiana, the excavator C. Webb (1959) recognized in his preliminary investigations that the mound was stratified, with at least four habitation levels. Abandoning the traditional "vertical cake-slicing technique," Webb proceeded to excavate each habitation level as a natural unit.

Bison-kill sites in North America provide other instances of excavation by natural zones. Kehoe (1967) had exposed the stratigraphy of the Boarding School Bison Drive (Montana) in test excavations in 1952. Later, in 1958, excavation was done by "layer stripping rather than by arbitrary levels" (p. 13), using the profiles of the 1952 test cut as a guide.

Dibble (in Dibble and Lorrain, 1968: 19) relates the excavation technique used at Bonfire Shelter, Texas:

> The nature of the deposits at this site . . . provided an opportunity for prime reliance on a "natural level" excavation technique. After preliminary exploratory tests had made gross outlines of the deposits . . . reasonably clear, further excavation by arbitrary levels was abandoned. Proceeding in descending order of stratigraphic occurrence, four culture-bearing deposits were excavated primarily as vertical units.

Whether the excavator uses arbitrary levels or natural strata will of course depend on the internal structure of the site and the problems being investigated. As mentioned above, it may at times be advisable to combine the two methods (for example, a thick natural zone can itself be excavated in arbitrary levels), use other techniques, or even devise new ones. In the notes of any excavation, a careful statement on excavation methods should be set down in order that future workers may know how the materials were recovered.

EXCAVATING A GRID UNIT

The preceding discussions of excavation techniques have been fairly general. In order to give a clearer picture of the actual, practical application of these techniques in the course of ordinary excavation, it may be worthwhile here to describe the steps in the process of digging a hypothetical typical excavation grid unit. The proper or customary use of the tools mentioned earlier in the chapter can be taken up further here.

By a "typical" unit is meant one that shares all or most of the characteristics commonly found in excavation in an area. Actually such a unit will rarely be encountered; the vast majority will exhibit at least one special or unique feature.

The excavation unit, let us say, is ten feet square, and its limits will be defined, except under special conditions, by the intersecting lines of the coordinate system. Its four corners will be marked by stakes, each bearing a white tag giving its coordinate location.

Before starting to dig, one must decide where the excavated earth is to be thrown. It should not be piled on the surface of any other unit likely to be excavated later, or where it will be difficult to replace at the end of the dig.

Two considerations should be kept in mind at the beginning of every excavation. The first of these is the danger of cave-ins—not inconsiderable in very soft or unconsolidated site soils. Cave-fills, which are loose and relatively uncompacted, have a tendency to slump, and there are recorded instances of archaeologists being killed by the collapsing walls of deep trenches. As a general rule, in making any excavation likely to be carried to a depth where there is any danger of slumping, the walls of the pit or trench should be sloped inward, or "battered," to ensure their stability. Because of this slope, not all of the deposit contained within a unit as defined on the surface will actually be excavated. The earth lying between the theoretical and actual limits of the unit may, however, be removed when an adjoining unit is excavated. In such cases, care should be taken that materials recovered within this remainder are located, for the record, within their correct unit, according to the site map. Be sure to record in the field notes both the surface and base dimensions of the grid (or pit or trench) units that have been excavated with sloping or battered walls. You or the reader of your report may want to calculate the cubic content of the deposit excavated, and these measurements will be essential. The depth to which excavation will be carried in any unit can often be determined in advance from its position on the site and indications from nearby excavations.

Second, it should be remembered that the stakes marking the corners of excavation units must be used in recording the location of all materials subsequently recovered, and their location must therefore be carefully preserved. One way of doing this is to leave them standing on top of substantial columns of earth not to be excavated (i.e., broken down and examined) until the stakes can have no possible further utility. Again, since these columns will lie partially within four separate units, the location of materials eventually recovered from them should be carefully determined. Columns that obstruct the excavation of a burial or some other feature whose exposure is required will of course have to be removed.

An alternative system of placing the stakes marking the grid coordinate may be used. The rows of stakes are placed at equal horizontal distances along both sides of a trench, from 12 to 18 inches from the edges. In a trench five feet wide, with the stakes set laterally one foot, the rows of stakes would be seven feet apart. The elevation of each stake is determined by instrument from—or with reference to—the main datum point, and that elevation is marked on the stake together with its designation in the grid pattern (Atkinson, 1953: 152; Wheeler, 1954: 69). The location of any find within the trench or pit can then be determined by use of the measuring triangle, as explained in Chapter 6 under "Recording the Location of Artifacts."

The advantage of this sytem is that stakes are not driven into the edge of the trench or placed where they may be in danger of removal, but are securely set in firm ground back from the trench edge. One disadvantage in offsetting the stakes is that they may be covered by backdirt thrown out of the trench. In either case, care must be taken to protect the stakes from being moved or covered.

Often the uppermost stratum—up to six inches or so in depth—of an excavation unit will consist of topsoil. This is often sterile (i.e., lacking in archaeological material of any kind). The presence or absence of topsoil, which differs markedly from midden deposit, can easily be determined by test excavation. Even where topsoil is absent, the uppermost few inches of a site, often containing the root systems of a vegetation cover, may be sterile.

Obviously, the excavation of any unit must begin with a careful examination of the surface. The presence of surface finds is a signal that all deposit within the unit, from the surface down, must be examined. Where sterility has been absolutely determined (in earlier test cuts) the surface layer can be dug off with a shovel and thrown aside without examination. It should be remembered, however, that even though a surface layer is "sterile" in that it does not contain cultural material, it is still an important element in the depositional history of the deposit. The same, of course, is true for buried sterile layers separating cultural deposits.

When all sterile matter, if any, has been removed from the top of a unit, the business of actual archaeological excavation begins. In our "typical" excavation unit, this is done with a shovel. Working first along the base of one wall and systematically across to the base of the opposite one, the entire floor of the unit is turned over to a depth equivalent to the depth of the first arbitrary level. As each successive shovelful of dirt is dug, it is spread as thinly as possible over a clean section of the floor of the unit with the edge of the shovel, and it is carefully examined. If an artifact or other object to be recovered is revealed, its location should immediately be ascertained and recorded on the necessary form before excavation is resumed. The course of excavation is considerably simplified if this loose, excavated earth is thrown out of the hole at fairly frequent intervals and onto the backdirt pile—where it may either accumulate, if the adjoining square is not going to be excavated, or be carried away—rather than being allowed to collect at the bottom. Alternatively, the earth from the excavation can be thrown directly into a screen, or carried in a wheelbarrow to the screen for sieving. As each unit level is completed, the floor of the pit should be scraped clean and carefully inspected. As the excavation unit becomes deeper, the walls and floor should be watched for evidence of pits or stratification.

Much excavation in North America is conducted in the manner outlined above, where each unit is dug downward in successive levels to site bottom. However, special features that require refinements or modifications of technique are almost invariably encountered in the course of excavating any unit (see Fig. 5-11). The special excavation techniques employed in recovering burials, cremations, features, and artifacts are discussed elsewhere. If the

5-11. Care in exposing any feature from the moment it is encountered while digging is illustrated by these two finds made at the La Venta site in Mexico. Top: a haphazard deposit of shaped serpentine blocks. Bottom: two carefully and deliberately placed ceremonial offering ("caches") of stone celts. (Photographs by Robert F. Heizer, 1955.)

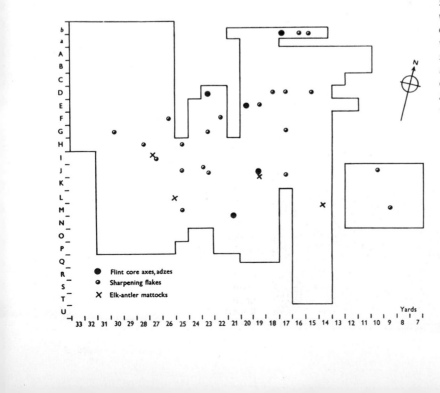

5-12. *Left above: density of worked flints enabling definition of occupation area within a letter-number grid system at Star Carr, England. Left below: distribution of certain tool types in the same area. Compare this distribution with the illustration above. (After Grahame Clark, 1954: Figs. 4, 9.)*

5-13. *Facing page: Plan of Zone A_1 (Mohammad Jaffar phase) at the site of Tepe Ali Kosh, Deh Luran plain of Iran. All tools larger than a flint blade are plotted in situ. (From Hole, Flannery, and Neely, 1969: Fig. 12; reproduced courtesy of Museum of Anthropology, University of Michigan.)*

object cannot be exposed without further large-scale excavation, it should be carefully protected while the latter is in progress. Trained excavators develop, before long, a "touch" or "feel" so sensitive that the slightest contact with an object is often sufficient for them to release pressure and avoid breaking it. Many experienced workers can tell, from contact, whether they have struck bone, burned clay, or stone.

A good deal of archaeology, of course, is not conducted with the shovel as the main excavating tool. Small hand trowels are often employed to work through the site earth, especially if it contains an abundance of artifactual materials (flint, potsherds, etc.), and in this case shovels are used only to remove the soil already examined. Wherever the use of shovels is inadvisable, notably at those excavations in which every attempt is made to leave artifacts in place until they can be plotted, work is done almost entirely with trowels. When artifacts are encountered, they are carefully exposed and their positions are recovered on a plan of the unit. This approach permits a precise examination of the spatial relationships between artifacts, debris, features, and other buried evidence. As illustrations of results of this procedure, see Figs. 5-12 and 5-13.

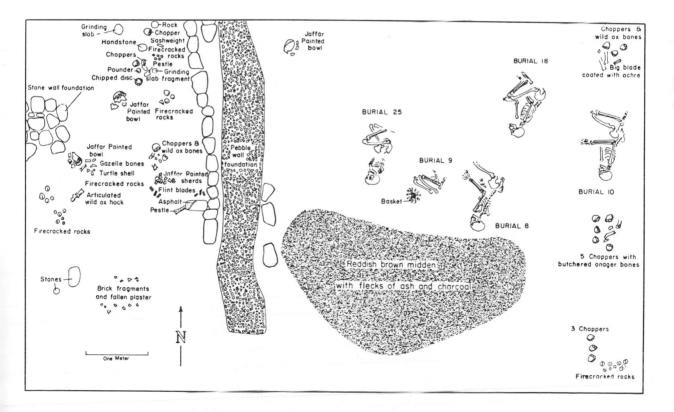

In some valley areas, where the average land contour is near sea level or the water table is very near the surface, ground water may be encountered above site bottom. Alluvial deposition may have elevated the surface of the ground, and a corresponding elevation of the ground water level may have the effect of immersing the lower portions of the site deposit. Unless a power-operated pump is available, there is no really satisfactory way of overcoming this obstacle. Wheeler (1954: 56) describes how, at Arikamedu, India, in 1954, he excavated to a depth of 11 feet below the water table by keeping the water out of the pit with pumps.

Whenever possible, units are excavated down to the base of the site or, in other words, to subsoil. (The difference between midden deposit, usually relatively dark in color, and subsoil is normally so marked that no excavator should have any difficulty in determining when he has reached the bottom of a site.) Nor can the subsoil safely be presumed sterile until it has been examined with care.

At the time of the site's earliest occupation, refuse, trash, and burials may have been mixed with or buried in the subsoil. For this reason, it is general practice to excavate the first foot or two of subsoil below site bottom in the same manner in which the midden deposit above has been excavated. Always be certain that the excavation of a unit has gone far enough into sterile or apparently sterile subsoil so that there is no possibility of missing burials or artifacts. Many excavators have stopped digging when they have reached a sterile layer, only to discover later that what they assumed to be the undisturbed base actually covered additional and older occupation deposits below. In every case, it is advisable to penetrate what is taken to be the base deposit to a depth that will preclude any chance of its being an interleaf in the archaeological deposit. Such deep testing can be done with a posthole digger or soil auger.

BACKDIRT AND BACKFILLING

Almost invariably, the archaeologist excavates a site under an agreement to leave the land undamaged or as it was. This means that when the digging is completed, all excavated earth must be replaced in the trenches and pits and the surface left level and smooth. Backfilling is one of the unavoidable consequences of archaeology, and its ultimate necessity should be borne in mind at all times in the course of excavation (see Fig. 5-14). A little foresight in the distribution of backdirt may save a great deal of trouble in backfilling.

In exploratory excavation, excavated earth is generally piled as compactly as possible on the surface at one side of the unit. Do not see how far you can throw the excavated earth—it must all be returned to the hole from which it came. To ensure sufficient earth to fill all excavations at the end of

5-14. *Top: the Paleolithic rockshelter of La Colombière, France. Note trench running into deposits and mine cars for earth removal. (From Movius and Judson, 1956: Fig. 44) Bottom: backdirt removal from Pompeii excavations, 1864.*

the dig, any area on which backdirt is to be thrown should be *completely* cleared of vegetation or other cover. Otherwise, a considerable amount of dirt may settle and become packed among the plants or other matter and be very difficult to move.

As already noted, excavated earth should not be put where it covers the surface of units that are likely to be excavated later. Very large piles should be avoided as they are difficult to handle and may necessitate moving the dirt a considerable distance when it is replaced. Unless a stratigraphic profile is to be preserved, earth can simply be thrown from one unit into another that has been completely excavated and its profile noted. The main point is to keep some pattern of backfilling in mind at all times during the course of excavation so that at the end of work every pit or trench can be refilled with loose earth piled as near at hand as possible.

5-15. *Using a "scraper" to backfill a southern Texas excavation. The device can be easily constructed using scrap lumber and can be linked, by ropes, to a vehicle.*

The backfill should be packed in so that it will not settle too much in subsequent rains. As a hole is being filled, the earth should occasionally be tramped on and probed with shovels to pack it down firmly.

Backfilling almost always takes longer than you think. Be sure to allow enough time for it when setting up an excavation schedule, especially if you have a deadline. On the average, for instance, it takes one worker with a shovel from two to three hours to completely refill one five-by-five-foot unit that has been excavated to a depth of five feet.

A digging crew can sometimes borrow a Fresno scraper or "Mormon board" scraper from a local rancher (cf. Fitting, 1973a: 7). Either of these, hooked to a team of horses, a jeep, a pickup truck, or even a passenger car, will fill a site more easily and rapidly than workers with shovels. In addition, the crew can construct a simple scraper (see Fig. 5-15). Large excavations—where the time required for labor to clear, remove overburden, or refill pits and trenches is prohibitive—can often be cleared or filled with a bulldozer secured on hire or loan (Daugherty, 1956: 231; Wedel, 1951). A good excavator will keep this in mind and, during the course of digging, will try to make arrangements for securing machinery on loan from someone whose interest in the excavation has been cultivated.

Archaeologists often throw bottles and other nonperishable camp debris into the bottom of excavation units prior to backfilling. These serve as markers to any later excavator who might happen to dig in the same spot. It is not difficult to conceive of some future processual archaeologist uncovering these remains and trying to reconstruct, from this evidence, the dietary habits of his or her archaeological predecessors. Based on such a biased sample, the study will no doubt conclude that earlier field camps subsisted largely on alcoholic beverages.

Even pothunters sometimes have the forethought to mark their plunderings by placing some modern object in their pits. McKern (1930: 443), during his excavations at the Kletzien mound group (Wisconsin), came across a bottle containing a slip of paper bearing the date "Oct. 11, '96," apparently a record of some early relic-collector's explorations.

CAVE AND ROCKSHELTER EXCAVATION

The excavation of cave and rockshelter sites involves a great many special considerations not applicable to open sites and thus requires specialized techniques. Limited space, lack of light, the distinctive character of the deposit, the problem of dust, and especially the far better preservation of perishable cultural materials in dry caves are all factors that profoundly affect methods of excavation. Cave excavation may be a hazardous undertaking. Bats may be carriers of rabies; loose sections of ceiling may be dislodged and fall; and dust can cause serious respiratory difficulties. An exhaust fan, run by either a gasoline engine or an electrical generator, dust-filter masks, artificial lighting (Heizer and Napton, 1970: Pls. 8–11), and timber cribwork to prevent cave-ins (Harrington, 1933) may be necessary.

Caves containing evidence of human occupancy occur in many areas. In drier regions, these sites may yield normally perishable materials such as leather, wood, and the like. Small caves represent less of a problem in excavation than large ones. For examples of small cave excavation, see Wallace and Taylor (1952) and Baumhoff (1955). See Fig. 5-16 for an illustration of the stratigraphy revealed in the excavation of a rockshelter. The following is a list of references containing further information on the methods and problems of excavating in caves: Aikens (1970: 2–3), Alexander (1970: 15–19), Champe (1946: 10–14; Fig. 3), Collins (1969: 2–4), Cooke (1963: Fig. 1), Cressman (1942:

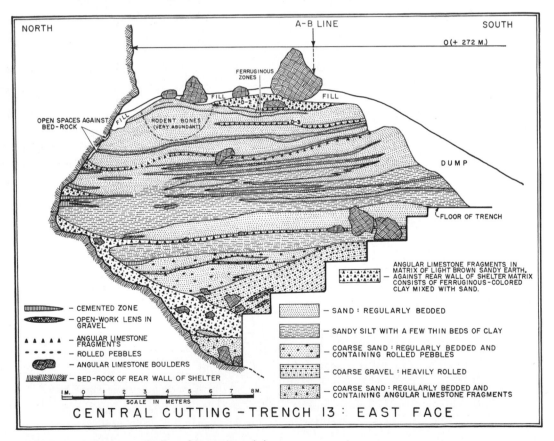

5-16. *A carefully drawn stratigraphic section of the Paleolithic rockshelter, La Colombière, France (from Movius and Judson, 1956: Fig. 10).*

22; Figs. 3-10, 22, 63, 64, 75-79), Cressman, Williams, and Krieger (1940: 3-5; Figs. 1-4, 11-14), Fowler (1959), Harrington (1933: Pls. 8, 12, 15, and text figures *passim*), Heizer and Krieger (1956), Heizer and Napton (1970: 14-15; Fig. 9), Lehmer (1960: 136-139), Logan (1952), Loud and Harrington (1929: 1-123; Figs. 1-6; Pls. 2, 3, 7-9), Malan (1945), Martin *et al.* (1952), Movius (1974: 105ff.), Movius and Judson (1956), Steward (1937a: 8-9, 91-93, 107; Figs. 1, 2, 39, 40, 44, 45; Pls. 1-5), Word and Douglas (1970), Zingg (1940: map facing p. 5).

UNDERWATER ARCHAEOLOGY

The rise of sea level in the most recent postglacial period has covered the shallower parts of the continental shelf (Shepard, 1964; Fairbridge, 1958; Emery, 1966). Geologic subsidence of coastal margins has also occurred, drowning any archaeological materials present. Shipwrecks have strewn artifacts over the ocean floor. These and other processes make the bottoms of lakes, seas, and oceans a rich source of archaeological materials.

Underwater archaeology has already accumulated a very large literature (Kapitan, 1966), from which we cite the following works on techniques and kinds of materials recovered: Andersen (1969), Bass (1963, 1964, 1969), Borhegyi (1958), Clausen (1967), Cleator (1973), Dumas (1962), Frost (1963), Goggin (1960), Green *et al.* (1971), Hall (1966, 1970), Marshall and Moriarty (1964), Olsen (1961), Peterson (1965), Ryan and Bass (1962), Silverberg (1963), Throckmorton and Bullitt (1963), Taylor (1965), and Tuthill and Allanson (1954).

STRUCTURAL REMAINS

Structural remains discovered during excavation are of great interest and potential significance. Simple structures constructed largely of perishable materials may leave only minimal traces behind them. Excavators must therefore be constantly alert for these traces—postholes, wall trenches, packed earthen floors, and the like.

Once recognized, such remains rarely present problems that cannot be dealt with adequately by standard field procedures, if these are perceptively applied; the remains will usually be treated and recorded with the same care and in the same detail as smaller features of special importance. Particular attention will be given during the clearing of the floor to any evidence of wall or roof materials. Often sizable fragments of the walls or roof fall to the floor and are preserved by one or another agency. If the structure burned, charred fragments carefully excavated and recorded may go a long way toward reconstructing what the building looked like. Such remains should

A'

A

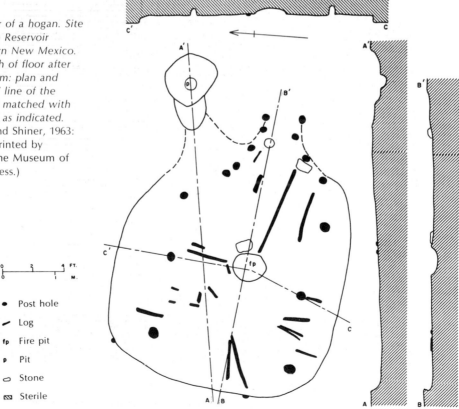

5-17. The floor of a hogan. Site LA 4199, Navajo Reservoir District, northern New Mexico. Top: photograph of floor after exposure. Bottom: plan and profile. The AA' line of the drawing can be matched with the photograph as indicated. (After Hester and Shiner, 1963: Figs. 10, 11; reprinted by permission of the Museum of New Mexico Press.)

● Post hole

╱ Log

fp Fire pit

p Pit

⬭ Stone

▨ Sterile

be photographed and drawn *in situ*. Postholes, wall trenches, possible entranceways, evidence of hearths, and other items of importance must be carefully studied and recorded (see Figs. 5-17–5-19). Cache and storage pits, burials beneath the floors, and subfloor deposits should be diligently searched for. The location of all artifacts, animal bones, and other objects found on the floor must be precisely recorded, as their distribution may help locate various activities within the structure (see Figs. 5-12 and 5-13).

The best procedure for excavating a floor once it has been discovered is usually to remove the overburden to within a few inches of the floor, where structural materials begin to appear or, in any case, before floor-level artifacts and features appear. The deposit immediately overlying the floor can then

5-18. *Excavation of a structure in the village area at the George C. Davis site (Texas), 1970. Diameter of structure is approximately 11 meters. (Photograph courtesy of Dee Ann Story.)*

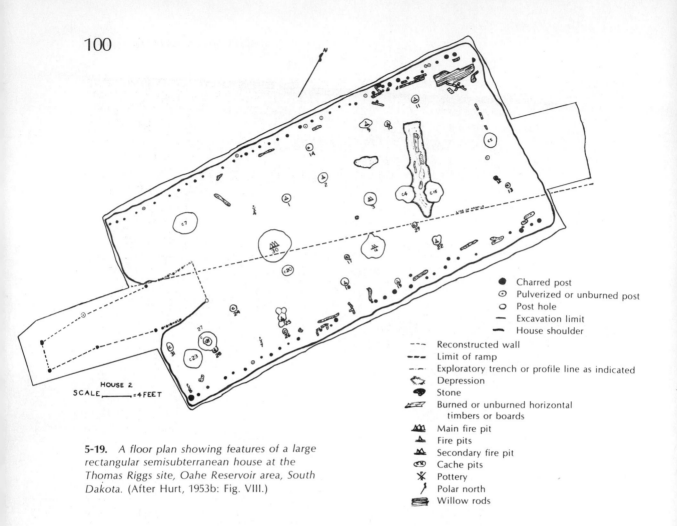

5-19. *A floor plan showing features of a large rectangular semisubterranean house at the Thomas Riggs site, Oahe Reservoir area, South Dakota.* (After Hurt, 1953b: Fig. VIII.)

● Charred post
⊙ Pulverized or unburned post
○ Post hole
— Excavation limit
━ House shoulder
--- Reconstructed wall
━━ Limit of ramp
─·─ Exploratory trench or profile line as indicated
🐚 Depression
🍳 Stone
▰▰ Burned or unburned horizontal timbers or boards
⋀⋀⋀ Main fire pit
⟁ Fire pits
⋀⋀ Secondary fire pit
⊗ Cache pits
✗ Pottery
⌿ Polar north
▤ Willow rods

HOUSE 2
SCALE _____ = 4 FEET

be excavated meticulously with a trowel. If the structure is a pit house, its existence may be apparent before excavation. In this case it may be desirable to sink a pit off center until the floor is located. From this pit a trench or trenches can be dug to locate the walls, which can then be outlined. Overburden will be removed next, and the floor surface deposit finally dissected by careful horizontal digging. If pit houses are suspected but are not evident from the surface, it may be desirable to dig a test pit outside the site area in order to test the depth and character of the undisturbed subsoil. Test pits can then be dug in a grid to determine where disturbed deposits continue below the expected natural level. This may indicate pit house fills to be excavated in the manner described. Sometimes a soil auger can locate floors and save digging pits.

In a site occupied over a long period of time, later house pits may be cut through earlier ones (see Figs. 5-20 and 5-21). Such complex situations require the greatest care in the recording of details and a perceptive overall handling

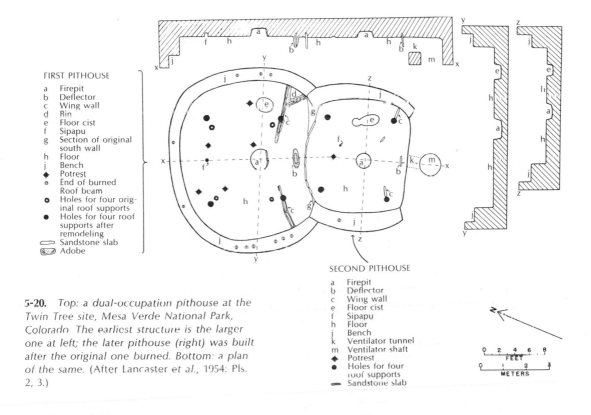

FIRST PITHOUSE

a Firepit
b Deflector
c Wing wall
d Bin
e Floor cist
f Sipapu
g Section of original
   south wall
h Floor
j Bench
◆ Potrest
◐ End of burned
   Roof beam
◎ Holes for four orig-
   inal roof supports
● Holes for four roof
   supports after
   remodeling
⬭ Sandstone slab
▨ Adobe

SECOND PITHOUSE

a Firepit
b Deflector
c Wing wall
e Floor cist
f Sipapu
h Floor
j Bench
k Ventilator tunnel
m Ventilator shaft
◆ Potrest
● Holes for four
   roof supports
⬭ Sandstone slab

5-20. *Top: a dual-occupation pithouse at the Twin Tree site, Mesa Verde National Park, Colorado. The earliest structure is the larger one at left; the later pithouse (right) was built after the original one burned. Bottom: a plan of the same. (After Lancaster et al., 1954: Pls. 2, 3.)*

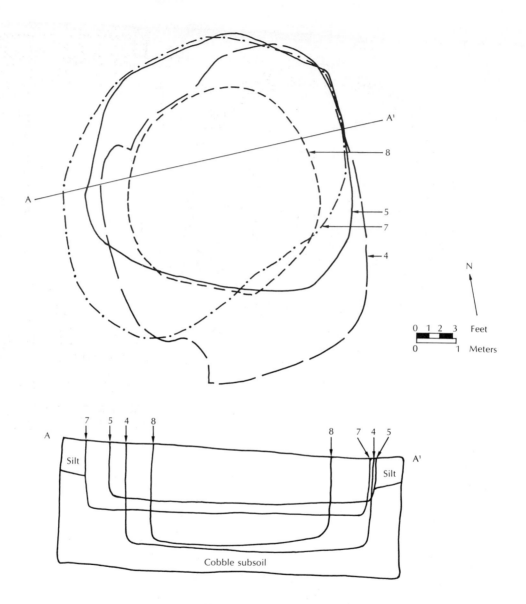

5-21. *A serially occupied pithouse at the Serrano site, Colorado. The earliest structure was No. 4. Successive constructions on the same spot follow the sequence 8, 7, and 5 (the latest). Top: plan of pithouse outlines. Bottom: profiles of pithouse walls and floors. (Simplified after Dittert and Eddy, 1963: Fig. 24.)*

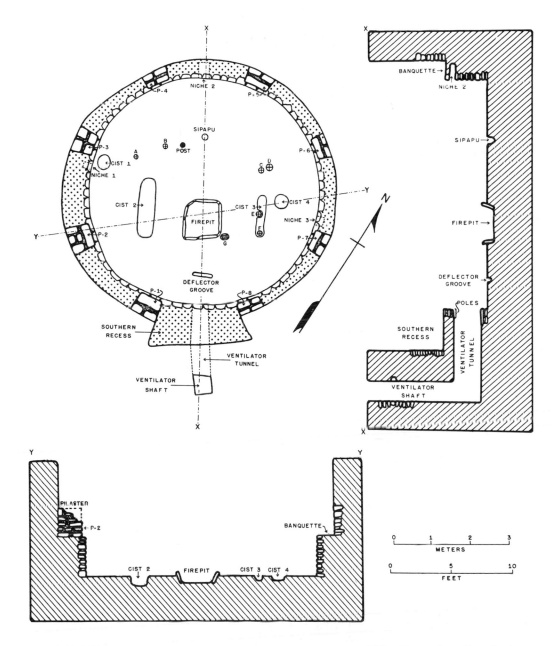

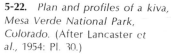

5-22. *Plan and profiles of a kiva, Mesa Verde National Park, Colorado.* (After Lancaster et al., 1954: Pl. 30.)

of the excavation. Since pits were sometimes dug for clay or other materials and then filled with trash, care must be exercised not to confuse such features with pit houses. In recording all house excavations coordinate (usually north-south and east-west) cross sections must be drawn and shown on the plan of the structure (cf. Figs. 5-20–5-22).

Lewis and Kneberg (1946: 49–54) describe the archaeological evidence for houses of flexible small-pole framework as opposed to that in the rigid large-log houses found at Hiwassee Island. See also Calabrese (1972: 8), Hurt (1970: 171, 173), Sperry (1968: 8–9), Strong (1935: 73–74), and Wood (1969: 65, 67) for the technique of Plains house and earth-lodge excavation.

Archaeological sites with very complex structural or monumental remains require highly specialized techniques and methods of investigation. A notable example is the great temple-pyramid at Cholula, Mexico, where more than five miles of tunnels were dug through the mass in order to study earlier structures concealed within the mound (Marquina, 1951). Excavating elaborate structural remains may be further complicated by the legal requirement or moral obligation to consolidate or even restore the remains as permanent monuments of ancient peoples and their works (Bernal, 1963). Such monuments require carefully trained and thoroughly experienced excavators and excavation procedures that are outside the scope of this general guide. We complete this section with some very general observations on excavating structures of moderate structural complexity.

The presence of such remains is generally indicated by the mounding that results from the collapse of a roof, upper wall, or other superior portions of the structure and the subsequent erosion of the debris. Confronted with a mounded feature, the archaeologist's immediate task is to determine whether it is architectural in nature. Structures built of stone are sometimes obvious from building stones present in the debris of the mound, but features of earthen construction are seldom so evident. Similarly, rubbish heaps form mounds. These will usually turn out to be formless, but since rubbish was often used to build platforms and foundations, the issue may remain clouded until actual excavation is undertaken. The regularity of the mound form, its alignment or grouping with other mounds, the presence of a nearby borrow pit, and construction patterns in the area will usually provide clues to identification.

The excavation methods to be applied will depend upon the nature of the structure and the way it was built, the specific objectives of the excavators, and the limiting factors of resources at hand versus the magnitude and complexity of the structure. In general, the basic principle in excavating stone or adobe structures is "work from the known to unknown." Thus a pit, perhaps two meters square, is usually dug some distance outside the mound periphery to locate a plaza or court floor, an old ground surface, or occupational level, and to determine the nature of the subsoil deposits. The pit is

5-23. *The Maya site of Becan (Campeche, Mexico). Note the large fortification ditch (1.2 miles in circumference), from which 177,607 cu. m. of fill was removed. Late Preclassic. (Photograph courtesy of R. E. W. Adams and the National Geographic Society.)*

then expanded into a trench dug into the side of the mound, penetrating first the surface soil and humus of the present mound, then the collapsed and eroded debris from the upper portions of the structure, and finally the base of the structure's exterior wall.

Once the archaeologist has discovered and exposed this element of the structure, side trenches may be opened to follow the wall to the left and right. Where construction is not well preserved, the trench should not turn a corner at an especially poorly preserved section of the wall, but continue well beyond the corner before making the turn. From the amount of fallen wall stone and the preserved height and contour of the mound, it should be possible to determine approximately the original wall height. In clearing the walls, any fallen ornamental or decorative features should be noted and carefully recorded. Evidence of the original wall facing or surface treatment may be preserved at the base of the wall.

If the exterior walls enclose rooms, these may be excavated next. As discussed above, over burden is usually removed to within a few inches of the floor, with the floor zone then carefully dissected by trowel excavation. If the walls are part of a substructural platform, excavation must then turn to the upper terraces or superstructure. These walls are located as before by trenching in from the side of the mound where the upper floor level should be located. If a foundation platform is present, it is usually desirable to sample its fill and to investigate the possibility of earlier construction or a tomb within. Although this is sometimes done by pit excavation from above, the greatest control is maintained where a trench can be excavated in from the side along the base level. In this way features will be exposed where they should be best preserved and the chance of missing or damaging features is minimized. In excavating foundation fill, the investigator must be careful not to mistake temporary retaining walls and makeshift stairways used in building up the fill for earlier interior construction. Indeed, these construction techniques used in building up the fill should be noted as Ford and Webb (1956: 37–38) and Morris, Charlot, and Morris (1931, 1: 146–148, 204–206) have done.

Where construction is of adobe, distinguishing the walls and other structural features from debris composed of the same material can often be painfully difficult. Kidder, who excavated an adobe platform structure at Kaminaljuyu, Guatemala, reports that it was sometimes impossible to see the juncture or separation lines between buildings approached in cross section in a penetration trench. The problem was resolved by having workers use the pointed end of a hand pick for all advance or exploratory work. Since fill did not bond or fuse with the adobe walls it covered, the pick was used to rip dirt loose and pull it forward, causing material to fall away at the cleavage line between fill and wall, and exposing the wall (Kidder, Jennings, and Shook, 1946: 27–28, 90, 92). Braidwood and Howe (1960: 40–41) discuss a similar problem in the excavation of *tauf* walls.

As mentioned earlier in this chapter, earthen burial mounds in the Eastern United States are frequently excavated in a series of vertical slices removed as the excavators dig in from the side along a broad exposure equivalent to the mound's diameter. In this approach the excavators are repeatedly digging into a lateral profile of the mound, but, obviously, no cross-profile is presented. An alternative method shown in Fig. 5-3 above preserves standing coordinate axial profiles of the mound (Lewis and Kneberg, 1946: 21–22). An exceptionally detailed and well illustrated account of a burial mound excavation is given by Dragoo (1963: 9–22).

Lewis and Kneberg (1946: 28–29) have described and we summarize a usually valuable method of excavating earthern platform structures. In the hypothetical profile on page 107, a premound village deposit, resting upon subsoil, is buried beneath an earthen platform, which in turn is buried be-

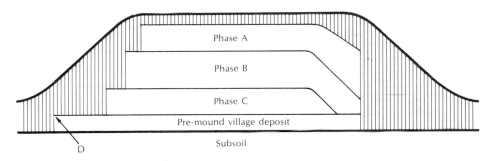

Diagram of substructure mound excavation technique (After Lewis and Kneberg, 1946).

neath two successive enlargements. A grid system of 10-foot squares is first laid out on the surface of the mound to provide spatial control. Four test trenches five feet in width are dug into the mound along the coordinate axes from points well beyond the periphery of the mound. In the diagram the trench begun from the left, indicated by the hachured lines, is dug to subsoil and then expanded into the mound by vertical slicing. Upon encountering the pre-mound village deposit (at point D) the excavators step the trench up to the surface of the deposit, thus preserving postmolds and other features possibly present there for later study. The trench is carried forward along this surface until the summit of Phase C becomes apparent in the side and end walls of the trench. The trench is then stepped up to the level of this summit and carried forward until the summits of Phases B and A are successively reached and stepped up to in the same fashion. Next, the test trench at the opposite end of this axis is begun as shown by the hachured lines on the right. In the hypothetical example shown above, the summit of Phase A appears in the side and end walls of this test trench before the summits of the lower phases. Thus the trench is stepped up from the subsoil to the Phase A summit where it is carried forward to meet the trench previously dug from the opposite side. The procedure is repeated in the digging of the other two test trenches.

When the four trenches intersect on the summit of Phase A, the resulting four quadrants of the mound's surface mantle are removed, completely exposing the summit of Phase A. After the architectural and other features are recorded, the four test trenches are carried down through the fill of Phase A to the summit of Phase B, which is then also completely exposed. The profiles of both coordinate axial trenches are recorded phase by phase and serve as a control for the horizontal stripping of the fill from the successive summits and for the removal of the fill from the side slopes. Since the side slope fill is removed at the same time as the fill overlying each building unit, the form of the structure during the successive periods is revealed. The combination of vertical and horizontal excavation provides a complete series of vertical profiles along the north-south and east-west axes and exposes entire building units at one time. Finally, the complete surface of the pre-mound refuse deposit is exposed for study and separate excavation.

In conclusion it should be noted that although building plans and reconstructions generally seem clear-cut and obvious in published reports, the student will find the situation in the field is often quite the opposite, and he or she will constantly face difficult interpretative and procedural decisions of the greatest importance. Even recognizing and interpreting such basic architectural features as walls and floors can be difficult. Where alterations occurred in ancient times, the remains will often present a confusing array of fragmentary structural features—see, e.g., Structure A-5 Complex at Uaxactun, Guatemala (A. L. Smith, 1950: 15–44; Figs. 1–38, 58–81), and North Acropolis at Tikal (Coe and McGinn, 1963)—the earlier remains represented, if at all directly, by the merest remnants. It will be the excavator's task to retrace precisely the various steps in the sequence of events. A sound knowledge of building patterns and methods in the area is obviously necessary.

Cultural deposits in architectural remains are also complicated by repeated occupations of a site, especially if the structures are remodeled or become the foundations of other buildings. Ancient as well as contemporary rubbish deposits, because they are usually nearby and easier to dig in than undisturbed earth, are often used as fill in platforms and foundations. Such rubbish may be scattered about and subsequently incorporated into other deposits or into structures at some distance from where they originally lay. Such confused deposits require perceptive ordering through correct interpretation of the structural events; careful and constant attention together with precise recording will be required to work out these events and their correlations.

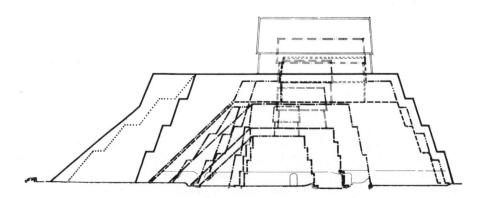

Architectural cross section of the principal pyramid at Tenayuca, Mexico, showing succession of building enlargements. (After Marquina, 1951: Lam. 50.)

SOME HAZARDS IN FIELD WORK

We venture to add this final section to remind students that field investigation can be dangerous. Ordinary city life also has its hazards, as we all know, but they will not prepare anyone—especially most Americans—for the unfamiliar hazards to be met on an expedition.

Outside the continental United States there is always the risk of contracting a local disease that, if left undiagnosed or if incorrectly treated, may cause severe health problems. Several diseases may be contracted from eating food prepared in an unsanitary manner. Water is often contaminated and should always be boiled or otherwise purified if this is known or suspected to be the case (good portable drinking water purifiers are available for under $30). A well-trained local doctor usually can recognize infections and know how to treat them.

When you are in another country you are well advised to behave in a manner that will not give offense to the local people. What seems funny to you may offend if you laugh too loudly. This caution applies particularly to some parts of Latin America, as many inexperienced Americans have learned to their sorrow. If you encounter aggressive drunks in a foreign country, try to extricate yourself as quietly and speedily as possible—if there is trouble, you will not find many among the onlookers who will help you out of the situation.

In the United States there are the usual rural dangers such as rattlesnakes, range cattle, bulls, and over-friendly, possibly rabid wild animals. In some rural areas it is an invitation to trouble to hang around the local bar in the town where you get mail and buy groceries.

Valley fever is an endemic disease contracted by breathing dust from soil containing the fungus *Coccidiodes immitis*. It consists of an unpleasant, though rarely fatal, lung infection (Werner et al., 1972; Werner, 1974). The range of this fungus is in a belt from northern California southwestward through southern Nevada, Arizona, southern New Mexico, and Texas to the Gulf Coast.

Cave bats are under suspicion as carriers of rabies. There is evidence that even healthy bats can communicate the disease to other mammals through their urine, which they release while flying (*Time* Magazine, September 29, 1961, pp. 50-51).

Working in dry and dusty caves may lead to serious problems of lung congestion. The Harvard archaeologist S. J. Guernsey reportedly died as a result of digging in one more of these sites than he should have.

Camp dangers are common—tripping over tent ropes, eating tainted food or preparing food in dirty field kitchens, falling into the camp fire, and the like. Pressure gas lanterns are known to release toxic fumes from the beryllium in the incandescent mantle (Griggs, 1973).

As we have already suggested, cave-ins of deep trenches or pits can occur in all kinds of sites, but especially in caves. Several archaeologists have died in cave-ins. People have had their skulls damaged beyond repair by heavy double-ended picks wielded by careless workers. Unskilled use of axes in chopping has also claimed its share of victims. Guns should be prohibited in all field camps unless they are required for defending the camp against dangerous animals or shooting game for food.

Protection against tetanus infection is always advisable since the organism can live in the soil.

RECORDING
EXCAVATION DATA
AND COLLECTING ARTIFACTS

6

Excavators must keep in mind that the site itself is, in a larger sense, an artifact of human activity. Under most circumstances digging destroys this artifact, and it is therefore necessary that archaeologists record in their notes as complete a description as possible of the site as it is being dug. They must always remember that their observations will be the only source available for reconstructing the former occupation of the site, once excavation has been completed. Excavation notes must include not merely what is found, but a running commentary on what is done and how it is done. The notes should be a record of technique as well as of results, so that future work may be guided by past achievements and errors.

From Taylor (1948: 191) comes the following statement.

It is possible to say without injustice to any particular field worker that, however carefully the archaeologist preserves his findings either in the form of notes or specimens, he always finds that there is information which he needs for his analysis but which he does not have in his records. Critical details will beg for elaboration and clarification during laboratory study, but there will be no way of bettering the situation. Only experience and the failings of former jobs will tell the archaeologist what he should be on the lookout for in his next investigation. For these reasons there is only one axiom to be remembered: when in doubt, preserve! Many things which may seem trivial and merely an added burden at the time of excavation may turn out to be of great importance to a full-blown cultural picture. It is worth preserving these data at the expense of a little extra labor and the following out of a few blind leads. When in doubt, preserve!

Notes should be kept in a bound notebook to prevent the loss of pages. The kind of notebook used by surveyors, in which one side of each page is cross-sectioned, is extremely useful, for it provides an immediate scale that can be used for mapping or for drawing artifacts in proper proportion. Another type of bound field notebook now available has gridded polyethylene pages that can be written upon in any environment, even under water. A soft, dark pencil of at least No. 2 hardness is most convenient for writing, as it is easily read and relatively permanent. Attention should be paid to legibility, particularly of numbers, and esoteric symbols should be avoided. Notes should be kept in such form that they can be understood by anyone referring to them, and as clean as possible under field conditions. Any necessary elaborations of the data recorded briefly on the site survey form or site map should be placed in the notes. Details such as the datum location should be entered, and an abstract of the plan of the grid layout noted. While the excavating is being done, particular attention should be accorded depths, stratification, and concentrations. Many excavators make carbon copies of all notes and file them separately as insurance against losing the originals. Others photograph all notebook pages with a 35 mm. camera at the end of a dig. The investment in film is nothing compared to the value of the single-copy originals. There have been enough lost field notes to make such precautions worthwhile.

The presence and depth of culturally sterile topsoil should be carefully noted at horizontal intervals frequent enough to demonstrate any variation. Depth of plowing or other surface disturbances, such as those caused by house foundations, posts, or pits, are also important. The depth of unit levels (whether arbitrary or natural) should be entered and any change noted. The midden deposit should be described as to composition (shell, sand, ash, clay, etc.), contents (bone, artifacts, stone, etc.), color, consistency (degree of compactness or friability), moisture content, and amount of disturbance by rodents. These factors should receive constant attention and any variations should be noted. Any indication of natural causes should be stated. For example, moisture content may vary considerably, and, while the date will indicate the season, any recent natural or artificial irrigation (rain included) should be recorded.

Stratification (Chapter 7) is of the utmost importance. It may be visible in the walls of the excavation as a sharp change in the color of the midden, as layers of different composition and contents, or as a change in consistency. Whatever its nature, an exact depth can usually be given at frequent intervals. Or stratification may be a gradual transition, lacking distinctness, to be discerned by more subjective measurement, such as of a gradual color change, a varying compactness of deposit, etc. If no physical stratification is apparent, this fact should be stated.

The tools used should be noted in the record. If one level is screened and others are troweled or spaded, a difference in the number of recovered artifacts may result, and the several techniques must be taken into account

(Meighan, 1950) when the excavated materials are analyzed. The methods used to handle special problems should be included in the notes. For example, if the midden extends below the water table, it should be stated whether water was pumped or bailed out of the pit, the muck placed in screens and washed, or what other means of excavation were used. Such records, made at the time and on the spot, are often of great help to the person studying the materials recovered. Not all the questions that will arise during analysis can be anticipated, but a full record of what was done during excavation may help to answer them.

One of the most important purposes of the notes is to record artifacts not included in the permanent collection from the site. This includes such variable data as the size, condition, and other details of fragile artifacts that could not be preserved; sketches; inferential evidence such as imprints; the number and nature of ash concentrations encountered; localized changes in midden consistency; or other phenomena lacking sufficient definition to be recorded as features. Occasionally, artifacts are so large, or of such common occurrence and uniform type, that it would be impractical to collect and retain them in a museum. In such cases, a full notebook and photographic record should be kept of the number, amount of variation, and provenience. For large artifacts, drawings with dimensions and cross sections should be made in the notebook. It is also useful to place check references in the notes on the number and location of soil samples obtained, the manner in which they were collected, and any special pedologic tests that were made and results obtained.

After the return from the field, a permanent copy, preferably typewritten, should be made of the notes and filed where it will be accessible to other students. Problems arise repeatedly from special studies made of the site or its contents, and field notes are of great value in solving them.

RECOGNIZING AND HANDLING ARTIFACTS IN THE FIELD

An artifact may be defined as anything made or modified by human beings. Artifacts such as projectile points, potsherds, and seed-grinding implements are easily recognized. Difficulty usually arises from fragmentary pieces or crudely made specimens, but there should be some clue in the shape, material, or method of manufacture to tell whether or not the piece was made by humans.

Difficulty also arises when the definition is extended, as it often is, to include modification by use as well as by manufacture. Thus the wastage from the making or use of tools is in the artifact class. The refuse deposit in which the tool is found is an artifact, because it is the product of human activity. Where, then are the limits? Is imported pottery-tempering material, which is crushed and mixed with the clay, an artifact? Technically it is, but practically it is an ingredient or constituent of a composite artifact (the pot). Is an unmodified seashell, found in an inland site far from the ocean, an artifact? Since it was collected and transported by man, it is artifactual in nature, but being unmodified, it is not an artifact. Still, by reason of being a natural object occurring through human intervention in an archaeological site, it is different from a stone pebble deposited there by an ancient river, and cannot be ignored as evidence of human action.

As another example, take the impression of basketry recorded on a piece of damp clay later fired into pottery. The now nonexistent basket, size and shape unknown, can be identified as having been made by the coiling technique, with *n* stitches per centimeter, direction of work going down to the right, etc., etc. In short, we can determine many technical details about a basket where actual physical evidence has quite disappeared. But since it no longer exists, the basket *per se* is of course not an artifact. Similarly, the imprints of seeds in pottery yield important information on what cereals were being grown in certain areas at certain times (Helbaek, 1953). Seeds, of course, are not artifacts, but their presence gives clues to how other objects found at the site might have been used—in cultivation or food preparation, for example.

The question becomes even more difficult if we try to decide whether human fecal pellets (coprolites) are artifacts or not. These remains (often preserved in dry cave deposits) are produced by the infinitely complex but wholly natural (i.e., biological) process of human metabolism. But they may contain bones of fish (caught with hooks or nets), husks of seeds (collected, ground, cooked, and eaten), and other items that could not possibly occur in the feces of non-culture-practicing animals. Are these coprolites artifacts? No, but they contain clear (and extremely interesting) evidence of the operation of culture. The noncultural fishbone and seed husks are perhaps best described as evidence of the existence and operation of culture. So we see that evidences of cultural pursuits or practices may themselves be noncultural in form, but they are nonetheless of the greatest interest to the archaeologist who is studying human action in prehistoric times. The problem of definition is put nicely by Childe (1962:11) who writes:

> The most obvious results of human behaviour, the most familiar archaeological data, may be termed *artifacts*—things made or unmade by deliberate human action. Artifacts include tools, weapons, ornaments, vessels, vehicles, houses, temples, canals, ditches, mine-shafts, refuse-pits, even trees felled by a woodsman's axe and bones intentionally broken to extract the marrow or shattered by a weapon. Some of these are movable objects that can be picked up, studied in a laboratory and perhaps exhibited in a museum; such may be termed *relics*. Others are too heavy and bulky for that treatment or are absolutely earth-fast like mine-shafts; all these may be designated *monuments*. But many data are not strictly artifacts, are neither relics, nor monuments. A Mediterranean shell

in a mammoth-hunter's camp on the middle Don or in a neolithic village on the Rhine is a precious document in the history of trade, though not an artifact. The deforestation of Southwestern Asia and the conversion of the prairies of Oklahoma into a dust-bowl are results of human action. Both are historically significant events and by definition archaeological data. Yet their short-sighted authors in neither case consciously envisaged or deliberately planned the regrettable results. If an irrigation system is an artifact, an accidentally produced desert is not.

A large portion of man's handiwork is unobtrusive, often resulting without conscious intent from the use of some implement. The solution to such problems of definition depends largely on the experience of the excavator, and this can come only from handling and observing actual specimens. This discussion will emphasize certain observations that should be made before an object is discarded as unmodified. Careful inspection is the most essential requirement. The eye soon becomes experienced in noticing scratches or a meaningful luster, so that a comprehensive glance is usually sufficient to indicate the possibility of human modification and the need for more careful scrutiny.

If the excavator cannot decide at once whether a find is an artifact or not, perhaps because it seems so crude, the specimen should be saved until it can be examined more carefully.

Stone   One of the most common manufacturing techniques encountered in archaeology is that of chipping or flaking stone (Squier, 1953; Holmes, 1919: 278ff.; Watson, 1950; Oakley, 1956; Braidwood, 1963; Leakey, 1954; Goodman, 1944; Ellis, 1965; Crabtree, 1972; see also a bibliography on this subject published by Hester and Heizer, 1973b: 19–20). At times it is very difficult to decide confidently whether flakes were removed from the edge of a stone by human or natural action (Engerrand, 1912; Warren, 1923; Barnes, 1939; Hester and Heizer, 1973b: 20–22). If the doubtful stone is found associated with many undoubted chipped implements, the decision may be no less difficult but far less important than if the stone is one of only a few—all doubtful—at a very old site where human presence is still in question. Has the excavator discovered a very ancient, rudimentary, lithic tool industry or not? Carter (1950, 1957) decided that he had, and announced that he had found evidence of Third Interglacial man on the San Diego County coast of Southern California. Haury (1959), Krieger (1958, 1959), and Johnson and Miller (1958) concluded, to the contrary, that the fractured stones taken by Carter to be artifacts were of natural origin.

A similar situation is that of the Calico Hills locality, also in Southern California; excavations by R. Simpson and others (Leakey, Simpson, and Clements, 1968) produced chipped specimens they interpreted as artifacts dating back 100,000 years. Haynes (1973) has since published new data indicating that these are naturally flaked rocks, or "geofacts."

It is an historical fact that unsupported claims of great human antiquity arise more frequently in California than in any other part of the New World. Whether the infamous hoax of the Calaveras skull set this local phenomenon in train, or whether the Golden State produces more archaeological freaks, or whether the citizens of that element of the Union are simply uncommonly gullible, we do not know. But the situation does exist and is likely to continue, and therefore it becomes an integral consideration in practicing and evaluating archaeology in California. Other states probably have their own special archaeological anomalies.

An interesting investigation into whether human action was involved in the production of some or all items in a large surface collection of fractured stones in certain Arizona localities has been done (Ascher and Ascher, 1965; cf. additional comments in *Science* 148:167–168, 1965). The student interested in other studies of the same problem is referred to Bourdier (1953), J. D. Clark (1958, 1961), Harner (1956), Warren (1914), Lacaille (1931), Leakey (1953: 45–48), and Watanabe (1949).

At times, even the most experienced, practiced, and reliable authority must admit that the usual test criteria for distinguishing natural from man-made objects fail to provide a clear answer, but such instances are, happily, rare. Leakey (1953: 46), in discussing the differences between natural and human flaking, writes, "How, then, can these results of pressure flaking by natural agency be distinguished from humanly made tools? Often they cannot. Consequently, many specimens that *may* be due to human workmanship, but which have been obtained from a geological stratum, have to be discarded as doubtful specimens." Because, in North America, extremely simple chipped stone objects have been reported from geologically datable deposits, and because some recent workers have proposed a "pre-projectile point stage" in American prehistory (Krieger, 1964a; cf. the penetrating comments on the "American Eolithic" by Greenman, 1957), the problem of people or nature as the producer of certain modified stones is a real, not hypothetical, one for American archaeologists.

Another large class of stone artifacts comprises those resulting from abrasive action. Here again, as with the chipped stone, arises the question how the modification occurred—by natural or human agency. Wind-driven sand can modify stones so that they may be mistaken for artifacts (Whitney and Dietrich, 1973). Sea worms and clams can bore holes in stone. Knowledge and experience do help, however. The holes or cavities produced by clams and sea worms are usually set at angles and have parallel sides, unlike holes drilled by human beings, which usually have a conical cross-section and show evidence of the tool used in the drilling. Often the altered surface of a stone or bone is so localized or in such a position that natural causes are impossible. Smoothness is often a useful determinant if the object is not waterworn.

Differences in color and luster are also frequent guides, especially for edges. A new student should become acquainted with the appearance of smoothed surfaces of manos, metates, abrading slabs, and similar artifacts before going into the field.

Roughened, macerated edges or ends may indicate that a stone was used for pounding. These modified areas are frequently the only identifying feature of hammerstones, mauls, and crude pestles.

Care must be taken in distinguishing between natural and artificial scratches on stone. People usually make incisions in some regular pattern or in such conflicting directions that no natural agency could be responsible. Grooves made by humans frequently reveal an unnatural smoothness, polish, or regularity, whereas notching usually occurs in some pattern.

Particular attention should be paid to evidence of decoration. Smooth flat surfaces can be held to the light and examined for incising, punctate designs, or applied color. Color is often easier to see when the artifact is wet, but the excavator should remember that not all color is fast and may be dissolved by water; cleaning of such specimens should be done under laboratory conditions.

Geology is so important to archaeologists that they should have at least the solid background of an introductory college course in it. Zeuner's (1950) general article on the relationships between geology and archaeology is worth reading.

Bone and antler   Before any bone is classified as unworked, it should be examined carefully for traces of modification, especially at the ends. Bones often became cut or scratched in the quartering of a carcass, leaving unmistakable marks. The reader is referred to Kidder (1932: 197; Fig. 166) and Hodge (1920) for examples of such bones.

The transverse cutting of long bones was a very frequent process. A V-shaped channel was made deep enough to allow breakage, leaving a characteristic lip (see Kidder, 1932; 201; Fig. 170). As the articular ends of long bones were occasionally prepared for various uses by removing the cancellous interior, they should be examined for such evidence. The cannon bones of hoofed quadrupeds were often split by "sawing" along the line of the natural medial groove. Specimens are commonly found on which this process was only partly finished. Excavators should become familiar with bone in its original, unmodified form, and inspect all bones encountered for man-made changes.

Animal bones sometimes look as if human beings had shaped or modified them, whereas only other animals or natural forces have actually been at work. Gnawing by rodents and carnivores, for example, often produces marks on bones that suggest deliberate human workmanship. For further discussion of this subject, the student is referred to the papers of Brain (1967), Koby (1943), Nelson (1928), Pei (1938), Sadek-Kooros (1972), and Sutcliffe (1970).

Rounded surfaces and polish are the best evidence for distinguishing tools from unmodified fractured bones. All edges and tips should be examined for smoothness and luster; such inconspicuous artifacts as splinter awls, bone tubes, and scapula tools can easily be overlooked.

Natural foramina should be distinguished from artificial holes, which are often conical or bear traces of cutting. Similarly, teeth with normal polish and grooving from wear should not be confused with artifacts. Incised bone should not be confused with marks resulting from gnawing by rodents, and the etching of bone by root action should not be mistaken for evidence of artistic expression.

Perishable artifacts   Wood, fibers, and other plant materials buried in open sites, which are generally subject to alternate wetting from rain and drying in nonrainy warm seasons, will not be preserved any length of time. However, these objects are often preserved by special conditions. One of these is incomplete burning (i.e., carbonization). Such artifacts as baskets, string and other textiles, and various wooden objects are preserved by being charred. Ash concentrations should be examined carefully for traces of such remains. Another special condition is dessication. In dry caves, ordinary organic material fails to decay. Thus such caves provide one of the best opportunities for reconstructing former cultures. All pieces of wood found in caves should be examined for sharpened ends, evidence of cutting or pounding, and burned pits or ends. The cultural deposit may be screened and bits of textile, scraps of leather, quids, plant remains, and fecal matter recovered. Many societies were less concerned than we are with disposing of their excretory wastes. Human feces are often abundantly present in well-preserved (desiccated) condition in dry archaeological deposits and can provide a surprising amount of useful cultural information not otherwise obtainable. A review, with citations to older published materials, of this kind of information on prehistoric diets is presented by Ambro (1967), Bryant (1974), Fry (in Aikens, 1970), Heizer (1960, 1967), Heizer and Napton (1969), Napton and Heizer (in Heizer and Napton, 1970), Nissen (in Heizer and Hester, 1973), and Roust (1967). Other reviews and data are contained in Callen (1963, 1965) and Callen and Cameron (1960), who report on materials from the Mexican and Peruvian areas. Surprisingly, large amounts of identifiable pollen grains are preserved in desiccated feces (Martin and Sharrock, 1964; Riskind, 1970), so that a new source for palynological data, tied directly to man, is now available for those areas where feces are preserved in dry deposits.

Miscellaneous objects   Any objects of European manufacture may be of extreme importance in dating a site if they are definitely associated with the cultural deposit and not a later intrusion (cf. Woodward, 1965).

Another large class of objects should perhaps be discussed here, even though they cannot be classed as artifacts. Like the seashell mentioned above, they are found where they do not occur naturally. When it appears—either by logical deduction from this occurrence out of context *per se,* or by definite association with other remains—that human beings transported them, such objects become important in the analysis of a site.

One thing that will often be found thus out of normal context is unmodified animal bone. Its presence in a refuse deposit is usually the result of man's quest for food and raw materials. However, natural death or animal predators may account for animal bone found in cave middens and in open sites; the explanation depends on the articulation and completeness of the bones, on the species represented, and on other evidence of animal occupation of the cave. Likewise, most of the seeds, grass, and other plant remains from cave middens should be saved or noted, unless they can safely be ascribed to nonhuman residents. Wood rats (genus *Neotoma*) are scavengers and will collect an amazing variety of objects which they use to build their "nests" or houses (Heizer and Brooks, 1965: 160, 162). When man and wood rats have lived, either as commensals or in turn, in caves or shelters, artifacts may be found in the rat nests. We mention such instances since they can be of archaeological importance under certain conditions (Heizer, 1960: 115, 136). Unmodified stones are meaningful in sites in a fluvial delta area and in shellmounds, where their presence can usually be assigned to the actions of the former inhabitants. Quartz crystals, concretions, and foreign minerals are other examples of meaningful objects. In order to recognize the significance of such exotic objects, archaeologists must know the geology of the region and be familiar with any previously excavated archaeological sites of the region, and their contents.

Some objects are meaningful through definite association. The most significant associations are those involving burials; even unworked objects derive meaning from their position in relation to the human remains or modified artifacts.

Nonnatural or patterned concentrations of unmodified objects are treated as features, examples being fireplaces, cooking stones, and caches of charred seeds. Sometimes an unmodified object becomes an artifact through use, e.g., a shell used as a container, a river cobble used as a hammerstone, a deer or elk antler used as a digging tool, a flat scapula blade used as a hoe or shovel, the lower jaw of an ungulate used as a saw or grass-cutter, etc., etc.

THE EXCAVATION OF ARTIFACTS

Various tools are used in excavating artifacts; several different tools will sometimes be need for extracting a single object, depending on the material from which the particular artifact is made, on the enclosing medium, and on individual preference. The trowel is an all-purpose implement, but certain kinds of artifacts and conditions sometimes require other devices. Carbonized textiles, for instance, are a special problem. If the surrounding soil is soft and dry, a stream of air is often a satisfactory means of exposure. If the work is below water level or the earth is wet and sticky, a small stream of water may be useful in removing the coating of mud. Hand picks or railroad picks may be required to cut through heavy clays or lime-indurated layers.

All artifacts encountered should be treated as fragile until the excavator is certain of their condition. Direct contact of the excavating tool with the artifact should be avoided, the enclosing medium being removed by lifting, brushing, or blowing—seldom by scraping. Shell ornaments, antlers, and micaceous sheets, especially when wet, require extreme care in excavation to prevent their disintegration.

Whenever possible, an artifact should be exposed *in situ* and not extracted until it has been completely exposed and all its associations have been noted. No matter what the material, it may break, if pulled or pried. Equally important, associations may be lost if an object is pulled out before it is fully exposed and the immediately surrounding area on the same level is cleared. Before the artifact is removed, its position should be plotted and analyzed, including its relationship to other artifacts or features, its stratigraphic position, and its possible disturbance or conveyance by rodents or other indications of change after deposition. A photograph and a sketch are desirable if there is a significant association suggesting the use of an object, its time of deposition, or its relation, through proximity, with other artifacts or features. If there is an implication of geological antiquity in the associations or stratigraphic position of an artifact, it should not be removed at all, if this is practicable, until competent authorities have viewed it in its undisturbed condition and position.

RECORDING THE LOCATION OF ARTIFACTS

After an artifact has been exposed, its position must be recorded. This information is as significant as the artifact itself. No excavation can be adequately analyzed unless each artifact can be accurately placed in relation to all other cultural remains. Clustering of artifacts from which some former activity may be inferred may provide essential evidence for dating the site and for determining the nature and extent of cultural activity and change during the occupation of the site.

Even fragments with little or no diagnostic value (e.g., tips or medial sections of projectile points or awls) must be collected and located. If cultural stratification is known to be present and some common object does not conform to the normal distribution, a record of the exact depths of the aberrant specimens is necessary.

There are, of course, exceptions to these exhaustive procedures. If an object has no associations, its location may be relatively unimportant. Sites with a great abundance of flint-flaking debitage or whose soils are loaded with potsherds could never be adequately examined if the exact location of every flint scrap or every pottery fragment were plotted. This is not to say, however, that such commonly occurring items should be treated as unimportant. Indeed, at many Paleolithic sites, each bit of chipped stone is carefully plotted (cf. J. D. Clark, 1969: Fig. 15). The excavator's judgment— and the research design—must determine whether or not an artifact may be approximately rather than precisely located.

An example of what would seem to be the proper measure of care in recording, consistent with the importance of flint-reject material, is the work of Grahame Clark (1954) at the Mesolithic site of Star Carr in Yorkshire, England. By plotting the frequency of worked flints per excavation unit (Fig. 5-12), Clark was able to define the area of activity in flint knapping at the site. Similar plots showing frequencies of specific kinds of objects recovered have been published for the Pomongwe Cave site in Southern Rhodesia (Cooke, 1963), the El Inga site in Ecuador (Bell, 1965), and in sites of the DeCordova Bend area of north-central Texas (Skinner, 1971). These plots provide a visual impression not obtainable from a table of numerical occurrence.

The so-called level bag, in which is collected all the unworked animal bone, flint scrap, etc. recovered from a given level or layer, should always bear the site designation, excavation unit, and date. Make it a regular practice to label the level bag *before* it is set on the pit edge and filled with finds. Any delay will inevitably result in some bags remaining unmarked and their contents therefore made useless.

An artifact slip should be made out for all complete specimens and for those fragments that retain enough recognizable characteristics to allow typological identification. The primary purpose of this slip is to preserve the record of the location and any remarks on the occurrence of an artifact until such information can be entered in the field catalog or on the artifact itself. The advantage of a separate record makes artifact slips preferable to notes written on artifact bags. The notebook record may also, in many cases, include information about the specimen, and after the specimen has been assigned a number in the field, this number should be entered in the pertinent notebook record. If a slip is not used, the data entered on the artifact bag should be full and complete, including a sketch of the object. Regardless of what system is used, it is essential that each item recovered be afterward identifiable. Otherwise, confusion may arise over exactly which item the data refer to.

A sample artifact record form is shown in Fig. 6-1. Such forms can easily be made in quantity by preparing copy on a mimeograph stencil so that six or eight can be printed on a single sheet and then cut out. The excavation unit must always be stated. Horizontal measurements are consistently taken from some corner stake agreed upon before the beginning of excavation and are added to the total distance from the datum point. (The compass direction of the reference corner should always be recorded.) These measurements are taken from the string stretched between the stakes, parallel to the unit walls, and are usually expressed in terms of the cardinal directions. Either direction, north-south or east-west, may be taken first, but as a convenience in later cataloguing and study it is preferable to use one order or the other consistently.

Pertinent remarks on association, position, or condition should be entered. When possible, a tracing or sketch of the artifact should be made on the back of the record form or in the notebook. This is useful for distinguishing duplicate specimens, such as projectile points or shell ornaments, placed in the same artifact bag. When completed, the slip should be checked

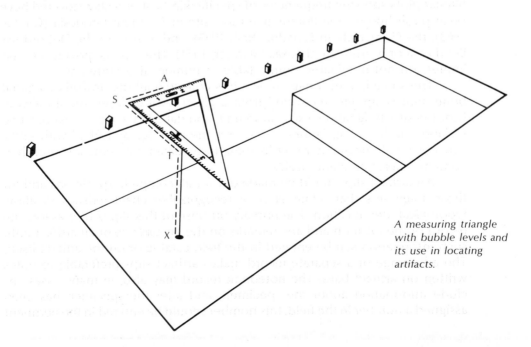

A measuring triangle with bubble levels and its use in locating artifacts.

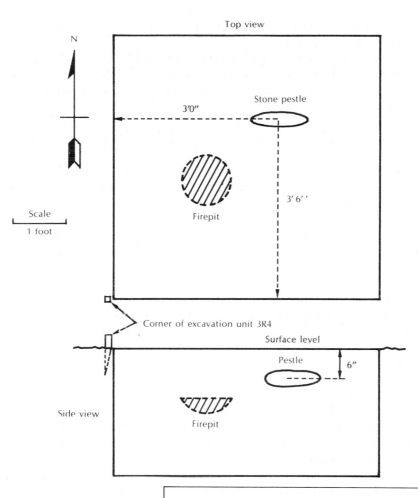

6-1. *Plan and profile of a 5 × 5 foot excavation unit showing one method of triangulation used in locating artifacts, and an artifact record form containing information on the location of the pestle found in excavation unit 3R4. The measuring tape may be hooked onto the corner stake by a nail driven into the top of the stake. The tape should be held level and the object's position determined with a plumb bob. Location by triangulation must be done as carefully as possible to insure accuracy.*

Artifact Record

Description Stone pestle (complete, length 10", diameter 4")

Site Sol-2   Date 3/4/49

Pit or Tr. No. 3R4   Depth 6"

Location 3 ft. 6 in. N of Datum SW Corner
          3 ft. 0 in. E of Datum SW Corner

Remarks Near firepit (recorded as Feature 21)

Recorded by AB Lord Field No. Sol-2-439

for any omissions, then folded to prevent soilage, and placed in the same container with the artifact.

The system shown in Fig. 6-1 for locating artifacts has some shortcomings since it is not always precise. The technique next described is somewhat more complicated (and therefore slower) but more precise. In this method, the rows of stakes bordering the trench are set back one foot from the edge of the trench and are placed no farther than five feet from each other. Each stake is marked with its location and elevation relative to the central datum point.

When a find is made, a measuring triangle is used to determine its location, as shown in the accompanying diagram. This is a right triangle made of wood, with one arm three feet and the other arm four feet long, and each arm equipped with a fixed spirit level.

The position of a find in the excavation unit is recorded by holding the triangle level, with the short side resting against the nearest stake and along the baseline string running along the line of stakes, and the outer edge of the long side of the triangle positioned vertically over the find. A painted cloth tape with a plumb bob attached to the zero end is held against the long side, directly over the object, and the vertical distance is measured. In the diagram the three coordinates are S-A, S-T, and T-X. For other descriptions of this method of locating finds, see Atkinson (1953: 152–153) and Wheeler (1954: 68–71).

Another method of three-dimensional recording has been suggested by Schwarz and Junghans (1967). From his work on an underwater shipwreck, Andersen (1969) has proposed a technique for field measuring that involves the use of three base points placed around a site and computer processing of the data obtained. Christensen (1969) has commented on the limitations of Andersen's technique.

Some archaeologists prefer to designate depth in terms of both the actual surface and the datum plane, but even where the depth from datum plane appears irrelevant to the stratigraphic situation, it may have to be used because the actual surface above the find spot is no longer present, having been removed by excavation. To obtain datum-plane depth, one person holds the leveling rod with its lower end at the find spot, a second person sights with the hand level (or alidade or dumpy-level) from the leveling station and the reading is subtracted from the datum elevation. If the contour map has been made with sufficient care, actual depth from surface can be determined by reference to the map. A level line, run from the nearest grid stake (whose position and elevation are already recorded) will enable a depth measurement to be made, or a string run over the excavated area between two points on the original surface allows the surface directly over the find spot to be extrapolated (see Fig. 6-2).

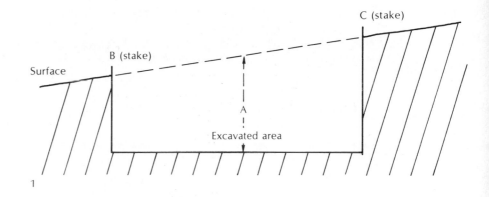

6-2. *Three methods of recording the depth of an object encountered during excavation:*

1. A taut line, stretched between stakes B and C at the surface level of deposit, will give the original surface level at a point immediately above find. The depth from the original surface is distance A.

2. A level line (its plane verified with a line level) is extended from the base of stake C to give the depth measurement B. An alternative is to run a level line from the base of stake D to give the depth measurement A.

3. The depth of an object from the datum plane is determined by taking a level line of sight, B–C, from instrument B, reading distance A on a measuring rod, and subtracting D, the height of instrument

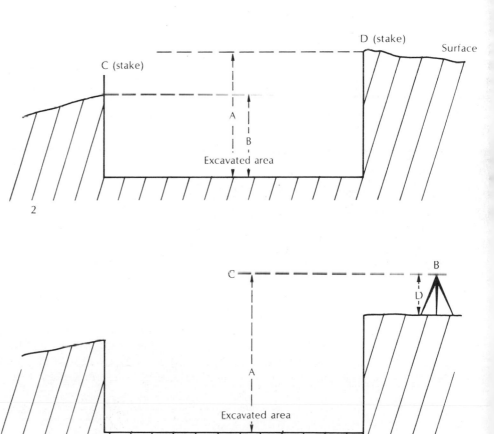

6-3. *Top: a partially exposed house floor showing postholes on the edge and interior. The house floor was originally about 8 × 9 meters. Note the grid stakes replaced for purposes of accurate location and recording. The picture's major fault is that it lacks a scale. (After Hatt, 1957: Fig. 66.) Bottom: exposed floors of two rectangular Iron Age houses at the Nørre Fjand site, West Jutland. Note the neatness of excavation and the replaced grid corner stakes to aid in recording. (After Hatt, 1957: Fig. 101.)*

If finds are made in an area opened up so far that it is difficult to record their location from the still-standing grid coordinate stakes, one can reset the grid stakes within the open area (see Fig. 6-3), stretch strings, and record the finds. This is nicely illustrated in Meggers, Evans, and Estrada (1965: Pl. 12), and Ford (1963: Pls. 2, 3).

The proper collecting or field-storage container is determined by the size, quantity, material, and condition of the artifact in question. Large stone objects should be kept separate to prevent damage to fragile shell, bone, or flaked specimens. It is usually safest to wrap shell artifacts or objects first with appliqué, adhesive, or inlay, then with tissue paper or toilet paper, and place them in individual boxes or sacks. Any small objects, especially beads, should be wrapped or boxed so they will not escape notice when the sack is emptied. Charred textiles should be placed in cardboard boxes and carefully packed so as not to be crushed. Long bone artifacts should be arranged so that no strain will be placed on them. Packing of specimens in crushed paper is often advisable.

The archaeologist should always bear in mind that artifacts are basic to the reconstruction of the life and cultural pattern of the former inhabitants of a particular site. Equally important, as noted above, is the position of the artifacts in the site, since position provides evidence of the changes that took place in the activities of the former occupants—evidence that, in turn, may contribute to our understanding of the dynamics of culture.

Childe (1962: 14-15) discussed the important matter of association and its significance in archaeological interpretation:

> Archaeological data are said to be associated when they are observed occurring together under conditions indicative of contemporary use. A classic example is provided by a pagan burial. Take a warrior with his accoutrements and insignia, provided with food and drink and a complete table service, laid on his back in a coffin hollowed out of an oak trunk which is then covered by a barrow (burial mound). In this instance the skeleton, the burial ritual and the several items of mortuary equipment are associated; they constitute what we may term an assemblage. In the same way all objects left on the floor of a hastily abandoned house, together with the house itself and its fixtures, are considered associated and termed an assemblage. On the other hand, this term cannot be applied without reservation to everything found on the site of the house, in a single rubbish-pit, or in the same bank of river gravel. If the house had been occupied for several generations, objects of different age may have got trampled into the floors or lodged in chinks and crannies. The contents of the local rubbish-pit may be equally varied. In both cases modern techniques should enable an excavator to distinguish and collect several consecutive assemblages from the pit and house-site. Not so with the gravel bank. The same bed of river-laid gravel may contain stone implements made and lost by men actually encamped beside the river's course together with other implements that had been lying about the ground within the catchment area for 100,000 years before the flood-

waters picked them up and bore them to the gravel bank. In such an *aggregate* no excavation, however expertly conducted, would distinguish assemblages of associated types.

FIELD SPECIMEN CATALOG

An important part of the procedure of recording field data is the keeping of a field catalog. Future reference to artifact location will depend upon the information contained in such a record, and from it will come the entry in the permanent museum catalog. It should always be kept in mind that, though you are the present excavator, and familiar with the site, some other person may later work with your collections, observational data, and records (Wheat, 1956). The method of recording specimens in a field catalog depends, in part, upon the type of site and the nature of the data to be recorded. Once a specimen has been unearthed and the necessary find data are recorded, it is ready for field cataloguing.

Actual field cataloguing is generally done in the evening when in camp; however, it may be done at any time or by any individual who has been left in charge of the camp for the day. Or, on an excavation where there are enough supervisory personnel, a field laboratory may be established in which all finds are received, cleaned, repaired, and catalogued.

It is recommended that the field catalog be kept in a book with pages that are bound or clamped, rather than in a loose-leaf ring binder, and that all entries be recorded in black India ink. When an artifact being catalogued is found to lack some of the required information on place or conditions of occurrence, make a record of this lack and the reasons therefor.

When a daily field catalog is being made of artifacts recovered from more than one site, it is advisable to prefix the specimen number with a site number. Thus specimen number 8122 from site Sac-6 would appear on the specimen and in the catalog as Sac-6-8122. Blocks of pages may be reserved for separate sites so that no page contains data on specimens from more than one site.

Select a clean, inconspicuous spot on the specimen for the field catalog number. A second, permanent museum number will be applied later, and space should be reserved for this. After the ink dries, it is advisable to cover the inked number with a thin coat of celluloid and acetone for protective purposes. On dark specimens such as slate or obsidian, an undercoat of white India ink may be applied to provide a contrasting surface for the field specimen number. When quantities of shell beads are recovered, it is advisable to tag several specimens of the lot and to number the box in which they are kept. Carbonized material should be tagged after a preservative has been applied and the box numbered. Organic remains (textiles, charcoal, bone, shell, etc.) collected and saved for possible dating by the radiocarbon method, should not be subjected to any preservative treatment. A note should be affixed to the container, cautioning against the use of organic preservatives, and stating that the contents have not been treated because they may later be used for radiocarbon dating. This will prevent an overzealous museum preparator from applying preservative substances.

Any box containing fragile specimens should be so labeled. Instructions for careful handling or repair or directions not to clean or wash particular specimens should be clearly stated on a red-bordered gummed tag attached to the box containing the specimens. Many finds have been ruined by museum preparators who did not realize that they needed special treatment.

As artifacts are catalogued, they should be wrapped and packed in boxes suitable for their transport from the field to the laboratory or museum. Boxes to be shipped by freight should be of wood and should have a wire binding. Always place an extra address label inside in case the outer label is damaged or destroyed. Pack small, light pieces together and heavy, unbreakable objects (pestles, stone choppers, etc.) in separate boxes. As boxes are filled, a packing list should be prepared and the box numbered so that the whereabouts of all specimens are known. File the packing lists with the catalog so that a check may be made when the boxes are unpacked and the final layout of material is made in the laboratory or museum.

The mimeographed field specimen inventory record (page 130) has proved useful and may be recommended as containing space for all essential find-data. Number the sheets for each site consecutively, write the site's name or number on each page, and enter the date the page was filled out. The vertical columns contain entries for specimen number, description of the item, provenience, depth, association with a feature, stratigraphic level, and the like, a "remarks" column, and a column where the permanent museum number may be added later. Some archaeological projects may entail the collection of materials and information not anticipated in the field specimen inventory record discussed here. In this event a special form can be devised to accommodate the required data.

After the field catalog numbers are assigned, all notebooks, burial and feature record sheets, artifact slips, and photographic record sheets should be reviewed and field specimen numbers entered on them for cross reference and identification. This procedure is an absolute necessity if the field records are to be complete and understandable.

Many organizations have devised series of cross-reference card files for artifacts. One file may order finds by the material of which they are composed (obsidian, flint, bone, stone, pottery, etc.); a second by excavation unit or section of the site; a third by chronology, and so on. Such multiple systems represent a good deal of work, but their advantages for future study and for publication are obvious.

ARCHAEOLOGICAL FIELD SPECIMEN INVENTORY RECORD

SITE _____ COLLECTOR _____ DATE _____ Sheet No. _____

Field Spec. Number	Description	Location	Depth	Association	Remarks	Mus. No.

RECOGNIZING AND RECORDING FEATURES

The word "feature" is ordinarily used to denote those material and visible items in or about archaeological sites that are either atypical of the general run of the deposit or not frequently encountered on the surface or in the vicinity of an aboriginal habitation. Generally speaking, features are things that are not brought back to the laboratory or museum. Thus ash lenses, house floors, caches of unworked stones, earth ovens, storage pits, and the like are generally called features (see Figs. 6 4 and 6 5). Groups of things such as a cache of charmstones, flaked blades, net-sinkers, raw implement material chunks found together, or an animal burial in a site may also be called features (cf. Fig. 5-8).

Most sites in an area will follow the same general pattern as to material nature of deposit and artifact occurrences, but no two archaeological sites are the same; and even the trained archaeologist can foresee little before the shovel work starts. Recognizing features in any site depends, in large part, upon close observation and careful excavation. In examining a new site, especially in a region where little previous work has been done, every object encountered should initially be considered a potential artifact or feature. The find should then be exposed with trowel and brush until its nature can be determined. Too often, features are recognized as such only after they have been partially or completely removed or destroyed. Students will learn that experience, patience, and good judgment are their best aids.

All features should be recorded on a standard feature sheet, a photograph should be taken, and, if possible, a sketch should be placed on the back of the data sheet. If a complex of artifacts is associated with a given feature, it should be observed and collected as a unit, and the association entered in the field catalog in the "Remarks" section. The following are some of the main categories of features usually encountered.

Surface features Although many of the surface features may be included on the site survey sheet, others require additional and more detailed study. A discussion of some common surface features follows:

House sites Indicate on a scaled drawing the number of houses, their location on the site and their relation to one another, orientation of door-ways, and any architectural features present (see Fig. 4-3).

Borrow pits Borrow pits are rare but do occur. They may be confused with depressions marking the location of large semi-subterranean houses or ceremonial chambers. Excavation will settle the point. Occasionally, auxiliary sites contain earth borrowed from the main deposit. If such sites occur, they may explain depressions on the surface of the larger site.

6-4. *Top: a stage in the exploration of a large and complex buried feature at the La Venta site, Mexico. After careful recording, the stones will be removed and the excavation will proceed to greater depth. Note the retention of a standing stratigraphic control wall. Bottom: the same feature after further exploration. At right center, two stone blocks are embedded in the stratigraphic control wall. These are elements of the series of stone blocks that appear in the foreground of the top photograph. (Photographs by Robert F. Heizer, 1955.)*

6-5. A complex feature of superposed elements at the La Venta site, Mexico. Top: a photo taken at moment of discovery of a foundation of unshaped stones lying beneath the mosaic mask. The pickman at left is on the point of encountering the foundation layer. Bottom: after removal of the mask, portions of the first four stone layers were exposed in the right half of the pit; in the left half of the pit, the fourth layer was exposed. In all, twenty-eight of these stone layers were encountered before workers reached the bottom of the pit in which the feature was constructed. (Photographs by Robert F. Heizer, 1955.)

Bedrock mortars   If a rock exposure occurs near a site and contains mortar holes, the type of rock, the number of holes, their depths, and the shape of the mortar cavity should be noted.

Quarry sites   Sometimes sites may be found near lithic outcrops that the occupants were exploiting. At such sites the quarry material should be identified, samples taken, and the amount of quarry refuse estimated. If a working face or any of the mining tools used can still be identified, they should be mentioned. Since quarries often have associated workshops, these should be plotted on a map of the site area. Not only the worked stone in the form of waste or debitage, but stone-working tools such as hammerstones may occur and should be noted (Bryan, 1950; Bucy, 1974; Parker, 1924; Spence and Parsons, 1972; see also a bibliography of lithic quarry studies in Hester and Heizer, 1973b).

Workshops   The word "workshops" implies that some material such as flint, jade, or shell was transported to a site to be used in making something. Such areas, as noted above, may themselves constitute a site, or they may occur as concentrations or areas of specific activity in a large habitation site. Such workshops should be carefully plotted on the site map, the size of the work area should be determined, and the type, nature, and amount of material used should be recorded.

Pictographs and petroglyphs   These, whether directly on or near a site, should be recorded and written up on a separate record form (see Figs. 6-6, 6-7 and the Petroglyph Record Form on p. 137). Pictographs and petroglyphs may also occur alone, and by themselves constitute a site (Cain, 1950; Cressman, 1937; Steward, 1929; von Werlhof, 1965; Heizer and Baumhoff, 1959, 1962: Appendix A; Jackson, 1938; Kirkland and Newcomb, 1967; W. Smith, 1952; Kühn, 1956; Grant, 1965; Schaafsma, 1963, 1972; Turner, 1963).
Methods and special techniques for recording such sites are discussed by Anati (1960: 36–38), Ayres (1961), Burton (1969), Cooke (1961), J. W. Clark (1967), Fenenga (1949), Gebhard (1960: 14–18, 78–79), Goodwin (1953: 132–138), Gorsline (1959), Grant (1965: 98–100), Hedden (1958), Heizer and Baumhoff (1962: 273–278), Johnson (1958), Knight (1966), Roefer, English, and Lothson (1973), and Swartz (1963).

Subsurface features   Any unusual item or association of items found during the course of excavation should be recorded in the field as a "feature," regardless of its apparent unimportance at the time of discovery. As with artifacts, the method of exposing buried features varies according to the nature of the material.

6-6. *Two petroglyphs from Nevada. The top rock (at site NV-Mi-4) has had the pecked designs filled with ordinary white chalk to emphasize discrete elements. (Photograph by Robert F. Heizer, 1958.) The bottom photo is of an unchalked rock (at site NV-Wa-68), and the designs are much more difficult to distinguish. (Photograph courtesy of Archaeological Research Facility, Berkeley.)*

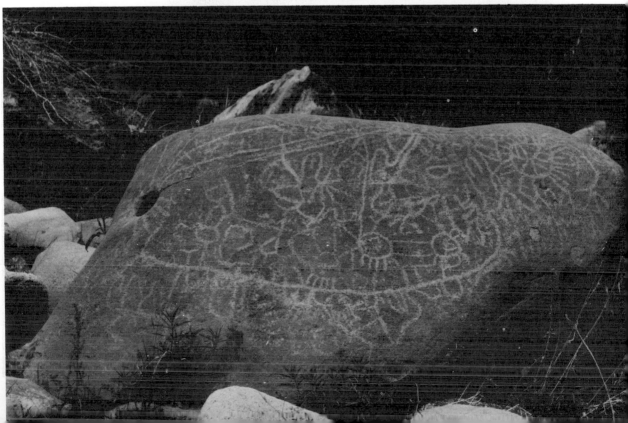

Facing page: A form sheet for recording petroglyph and pictograph information. Methods and special techniques of recording are discussed by Anati (1960: 36–38), Ayres (1961), Fenenga (1949), Gebhard (1960: 14–18, 78–79), Goodwin (1953: 132–138), Gorsline (1959), Grant (1965: 98–100), Heizer and Baumhoff (1962: 273–278), and Swartz (1963).

6-7. *Top: a common form of site vandalism; site NV-Li-9, a petroglyph locality. Bottom: chalked petroglyphs at site NV-Li-7 showing bighorn sheep, two costumed hunters holding atlatls and a spike-headed humanoid figure. Scale is 1 foot. (Photographs by T. R. Hester.)*

PETROGLYPH RECORD

1. Site_____ 2. Cross reference survey record_____

3. Face_____ 4. Dimensions of decorated area_____

5. Horizontal location_____

6. Kind of rock_____

7. Position of rock_____

8. Method of decoration: pecked( ); rubbed grooves( ); painted( ); other( )

9. Colors_____

10. Design elements_____

_____

_____

11. Superimposition_____

12. Natural defacement_____

13. Vandalism_____

14. Associated features_____

15. Additional remarks_____

_____

_____

_____

_____

_____

_____

16. Published references_____

_____

17. Sketch_____ 18. Scale of sketch_____

19. Photo nos._____

20. Recorded by_____ 21. Date_____

A grid frame (shown below) is useful in recording small features. The apparatus should be of convenient size, e.g., about four feet (or one meter) on each side. The sides may be made of wooden strips (1 × 2 inches) fastened together at the ends by means of angle irons. Around the edges of the aperture thus formed, nails, tacks, or screw eyes are set at regular, carefully measured intervals, say every five inches (or some similar subdivision in the metric system). Fine cord or flexible wire is stretched tautly from one nail to another, either in one continuous piece or in separate pieces, so that a square grid is formed as shown.

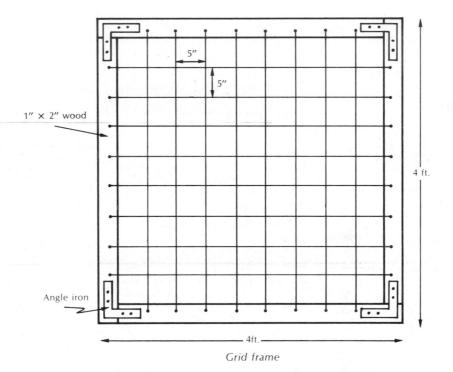

Grid frame

When laid over a feature, skeleton, or any find requiring a detailed plan drawing, the grid frame makes it easy to draw an accurate scale sketch on cross-ruled paper. If a five-inch grid is used, the drawing may conveniently be made on a common size of graph paper, i.e., one that is ruled ten squares to the inch. Photographs of this device being used in the field are shown by Bruce-Mitford (1956: Pl. 31b), Cole and Deuel (1937: 271), Cotter and Corbett (1951: Pl. 15), Mason (1942: Pl. 5), and Shafer (1971b: Fig. 18). See also Fig. 6-8.

Floors Whether floors seemed intended for domestic or ceremonial use, the nature of the surfacing material, as well as the thickness, density,

6-8. *The careful excavation of a living floor at the San Creek site, west central Texas. Note measuring frame used for recording. (After Shafer, 1971a: Fig. 18a; photograph courtesy of Harry J. Shafer and the Texas Archeological Survey.)*

configuration, and area of the floor should be recorded (see Chapter 5). Of course, any associated features, such as postmolds, hearths, clusters of objects on the floor (see Fig. 6-8), etc., have to be mapped and carefully recorded (cf. Binford *et al.,* 1970: Fig. 7).

Storage pits Settled communities often stored surplus food in pits dug into the earth. The Mohave Indians of the Colorado River area stored melons in deep pits lined with reeds (Forde, 1931: 111–112), and many of the agricultural groups of the Eastern United States stored maize in cache pits (Will and Spinden, 1906: 157–158; Wilson, 1917: Chap. 7; Robbins, 1968), and prehistoric village sites in the Great Plains area possess such pits (Bell, 1936; Calabrese, 1972; Karklins, 1970; Sperry, 1968; Wedel, 1961; Wood, 1971).

Since storage pits usually became repositories for trash and garbage after they were no longer usable for storing foods, their contents can provide most interesting information. These pits must be measured, their contents documented, the nature of the fill recorded (see Robbins and Irving, 1965: 158ff.), and their locations within a prehistoric community plotted. See Grebinger (1971: Figs. 1 and 7) for a good example of the spatial distribution of various types of pits at a site in Arizona; for a well illustrated example of the excavation and interpretation of what are interpreted as stone-filled cooking pits, see Shafer (1971b: 113–127).

Hearths Many items may be noted about a hearth uncovered during excavation (or in the recording of a surface hearth; see Varner, 1968; Epstein,

6-9. *Recording a hearth with the use of a 20 cm. grid.* (Photograph by T. R. Hester.)

1969: 12): the type, amount, and size of rock present; the amount of ash; evidence of food remains (mammal and bird bone, shellfish, carbonized plant remains, etc.); relation to house floors, if any, and artifacts or materials found distributed around, and possibly associated with, the hearth. Hearths are often an excellent source of carbonized wood (charcoal) that can be used for radiocarbon dating (see Chapter 14). The recording of a hearth and objects associated with it can be made easier by laying out a small grid (perhaps 20 cm. squares) over the feature (see Fig. 6-9).

In addition, such finds as the following should be noted and written up as features: shell lenses, concentrations of stones or artifacts, concentrations of animal or bird bones, intrusive pits, and animal and bird burials. Though the burials may be recorded on a standard burial form, they nevertheless constitute a special feature in the site (Heizer and Hewes, 1940).

To facilitate recording of essential data regarding surface or subsurface archaeologic features, a prepared sheet may be used. The feature record form on page 142 was devised for use in California. Since sites and their contents vary widely in different areas, such a form, if used, should be amended to fit regional conditions. An example for the American Southwest is shown by Dittert and Wendorf (1963: Figs. 9-10) and reproduced here with entries numbered to facilitate cross reference.

1. Features are numbered sequentially (1, 2, 3, etc.) *as they are recorded.*
2. Site name or number.
3. Depth from surface directly above the feature. If the feature itself has a thickness, note whether measurement refers to the top, bottom, or midpoint of the feature.
4. If the datum-plane level is employed rather than the actual surface, enter the depth.
5. Designation of excavation unit (trench, pit number, etc.).
6. Coordinate location in feet and inches from a datum point.
7. Name, type, and identification of feature.
8. Itemization and brief description of objects or components of the feature.
9. Length, width, thickness (horizontal and vertical extent).
10. Association with, or relation to, stratigraphic levels.
11. Further observations, if space is needed.
12. Name of person responsible for exposure and clearing of find.
13. Name of recorder.
14. Date of recording data on this sheet.
15. Photograph number. If no photograph is made, so specify.
16. Location of sketch (reference to notebook, separate sheet, or reverse side of feature record).

ARCHAEOLOGICAL FEATURE RECORD

1. Feature no._____ 2. Site_____

3. Depth from surface_____ 4. Depth from datum plane_____

5. Excavation unit_____

6. Horizontal location_____

7. Definition_____

_____

_____

8. Associated objects and features_____

_____

_____

_____

_____

_____

9. Dimensions_____

10. Stratigraphic notes_____

_____

11. Additional data_____

_____

_____

_____

12. Exposed by_____ 13. Reported by_____

14. Date_____ 15. Photo_____ 16. Sketch_____

COLLECTING NON-ARTIFACT SAMPLES

In most excavations, the need will arise to take samples that are non-artifactual in nature. Such samples may include charcoal or other organic materials needed for radiocarbon dating, midden samples for palynological, chemical or pedologic studies, and the like. Many of these kinds of samples can be analyzed by the archaeologist, but others require the services of specialists.

Pollen sampling   (see also Chapter 14). Soil samples can be taken for subsequent palynological analysis, in the hope of obtaining evidence on paleoenvironments. Each sample should be taken from a freshly cut exposure, using a clean trowel, sterile plastic bags, and external tags (Bryant and Holtz, 1968). Samples can be in a "column," i.e., in a vertical row, one or more from each natural stratigraphic unit or at arbitrary intervals (for example, one sample every 5 or 10 centimeters, from the top to the bottom; Kautz and Thomas, 1972: 45).

V. M. Bryant, Jr. has told us (personal communication) that the size of the soil sample collected in the field varies with the type of site under excavation. For example, in alluvial sites, palynologists ask for a minimum sample of 250 milligrams and would prefer a sample of around 500 milligrams. In caves and rockshelters, the sample size needed often depends on how much material has been deposited in the site by wind and how rapidly the deposits have accrued. However, about 10 grams per sample is often sufficient. A general rule is that you can never collect too much. If reconstructing the paleoenvironment by means of analyzing pollens is a major part of your research design, soil samples should be taken early in the field season and forwarded to a palynologist. Thus the samples can be analyzed while the rest of the excavation proceeds and the palynologist can tell the archaeologist, before he or she leaves the site, whether further samples should be collected, in what quantities, at what locations, and so forth. If no pollen is present at the site itself, one can obtain paleoenvironmental data by pollen sampling in nearby lake deposits or bogs (a "Hiller borer" or "Livingston sampler" is recommended).

Charcoal sampling   In obtaining charcoal samples for radiocarbon analysis, the precise cultural and stratigraphic position of the sample is most important. *In situ* samples of charred material are, of course, the best, but small bits of charcoal can be extracted to form a sample. Ralph (1971: 8–9) dispels the old adage that a potential radiocarbon sample should not be touched with one's bare hands. She does recommend, when available, a "clean trowel, spatula, or tweezers" to remove particularly small samples of charcoal, especially those mixed with earth. On balance, she points out that extracting the charcoal in the field (either by hand or with the tools mentioned above) is better than packing and shipping a large quantity of mixed charcoal and earth, as such shipment often leaves the material badly broken and even more completely mixed. Michels (1973), on the other hand, states that if possible, only glass or metal should come in contact with the sample in the field:

> The tools and containers should be clean and free from all organic material, greases, lubricants, preservatives, etc. Samples should be removed with clean metal trowels or spatulas, and placed directly in new aluminum foil. After being wrapped in foil, the sample should be placed in a glass or metal container. . . . If a piece of the sample drops to the ground, it should be discarded (Michels, 1973: 164).

Most radiocarbon laboratories have procedures by which contaminated charcoal samples can be satisfactorily cleaned (cf. Davis, Srdoc, and Valastro, 1973: 24). Naturally, the archaeologist who thinks a sample may be contaminated in some fashion, should make this clear to the laboratory.

The necessary sample size for radiocarbon dating varies according to the type of organic material in question (see Michels, 1973: Table 9). For example, the desired amount of charcoal is 8–12 gms., and of wood, 10–30 gms. For additional information on the kinds of organic materials that can be radiocarbon-dated, and the sample sizes required, see Michels (1973) and Polach and Golson (1966).

Archaeomagnetic samples   A relatively recent dating technique, archaeomagnetism, operates on the principle that the direction and intensity of the earth's magnetic field will vary over the years. When clay and clay soils containing magnetic minerals are heated to a certain temperature, these minerals will assume (and retain after cooling) the direction of the magnetic field surrounding them. By measuring these quantities, the age of the sample can be determined, but only if the sequence of changes in the earth's magnetic field at that particular location is already known (see Bucha, 1971; Michels, 1973: 130; and Chapter 14).

Archaeomagnetic samples are usually taken from hearth areas within a site. At the present time, there is but one laboratory in the United States analyzing these samples, and this is at the University of Oklahoma (under the direction of Dr. Robert DuBois). Collecting archaeomagnetic samples is a fairly complex task, best left to experts (see Bucha, 1971: 85–87).

Matrix sampling   Taking samples of the midden deposit for later microanalysis in the laboratory can be accomplished in a variety of ways. "Column sampling" is one procedure commonly employed (Ascher, 1959; Brooks, 1965; Meighan *et al.*, 1958; Salwen, 1962). Story (1968: 8; and Fig. 4b) describes column sampling in her report on excavations at a shell midden on the central Texas coast:

> A total of eight column samples were collected, each by removing a section roughly 0.5 feet wide and 0.5 feet deep from an exposed wall. . . . These samples extended from the surface or from just beneath the surface . . . to, or near, the base of the excavations. Each column was divided and bagged separately by stratigraphic unit, and within a (stratigraphic) unit, by arbitary levels.

Cores of midden deposit can be obtained from various depths by using a soil auger (this is comparable to column sampling; see Casteel, 1970).

So-called whole samples can be collected, as when an entire lens in a rockshelter deposit is removed to the laboratory or when large segments of the more extensive strata at a site are taken up and put into large plastic bags, which are then sealed and labeled (cf. Collins, 1969: 4).

In some cases, midden constituents can be separated or sorted in the field by water-flotation techniques. Flotation can be used to recover seeds, tiny animal bones, and other remains that might normally be lost in screening (see French, 1971; Jarman, Legge, and Charles, 1972; Hammond, 1971; Payne, 1972; Renfrew, 1973: 21–23; Schneider and Noakes, 1970; Schock, 1971; Struever, 1968a; Williams, 1973).

Further discussion of constituent analysis of midden deposits can be obtained in the references found in Chapter 5.

Finally, several kinds of *chemical sampling* techniques are used in the course of field work. The most common of these is phosphate analysis (see Ahler, 1973; Cook and Heizer, 1965b; Cornwall, 1958; Provan, 1971; Schwarz, 1967), used to detect soils that have been chemically enriched by human activities. Soil phosphate content can be analyzed on a "spot test" basis, using an auger to obtain soil samples and a small set of field equipment to test the samples (cf. Eidt, 1973: Fig. 1). Eidt (*ibid.*: 210) reports that such instant chemical testing of site deposits "can be employed to create phosphate map patterns depicting the extent and type of settlement features along with their relative length of duration."

Other chemical tests can be used in the field to identify postmolds and rodent burrows (van der Merwe and Stein, 1972), to identify catlinite (Sigstad, 1970), and to distinguish black discolorations caused by manganese dioxide from those caused by charcoal (Alford, Bundschuh, and Caspall, 1971). In the laboratory, phosphate analysis of the earthen contents of pottery vessels has been done in an effort to determine the original purpose of the pot, and Duma (1972) has proposed phosphate analysis of the pottery itself.

For a general review of many of the major sampling techniques, see Hester and Conover (1970). Although their paper describes ecological sampling for Northwest Coast shell middens, it provides examples of collecting procedures for a variety of samples, methods for processing the samples, and archaeological applications of the data derived from the analyzed samples (for other examples of midden sampling in coastal sites, see Rappaport and Rappaport, 1967, and Shawcross, 1967).

STRATIGRAPHY

R. E. W. Adams

7

The tyme, that may not sojourne
But goth, and never may retourne,
As water that down renneth ay,
But never drope retourne may;
Ther may no-thing as tyme endure,
Metal, nor erthely creature;
For alle thing it fret and shal
The tyme eek, that chaungeth al,
And al doth waxe and fostred be,
And alle thing destroyeth he.

—CHAUCER, *The Romaunt of the Rose*

 Archaeologists are repeatedly confronted during their excavation careers with maddeningly complex physical situations. In the American West they may find that a herd of bison was driven into an arroyo and some 190 of them killed and then butchered, leaving a bewildering mass of bones and artifacts, the whole later modified by erosion. That was what Wheat and his associates encountered at the Olsen-Chubbuck site (1972). In the Middle East, they may find multi-layered jumbles of mudbrick walls intermingled with burials, trash, burnt-down buildings—all modified by later construction, casual looting, and prehistoric antiquarianism. Dry caves and deserts may yield exquisitely preserved materials and plant remains, but often in the context of dust as fine as talcum powder and sand that runs like water when disturbed. Shell middens in North and South America, geologically rearranged deposits in East Africa, pithouse villages on the Missouri River, and Mayan ruins in Yucatan all present their own unique problems of excavation.

In all of these situations, however, the basic purpose is always the same—to elicit order from the apparent chaos. A primary means of accomplishing this purpose is stratigraphy, analyzing the strata or layers of archaeological sites much as geology analyzes the strata of the earth. For the professional archaeologist, there are few satisfactions to match that of reaching a complete, rational, and tested explanation for a complex stratigraphic problem. It is upon such data that the most important goals of archaeology are based, the studies of cultural history and of cultural process.

Both the stratigraphic principle and the practice of stratigraphy were recognized long ago, perhaps as early as Classical Greece. Then they were apparently lost, not to be rediscovered until the eighteenth century. William Smith, who recognized a sequence of deposits in Kent's Cavern in England in the 1790's, is probably one of its earliest rediscoverers. Metric or arbitrary level stratigraphy (a technique for dealing with weakly stratified or apparently unstratified sites by establishing levels of arbitrary depth) was introduced to the New World probably by Boas through his colleague Manuel Gamio, who excavated in such a manner in 1911. Nels Nelson's use of the technique probably stemmed from his Old World experience with Palaeolithic archaeology, gained while excavating with Obermeier and Breuil. In 1914 Nelson applied this principle to sites in the Galisteo Basin of New Mexico. Nelson's work was much better publicized than Gamio's and had an immediate impact on field workers. A. V. Kidder, Sr., used the method in his work at Pecos, New Mexico, and it became standard in the 1920's (Willey and Sabloff, 1974: 89–96).

DEFINITION

Phillips, Ford, and Griffin (1951) have provided perhaps the most succinct definition of stratigraphy, along with a useful distinction: stratification is what you find; stratigraphy is what you do with it. As already noted, the term and the basic method come from geology. Some of the basic assumptions come from geology, too, such as uniformitarianism. Uniformitarianism is the assumption geologists make of uniformity or continuity in the processes forming the strata of the earth. In other words, when volcanoes erupt today, they lay down layers of ash. Geologists assume that ancient volcanoes did the same.

Similarly, archaeologists assume that human behavior (the force that forms archaeological deposits) is much the same today as it ever was. For example, most modern communities have a dump for their rubbish and garbage. Archaeologists routinely encounter mixed deposits whose likeliest origin seems to be their having served as the trash heap of a primitive people. A. V. Kidder, Sr., digging into the Andover, Massachusetts, town dump in 1922, found layering and change there markedly similar to those found in the much older trash deposits at the prehistoric Southwestern ruin of Pecos.

PRINCIPLES

There is really only one major principle in archaeological stratigraphy. This is the *law of superposition*. In other words, under most conditions, as common sense would suggest, the earliest layers are on the bottom and the latest layers are on the top. A sequence of events, physical and/or cultural, producing the layers is represented by the changes from bottom to top. The excavator should also be aware of the possibilities of "reversed stratigraphy," deposits in which normal stratigraphic processes may have been disrupted (such modifications can be caused by digging of storage pits or graves, animal burrowing, and the like; cf. Hole and Heizer, 1973: 147; additional examples are provided by Colton, 1946; Pydokke, 1961; and Tolstoy, 1958).

Even normal stratigraphic conditions, however, do not make excavation simple. Strata may be either horizontal, slanting, vertical, deformed, or a combination of these. They may be sharply distinguished from one another by color or consistency or contents, or they may grade very subtly into one another. Preservation contexts range from the best (dry caves and deserts) through architectural stratigraphy and open sites to geological deposits, usually the worst for preservation. The physical nature can range from talcum powder-like dust to heavy clays and stone.

GOALS

Whatever the nature of the site and its strata, the minimal goal of archaeological stratigraphy is to work out the sequence of individual samples of deposits and to elicit the events producing them. In other words, one aims at producing a depositional history for each excavated sample or group of samples.

A middle-range goal of stratigraphic work is to establish a site chronology and culture history by synthesizing the histories of the individual deposits.

The ultimate aim is to establish a regional sequence into which individual events and site sequences are keyed by means of common factors. Usually it is only at this point that one can begin considering problems of culture process, although they may be anticipated earlier.

TECHNIQUES OF EXCAVATION, LABELING, AND RECORDING

Test pits excavated by arbitrary levels are usually the first means of revealing stratification in the deposits at a site. The arbitrary levels in such pits necessarily cut across any natural levels present. In an extensive test-pitting program, most pits will not be re-excavated according to natural levels, and therefore the recording of the stratigraphic sequence in these pits is mainly accomplished after arbitrary excavation. During excavation, whether of test pits or of the main site, extensive and detailed notes should be kept, including schematic drawings on gridded paper showing stratigraphic features as they appear. These features often fade in both color and contrast after exposure, and it is vital to note them promptly as a guide to the final recording procedure. Soil color is usually an important aspect of the stratigraphy, and description should be done using the Munsell soil-charts (Munsell, 1954).

When a unit has been completely excavated, the walls of the pit should be thoroughly cleaned to make the strata easier to see. If the walls are stable, a combination of scraping with a sharp trowel and light brushing with a whiskbroom or a lighter-weight brush will work; otherwise, a method must be improvised to suit conditions. In dry cave deposits, an atomizer may be used for final cleaning. In permanently damp sites such as Star Carr, Grahame Clark thinks that water jets might help in excavation (1974: 50). Air-compressed brushes may be helpful at times. Wetting with a back-pump sprayer will often freshen and rejuvenate features in the walls for recording.

Labeling is necessary at least during the final stages of recording. This may be done by using numbered pieces of note card attached to the wall with nails. Various other, more ingenious, means of labeling are available, such as the use of cutout plastic numbers and letters that can be attached to vertical surfaces by nails. The aim is to produce a visual reference system for use during recording. At this point a Polaroid color photograph may be taken in order to guarantee that something of an objective record is made. The labeling system used will naturally depend on the field system in use by the project. It is very convenient to use label numbers that are also the lot numbers assigned to materials from those layers. Thus the excavator and the artifact analyst (if they are not the same person), can talk more easily about their various conclusions. See Fig. 7-1 for an illustration of labeled cave deposits at Arenosa Shelter in Texas.

Stratigraphic recording can be done in a number of ways. However it is done, some sort of scaled reference system will be needed. American archaeologists have traditionally stretched vertical and horizontal strings across the face of an excavation to create a grid, using a line level to achieve horizontal levels and a plumb bob to achieve vertical ones. All measurements should be metric, and millimeter-ruled paper should be used for scale drawings. Long rolls of grid paper that can be cut are preferable to 8½" × 11" notebook size. Scale drawing has been the traditional method of recording stratification, and is very good indeed when it is well done. Detailed notes may be made on or at the margins of the drawings. Each layer should be described according to color, composition, unusual features, and content.

7-1. *Upper half of the stratigraphic profile at Arenosa Shelter (41VV99).* (Photograph courtesy of David S. Dibble and Texas Archeological Survey.)

Again, a picture is worth a thousand words. Color photographs with Polaroid and regular cameras are absolutely necessary. Such photographs should be made either on an overcast day or with the wall shaded. A canvas can be held over the excavation for this purpose. Overall shading avoids the high contrast of a partly shaded wall or the dappling effect of tree shade, and makes the light value more or less uniform over the entire surface of the wall. Thus, not only will the entire surface be more faithfully recorded, but there will be no variations in color, texture, or reflectivity except those attributable to stratification. Since color photos are expensive to reproduce, final and detailed shots should also be taken of the wall with black and white film. Detailed shots may be made in 135 mm., but overall final shots should be made using film no smaller than 120 mm. This allows for blowups without much loss of significant detail. Although it is frowned upon in some quarters as modifying what one is seeking to record, outlining the strata by cutting lines in the face of the wall with a trowel will make the strata much more distinct, the boundaries between them more visible. More revealing photographs can then be taken. Should this be done, however, the unmodified excavated face should be photographed beforehand.

Finally, scales and labels should be included in all photos. A numbered sequence should be used to account for all film used in the project. The number of the roll and of the frame should somehow be recorded either in notes or on the drawings.

Photogrammetry is a potentially very valuable means of recording stratification to scale. The use of this aerial photo and mapping technique in archaeology has been pioneered by Prof. Jesse Fant and Dr. William MacDonald of the University of Minnesota Messenia Project in southwestern Greece (Fant and Loy, 1972). Briefly, cameras (two 120 mm. Hasselblads) are placed at opposite ends of a bar mounted on a bipod. The cameras are aimed so that the photos they produce overlap by about 20 percent. The distance from the film in the cameras to the trench wall is recorded. This information is fed into a device called a second-order stereo-plotter, which uses the two overlapping negatives to make scale drawings, at any scale desired, of the trench wall. Although the technique demands a big capital investment in cameras, it is cheap and efficient when one considers the saving in excavators' time and energy. Stratigraphic profiles can be recorded in a fraction of the time required to draw them by hand—and more objectively. The drawback to the method is that no detailed record of the stratigraphy is immediately available. The second-order stereo-plotters are seldom located near enough to the field to be immediately usable. This handicap might be overcome by supplemental use of Polaroid shots and schematic drawings.

Because of the press of field conditions and multiple demands on his attention, the archaeologist should have either a form that supplements the stratigraphic drawing, or a checklist of data that should be recorded. Either in notes or on a form, cross references should be made to all associated drawings, photos, lot numbers, burials, and any other pertinent data.

The arbitrary-level test pit is not only the most common but the simplest recording and labeling problem that the archaeologist will face. Should the deposits be deep, rich in artifacts, and distinctly stratified by soil color, however, then it is mandatory to take a sample by *natural-level excavation*. A column is first isolated on three sides by digging three pits with arbitrary levels. The isolated column is then excavated by natural levels, which are correlated with the arbitrary units around it, thus increasing the size of the artifact sample. An example of this sort of excavation as done at Altar de Sacrificios, Guatemala, is illustrated in Fig. 7-2.

An example of interesting and significant stratigraphy excavated entirely by arbitrary levels within a series of adjacent five-foot squares is the Devil's Mouth site in the Amistad Reservoir region of southern Texas (Johnson, 1964;

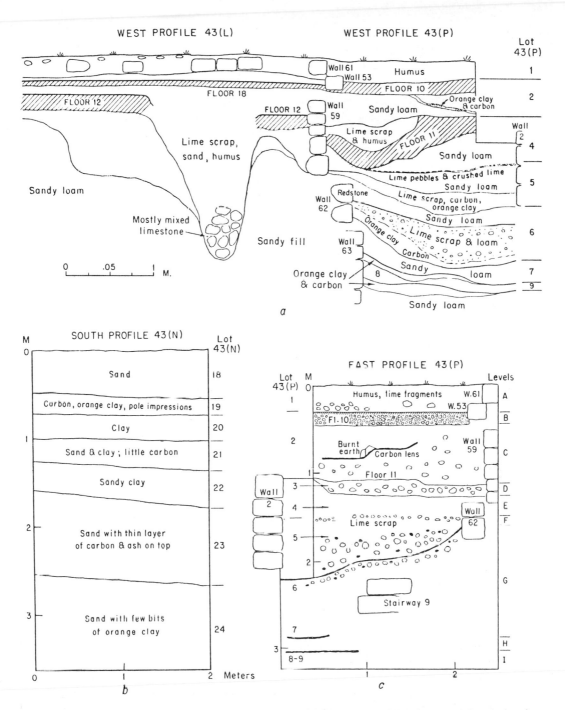

7-2. *Two profiles of the 43(P) column at Altar de Scarificios, Guatemala. This column was first isolated on three sides and then taken out by natural levels. The rich deposits of many types of potsherds in the changing levels were crucial in setting up the Altar ceramic sequence. (A. L. Smith, 1972: Fig. 15; reprinted courtesy of Peabody Museum, Harvard.)*

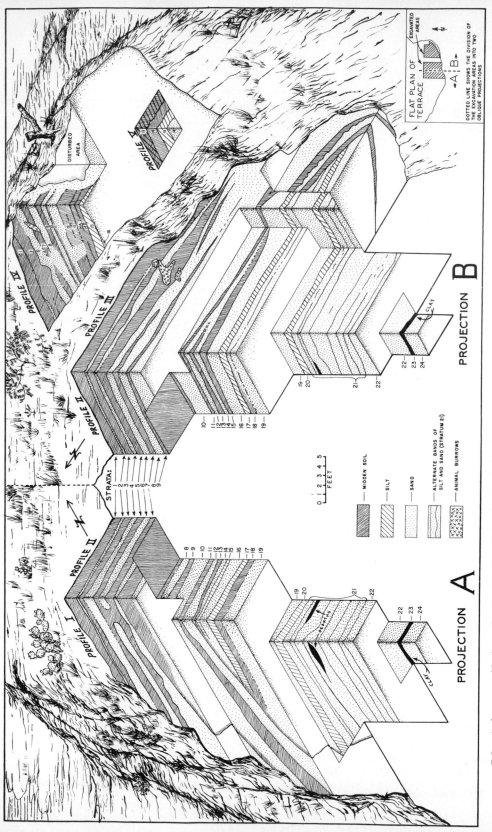

7-3. *A drawn profile from the Devil's Mouth site in the Amistad Reservoir of Texas. Note the technique of presentation and the correlation of deposits from pit to pit.* (Johnson, 1964: Fig. 5; reprinted courtesy of Department of Anthropology, University of Texas, Austin.)

see Fig. 7-3). Note that the illustration synthesizes the results of all 23 squares. This illustration emphasizes again a primary aim of stratigraphy, which is to elicit a depositional sequence *in its own terms*. Johnson's notes and drawings during excavation were undoubtedly kept according to the individual squares excavated, but were later correlated, synthesized, and presented in terms of depositional history.

Trenches reveal long stratigraphic profiles. In recording, labeling, and controlling stratigraphic data from trenches, one should be aware of the arbitrary nature of the separation between sections of the trench. Essentially the same techniques are used for trenches as for pits, the major difference being the quantity of data to be handled.

Architectural elements within any excavation complicate matters and necessitate distinctive approaches. Structures are often excavated by the natural levels; i.e., the space between two plaster or beaten earth floors or between two walls. However, rooms or open spaces within architectural complexes must be subdivided both horizontally and vertically.

Stratigraphic situations found in association with architecture are the most complex of all and require infinite patience and a distinct recording system. One workable system is to record by strati-units as opposed to functionally designated units. Strati-units are physically distinguishable units that are clearly the result of a single activity. For example, a stone wall is a strati-unit. The functional or interpretative unit, however, might include not only the stone wall, but the plaster floor that turns up to it, and the ceiling that lies above it, if that should survive. By this system, recording is done on the strati-unit level that, in effect, is a natural stratigraphic level. The distinction between this and non-architectural stratigraphy is that here one may have several strati-units in the same horizontal level.

An analogy from linguistics may be useful here. The phonetic unit is the smallest distinguishable unit (as is the strati-unit), and the phoneme is the smallest functional unit (as is the interpretative unit). Each functional unit is based on interpretation of the physical evidence, which in turn allows an interpretation of an event. This event, the building of a wall and associated floor, also represents a period of time, which can be designated a "time-span" (Coe, 1962: 506). If one uses this system of excavation, labeling, recording, analysis, interpretation, and synthesis, one ends up with a depositional history. These may be phrased in terms either of interpretative units or of time-spans.

SPECIAL SITUATIONS

Multiple and complex architectural units should be designated by some system such as nonsense names. This allows reference to the strati-unit or interpretative unit in notes without the implied sequence of numbering or

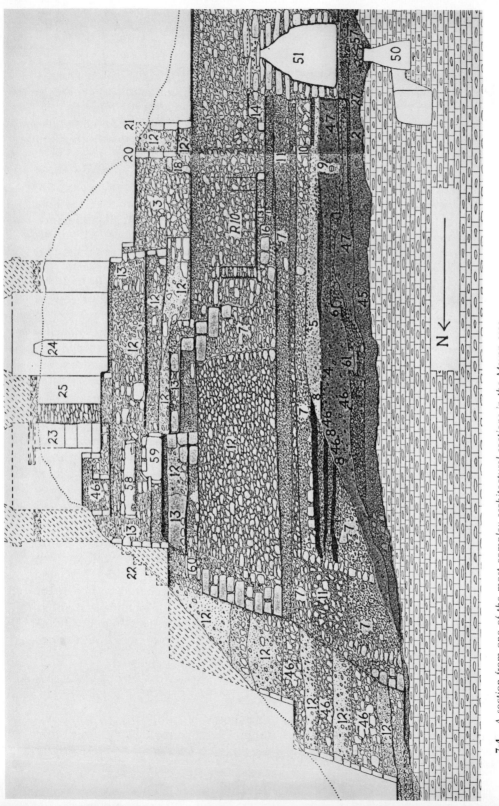

7-4. A section from one of the most complex architectural sections in the Mayan area, A-V palace at Uaxactun, Guatemala. E. M. Shook produced two detailed cross-sections; this is a fragment of one. Shook's extraordinarily accurate drawing is surely a tour-de-force of this kind of recording. (A. L. Smith, 1950, Fig. 70; reprinted courtesy of Carnegie Institution of Washington.)

alphabetics. With a number system one may number two sequent structures 1 and 2, only to find another structure between them or a building phase off to the side that came between. Rather than use 1a, 1b, etc., use the temporary designators of three words such as "cow," "zip," tek," etc. These nonsense tags can be discarded after excavation is finished and structures numbered or lettered in sequence. In this final designation system it is best to number from the latest to the earliest so that the highest-numbered structural unit is the earliest. Then if further excavation uncovers earlier phases, designations such as –1, and so forth, can be avoided.

In dealing with large *architecture* it is useful to break up an apparently homogeneous mass of fill into manageable units. Inevitably, the structural fill contains considerable ceramic material from several.phases. The stratigraphic evidence from pits and trenches is clearly the only way to order the artifacts within such fill. For example, we know that ceramic complexes given the names Blue, White, Red, and Black are contained within the structure. But we only know the relative age of these complexes (say, that Black is the latest complex, and all others are earlier) by evidence from undisturbed deposits excavated at another location. This sort of information is most reliable if it is replicated over and over within the segregated blocks of building fill. Those blocks nearest the surface are naturally most open to mixing with material earlier than Black complex, but segregation of blocks of structural fill will indicate this as one proceeds more deeply into the structure.

Burials are often found within structures, or other deposits, as well as isolated in cemeteries. Artifacts included in burials were clearly *in use* at the time the person was buried. However, heirloom pieces may have been *manufactured* long before. Sequences based on burial lots may also be faulty if special items were made for the funeral, or brought from outside the region to the funeral. The latter may have happened in the case of far-flung kin groups. Burials are often made under disturbed deposits, and these can date the burial independent of the items contained as offerings. This information is gained by the use of the "not-earlier-than" technique used in connection with the evaluation of structural fill (see, for example, Adams, 1971: 59–78).

Vertisols are a bothersome aspect of archaeological and geological stratigraphy in parts of the world, including the south-central United States and parts of Texas (Duffield, 1970), Africa, India, and Australia. These soils are especially susceptible to heaving and cracking and carry artifactual material with them, thus disturbing the original stratigraphic situation.

THE PROBLEM OF SAMPLING

All of archaeology can be viewed as a vast sampling game (see Chapter 15). The reliability of the information gained from stratigraphy is directly related

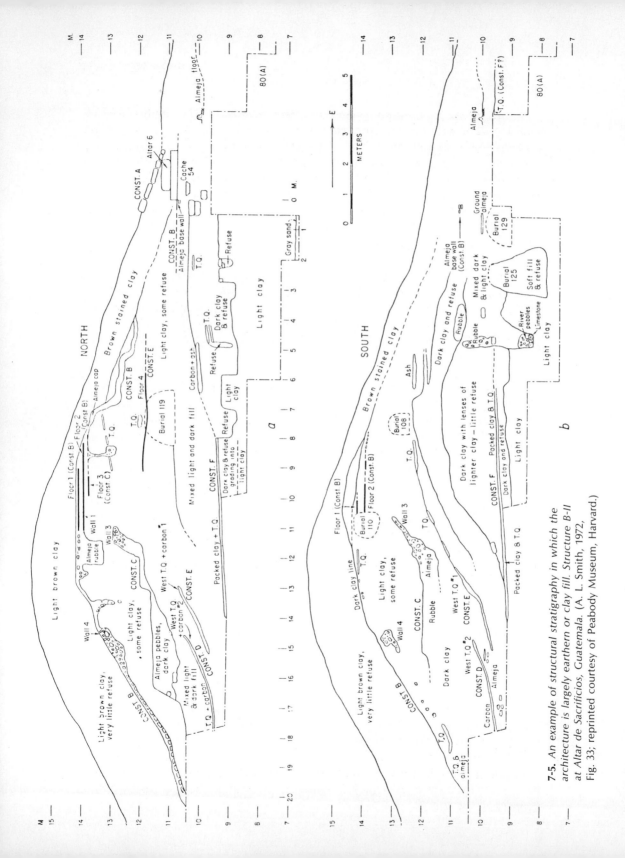

7-5. *An example of structural stratigraphy in which the architecture is largely earthen or clay fill. Structure B-II at Altar de Sacrificios, Guatemala. (A. L. Smith, 1972, Fig. 33; reprinted courtesy of Peabody Museum, Harvard.)*

to the size of the sample. In other words, the more you dig, usually, the more reliable your conclusions. And, relatively speaking, archaeologists dig very little. It has been calculated that in the case of a moderately large Mayan site, Altar de Sacrificios, only 2–3 percent of the deposits theoretically present were sampled in 15 months of digging. The Jarmo excavations produced only about a 4 percent sample on a relatively small site, one with about 2,000 square meters of scatter showing on the surface (Braidwood, 1974). At the site of Momíl in Colombia, the Reichel-Dolmatoffs' (1956) excavations produced a 1/6,000th sample from total theoretical deposits of about 360,000 cubic meters.

Another way the point can be made, is that rarely does one get the chance of replicating information by further excavation. The hoary tales of the most interesting finds being made in the final days of a project are true.

Another disquieting aspect of stratigraphic sampling is that so much of the information produced is anomalous, confused, and understandable only by means of digging into undisturbed locations with long sequences under them. The latter are statistically rare in any excavation. Thus, a systematic and rigidly based sampling system is not necessarily the best means of *sampling* for stratigraphy. Such a system is excellent for *locating* stratigraphy. For purposes of increasing the size and reliability of the sample, however, one must differentially exploit the best-ordered deposits and those with the longest sequences. There is no mechanical cookbook approach to field work that will infallibly yield reliable results. One must approach each situation with a willingness to apply the most appropriate from a full arsenal of techniques ranging from the most subtle and painstaking to the most rapid and narrowly objective-oriented.

The archaeologist must approach his peculiar and specific situation with technical finesse and theoretical sophistication. Obviously, the extremely detailed and careful approach demanded by a Paleolithic rockshelter (Movius, 1974) is not appropriate for one of the many apartment houses in Teotihuacan. The fact that there are many fewer Paleolithic rockshelters in all of Southwestern Europe (about 500) than there are apartment houses (over 2,100) in the single Mexican site of Teotihuacan alone dictates the approach to their respective stratigraphic problems. In a sense, then, this is another aspect of the sampling problem.

SPECIAL AIDS

Soil samples from the walls of pits or trenches can be taken by various techniques. The wall should always be cleaned immediately before sampling. A simple technique is to dig out the sample from each stratum with a clean knife, putting each sample into a sterilized mason jar and labeling the jar. Another technique is to paint the wall with a vertical stripe of latex rubber.

Several coats of the rubber will form a strip sufficiently strong to peel off with samples of the various strata adhering to the underside. The sample side can then be protected by covering it with cellophane wrap and the whole thing placed in a box, either entire or in sections. For purposes of faunal and floral analysis, about a 4-inch-(10 cm.)-square segment as deep as the deposit should be taken. Soil samples can be processed in the field or in the laboratory, washing them through 30-micron screens. However, water should not be used under pressure, but merely to float away the plant and animal remains, as in tubs. The residue is then bottled in sterile jars, labeled, and saved for analysis. Soil samples for pollen analysis should be bagged in heavy plastic and boxed in wooden cases to prevent drying and distortion. For equipment and techniques involved in getting palynological samples see Chapter 6.

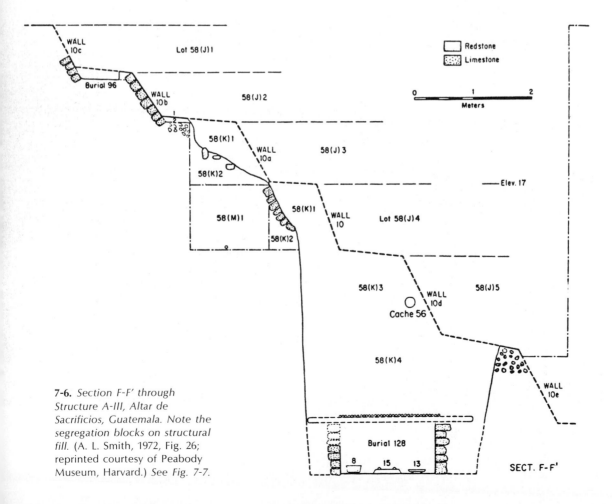

7-6. *Section F-F′ through Structure A-III, Altar de Sacrificios, Guatemala. Note the segregation blocks on structural fill.* (A. L. Smith, 1972, Fig. 26; reprinted courtesy of Peabody Museum, Harvard.) *See Fig. 7-7.*

7-7. Section F-F' and Altar Burial 128 looking at the
interior structure. Materials had been removed from the
tomb during excavation and were partially replaced for
this posed picture. For original aspect of the tomb see
A. L. Smith, 1972, Fig. 49. (Photograph courtesy of Ricardo
Mata, Guatemala.)

Coring tools, especially hand-operated augers, are useful in testing sub-surface deposits when one has reached the bottom of a deep pit. Too many archaeologists have assumed that a sterile lens encountered at respectable depth was the bottom of cultural deposits, only to find through later excavation that the most interesting material lay just below. Auger work can indicate the presence of such deep deposits (cf. Johnson, 1964; Drucker, Heizer, and Squier, 1959).

Air jets and water jets, mentioned above, both run by portable engines, can greatly aid in excavation. Air jets may be especially useful in outlining mudbrick architecture in which it is often difficult to distinguish between the matrix soil and the structure.

For European Mesolithic sites, Clark (1974) recommends securing the collaboration of paleobotanists in order to make sure that the stratigraphy has been interpreted correctly. Indeed, the older the site and the more dependent the archaeologist on ecological data to explain cultural matters, then the more urgent is the need for cooperative colleagues from the natural sciences. Archaeologists should not attempt to acquire all of the skills necessary to do palynology or a similarly complex analysis. They will not only spend valuable time on a secondary commitment, but will find that their analyses carry less weight than if done by a specialist.

The following are useful treatments of various stratigraphic problems.

Cave excavations   Sheep Rock Shelter, Eastern United States (Michels, 1973); Danger Cave, Western United States (Jennings, 1957); Abri Pataud, France (Movius, 1974); Tularosa Cave, Southwestern United States (Martin *et al.*, 1952, and Martin, 1974); Eduardo Quiroz Cave, British Honduras (Pendergast, 1971).

Open camp and kill sites   Olsen-Chubbuck site, Western United States (Wheat, 1972); Lehner site, Southwestern United States (Haury, Sayles, and Wasley, 1959); Momíl shell-midden, Colombia (Reichel-Dolmatoff and Reichel-Dolmatoff, 1956); Nap-32, Central California (Heizer and Squier, 1953).

Village-sized sites   The SU site, Southwestern United States (Martin and Rinaldo, 1947); George C. Davis site, East Texas (Newell and Krieger, 1949); Oahe Dam sites, Middle Missouri (Lehmer, 1954); Issaquena sites, Lower Mississippi (Greengo, 1964); Jarmo, Middle East (Braidwood and Howe, 1960).

City- and town-sized sites with civic architecture   Jericho, Middle East (Kenyon, 1957, see esp. Fig. 4); Beidha, Middle East (Kirkbride, 1960); Chatal Hüyük, Turkey (Mellaart, 1962–64); Altar de Sacrificios, Maya lowlands (Smith, 1972); Uaxactun, Maya lowlands (Smith, 1950); San Estevan, Maya lowlands (Bullard, 1965); Poverty Point, Lower Mississippi (Ford and Webb, 1956); Winchester, England (Biddle, 1974).

EXCAVATION AND RECORDING OF HUMAN PHYSICAL REMAINS

Michael B. Collins

8

The day may come when, contemplating a world given back to the primeval forest, a human survivor will have no means even of guessing how much intelligence Man once imposed upon the forms of the earth, when he set up the stones of Florence in the billowing expanse of the Tuscan olive-groves. No trace will then be left of the palaces which saw Michelangelo pass by, nursing his grievances against Raphael; and nothing of the little Paris cafés where Renoir once sat beside Cézanne, Van Gogh beside Gauguin. Solitude, viceregent of Eternity, vanquishes men's dreams no less than armies, and men have known this ever since they came into being and realized that they must die.

— ANDRÉ MALRAUX

 Archaeologists will generally encounter two broad categories of human physical remains: those that were intentionally disposed of, and those that were not. Remains in both categories are culturally and biologically informative, particularly when viewed in evolutionary perspective and investigated as part of well-formulated research problems. Human remains should always be investigated with care and under thorough archaeological controls. Also, the investigator is obligated to study and proceed according to all local statutes regarding human remains.

Human evolution is both biological and cultural (Garn, 1962; Washburn, 1951; Hainline, 1965). A human group survives because enough of its members are biologically and culturally equipped to cope with their living situation, including conditions of their own making. Any change in this situation will evoke cultural or biological responses—and so closely are the two interrelated that it is virtually impossible to conceive of a cultural response to an adaptive need that would not involve a biological response, or vice versa. No aspect of archaeology touches so directly upon human biological adaptation and its relation to cultural adaptation as does the investigation of human physical remains. As a source of data for testing hypotheses about human microevolution, the archaeological record has two strong qualities to recommend it: it deals in centuries or even millennia, and it makes available for analysis physical (usually skeletal) variables that are not easily studied in living populations. Both environmental conditions and human behavior affect the biology—and therefore the bodies—of a population. Disease, diet, reproductive behavior, occupation hazards, and genetic conditions, for example, may all be reflected in physical remains (Krogman, 1940; Neumann, 1940; Angel, 1946; Snow, 1948; 498ff.; Goldstein, 1957; Roney, 1959; Anderson, 1962: 145–157; Wells, 1964; see also Brothwell, 1965). Many cultural practices may likewise be illustrated by human skeletal remains. Cannibalism, trephining, scalping, head-taking, and violent death may all be inferred from such materials.

Remains that were intentionally disposed of may reveal much about how the culture in question treated death. Artifacts and features associated with the dead, taken together, will help reconstruct burial patterns. The method of disposal chosen and the way corpses were prepared for it may reflect not only a culture's religious beliefs and mortuary practices but, since death is usually accompanied by strong emotional reactions, something of its popular psychology as well. The dead were often laid to rest with some of their possessions, and additional offerings may have been placed in the grave by relatives and friends. Observable patterns in the arrangement or nature of such items—like patterns in any archaeological materials—derive from, are attributable to, and thus reflect the ideas, social behavior, and cultural behavior of the people being studied (e.g., Binford, 1962, 1971).

Up to this point, we have considered human remains on an individual basis. But humans, like other species, adapt as populations, and remains must also be considered as parts of populations whenever this is possible. Physical anthropologists who study excavated human remains cannot expect fully satisfactory results from any narrower perspective (Garn, 1962; Washburn, 1951; Fry, 1965), and a new discipline has arisen in response to this need.

PALEODEMOGRAPHY

Integrated cultural and human biological data allow us to do statistical studies of past populations. As the value and the complexity of such studies were recognized, paleodemography became a distinct subfield of anthropology (Angel, 1969; Brothwell, 1971; Hole and Heizer, 1973: 363–372, 452–454). Paleodemographic research aims to determine the size, geographical distribution and density, growth rates, health, and age and sex ratios of a vanished population.

Wherever possible, these essentially biological data may be viewed in the context of behavioral evidence (such as role, status, dietary practices, etc.) and environmental setting. Usually these determinations are concerned with the dynamics of the population's adaptation, but static estimates are also made. Among the numerous treatises on paleodemography, the following are noteworthy examples: Dobyns (1966), Cook (1947 and 1972), Acsádi and Nemeskéri (1970), Naroll (1962), Anderson (1962), Wells (1964), Roney (1959), Goldstein (1953, 1957), Krogman (1940), Neumann (1940), Snow (1948), Howells (1960), Vallois (1960), Angel (1947), and Carneiro and Hilse (1966).

Archaeologists cannot excavate a population, of course, but they should recover as much information as possible to aid in appraising the significance of any recovered remains relative to the population of which they were a part. The theoretical Mendelian population does not exist in nature. Therefore, a researcher must choose a human group, establish certain parameters for the group (or "population"), and decide, somewhat arbitrarily, whether the "population" is sufficiently close to the model to justify Mendelian procedures of analysis.

Among living peoples, the primary requisites of the model are endogamy (breeding restricted to tribe or clan) and panmixia (random breeding) within those limits; of next importance is infinite size (Deevy, 1958; Dobzhansky, 1965. 115, Harrison, 1964: 150–161; Falconer, 1964: 48–49). Totally endogamous units seem not to exist, at least for any length of time (Dobzhansky, 1962: 219–250). Investigators must attempt to determine the level of endogamy in their groups and consider them adequately endogamous if an arbitrary level (say 70 percent) is observed. Ironically, the total human population is composed of units that are divided, subdivided, and further subdivided by degree of panmixia, and it is the smaller units that more closely approach panmixia (Wallace and Dobzhansky, 1967: 22-23). The "population" under consideration, then, must strike a compromise between size and randomness of mating; that is, it must be large enough that genetic drift is unlikely and yet it must be composed of people who are sufficiently close in geographic location, economic status, language, education, and occupation that their mating will be relatively endogamous and random as regards any genetic factors under examination.

The remaining characteristics of a perfect Mendelian population are as follows: each genotype must contribute equally to the gene pool of the following generation; there must be clear-cut generations; there must be an equal sex ratio; and there must be no mutation. None of these conditions will be met. In fact, the Mendelian population model stands as a Null Hypothesis in the inquiry, and the group under consideration can be evaluated as to deviation from the model. Sex ratio, for example, may be determined and its degree of variance from equality can be measured.

In general, in an extant breeding group of humans, various social and cultural as well as biological and environmental factors will cause deviation from the ideal Mendelian model (Morton, 1968). Population geneticists must identify as many of these factors as possible before they can fully understand the evolutionary status of the people being observed (Spuhler and Kluck-hohn, 1953: 295–317). This requisite of understanding applies to archaeological materials also, but the problems of data recovery are greatly magnified. It is never certain that any archaeological assemblage with which human remains are associated reflects a distinct society. Even when it seems clear that a single society is represented by a distinctive archaeological assemblage (e.g., Broken K Pueblo; Hill, 1970), the level of endogamy and the degree of panmixia are unknown.

An archaeological "population," then, is a collection of human remains recovered from a context interpreted as representing a single social system. It is obvious that the archaeological "population" is greatly removed from the Mendelian model, first by human breeding behavior, and second by the substitution of archaeological interpretation for more direct measures of the breeding status of the individuals.

If human remains are viewed as an essential part of the evidence of a total adaptive system and are recovered under sufficiently close archaeological controls that their status as a "population" may be evaluated, the physical anthropologist can contribute to the elucidation of many aspects of human prehistory. This is because the human phenotype includes genetically determined variation that provides information about the genetic characteristics of the "population" as well as other kinds of variation that can provide information about the environmental conditions under which the "population" existed.

The fundamental and, unfortunately, most difficult task of paleodemographic analysis is recovering an adequate sample of remains to constitute a population (Collins and Fenwick, 1974). It must be demonstrable that the individuals whose remains are under examination lived close enough together in culture, politics, social organization, geography, and time to justify their inclusion in a single unit of demographic analysis. Of course, such a unit may be the individuals occupying a single tiny village or an entire continent, but the archaeological context must be appropriate to permit definition and analysis of any such unit.

Below are discussed some of the kinds of archaeological human remains as well as the procedures whereby they may be recovered.

TYPES OF REMAINS

By far the most commonly encountered human remains in archaeological sites are bones and teeth, although where conditions of preservation are especially favorable, soft tissue may also be present. Hair, skin, and internal organs, when recoverable, are valuable sources of information. Data on hair form, fingerprints, soft-tissue pathology, stomach and intestinal contents, tattooing or scarification can be derived from studies of soft tissue (Glob, 1969; Robbins, 1971; Mongait, 1961; Taylor, 1966). As desiccation is frequently the cause of preservation, most soft tissue found is very easily recovered and preserved. So long as it is kept dry, it will keep indefinitely. In cases where embalming or burial under permanently moist conditions has preserved soft tissue (as in bogs, where chemically charged ground water acts as a preserving agent), specialized techniques will be required to stabilize the tissue condition (Glob, 1969). Many of the kinds of information to be gleaned from preserved soft parts are of a genetic nature (hair form or fingerprint patterns), others are of environmental significance (parasites or ingested materials), and some are cultural (dietary practices, tattooing, or calluses).

Bones and teeth may be in excellent condition or in any state of deterioration. Generally speaking, four kinds of damage may be evident in skeletal material: mechanical fracturing, chemical alteration, gnawing by animals, and warping; and any group of remains will usually exhibit damage resulting from some combination of two or more of these processes. In addition, skeletal material may become displaced or mixed by the activity of animals or humans or by other disturbances. The potential loss of data by displacement or breakage can often be overcome by careful field and laboratory techniques; however, gnawing, chemical alteration, and warping may permanently destroy some skeletal information.

Physical anthropologists are interested in the size and shape of bones, in the presence or absence of certain bones or features on bones, in the status of age and sex criteria of bones, and in the health of the person insofar as it can be judged from the bones.

Measurements of bone size and shape (indices and angles) are fundamental to the description of any skeletal collection. The size and shape of various skeletal elements are useful parameters in determining the genetic as well as the environmental status of the population. For example, stature is considered highly heritable (Dobzhansky, 1962: 85; Furusho, 1968, Newman, Freeman, and Holzinger, 1937: 72–72; Tanner, 1964: 344–345), but it is affected by the diet and health of a population, and in skeletal material, stature is estimated from measurements of long bones (Krogman, 1962; Trotter and Gleser, 1958). For these reasons, bones must obviously be recovered in the most complete condition possible.

The normal human skeleton (Fig. 8-1) is a complex of 182 bones plus a skull made up of 32 teeth and more than 24 bony parts. However, an individual may be born with more or fewer than the normal number of elements, he or she may lose skeletal parts during life, preparation for burial may remove parts, or bony parts may be separated from the rest of the skeleton after burial. Thorough observation and documentation of the skeleton and its adjacent matrix are essential to reveal these numerical anomalies and record evidence that may help the physical anthropologist in assessing their cause.

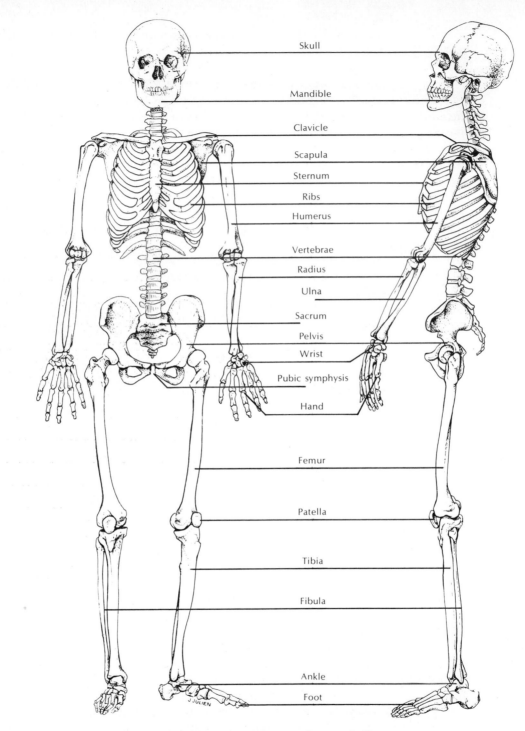

Skull

Mandible

Clavicle

Scapula

Sternum

Ribs

Humerus

Vertebrae

Radius

Ulna

Sacrum

Pelvis

Wrist

Pubic symphysis

Hand

Femur

Patella

Tibia

Fibula

Ankle

Foot

8-1. *The major bones of the human skeleton.*

For example, one of the genetically determined sources of numerical variation is polydactylism (extra fingers and toes), which results in more than the usual 19 toe or finger bones per hand or foot (Stern, 1960: 298–299). In multiple graves, these small bones might be misinterpreted as mixing if not observed in their anatomical position before the skeleton is removed. Since the inheritance of polydactylism is fairly well understood to be a dominant trait, biologically related individuals might be identified from grave data and from the distribution of this genetic trait. Similarly, the genetically determined shortening of the middle bone of the little finger (brachymesophalangy 5) is a biological marker (Hertzog, 1967; Stern, 1960) whose potential usefulness is lost unless skeletal materials are collected with extreme care.

People often mutilate themselves by cutting off fingers or knocking out teeth. These practices can be identified as cultural rather than idiosyncratic if a pattern of such losses can be established, which in turn can happen only if the excavations are meticulous. Cut marks on bone may indicate dismembering before burial (McGimsey, 1956: 158).

Many more examples of this kind could be listed, but in all cases, the message is the same—careful exposure and thorough documentation of skeletal materials can provide a wealth of data on the biology, culture, and environment of the extinct cultural system whose remains are being excavated.

Basic data in any demographic description of an archaeological population are the ages and sexes of the individuals represented. Age changes in bone are many. Long bones grow until the shaft of each bone fuses to its epiphyses (or ends). Until then, the bone is composed of three bony segments (the shaft and two epiphyses) and intervening cartilagenous tissue where longitudinal growth occurs. The approximate age at which fusion takes place is known for each bone, and in juvenile material where fusion is incomplete, it is important to recover all of the small epiphyses. Tooth eruption and fusion of the bones of the skull are other age-related changes that can help determine the age of skeletal remains.

One of the single most important age changes in the skeleton involves the pubic symphysis (see Fig. 8-1). During life, the medial surfaces of the pubic bones undergo a series of identifiable changes that can be used to estimate age of skeletal material (McKern and Stewart, 1957). It is extremely important in excavating skeletons to avoid damage to, or loss of, the pubic symphyses. In most cases, it is best if these surfaces are not cleaned in the field but transported to the physical anthropology laboratory for cleaning and restoration. Also, except in extreme cases, preservatives should not be applied.

Sex criteria in the skeleton include variation in size, shape, and robustness of bone. Although the skull and long bones are of use in determining sex, the pelvis is of the greatest value. Adult pelves are made up of three bones (two innominates and a sacrum) that are susceptible to damage, particularly chemical or mechanical. It is desirable to learn the basic sex criteria (see manuals such as those by Anderson, 1962; Bass, 1971; or Brothwell, 1963) and make preliminary sex judgments in the field. As the excavator becomes more familiar with these criteria, he will appreciate the physical anthropologist's concern for proper excavation procedures.

Pathology is often revealed in bone. The health status of a population can be determined to a certain extent by analyzing skeletal pathology, and in most cases no specialized excavation techniques are required. Exceptions include bones that have been chemically weakened by disease and thus are fragile at the time of excavation. The above-mentioned manuals include useful introductions to the nature of skeletal pathology, and the bibliography published by Armelagos, Mielke, and Winter (1971) is an important resource for anyone wishing to pursue the topic further.

Microscopic features of bone are also important in skeletal interpretations (cf. Tappen and Peske, 1970). In most cases skeletal material that is going to be studied microscopically requires no special handling in the field, although as a general rule, hardening by the application of liquid preparations is undesirable as they may interfere with clear resolution in the microscope.

ADVENTITIOUS REMAINS

Human physical remains are often encountered under conditions suggesting unintentional placement. Teeth, small bones, and the like become displaced from burials and mixed with refuse in occupational sites. Teeth or limbs lost during life may have been thrown on the refuse heap to begin with. In most excavations these stray remains are infrequent and uninformative.

However, individuals have sometimes met with tragedy away from home or become lost and died and their bodies were never found by their tribe or kin. Unlike the intentional burials discussed above, the prehistoric miner who perished when a dislodged rock fell on him in Mammoth Cave, Kentucky (Neumann, 1938; Meloy, 1968), and the Neanderthal individuals of Shanidar Cave, Iraq, who evidently died when crushed under great rocks falling from the roof of the cave (Solecki, 1963: 179), were found in the place and in the position of death. Such remains may tell very little about the population they represented, but a great deal about the activities in which the individual was involved at the time of death.

TYPES OF INTERMENTS

Human groups have followed a great variety of burial practices in the prehistoric past. A complete classification of burial practices is beyond the scope of this chapter, and we suggest here only some of the main varieties that may be encountered in archaeological sites occupied by simple societies. In more complex societies, of course—civilization or strongly class-differentiated societies—the more important individuals may be buried in elaborate tombs. For a broad perspective on the study of burial practices, see Brown (1971).

Primary interments   Here the bones lie in the same anatomical relationship (articulation) as when the individual was alive, and the presumption is that the skeletal elements have not changed position significantly since the soft tissue disappeared. In dry cave or open deposits, corpses may be found in naturally "mummified" condition, as in Nevada (Loud and Harrington, 1929), Northern Mexico (Zingg, 1940), Arizona (Kidder and Guernsey, 1921), the coast of Peru (Mason, 1961), and predynastic Egyptian sites (Lucas and Harris, 1962: 270).

The body may be in a contracted or flexed position, an extended position, or a sitting posture, and may lie on its face, side, or back. If the exposed bones are carefully studied, the investigator will usually be able to describe the exact position of the corpse at burial.

A special kind of primary interment occurs when corpses are simply placed or thrown on a surface in a protected area (such as a shaft-type cave). These remains often become scattered (Collins, 1967: 16–17), but may remain in relatively good anatomical relationship (Arroyo de Anda, Maldonado-Koerdell, and Martínez del Rio, 1953).

Secondary interments   These include the so-called bundle burials, in which the bones are collected after the flesh has been removed by exposure or by bacterial decay, and then deposited in a grave. The bones are not in natural anatomical relationship, and some may be missing. Those present may reflect human alteration such as painting, breakage, or cutting (Collins, Hester, and Weir, 1969).

Multiple interments   Single graves containing the skeletal remains of several people are of two main types: those in which all were buried at once, and those in which corpses were added over a period of time. The simultaneous group burials are usually taken to result from the death of many persons by a single cause (disease or war). In the southeastern United States (Sears, 1961) and at Cocle, Panama (Lothrop, 1937), however, graves have been found containing not only a paramount individual but also retainers or servants or slaves, apparently killed to join their master. In many Old World megalithic chambered tombs or dolmens—but only rarely in the New World, as at San Agustin Acaguastlan, Guatemala (A. L. Smith and Kidder, 1943)—corpses were introduced into graves over the years as individuals died. A method for as signing bones from a mixed collection to individuals by the use of ultraviolet fluorescence is described by Eyman (1965), and by McKern (1958).

Cremations   If the dead were burned, earth may have been thrown over the ashes and cremated bones. More commonly, however, the ashes were sifted, the calcined bones collected and placed in a basket or in a pottery jar (Heye, 1919; Sayles, 1937: Pl. 27), and the container buried in a dug pit. At times, as in California or Arizona, the cremated bones were simply put into the pit and covered with earth (Sayles, 1937: Pl. 28). Special rectangular clay cremaory basins were used by the Ohio Hopewell people (Shetrone, 1930: Figs. 47–49) and at the Snaketown site in Arizona (Sayles, 1937).

EXPOSING THE BURIAL

When a burial is discovered, and must be exposed, the investigator will find knowledge of certain techniques and observance of certain precautions very helpful.

Not all the problems that might arise while clearing a burial can be discussed here; the individual worker's sense and ingenuity must be relied upon to cope with special contingencies. In the following discussion, it is assumed that the pit or other feature in which skeletal material is discovered will be recorded by the same procedures used to document other features (see Chapter 5 above).

As soon as a burial is discovered, the excavator must try to determine its position. Since the skull is usually highest, it will most often be discovered first in stripping operations, but several points on the skeleton must be found and identified in order to pinpoint its exact location and position. This should be done before further exposure is attempted, and should itself expose as little of the skeleton as possible in order to protect it from rough handling. A knowledge of the form and relative position of the major bones of the skeleton is obviously necessary for identifying the exposed parts (see Fig. 8-1). Until experience brings this knowledge, excavators should use one of the recommended guides, such as Anderson (1962), Bass (1971), or Brothwell (1963). Even beginners can readily visualize the probable extent and dimensions of the burial as soon as they have identified a few critical points, such as the skull, pelvis, knees, and elbows.

One of the most satisfactory methods of exposing a burial is by blocking it out as soon as the position and extent are determined; that is, by leaving the burial embedded in its matrix on a pedestal while the surrounding dirt is cleared away and a level floor established. The height of the pedestal will be variable, but a foot is about the minimum. This method not only gives a more convenient working height, but also prevents loose dirt from drifting back onto the burial. This technique may not always be feasible. Indeed it should not be used if any trace of the pit in which the burial was placed remains, for such evidence must be preserved. For example, burials in the sterile subsoil of a mound may reveal the grave pit outline by a difference in color and texture between the mound soil and the subsoil (Webb, 1946).

Burials should generally be exposed from the top downward. Since it is obviously inefficient to be continually sweeping loose dirt over previously cleaned areas, it is advisable to expose the central areas first, especially the cavities of the rib cage, abdomen, and pelvis. Once these are cleaned, it will be time to expose the arms and legs that lie on the outside of the burial. Arm and leg bones should be exposed from upper to lower, the hands and feet last. The hands and feet consist of numerous small bones that are easily disturbed after they have been exposed.

Certain areas within a burial should be given special attention. Nonperishable items of shell, bone, and stone that are worn as ornaments—either strung or on clothing—will remain after the perishable items have disappeared. Therefore, valuable clues may be gained by observing the exact location of such nonperishable objects before removing them. For example, necklaces may be indicated by beads or other perforated ornaments found around the neck and shoulders and upper rib cage; headdress ornaments may be found around the skull, wristlets along the arm, and waistband and skirt ornaments in and around the pelvic cavity. Ornaments or tools were often placed in the hands, and the areas around the hands should be carefully investigated. One item that beginners often fail to recognize is powdered red ocher. Occasionally found with burials, this red ocher or cinnabar may stain the bones a dull brick red color and may also tinge the soil surrounding the bones. Where the paint cannot be collected in pure lumps, a sample of red-stained earth will suffice for a mineralogical determination.

Complete cremations obviously present a different problem. The local accumulation of ash, charred wood, and calcined bone usually serves to delimit the area of the cremation, and careful troweling and brushing will define the horizontal limits of the cremation in the surrounding matrix. Once this is done, a vertical profile may be obtained by cutting down in the middle of the cremation, exposing a side view, and showing the depth of the ash-and-charcoal lens. This may also give clues to the exact cremating procedure if layering of charcoal and bone appears at different levels. The remains of a cremation must be exposed by careful brushing to see whether carbonization has preserved traces of normally perishable objects, especially wood.

At one time it was assumed that a pile of cremated bones was of no value since so little could be learned from it. However, charred bones can be used for radiocarbon dating (Chapter 14). Also, Gejvall's (1963) detailed technique for studying calcined bone fragments allows sex, age, and sometimes even pathology to be determined from them. This technique also offers

new leads to cremation practices. The excellent review of Hopewell cremation practices by Baby (1954), as well as the work of Atkinson, Piggott, and
Sanders (1951), Powell and Daniel (1956: Appendix B), Piggott (1962: Appendix II), and Wells (1960), can be recommended as examples of the kinds
of information that can be recovered from cremations. Cremated bones can
no longer be dismissed, but must be carefully collected and saved.

Badly preserved bone is difficult to expose and collect (cf. Wesolowsky,
1973: 342). Special care in brushing away the enclosing earth and preservative
solutions applied to the bones will permit a record of position and preservation of the bones. Ritchie and Pugh (1963) describe a special method of photographic recording of badly decayed skeletal materials.

If burials are found in a hard matrix, the excavator should not attempt
to remove the hardened materials from certain fragile areas on the skeleton
while it is in the ground. Such regions as the eye sockets, nasal cavity, ear
openings, scapula, pubic symphysis, and sacrum are easily damaged by sharp
tools and can best be cleaned later. The entire block containing the skeleton
should be removed intact to a more advantageous working site before further
exposure is attempted. This can be done by special techniques (Orr, 1942;
Antle, 1940).

Two successful methods for removing a complete burial are briefly
described here. The first preserves the burial *in situ,* so to speak, even while
removing it. The burial is partly exposed and isolated on a block or pier
of earth. About six inches beneath the bottom of the grave, the pier is cut
through with a coarse saw or long butcher knife. Then a flat sheet of heavy-
gauge galvanized iron is pushed and pulled through this cut to form a base
for the block. The sheet will be hard to push in, but must be inserted carefully
to avoid disturbing the bones. The upper sides of the block are then wrapped
around with wide layers of sacking and tied with string to keep the block
intact. In the meantime, a wooden box about eight inches deep has been
built with one long side left open. The skeleton, still encased in earth and
resting on the iron sheet, may then be pushed into the box and the side board
nailed on. The sacking can be removed, earth packed around the sides to
fill the box solidly, and the skeleton exposed by brushing away the earth
that covers the bones. After all the bones are fully visible, the remaining bed
of earth on which the skeleton lies may be saturated with dilute acetone-
celluloid or gasoline-paraffin. Such boxes containing skeletons are useful for
museum displays or to demonstrate burial positions or methods of exposing
a burial to students.

The second method is one once employed to remove the ceremonial
burial of a bear encountered in a prehistoric California cemetery (Heizer
and Hewes, 1940: Pl. 1). The bones were first fully exposed. Next a careful
scale drawing of the burial was made on a 24-×-30-inch sheet of cross-
section paper (the scale used was one-half actual size). Then, at each end of

the long axis of the skeleton, a datum stake was set up. The tops of these two stakes were of exactly equal height, and a wire was extended between them over their tops. Employing this level wire as a datum plane, the excavators determined the elevation of each end of every visible bone, and recorded these measurements on the drawing. After the burial was photographed, the bones were taken up and marked as right or left side. The field crew then spent several evenings reconstructing the burial within a box. When completed, it was taken to the museum in an expedition truck. This method has an advantage over the technique of removal *in situ,* since the box is not so heavy; it is, however, much more time-consuming. Any boxes made to receive skeletons should be screwed together and reinforced with angle irons.

BURIAL RECORDS

Sketching the burial often presents a serious problem to beginning students. A sketch is never omitted, although the amount of detail may vary according to the time available and the skill of the recorder. In general, the sketch must be as complete and as accurate as time and skill permit. Anyone can sketch a burial, for patience and practice can compensate for lack of formal training and artistic ability. Anatomically correct sketches are preferable to stick figures. These can be done, regardless of drawing ability, by sitting down in a position with a good view of the burial and drawing each bone exactly *as it appears from that position,* attempting to reproduce perspective by relative size. It must be emphasized that the sketcher must make the drawing from one position only, for the perspective will change with different views. Deep shading and hachuring tend to obscure the drawing. All artifacts are sketched in and also labeled, either by key numbers or by listing in the margin. An arrow designating magnetic north must appear in the sketch. The most convenient place for the sketch is on the coordinate-ruled back of the burial record sheet.

Sketches and photographs may seem to duplicate each other but no one can be certain of the quality of a photograph until it is developed and printed. If one or more photographs should be ruined, the sketch may be the only record of a given stage in the excavation or of a certain artifact's original position. Also, small details and especially artifacts are often difficult to identify in burial photographs taken under adverse conditions. These can be easily identified on the sketch, which is thus a necessary supplement to the photographs.

The accompanying burial record sheet contains entries for the various items of pertinent information, usually deemed necessary for a complete recording of a burial. A brief explanation and guide to the use of this record form, according to the numbered entries, follows:

1. List by site (usually a sequential numbered series is assigned to graves from each site).
2. Give name and/or number of site.
3. Specify pit or trench, etc., in which burial occurs.
4. List feet and inches by direction (e.g., 50′ 8″ N, 18′ 4″ W). Use nearest datum (specifically identified in this entry), measuring to a point on burial (usually the skull) that is specified.
5. State in inches (or meters or centimeters) to center of burial or bottom of grave. Record precisely what point the depth measurement refers to and from which point it is taken.
6. See Chapter 4. The depth is commonly measured to skull. Often this measurement is not made.
7. Designate stratum in which burial occurs.
8. Specify type of soil around burial (shell midden, ashy midden, sterile subsoil, etc.).
9. Designate poor, fair, good, or excellent.
10. Delete the inappropriate one; only a rough count is needed.
11. Leave blank unless certain, or if your determination is uncertain, indicate this with a question mark. Refer to the end of this chapter.
12. Leave blank unless certain, or query your identification if it is only a guess. Refer to the end of this chapter.
13. List only obvious and striking features.
14. See pages 170–72 for details.
15. See pages 170–72 for details.
16. See pages 170–72 for details.
17. Insert side or check appropriate blank: give direction in which frontal part of body is facing.
18. State the direction in which the head lies in relation to a line between the skull and center of the pelvis. An accurate compass reading is advisable.
19. Give the two largest dimensions at right angles.
20. List artifacts and features. Give field catalog numbers if possible.
21. List any observation not covered above that might be useful as part of the record.
22. Give full name.
23. Give full name.
24. Enter photo number (see Chapter 12).
25. Indicate whether the sketch is on the reverse side or on a separate sheet.
26. Give date recorded.

ARCHAEOLOGICAL BURIAL RECORD

1. Burial No. _____ 2. Site _____ 3. Excavation unit _____

4. Location _____ of datum _____ to _____

5. Depth from surface _____ 6. Depth from datum plane _____ to _____

7. Stratification _____

8. Matrix _____ 9. Condition _____

10. Bones absent (or present) _____

11. Sex _____ 12. Age _____

13. Pathology _____

14. Type of disposal _____

15. Position of body _____

16. Left side _____ right side _____ back _____ face _____ sitting ___

17. Position of head _____ side _____ back _____ face, facing _____

18. Orientation _____ 19. Size of grave _____

20. Associated objects (itemize) _____

_____

21. Remarks _____

_____

_____

22. Exposed by _____ 23. Recorded by _____

24. Photo _____ 25. Sketch _____ 26. Date _____

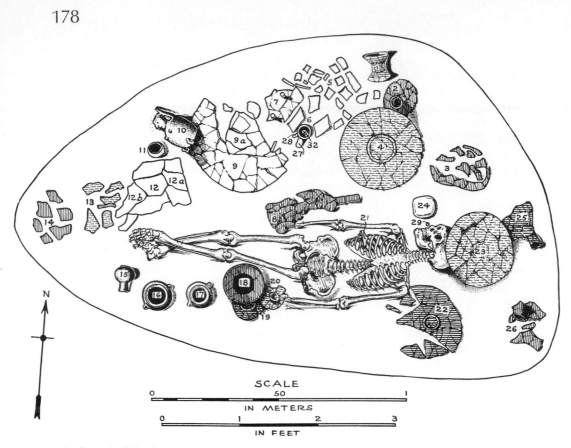

SCALE

8-2. *Grave in Sitio Conte, Panama.*
Somewhat better endowed than burials in
most of North America, this grave has been
depicted in an exemplary way. Numbered
items refer to objects found in association
with skeletal remains. (From Lothrop, 1937:
Fig. 226.)

REMOVING THE BURIAL

After the burial is exposed, recorded, and photographed, it should be removed in order to safeguard the skeleton and associated artifacts. Some
techniques for the care of the bones will be discussed here.

Wooden boxes, made to size, are the ideal containers for skeletons,
both in the field and for shipment to the laboratory. They afford far more
protection than cardboard cartons, and they do not fall apart when they get
damp. Once made, they will last for years of field work. The ends should be
made of ½-inch or ¾-inch stock, the sides, top, and bottom of ⅜-inch stock.
Experience has shown that the following *inside* measurements are adequate

for the skeletons of normal adults: 24 inches long, 9 inches wide, 8½ inches deep. A number of smaller boxes may be provided to care for the skeletons of children, and fragmentary or partial skeletons.

The burial number, skeleton catalog number, or other pertinent data should be painted on the box. Cards tacked or glued to the box are often lost in transportation. To be on the safe side, it is well to stick an identification or reference tag inside the foramen magnum (the opening in the skull through which the spinal cord passes) and to tie one onto a long bone as well.

Long bones can be wrapped separately in sheets of newspaper. The cranium, the mandible, the vertebrae, fragmentary bones, and the bones of each hand and foot should be placed in separate paper bags and labeled (e.g., "Bones of left hand, burial No. 12, site Sol-52"). This will ensure against the loss of small bones, teeth, fragments, etc. Shredded paper is a nuisance, both in the field and in the laboratory. Crumpled newspaper provides adequate protection and is both easily obtained and readily disposed of.

In packing, the cranium should be placed at one end, the heavy long bones packed next, and the lighter bones placed on top. These recommendations apply, of course, to skeletal material in a fairly good state of preservation. Friable, wet, or poorly preserved bones require special attention in the field.

Care must be taken to avoid breaking the bones while removing them from the soil. This is best accomplished by undercutting each bone with a trowel and lifting it all at once. Any bones on top must be removed first. Gradual and overall pressure is necessary on the larger bones to prevent snapping. Each bone is scraped as clean as possible as it comes out, and the dirt is left in the burial pit. Any beads or other small artifacts will mean that this dirt must be screened before it is thrown away. The skull and pelvis are most difficult to remove and must be handled with great care. A firm but not too hard material, such as split bamboo, is better than a metal trowel for this kind of work.

If time and water are available, bones may profitably be washed in the field. If the matrix is hard and calcareous, adherent soil can often be removed much more easily immediately after exposure than after it has dried. A tub or bucket of water, brushes, small dull knives (or bamboo splints), and ice picks are usually sufficient to clean the bones in the field. Each skeleton must be kept separate while being washed. Drying is best done on screens to facilitate drainage and in the shade to prevent cracking and peeling.

Unless a complete field laboratory is set up, there is little sense in mending broken bones in the field. Very brittle and friable bone can be strengthened for shipment by applying several coats of very thin cellulose dissolved in acetone. The bones should be clean and dry, since this type of binding is markedly less satisfactory on damp material (Bentzen, 1942).

The age, sex, and pathology of a skeleton become clearer after the bones have been removed and the critical points noted. Since field determinations of sex, age, pathology, etc., are often done hastily and by nonexperts, they should always be checked in the laboratory by qualified specialists, and these more accurate findings attached to or filed with the burial record made in the field. Even in the laboratory, two expert physical anthropologists cannot always agree on sex and age determinations of prehistoric skeletons. An interesting discussion of differences in such estimates is given by Hooton (1930: 20–21, 29–30) in his monumental study of the skeletal materials from Pecos, New Mexico.

ESTIMATING AGE AND SEX OF SKELETAL MATERIALS

It is possible to estimate the age of the person buried by examining the skeletal development, if the bones are in reasonable condition. The age groupings listed below are given as one example of age divisions; the student should consult the works of Hooton (1946), McKern and Stewart (1957), Stewart (1934), Todd (1920–21), Todd and Lyon (1925), Stewart and Trotter (1954), Anderson (1962: 128–140), and Genoves (1963b) if more accurate groupings are desired.

1. Infant (birth to 3 years): to complete eruption of deciduous dentition.

2. Young child (3 years to 6 years): from complete deciduous dentition to eruption of first permanent teeth, usually first molars.

3. Older child (6 years to 12–13 years): from first eruption of permanent dentition to eruption of second molars. No long-bone epiphyses united as yet.

4. Adolescent (13 years to 18 years): from eruption of second molars to eruption of third molars. This is quite variable and the end of this period should show almost all epiphyses joined to the long bones, except the head of the humerus, the lower end of the radius and ulna, and the upper crest of the pelvis.

5. Sub-adult (18 years to 21 years): the third molar may be erupting and the epiphyses mentioned in 4 united. Closure of the sagittal suture of the skull begins near the end of this period.

6. Young adult (21 years to 35 years): all epiphyses except the medial end of the clavicle are united. This latter unites within this period. The sagittal suture is usually closed near the end of this period. Other sutures show beginning of closure.

7. Middle-aged adult (35 years to 55 years): cranial sutures show marked closure and some obliteration. In California, tooth wear is marked, and some teeth are usually lost. This class of skeletons probably provides the largest number of adult burials.

8. Old adult (55 years to 75 years): all sutures very advanced and many obliterated. Tooth wear is excessive and few teeth remain at death. Pubic symphysis shows marked erosion of surface.

9. Very old adult (over 75 years): very few skeletons will fall into this group. All sutures are obliterated and teeth will probably be entirely lacking.

Pelvic Sex Characteristics

	Male	Female
Subpubic arch	Narrow	Broad, diverging
Greater sciatic notch	Narrow, deep	Broad, shallow
Acetabulum	Large	Small
Pelvic inlet	Small, narrow	Large, broad
Pelvic wings (ilia)	Large, vertical	Small, flaring
Sacrum	Long, narrow	Short, broad
Muscular impressions	Strong, heavy	Light, smooth
Ischium-pubis index	Small	Large

Cranial Sex Characteristics

	Male	Female
Supraorbital ridges Mastoid process Occipital crest Malars Supramastoid crests Mandible	Large, well developed	Smaller, less developed

Long-Bone Sex Characteristics

	Male	Female
Muscle attachments	Larger, rougher	Smaller, smoother
Femur head diameter	Generally more than 46 mm.	Generally less than 46 mm.
Articular ends of bones	Larger	Smaller

A trained observer's sex determinations in adult skeletal material can be accurate in 80 to 90 percent of all complete burials. Sex of sub-adult specimens can rarely be accurately determined. The regions giving the most reliable results are, in order of their importance: the pelvis, the skull, and the major long bones. In every known sex criterion, there is a gradual transition from hyperfeminine to hypermasculine expression, with the middle ground indeterminate. Since it is not uncommon to find typically feminine characteristics in an otherwise masculine skeleton and vice versa, determination of sex depends on the *preponderance* of traits characteristic of one or the other sex. The primary rule is to assess as many characteristics as possible before making a judgment. Also, in larger collections where "population" characteristics can be determined, sex determination is likely to be more reliable.

It is not feasible to attempt sexing solely on the basis of the brief checklist given here. Since accurate sex determination is largely based on experience, it is advisable to handle numerous skeletal specimens of known sex. If this is not possible, the student must at least study drawings of skeletal material, mainly of the pelvis, found in all good anatomy texts, and take into the field some illustrations of osteological sex differences. Further information on sex characteristics of bones may be gotten from the works of Heyns (1947), Hooton (1946), Hrdlicka (1948), Krogman (1939), Washburn (1948), Brooks (1955), Stewart and Trotter (1954), Stewart (1954), Anderson (1962), Hanna and Washburn (1953), Thieme and Schull (1957), Genoves (1963a), and Bass (1971).

Archaeologists have failed to exploit graves as fully as they might as a source of data for prehistoric human behavior patterns and beliefs. Kroeber (1927) suggested that the pattern of disposal of the dead was more probably subject to change or "fashion" than is commonly assumed. Gould (1963) tried to examine this question, using archaeological data from California. If archaeologists wish to use this important source of information to illuminate prehistoric beliefs, they will have to think about the problem before they excavate in order to know what kinds of information they should collect.

RECOVERY AND SIGNIFICANCE OF UNMODIFIED FAUNAL REMAINS

Alan C. Ziegler

9

Nothing is foreign; parts relate to whole
One all-extending, all-preserving soul
Connects each being, greatest with the least;
Made beast in aid of Man, and Man of beast;
All serv'd, all serving: nothing stands alone;
The chain holds on, and where it ends unknown.
—ALEXANDER POPE, *An Essay on Man*

 Bone and shell are the normal raw material of a faunal analyst because they usually survive in archaeological sites even where skin, horn, and other softer animal parts have long since disintegrated. Since, these skeletal parts are usually numerous and relatively evenly distributed over many sites, sampling error is at a minimum. Any routine competent identification of preserved faunal remains—both hard and soft parts—from an archaeological site can reveal which species of animals are represented in the excavated material. But a proper faunal analysis merely begins at this point, and goes on with appropriate analytical techniques, to make a truly significant contribution to the overall understanding of a site's prehistory.

For instance, a thorough faunal analysis could help determine how the remains of each species present in the deposit were introduced there; the dietary and culinary preferences of the aboriginal inhabitants; customary hunting areas and seasons for different types of game; the approximate population of the site and how long the occupants had been there; which parts of the site were in use at which times; ritual or totemic uses of animals; climatic or other ecologic changes in the site region; the existence and extent of prehistoric trade routes; and even aboriginal domestication practices and animal diseases.

It will seldom prove practical or even desirable to use all of the various analytical techniques to be mentioned in this chapter for any one site analysis. But a faunal analyst should at least be aware of them so that the more appropriate can be selected, modified, and improved for use as needed. Most of the techniques noted in this chapter are described in more detail in Ziegler (1973). Certain biochemical, microscopic, and other valuable procedures that are not covered here may be found in Brothwell and Higgs (1970). Basic statistical methods for treating simple faunal data are described in Simpson, Roe, and Lewontin (1960), whereas Davies (1971) provides an introduction to the desirable application of computer methods in biology.

EXCAVATION AND PRE-ANALYSIS PROCEDURES

Handling faunal specimens   As much osseous and other faunal material as possible should be saved from an excavation, not just entire shells, and bones, or bone fragments bearing articular surfaces. This material should be washed free of matrix and placed in containers bearing identifying site, pit, and stratigraphic data. The faunal analyst should also obtain the following three sets of data:

a)   the specific location of the site, in order to be able to draw general conclusions regarding the types and/or species of animals that would—or would not—reasonably be expected to appear in the faunal inventory;

b)   a three-dimensional representation of the site, along with the volumetric relationships of the excavated portions to each other and to the unexcavated remainder, in order to correct or compensate for stratigraphic and volumetric irregularities of the bone-bearing matrix; and

c)   the method used for retrieving the osseous sample, so that possible collection bias introduced by factors such as the mesh size of the recovery screen can be identified and suitably treated.

Identification   In the identification process described here, the analyst handles the containers representing a single pit and level of a site one at a time, thus avoiding the time-consuming job of individually numbering each bone fragment. All of the bones from the first container are initially sorted into apparent species or types of animal. The bones in each such species grouping are then compared one by one with the bones of identified reference skeletons assembled in the immediate work area. Bone atlases and related publications are available (for example, Gilbert, 1973; Olsen, 1971; Schmid, 1972; Cornwall, 1956; Howard, 1929) but these visual aids are best used as general guides to the possible type of animal—or individual bone—represented rather than as a substitute for final bone-by-bone comparison.

For a beginning investigator, accurately identifying bones to the species level may seem difficult, but generally such identification merely involves

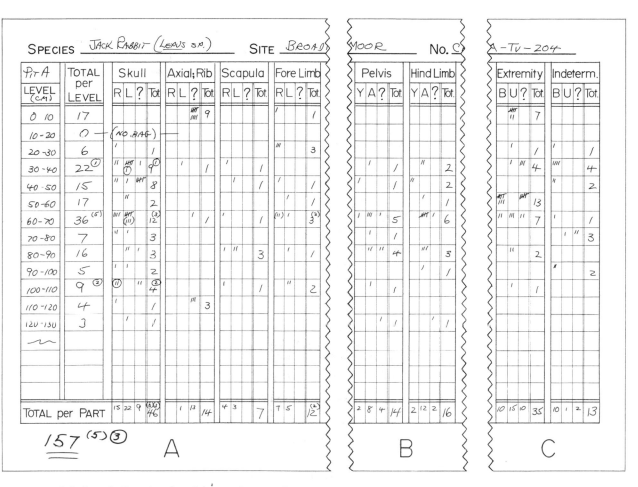

9-1. *Sample "species sheet" for use in recording identified bone frequencies. Three possible variations of column subdivision are shown: A, right or left side of body, B, young or adult individual; and C, burned or unburned condition. The underlined figure at the lower left indicates the grand total of this species' bones in the pit, and parenthesized or circled numbers indicate subtotals of bones exhibiting particular conditions of special interest to the analyst. Reprinted by special permission from Ziegler,* Inference from Prehistoric Faunal Remains, *A-W Module, 1973, Addison-Wesley, Reading, Mass.*

first determining what bone of the skeleton is represented, and then directly comparing the unknown bone with the corresponding one of known species in the general size range suggested. It is best, especially at the beginning, to err on the conservative side. That is, if deciding whether a fragmentary bone belonged to a black bear (*Ursus americanus*) or a grizzly bear (*Ursus horribilis*) appears difficult, do not hesitate to label it simply "bear (*Ursus* sp.)."

Species sheets (see Fig. 9-1) should be prepared for recording all bones identified for each species or general type of animal discovered in a site inventory, and all material can then be recorded on the appropriate sheet as it is identified. Notations of condition, position, or status (burned, unburned, right, left, adult, immature, etc.) may be set up as column headings on these sheets as they are needed for each particular site.

After being identified and recorded on the species sheet, all bones from the same original container should be divided into a number of smaller containers, one for each of the animal categories used on the species sheets. Uniform-sized containers, appropriately labeled as to species and excavation data, should be used, so that each lot of bones can later be weighed without opening and emptying out each of these species containers.

The identification procedure then continues with the opening of the second original site container, and the identification, recording, and repackaging of its contents in the same manner. Note that in this suggested identification and recording procedure, all bone material from a site is assigned to *some* faunal category, even if the category must necessarily be as generalized as "indeterminate fish," "small vertebrate," or "large mammal."

Adjustments of raw data   After this procedure has been completed, a minimum-data table similar to the accompanying table can be prepared for each excavation unit of a site, and no less than this amount of faunal information should be included in every site report.

However, a few adjustments to these raw data are usually necessary before the identified faunal remains can be analyzed accurately. These adjustments, more fully described below, may prove to be required because of variations in

a)   depth of excavation pits;
b)   volume of material excavated from pits or stratigraphic levels;
c)   estimated rates of matrix deposition in sites or site subunits; and
d)   recovery ratios for bones of various-sized species.

Varying depths of excavation pits can usually be identified and compensated for by reference to a cross-sectional diagram of the site. As merely one example, the arbitrary excavation unit 10 to 20 cm. below datum in the uphill portion of a certain sloping site might be obviously equivalent (i.e., contemporaneous) to the 40–50 cm. level in the downhill part of the site. In

Site CA-Nv-144 Pit SW-1	Depth in cm.											Total per species
	0 to 10	10 to 20	20 to 30	30 to 40	40 to 50	50 to 60	60 to 70	70 to 80	80 to 90	90 to 100	100 to 110	
Black-tailed jack rabbit (*Lepus californicus*)	1	3	5	5	7	8	3	3	1	3	1	40
Cottontail or brush rabbit (*Sylvilagus* sp.)	—	1	1	—	2	—	—	2	1	—	—	7
California ground squirrel (*Citellus beecheyi*)	1	5	3	3	2	4	9	2	1	4	2	36
Wood rat (*Neotoma* sp.)	—	—	—	—	—	—	—	—	—	1	—	1
Raccoon (*Procyon lotor*)	3	4	8	1	1	2	1	7	5	—	—	32
Deer (*Odocoileus* sp.)	2	9	5	2	4	3	8	8	4	3	1	49
Medium artiodactyl (Deer, sheep, etc., size)	13	8	12	3	12	9	18	11	9	12	4	111
Medium mammal (Coyote size)	—	—	5	7	1	—	—	—	—	2	—	15
Duck (genus indeterminate)	7	—	—	2	1	—	—	3	1	—	1	15
Snake or lizard (family indeterminate)	—	—	1	1	—	—	—	—	—	—	—	2
Total per level	27	30	40	24	30	26	39	36	22	25	9	308

Sample "minimum data" table for a collection of unmodified faunal remains from one excavation unit of a hypothetical site. Excavation depths appearing here have been corrected for contemporaneity as explained in text. Figures given for faunal remains indicate raw numbers of identified bones and bone fragments. (Ziegler, 1973: Table 1, reprinted courtesy of Addison-Wesley Publishing Company.)

such a case it would probably be desirable to adjust the various levels noted in the minimum-data table to indicate this age-contemporaneity. The fact that this adjustment had been made should be clearly stated in the report.

Differences in the volume of excavated material from various excavation pits or stratigraphic levels of a site must be recognized and adequately compensated for if raw numbers of bones recovered from each unit are to be directly compared. Thus, the recording of twice as many deer bones from the 20–30 cm. level as from the 90–100 cm. level of all pits has little meaning *unless* the volume of material excavated from each of the two levels is also considered. As an obvious compensation, if twice as much material was excavated between 20 and 30 cm. as between 90 and 100 cm., the raw number of deer bones (and all other items) recorded from between 90 and 100 cm. can be doubled.

It should be stressed here that these material-volume discrepancies are significant because the analyst wants to know how many deer (and other) bones per year were being deposited at the time of the 20–30 cm. level and at the time of the 90–100 cm. level. But since accurate time durations can seldom be obtained for each excavation unit of a site, such a Time Index is usually impracticable, and a Concentration Index (CI) is often used instead.

The Concentration Index for any item is simply the average number of that item found per given volume of excavated material. (It would be most convenient for comparative purposes if this volumetric unit could be standardized at one cubic meter.) The accompanying graphs, based on actual data from an Old World site, are introduced here to show Concentration Indices can reveal patterns (Graph B) within an apparently random set of frequencies (Graph A). Unfortunately, this density-determination method assumes that the matrix had been deposited at a constant rate for all portions of a site—or sites. Until Time Indices become more practical than they are now, however, Concentration Indices must be used.

To apply the Concentration Index method just described, the number of deer bones per cubic meter—instead of the uncorrected raw bone number of this species—found in each for the two excavation levels should be calculated and used for further comparisons. Thus, if deer bones (and matrix) had been deposited at the same rate in the two time periods represented by the two levels, the CI of deer bones would be approximately the same for the 20–30 cm. level as for the 90–100 cm. level, regardless of any volumetric discrepancies.

The fact that the matrix may actually have been deposited at different rates during various periods in the accumulation of a site midden is obviously a troublesome one. What has thus far been treated as a constant is actually a variable. The best approach to identifying and then properly quantifying this variable is to try to bracket as many stratigraphic levels as possible by absolute or relative age dates. This may be done not only by radiocarbon and

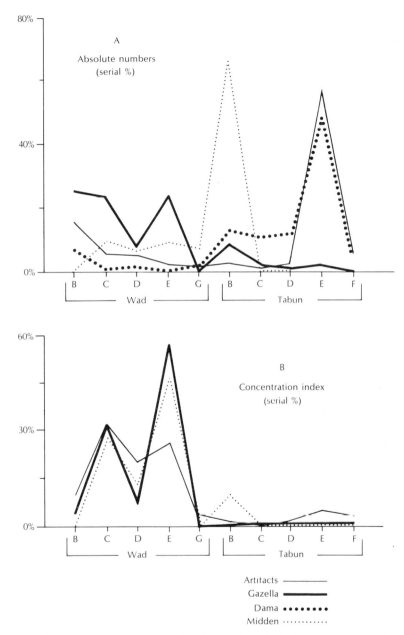

Comparison of serial percentage graphs of various archaeological categories from Mount Carmel, based on: A, absolute raw numbers; and B, concentration indices. Gazella and Dama are two different genera of Old World artiodactyls. Both graphs were constructed from the same set of numerical data appearing in McCown, 1961: Table 1. (After Ziegler, 1973: Fig. 7; reproduced courtesy of Addison-Wesley Publishing Company.)

other chemophysical dating methods, but also by noting such stratigraphic occurrences as the first and last appearances of a certain artifact type or animal species in a given geographic region.

To illustrate a faunal compensation based on this age-bracketing method (in the occasional case where it is possible), consider that a particular site made up of a single cultural layer has been sampled down to sterile subsoil by means of two excavation pits, and the deposit found to be twice as thick at Pit A as at Pit B. The depths sampled by the two pits, however, can reliably be dated to the same time span of 1,000 years. Also, for various reasons, at this site the volumetric discrepancy between the two pits can be attributed solely to a difference in the rate of matrix deposition.

Now, if deer bones had been deposited at the same rate in both areas, the raw total of such bones found in the entire complement of material excavated from each pit would be the same, and would require no compensation. But the bone number per arbitrary 10-cm. excavation level of Pit A would be only half that for a similar level of Pit B. Thus, for proper compensation, the CI for each level of Pit A deer bones would have to be doubled (or the CI of Pit B halved) before such concentration indices could be directly compared for analytical purposes.

Big bones are obviously easier to find than little bones. Thus if bones and bone fragments are hand-picked from a site, the faunal analysis may be biased toward large-bodied species. Screening the excavated earth for bones and other site material is usually more efficient, and is certainly statistically more reliable in that it allows relatively objective correction factors to be applied to frequencies of recovered bones.

Thomas (1969a) compared the recovery of bones from different-sized mammal species by two screen mesh-sizes, and recorded the correction factors he derived for various species from these comparisons. Ziegler (1973: 14–16) discusses Thomas' findings, and suggests average "recovery constants" by which to multiply the numbers of bones recovered from mammalian species of different sizes in order to adjust for the relative efficiency of various recovery screens. Briefly, all the skeletal bones of mammals above a live body weight of about 5 kg. will be recovered by one-quarter-inch or smaller mesh. But, as might be expected, significant numbers of such bones from smaller mammals will be lost through both of these screen sizes. For instance, the bone sample from a rat-sized species weighing less than 100 gm. must be multiplied by a recovery constant of about 3.5 for one-eighth-inch mesh and by about 70 for one-quarter-inch mesh, in order to approximate the true number of bones of this species originally present in the excavated material.

This procedure presumes there has been no differential survival rate of different bones (or teeth) from the same skeleton since interment, but Hole and Heizer (1973: 232) report an apparent instance of differential survival of milk teeth in comparison with adult teeth of the same species. Also, the faunal analyst should be aware that some sites or portions of sites may be partially or wholly deficient in bone simply because of high soil acidity. A pH below 7.0 is acidic, and Ritchie (1940: 10) and Bullen (1949: 106) have stated that bone may be destroyed in matrix with a pH of 6.3 or less.

ANALYSIS AND INTERPRETATION

Minimum number of individuals Since this figure is required for more than one of the analytical methods soon to be described, various ways of calculating it should now be explained.

The usual means of determining the minimum number of individuals of a particular species originally entering a deposit has been to consider this number equal to the highest number of any single skeletal element of the species identified in the faunal inventory. That is, four right humeri of porcupine (*Erethizon dorsatum*) would obviously indicate that at least four porcupines had once been there. This number can then sometimes be augmented by, for example, comparing the right porcupine humeri with the lesser number of left humeri also recovered. If one or more of the left humeri cannot be matched for size or age among the right ones, the presence of a corresponding additional number of individual animals is indicated.

If most of the animal bones in a site are fragmentary, the calculation of minimum numbers obviously becomes more complicated. But by using specific portions of bones—for instance, the head of the femur, the acetabular portion of the innominate, etc.—the same kind of calculation may still be done. Such computations can be further refined, if desired (see Watson, 1972; Chaplin, 1971: 70–75), but these refinements usually require prohibitive amounts of time and labor. For example, the exact portion of each bone represented must be recorded on the species sheets, or, if bones from all excavation levels or site areas are to be grouped for the necessary direct comparisons, each bone fragment must be individually numbered so that it can be returned to its original excavation lot.

A practical alternative method of calculating a relatively reasonable minimum number of individuals is available for many species and at many sites. If the average weight of the entire skeleton of a particular animal species is known, then the total weight of all recovered bone assigned to this species can be used to approximate the minimum number of individuals represented. Thus, a complete average porcupine skeleton weighs about 300 gm. (see Ziegler, 1973: Table 6, for skeletal weights of selected birds and mammals), so 100 gm. of identified porcupine bone from an excavation unit would indicate at least four average-sized individuals.

Of the several assumptions underlying this skeletal-weight method, two of the most significant are as follows. First, it has to be considered that all parts of the porcupine body had an equal chance of entering the deposit. This can be tested at least roughly by examining the distribution of identified bones on the species sheets. If the porcupine bone consists mostly of limb elements, then this method is clearly unsuitable because it will give a value far below the actual minimum number. Second, it has to be assumed that all the porcupine bones originally present in the deposit were recovered during excavation. And indeed, because an average live procupine weighs over 5 kg., this should be so, if the matrix was screened through a mesh no larger than one-quarter inch.

Two further assumptions are that the analyst correctly assigned all the bones of this particular species, and that the so-called average skeletal weight will actually be the average for all the various-sized porcupines entering the deposit.

Introduction of faunal remains   All bones in a site must have been deposited by either human or non-human means. If the bones were introduced by human inhabitants, this fact may be revealed in several ways. A burned condition of many bones—especially charring that suggests the bones were roasted while still largely covered with flesh—usually indicates deposition by man. The presence of identifiable bone or other animal remains in dried human feces (coprolites) is, of course, proof of human involvement (see Napton and Heizer, 1970, for recent investigative methods for coprolitic material).

A distribution skewed toward certain parts of the skeleton is usually also indicative of human activity. For example, with deer, if the trunk bones and the limb bones nearest the trunk are predominant, whereas skull bones and lower limb bones are virtually absent, human beings very likely dismembered deer carcasses elsewhere, and brought only selected portions to the site.

Signs of human "working" of bones fall into two main categories: butchering or skinning marks, and evidences of artifact manufacture. A good introduction to the identification of butchering and skinning marks—as well as examples of just how much ethnological data can be inferred from a thoughtful study of such marks—is available in Parmalee (1965) and Guilday, Parmalee, and Tanner (1962).

Finished artifacts of bone and other animal material are not normally turned over to the faunal analyst; and if they are, they should not be treated numerically or stratigraphically the way most unmodified faunal remains would be, because artifacts cannot be considered randomly deposited. However, much of the bone waste from the manufacture of such artifacts does often turn up in the "unmodified" complement of faunal material. Such debris may enable the faunal analyst to determine which animals provided the raw material for such aboriginal products as "splinter awls" or bone beads. These artifacts are so highly finished that they are largely unassignable to species. Also, the process by which the raw bone was fashioned into a specific artifact—and the tools needed to do it—can sometimes be deduced from various characteristics of the waste material. Fractured animal bones found in a site may also represent cultural items as opposed to, say, bones broken in a fatal fall or by a predator. The differences between bones intentionally broken by people for use as tools, and bones otherwise broken, are described by Sadek-Kooros (1972) and Bonnichsen (1973b).

Among the various non-human agents that may have introduced bone into a deposit, both mammalian and avian predators should be listed—especially for enclosed sites such as caves or rockshelters. If the site once served as the lair of a non-human carnivore or scavenger, the bone material recovered will tend to be noticeably gnawed or otherwise tooth-marked, especially on the borders or articular ends. (See Bonnichsen, 1973b, for more detailed information on this subject.) If dogs belonging to aboriginal human inhabitants can be discounted at the site for one reason or another, bones so marked would have been non-culturally deposited. Owls (like hawks, herons, and kingfishers) regurgitate pellets containing characteristic clusters of bones from their smaller vertebrate prey. These clusters, persisting after the softer material in the pellets has disintegrated, will consist of the mostly broken and matching bones of entire or partial skeletons, including complete upper and lower tooth rows, and are thus easily distinguishable from the relatively finely fragmented osseous parts remaining after the disintegration of human or other mammalian coprolites.

Entire skeletons or articulated major portions of the skeletons of animals found in a site deposit should be viewed by the faunal analyst with two general explanations in mind. Either the remains were intentionally—usually ritually—buried there by people (see Heizer and Hewes, 1940, and Cleland, 1966: 207, for examples), or they were not. If not, the animal may have died on the site or its carcass may have been brought there by non-human agency; in either case, the remains somehow became incorporated into the deposit. Relatively complete skeletons of burrowing mammals, small reptiles, and sometimes even amphibians such as toads and salamanders that have died in underground tunnels turn up with some regularity in certain sites.

Thomas (1971) has adapted an earlier paleontological technique to this problem of gaining insight into the deposition agent of bones of various species in archaeological sites. The underlying assumption in the archaeological version of this skeletal-completeness method is that skeletons of any species dying at a site naturally (i.e., in the absence of intervention by man or other predators) will tend to be more completely represented whenever found in any given excavation sample than those of species that died elsewhere (through whatever means) and were subsequently transported to the site. Obviously, during post-mortem transport and other handling skeletons would have more opportunity to be dismembered, dispersed, or otherwise destroyed before eventually being deposited among the other bones in the site.

Faunal analysts desiring to use this technique, should consult the more complete description in Thomas (1971) or in Ziegler (1973: 17–22), but the computation and analysis of skeletal-completeness data may be briefly summarized here as follows. The degree of skeletal completeness (CSI) is individually computed for each species identified in a site inventory, using the formula:

$$CSI = \frac{100 \times (\text{original raw number of bones})}{(\text{est. number of identifiable elements}) \times (\text{min. number of individuals})}$$

Of the factors in this formula, 100 is simply a constant multiplier; the original raw number of bones is the total for the species obtained from the appropriate species sheet; the estimated number of identifiable elements is that number of all individual bones of the particular species' skeleton that the identifier is competent to assign to this species; and the minimum number of individuals is, of course, the factor described just above.

When the CSI's for all identified species of a site have been determined by means of this formula, the results can be shown visually as in the accompanying graph (which, however, uses genera rather than species as its unit). Such graphs themselves are valuable analytical aids, allowing the collective CSI's for different sites to be compared at a glance. However, at this point in the procedure the CSI's of various species are still only relative ratings, indicating simply which species' skeletons are most well represented and which least. For translation into more useful information, the figures must somehow be related to the CSI of one or more species whose agent of deposition in the site either is known or can reasonably be deduced.

In the case of the site represented on p. 195, Thomas has previously determined on different grounds that two lagomorphs, the rabbit *Sylvilagus* and the jack rabbit *Lepus,* were eaten by the human inhabitants, and thus most of their remains recovered were probably deposited by human rather than natural means. The several species shown with CSI's noticeably lower than those of the two lagomorphs would be strongly suspected of entering the site deposit only after post-mortem transport. These species' remains should be further investigated (for butchering marks, for evidence of burning or of gnawing by carnivores, etc.) to determine their probable agent of deposition. On the other hand, the high CSI of the meadow mouse *Microtus* relative to those of the known human-deposited lagomorphs suggests that this species, as well as perhaps the other two small rodent species with relatively high CSI's, may be represented in the deposit largely as the result of natural deaths; or, depending on the physical or geographical situation of the site, one or more of these small rodent species might represent usual prey items of certain raptorial birds.

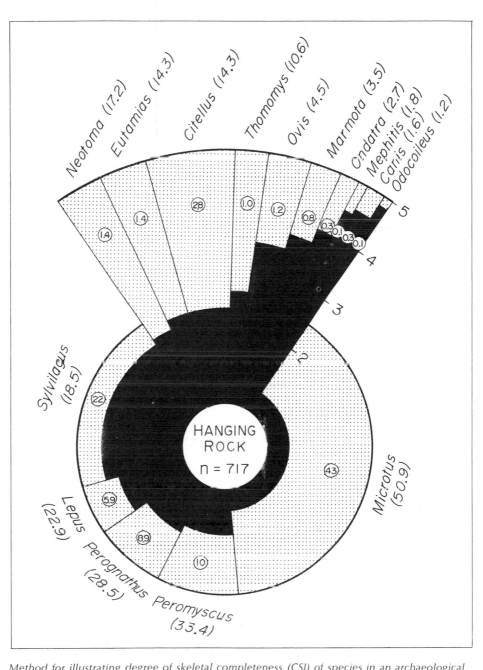

Neotoma (17.2)
Eutamias (14.3)
Citellus (14.3)
Thomomys (10.6)
Ovis (4.5)
Marmota (3.5)
Ondatra (2.7)
Mephitis (1.8)
Canis (1.6)
Odocoileus (1.2)

Sylvilagus (18.5)

Lepus (22.9)

Perognathus (28.5)

Peromyscus (33.4)

Microtus (50.9)

HANGING ROCK
n = 717

Method for illustrating degree of skeletal completeness (CSI) of species in an archaeological deposit. Figures in parentheses indicate numerical CSI, and radical length of black segments equals 5 − Log$_e$ CSI for each species. The site percentage of each species' remains is indicated by a figure in the stippled area. Also, the angular extent of each wedge is directly proportional to this percentage. For better visual discrimination in the case of this particular set of data, the angular extent for each of the ten wedges in the upper portion of the circle has been doubled. The original data are from Thomas (1971) and the graph is a slight modification of his Fig. 1. Reprinted by special permission from Ziegler, Inference from Prehistoric Faunal Remains, Fig. 5, A-W Module, 1973, Addison Wesley, Reading, Mass.

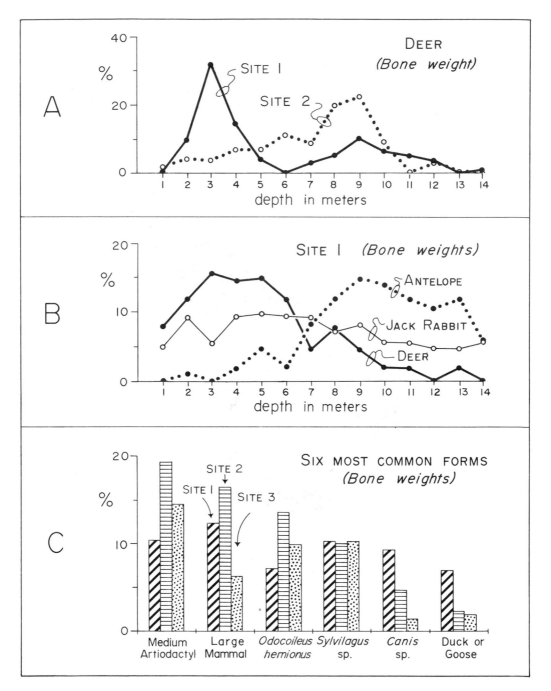

Three comparative uses of excavated bone weights. Graphs A and B are based on serial percentages, and C on site percentages, of the animals involved at these hypothetical sites. Reprinted by special permission from Ziegler, *Inference from Prehistoric Faunal Remains,* Fig. 6, A-W Module, 1973, Addison-Wesley, Reading, Mass.

Weights of bony remains   The total weight of bone (or shell) identified for each faunal category in a site, simply and conveniently obtained by procedures outlined earlier in this chapter, provides a set of objective data that may be very useful in many techniques the faunal analyst may want to use.

In most of the calculations a faunal analyst will make, the weights of bone are almost always more logical figures to work with than the mere raw numbers of bones or bone fragments recorded on the species sheets. For example, the weight of a well-preserved deer femur will be approximately the same no matter whether such a bone is recovered entire in one site or broken into six individually recorded pieces in another site. And this weight would be directly comparable between the two sites, whereas the two different raw numbers for femoral bone obviously would not.

The accompanying graphs illustrate three methods of plotting bone-weight distributions as an aid to interpreting such data. Graph A compares "serial percentage" of deer remains in two neighboring sites. (Serial percentage is the sequential distribution pattern of the total remains of one species throughout the stratigraphy of an entire site.) In using this kind of percentage note that the graph lines for the two sites are independent of each other because each relates only to the depositional history of the species *within that one site*. In other words, it cannot be stated from the data of this graph that the weight of deer bone at the 9-meter level of Site 2 was twice as great as it was at this same level in Site 1—in fact, it might have been only half as great, precisely equal, or three times as great. An allowable inference from the graph as a whole is, however, that in the entire history of the deposition of deer bones in this area—whether through human or non-human means—the greater *relative* intensity of this process shifted from Site 2 to Site 1 as time progressed.

Graph B compares serial percentages for three species at the same site. If all three are considered to have been taken and deposited by human beings, a possible inference is that most of the antelope represented in the site were taken in earlier times, and almost all of the deer were taken in later times, but jack rabbits were captured at a steady rate throughout the history of the site.

Graph C compares the "site percentage" of six kinds of animal found at three almost contiguous sites. (Site percentage is the percentage accounted for by each particular species in the total faunal remains found in a site. If only a single level of a site were being considered, this percentage would be termed "level percentage.") One likely inference from the similarity in their respective column profiles is that the bones now categorized as "medium artiodactyl" probably represent for the most part unassigned bones of the identified category *Odocoileus hemionus* (mule deer). Thus at each of the three sites the remains in these two categories might well be combined for purposes of certain additional computations, such as determining minimum numbers of individuals or calculating the edible meat weight originally represented by this skeletal material.

There appear to be relatively constant ratios between dry skeleton weight, live body weight, and edible fresh meat weight for particular kinds of animals (see, for example, Cook and Treganza, 1950; Cleland, 1966; or Parmalee, 1965). Thus if the skeletal weight is known, it can be converted to edible meat weight. Preliminary data (Ziegler, 1973, esp. Table 6) suggest that the appropriate conversion factors for relatively slim, long-limbed mammals such as canids and lagomorphs may be about ×8 or ×9; for stocky, shorter-limbed mammals such as bear and beaver, about ×14 or ×15; and for most wild birds, about ×15.

This edible meat weight can be further expressed in calories (at about 2000 per kg. of mammal flesh and about 1000 per kg. for bird flesh) to calculate, for instance, how long this single source of calories could have supported a given number of aboriginal inhabitants at 1,500 to 3,000 calories per person per day. Or, the approximate minimum daily human protein requirement (obtainable from a fresh weight of 150 to 250 gm. of vertebrate flesh) could be used instead of calories in such calculations. See Cook (1972: 23ff.), Baumhoff (1963), and Clark (1972: 25ff.) on ecologic determinants of aboriginal populations.

It is perhaps obvious at this point that other highly informative permutations of data on the relationship between edible meat weight and population numbers are possible if a time element is introduced. That is, if reasonable approximations of any two of these variables can be arrived at, the third can then be calculated. For example, White (1953) demonstrated how the probable numbers of aboriginal South Dakotan bison-hunters occupying a given number of single-family dwellings could be combined with estimated lengths of occupancy of the houses to estimate, among other things, how many bison had to be slain annually to support this prehistoric population.

Uses of the site The portion of the year during which a site was occupied—and the various purposes it served—can often be determined from faunal data. Remains of various migratory birds, fish, or even mammals taken for food indicate that the site must have been occupied during specific months of the year. For example, Howard (1929: 380–383) found abundant remains of winter-visitant species of ducks and geese in a prehistoric San Francisco Bay habitation area. Because bones of nestlings of summer-breeding cormorants (*Phalacrocorax*) were also present in the mound, Howard concluded that the site was occupied most—and possibly all—months of the year.

Most larger wild mammals bear their young during a specific relatively short period each year. And the ages of these young can be estimated to within a few weeks during the first year of life by looking at their tooth erup-

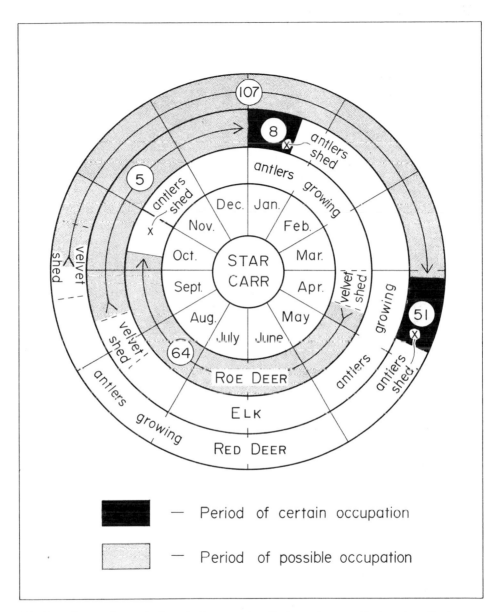

Working diagram for analyzing whether or not a site is used seasonally, based on the known annual antler cycles of three cervid species found at the European site of Star Carr. Figures in black portions of the circular tracks indicate relative numbers of adult male animals represented by excavated shed antlers and crania of individuals killed shortly after antler loss. Figures in stippled portions indicate relative numbers of adult males killed while still bearing full-grown antlers, and arrows indicate portions of the year during which these fully antlered animals could have been obtained. The diagram is constructed from data of Fraser and King (1954) and Clark (1972: 22). Reprinted by special permission from Ziegler, *Inference from Prehistoric Faunal Remains*, Fig. 11, A-W Module, 1973, Addison-Wesley, Reading, Mass.

tion and replacement. (See, as an example, the first-year age changes in the dentition of the mountain sheep, *Ovis canadensis*, recorded by Deming, 1952.) Thus, the presence in a site of such young mammals relatively accurately indicates specific months during which the killers of the animals were in the site area.

The known annual antler-growth and -shedding cycles of male cervids such as deer (*Odocoileus*), wapiti (*Cervus*), and moose (*Alces*), can similarly be used to fix the times during which hunters of these animals occupied a given site. The accompanying graph, although it represents European data, shows a method of recording and interpreting such antler-cycle information with regard to seasonality of site occupation. It is important to note that only two months (January and April) are indicated as *certain* occupation months— both on the evidence of *freshly shed* antlers in the site inventory. Although crania of all three cervid species bearing *still-unshed* antlers were recovered from the deposit, indicating that hunters could have been on the site any— or all—of the remaining months of the year, their presence cannot be determined on the basis of these unshed antler remains alone, and additional faunal or other appropriate data must then be consulted.

A heavy predominance of remains from a single type of animal, such as bison, sea mammals, salmon, etc., very often indicates that the site had limited uses. Possibly it was a temporary hunting or fishing camp. Further, if only certain bones such as head, manus, and pes of the dominant species are present, the site may have been a preliminary butchering point, from which the prepared carcasses were taken to a more permanent habitation site.

Demonstrating the intermittent occupation of sites, which often occurred on a seasonal basis when a particular food resource was abundantly present in the locality, can throw much light on the way of life of the people under investigation. This question can be approached in various ways, one of the chief ones being through the plant and animal remains left by the former inhabitants. Zoologists have in recent years begun to exploit the evidence of annual growth increments ("layers" or "rings" much like tree rings) that occur in mollusk shells and in the teeth and bones of reptiles, elasmobranchs, amphibians, fish, and mammals. The techniques for preparing the specimens for microscopic study are reasonably complicated, so such analyses are usually left to specialists. Not only annual but also monthly and even daily growth layers are detectable in many bony elements, and with sufficient study the age of the animal in years and months and days can be determined. These incremental growth layers can, therefore, often be interpreted to indicate the season in which the animal was killed, and from this the season of occupation by the men responsible for taking the animal for food. As an introduction to the subject the reader is referred to the works of Barker (1960), Casteel (1974), Clark (1968), Dobie (1971), Evans (1972), Gilbert (1966), Hall, Dollase, and Corbato (1974), Hederström (1959), Hewer (1964), Jonsgard

(1969), Laws (1960), McLaren (1958), Mitchell (1967), Pannella (1971), Pannella and MacClintock (1968), Peabody (1961), Rhoads and Pannella (1970), and Saxon and Higham (1969).

Faunal inventories can often be used to determine any temporal (i.e., vertical) or areal (i.e., horizontal) differences in aboriginal use of a site. Comparing the serial percentage profiles (as in Graph B on p. 196) of common types of animals for various parts and levels of a site is one useful technique. For instance, if the serial percentages of small food-mammal remains decrease from lower to upper levels of an excavation, while those of larger food-mammal remains increase, the site may have changed from an occasionally visited resting spot to a habitation site.

Comparison of faunal and non-faunal inventories can also reveal how a site or part of a site was used. In such comparisons the concentration indices described earlier are normally more convenient and accurate to use than either raw numbers or weights of inventory items. And if the *ratios* between concentration indices of the various items are used, differences in deposition rates of matrix—which so directly affect CI values—can safely be disregarded in many cases.

As an example, suppose a shallow site has been sampled by means of four pits, and the concentration indices of three items recovered were found to be as follows:

	Salmon bones (CI by wt.)	Acorn shells (CI by no.)	Obsidian waste (CI by wt.)
Pit A	2.4	10.7	45.2
Pit B	2.6	11.9	46.4
Pit C	17.0	11.4	45.0
Pit D	5.1	20.9	89.7

The ratio between the CI of the three items is approximately the same (1:4:18) for all pits except C, and therefore site usage—as regards at least these three items—was apparently similar for these three regions of the site. Also, even in Pit C the ratio of acorn-shell CI to obsidian-waste CI follows the pattern. This relative uniformity of ratios between various CI's simultaneously serves the purpose of a control: one that makes immediately apparent the unconformably high density of salmon bones in the Pit C region. Further analytical methods can then be employed to determine whether the Pit C area could have been where fish were boned or eaten.

Note the apparently doubled rate of deposition for all three inventory items in Pit D. Then, the analyst's problem is to determine on independent grounds whether this increased deposition rate is real, or whether matrix was for some reason being deposited much more slowly in this general area of the site. Note also that these relative densities of inventory items can be plotted on a plan diagram of the site in order to more clearly visualize or ascertain suspected differences in usage of various areas of the site. Clark (1954: Figs. 3, 4, 5; and 1972: Fig. 4; see also Fig. 5.12 of this volume) indicates how this has been done in the case of flint densities over the entire extent of the British site of Star Carr.

Past climate   Prehistoric changes in the climate of a site region may be inferred from faunal remains in two general ways: first, by the simple presence or absence in the deposit of species known or presumed characteristic of certain climatic conditions and, second, by changes in the relative abundance of such species through the stratigraphy of the site.

In making inferences from the climatic requirements of animals, it is obviously preferable to use species that survive today and whose ecological requirements can thus be known. Remains of an extinct artiodactyl, *Oreamnos harringtoni,* presumably closely related to the living mountain goat *O. americanus*, are found in an Arizona cave near southern Nevada. But before it can be stated that this find indicates very cold conditions in the area at the time represented, it must be proven that the climatic requirements of this extinct species were indeed very similar to those of its still-living relative. A better species to use for inferring past climatic conditions in this region is *Marmota flaviventris* (yellow-bellied marmot), now absent from southern Nevada but still present in mountains of the central and northern parts of the state. The appearance of this rodent species in southern Nevada site levels dating from several thousand years ago fairly surely indicate a colder climate than that now prevailing in the area.

Rather than simply stating that animal species found in a site inventory are characteristic of cold, wet areas, or of hot, dry ones, it is more convenient and specific to allocate the species to the appropriate Life Zones. These zones have been standardized by biologists in North America to designate successively higher (and thus usually colder and wetter) vegetation belts and associated "indicator" animal species. The Zones extend from near sea level to alpine vegetation line. Hall (1946) is a good reference for information regarding these Life Zones and their component biota in Nevada, for example.

It may often be possible to state at the conclusion of a faunal analysis that the climate of a particular site area appears to have changed from one characteristic of a certain life zone to one more similar to that of another zone. Cleland (1966) and Ziegler (1963) may be consulted for examples of this kind of conclusion regarding sites in the Great Lakes region and the northern Great Basin area, respectively. Casteel (1972) gives an excellent discussion of the use of fish remains as climatic indicators.

Certain smaller animals such as moles, shrews, rodents, amphibians, and desert reptiles are often more climatically limited—and thus better indicators—than are many birds and most wide-ranging larger mammals. Thus if such indicator species are found at a site, the analyst can be fairly certain of the climate in that area at that time. The converse, however—that if these species are absent from a site, the climate must not have been suitable for them—cannot be assumed. They may have been present in the region but not at the site because, for instance, of dietary taboos.

Inferences of past climatic changes tend to inspire more confidence when based on changes in relative abundance of several indicator or other animal species found throughout the strata of a site. In plotting and analyzing these changes, the characteristics of both *serial* percentages (discussed earlier in the section on weights of bone remains) and *level* percentages must be fully appreciated. The accompanying graphs show these two percentage methods illustrating the same set of faunal data, plotted in the form of the often-used variable-width columns rather than as graph lines.

Neither of the two graphs should be considered proof of particular climatic changes. There are simply too many variables involved to allow past climatic history to be inferred from any single set of faunal (or any other archaeological) data. However, Graph A (level percentage) gives some insight into the possibility of such changes, because it illustrates the ratio between abundances—expressed in this case as edible meat weight—of species *at each individual site level.*

Solely for the sake of simplicity in explaining this example, two very critical assumptions are made at this point. First, that all three species considered in the graphs entered the deposit in proportion to their true natural abundance in the site region at any given time and, second, that high deer numbers indicate wet conditions whereas high rabbit numbers indicate dry conditions. Thus, under these particular assumptions, the changing *ratio* between deer and rabbit numbers from Level III to Level I shown in Graph A could correctly be interpreted as indicating a change from dry to wet climatic conditions.

Note that the decreasing width of the deer column from earlier to later times in Graph B could be taken to indicate a change from wet to dry conditions—just the opposite of the conclusion from Graph A, and of the presumed true climatic shift. However, all that this serial-percentage deer column really indicates is the percentage of all deer remains represented in the site that entered during each of the three time periods. As emphasized when serial percentages were first discussed, such figures as those of Graph B cannot show how many deer remains *relative to rabbit remains* were entering the deposit at any time. Also, no one should conclude from Graph B that Level I was drier than Level III (under the two assumptions used here) unless he or she can explain why the serial-percentage values for the dry-climate rabbit decreased even more from Level III to Level I than did those for the wet climate deer.

A

Level	DEER		COYOTE		RABBIT		Total level %
I 2000 yrs.	79%	+	8%	+	13%		= 100%
II 500 yrs.	48%	+	14%	+	38%		= 100%
III 1000 yrs.	25%	+	25%	+	50%		= 100%

Level	DEER		COYOTE		RABBIT		Level total (edible meat wt.)
	Edible meat wt.	Level %	Edible meat wt.	Level %	Edible meat wt.	Level %	
I	300	79	30	8	50	13	380
II	100	48	30	14	80	38	210
III	400	25	400	25	800	50	1600

B

Level	DEER		COYOTE		RABBIT	
I 2000 yrs.	20%	+	4%	+	3%	
II 500 yrs.	27%	+	13%	+	16%	
III 1000 yrs.	53%	+	83%	+	81%	
Total serial %	100%	=	100%	=	100%	=

Level	DEER			COYOTE			RABBIT		
	Edible meat wt.	Time index	Serial %	Edible meat wt.	Time index	Serial %	Edible meat wt.	Time index	Serial %
I	300	0.15	20	30	0.02	4	50	0.03	3
II	100	0.20	27	30	0.06	13	80	0.16	16
III	400	0.40	53	400	0.40	83	800	0.80	81

Comparison of variable-width column diagrams of animal abundance at a hypothetical site, based on two methods of expressing the same numerical data: A, level percentage; and B, serial percentage. Level III represents the oldest time period, and Level I the newest. Reprinted by special permission from Ziegler, Inference from Prehistoric Faunal Remains, Fig. 10, A-W Module, 1973, Addison-Wesley, Reading, Mass.

Other possible inferences   Many other lines of investigation may be based primarily on the analysis of faunal remains. In fact, these other possibilities are limited only by the ingenuity and interest of the individual faunal analyst. A few of the more useful of these supplementary research lines will be mentioned here.

Probable trade routes among prehistoric populations can sometimes be retraced if species are found far out of their presumed normal ranges, as with marine shells excavated from a site far inland. Such probable extended lines of barter may in turn explain the presence of certain other species whose appearance at a site is difficult to explain on any other grounds.

Aboriginal conservation practices may also come to light in a faunal inventory. Do the recovered remains of a common food animal, for instance, differ significantly from the age or sex ratios found in nature, so that it becomes apparent that adult males were selectively taken more often than other individuals of the species? Or, as in the case of most cervids, were these adult males hunted more than females or young simply because of the bonus of useful antler material?

The search for conservation practices may well lead into an investigation of why a particular body or skeletal part of one species (or age-class or sex of a species) was used for a given type of artifact, while the same part of individuals of an equally available species was not similarly used. If, for example, eagle wings were used as fans in preference to the seemingly equally available wings of, say, geese, would this be best explained on totemic or purely utilitarian grounds?

Domestication of mammals and birds is not characteristic of many North American aboriginal groups, although some methods for identifying such a practice might prove informative elsewhere in the New World and at Old World sites. Reed (1961) and Clutton-Brock (1970) outline techniques to be applied to remains of potentially domesticated artiodactyls and canids, respectively. Also, any evidence of animal pathology (see Brothwell, 1970) might be further investigated for its possible relationship to domestication, or for its effect on other activities of an aboriginal population.

Finally, more ingenious analytical strategies might be devised to test whether there had been any "class" differences in the use of certain species or individuals of food animals. Such studies would of course require various non-faunal data in addition to the faunal data.

ARTIFACTS:
THEIR STUDY AND CARE

10

Let us not to be too particular. It is better to have old second-hand diamonds than none at all.

—MARK TWAIN

EXAMINATION OF ARTIFACTS
AND IDENTIFICATION OF MATERIALS

There are now available scores of what can best be termed "scientific methods" that can be applied to archaeological materials. Some of these examinations produce qualitative information about the chemical or elemental composition of the object being considered; others add a quantitative dimension. Some can be used (e.g., radiocarbon dating, paleomagnetism) to ascertain the age of the object; others tell us only what it consists of, and others reveal how much the item has changed since it was made or was alive.

Science in Archaeology (1963), a volume edited by Brothwell and Higgs, covers a number of these natural-science techniques that can be applied to archaeology, but the subject is so large that no single source could possibly speak of the many techniques and applications that are now known and that are almost daily being developed. See also *Science and Archaeology* (Brill, 1971); *The Application of the Physical Sciences to Archaeology* (Stross, 1971); *Methods of Physical Examination in Archaeology* (Tite, 1972); and *Archaeology and the Microscope* (Biek, 1963).

Because archaeological materials taken as a whole may include nearly

all of the kinds of palpable entities produced by nature (i.e., animal, vegetable, and mineral), it is often difficult for archaeologists to identify precisely
the bone or stone or vegetal material they have found. They may achieve this
identification through their own efforts, by using a published source written
by an expert, or by consulting an expert. Thus anyone wishing to learn what
kind of stone an object is made of may do so by asking an expert petrogra-
pher, or the hard way by checking in J. D. Dana's classic, *Manual of Mineralogy and Petrography,* A. Rosenfeld's *The Inorganic Raw Materials of Antiquity,*
J. A. Hedvall's *Chemie in Dienst der Archäologie Bautechnik Denkmalpflege,*
Read's *Rutley's Elements of Mineralogy,* Kemp's *Handbook of Rocks,* the
several volumes of R. J. Forbes' *Studies in Ancient Technology,* or H. Hodges'
Artifacts. Usually one secures more reliable information, and that more
quickly, by requesting the aid of an expert (cf. Taylor, 1957).

When a problem can be solved by learning the composition or source
of some object or material, the archaeologist who has some idea what kind
of inspection or analysis is applicable to the material is already started along
the way to an answer. All he or she must now do is to find someone willing
to make the examination. Biek (1963) is an excellent single source on techniques of examination.

Let us suppose that the archaeologist has found artifacts made of a type
of stone not found locally. The immediate question is where the stone came
from, since this will tell something about ancient trade or exploitation of
natural resources. If the imported stones are ten- to forty-ton basalt objects,
as is the case with the colossal heads, altars, and stelae at the Olmec site
of La Venta in southeastern Mexico, a search of the region may reveal their
geological source. This was done by one of the present authors with the aid
of an experienced vulcanologist, and the findings are published (Williams
and Heizer, 1965a). A similar investigation was carried out in the Oaxaca,
Mexico, area (Williams and Heizer, 1965b), and at Teotihuacan (Heizer and
Williams, 1965).

Similar petrographic-geologic studies aimed at determining the source
of stones used in prehistoric times have been done in highland Bolivia (Ponce
Sanginés and Mogrovejo Terrazas, 1970; Ahlfeld, 1946), New Mexico (Montgomery, 1963), Mexico (Ordoñez, 1892), and at Stonehenge (Thomas, 1923).
In England a long-term program of petrological examination of stone axes
has been under way for the last thirty years (see *Proceedings of the Prehistoric
Society,* Vol. 7, 1941; Vol. 28, 1962). The general method of petrological examination of archaeological materials is covered by Wallis (1955), Shotten (1963),
Jope (1953), and Fischer (1878). A bibliography of petrographic studies in
archaeology has been published by Hester and Heizer (1973b: 49–54).

Metal objects can be examined by chemical analysis (Samolin, 1965;
Coghlan, 1960; Coghlan, Butler, and Parker, 1963); their "impurity patterns"
can be determined (Pittioni, 1960); or the techniques that produced them can

be analyzed by electron spectroscopy (Fraikor, Hester, and Fraikor, 1971). By combining archaeological finds, ethnographic data, and laboratory analyses of metal objects, one can draw a picture of the development of ancient metallurgy—as, for example, for America (Bray, 1971) and the ancient Near East (Wertime, 1973). Neutron-activation analysis gives very precise and detailed information on the trace elements in metal artifacts (Friedman et al., 1966). Other metallurgical studies have been published by Bastian (1961), Butler and Van der Waals (1964), Easby (1965, 1966), Patterson (1971), Schroeder and Ruhl (1968), and Yao and Stross (1965). Articles on this subject can be found in the journal Archaeometry.

Petrography and the analysis of trace elements have also been applied to ceramic artifacts. These techniques can reveal much about the temper of pottery, the materials from which it was made, and the origins of ceramic trade wares. Petrographic studies include those of Dickinson and Shutler (1971), Shepard (1956), Williams (1956), and a great number of others, some of which are listed by Hester and Heizer (1973b:54–56). Neutron-activation analysis (trace-element studies), designed to provide information on the provenience of specific wares, have been carried out by Bennyhoff and Heizer (1958), Harbottle (1970), Johnson and Stross (1965), Perlman and Asaro (1969, 1970), and Sayre, Murrenhoff, and Weick (1958). Chemical and spectrographic techniques have been applied by Bouchard (1966), and Weymouth (1973) has recently used x-ray diffraction analysis in ceramic studies. A review article on the scientific analysis of ceramics has been written by Peacock (1970).

Obsidian, long used by man and limited in its natural occurrence, is an especially valuable material for studying ancient technology and trade relations. Trace-element patterns, as determined through x-ray fluorescence, neutron activation (Ashworth and Abeles, 1966), and other physico-chemical methods, of different obsidians are sufficiently distinct so that one can usually determine the source of an obsidian artifact (Cann and Renfrew, 1964; Cobean et al., 1971; Griffin, Gordus, and Wright, 1969; Heizer, Williams, and Graham, 1965; Hester, Jack, and Heizer, 1971; Hester, Jack, and Benfer, 1973; Graham, Hester, and Jack, 1972; Jack, Hester, and Heizer, 1972; Stross et al., in press; Weaver and Stross, 1965; see also the bibliographic listing prepared by Hester and Heizer, 1973b: 49–54).

Trace elements in flint and chert have also been analyzed in an effort to trace the geologic origins of artifacts (Aspinall and Feather, 1972; Luedtke, 1974); however, this particular application of the method still has many problems. Neutron-activation studies have been more successful with Egyptian quartzite artifacts. This research has focused on the Eighteenth Dynasty, particularly the colossal statues of Amenhotep III at Thebes. These statues, the Colossi of Memnon, stand 47 feet high, and each was originally a quartzite monolith weighing 720 tons. Trace-element analyses of samples from the statues, and from a series of Nile Valley quartzite quarry samples, have shown that the monoliths came from the Gebel el Ahmar quarries near Cairo, some 676 km. down the Nile from Thebes (Heizer et al., 1973; Heizer, Stross, and Hester, 1973).

Another kind of examination recently devised for stone artifacts, particularly tools, is microscopic analysis of patterns caused by use or wear. Detailed microscopic examination of striations, dulling, abrasions, etc., on the working edges of tools can provide meaningful evidence about what the tool was used for. The interpretation of such evidence rests heavily on replicative experiments and ethnographic analogy. The techniques used in analyzing wear patterns are reported by Biek (1963), Keeley (1974), MacDonald and Sanger (1968), and Mirambell (1964), and in the classic work of Semenov (1964). We cite below a few examples of the application of this kind of study: *North America* (Frison, 1968; Hester, 1970, 1974; Hester, Gilbow, and Albee, 1973; Hester and Heizer 1973a; Nance, 1971; Wilmsen, 1968; Witthoft, 1955); *Mesoamerica:* (Hester and Heizer, 1972; Hester, Jack, and Heizer, 1971); *Europe* (Bordes, 1969; Rosenfeld, 1971; Semenov, 1964). A detailed bibliography of wear-pattern studies is found in Hester and Heizer (1973b: 23–25).

Deliberate hoaxes in the form of something "planted" in a site are, one trusts, rare. The perpetrators of such *in situ* hoaxes are rarely malicious, but the practice is dangerous, and damaging to the necessary condition of trust among the members of the excavation group. Any worker caught playing this game should be asked to leave. The alleged planting of the Clovis point in one of the Lewisville (Texas) "hearths" has caused no end of doubt and confusion (Heizer and Brooks, 1965: 156), and there are many other instances, one of the best-known being the Piltdown skull (Weiner, 1955). This kind of juvenile behavior cannot be too strongly condemned.

Aside from having occasionally to deal with planted objects in excavations, archaeologists are often asked to state whether an isolated specimen is a genuine antiquity or a fake. This may involve identifying materials, style of decoration or form, making inferences about the kinds of tools employed in manufacture, etc. There is no good guide to this procedure, but the interested person can begin by reading the publications of Cooney (1963), Easby and Dockstader (1964), Ekholm (1964), Plenderleith (1952), Stross (1960, 1973), von Bothmer and Noble (1965), and Wakeling (1912).

CARE AND PRESERVATION OF ARCHAEOLOGICAL SPECIMENS

Leechman's advice (1931: 131) to "treat every specimen as though it were the only one of its kind in the world" is worth heeding, for the amount of information an object may supply is partly dependent on its condition. Following the exposure, photographing, and notebook recording of an artifact, burial, or set of animal remains, certain procedures may be necessary to ensure that the specimen arrives at the museum in the best condition possible. Failure to take necessary precautions may result in the disintegration or breakage of a specimen.

Field procedures for the care of specimens may be separated into three categories: preservation, repair, and cleaning. By preservation we mean the process of strengthening a specimen to reduce the possibility of deterioration. Repair, usually with some adhesive, means securing in position separated pieces of the specimen. In practice it may be better to pack the pieces separately and let them be restored in the museum under optimum conditions. Cleaning specimens in the field means removing dirt to facilitate handling, labeling, and shipping. The extent to which repair and preservation techniques should be employed in the field depends on such factors as local climate, distance of the excavation from a museum or permanent repository, and whether or not a field laboratory has been set up at the excavation. In any case, a minimum outline of materials and procedure is given below (see Brown, 1974; Downan, 1970; Garlake, 1969b; Keel, 1963; Mohammed Sana Ullah, 1946; Plenderleith, 1934; Rathgen, 1926).

Materials and equipment

Shellac and alcohol   Pure white shellac should be obtained, not orange or compound shellac. Depending on the use, the shellac may be thinned one-half to two-thirds with alcohol. This mixture is brushed or sprayed on specimens to harden them. If brushing is to be used, the solution may be kept in a mason jar or mayonnaise jar with a hole punched in the top to receive a round, half-inch brush.

Celluloid and acetone   This mixture is best carried in a stock solution and thinned before use with acetone kept apart for this purpose. "Duco" is the trade name for an adhesive product that is available in tubes and thus handier for small repairs. Another product is "Alvar" (polyvinyl acetate), which is soluble in acetone. The mixture of celluloid and acetone (or similar products) is useful as an adhesive and, in thin solution, to harden specimens.

Beeswax and benzine   Lumps of beeswax may be dissolved in benzine or gasoline. The mixture can be used to coat wet specimens.

Plaster of Paris   This product is supplied in several grades. The "slow-set" gauging variety is most useful, but any type will work. Mixed with water, it is useful for jacketing specimens, particularly burials, that are in very delicate condition or are to be preserved entire for exhibition or study. A washpan is desirable for mixing.

Burlap gunny sacks   These are used in combination with plaster of Paris.

Kleenex or similar tissue   Tissue is used in combination with shellac and alcohol for preserving "checked" bone.

"Lithiol"   This is a commercial liquid useful for preservation of stone that is disintegrating. Other hardening solutions are available.

Brushes   Paint brushes and whiskbrooms used in excavation are available for cleaning specimens. In addition, there should be an assortment of various sizes (half-inch and quarter-inch paint brushes and several water-color brushes) of brush for applying adhesives. These should be cleaned in the appropriate solvent after use.

Sprayers   Two devices adapted for spraying adhesives or hardening agents on fragile artifacts are the nose-throat atomizer and the plunger-type sprayer commonly used for glass-cleaning preparations. The second is easier to clean and less likely to break in the field than the first. After use, either type of sprayer must be thoroughly cleaned in the solvent of the adhesive. Liquid plastics under pressure in spray cans have also been found to be effective as hardening agents. With spray cans the cleaning problem is eliminated, although the total expense is greater than with the other types.

Any organic remains (wood, charcoal, bone) that have been chemically preserved thereby become "contaminated" and may prove to be useless for trace-element analysis or radiocarbon dating.

Field techniques   Procedures employed in the field may be separated according to the materials commonly requiring preservation or repair.

Bone   Bone specimens include unmodified animal and human remains and bone artifacts. Human skeletal remains will ordinarily be encountered as burials. After notation, sketching, and photography of each burial, the condition of the bones should be examined. Under ordinary circumstances the bones may be removed as they are and packed in such a way as to avoid pressure-fractures and friction. Even under the most favorable circumstances, however, teeth should be secured in their sockets with a dab of celluloid and acetone, or removed and placed in a separate bag or envelope labeled according to burial number and site.

If bone specimens are checked or cracked on the surface, the following treatment can be applied: while the bone is still in place, a coating of thin shellac and alcohol should be applied over and beyond the crack. Next, a single sheet of cleaning tissue is applied to the surface and stippled on with a brush that has been dipped in the mixture. After this has thoroughly dried, the bone may be removed and strengthened by the same process on the reverse side. Careful packing of such a specimen will be necessary. Remember that neither shellac nor celluloid will work properly on a damp or wet specimen.

When bone is extremely fragile and subject to rapid deterioration, it should be cleared of loose dirt *in situ*. Next it is saturated with acetone, then coated with a thin solution of "Alvar" and acetone. This coat is followed by others. When the solution has dried, the bone is removed and the reverse side is treated. In this way the bone is strengthened and sealed against moisture. An alternative method using polymerized vinylacetate is recommended (Anonymous, 1936). Careful packing and labeling are necessary (Lehmer, 1939:30; Antle, 1940; Burns, 1940; Jehle, 1957: 21–22; Keel, 1963: 15–17).

The following method of jacketing skeletal remains has been used successfully by paleontologists for years. It has been used less extensively by anthropologists, but it is the easiest method for removing entire burials, fragile bones, and artifacts intact (Camp and Hanna, 1937: 10–17; Antle, 1940; Clements, 1936).

When a specimen has been selected for removal in plaster, it must be prepared by careful excavation. Dig all around the burial, preserving the actual matrix in place and exposing as little of the bone as possible. In most soils the specimen will remain on a pedestal; in sand it will not be possible to excavate down the sides and ends of the specimen. If any bones are exposed, they should be coated with a thin solution of celluloid or shellac. Next the bones are covered with cloth or wet pieces of newspaper to prevent the plaster from adhering to the bones.

The specimen is now ready for jacketing. Take burlap sacks, like those used for coal or potatoes, and cut strips from two to six inches wide and from one to three feet long. Place these strips of burlap in water to soak. Then fill a washpan half full of water and sprinkle the plaster of Paris into it until the plaster comes slightly above the surface of the water. After the plaster has settled, stir the mixture slightly. Wring the water from a strip of burlap; dip it into the pan; wipe off the excess plaster; and place the strip across the burial at right angles to the main axis of the block. Press each strip firmly over the contours. Repeat the process, overlapping each strip slightly. When the surface is entirely covered in this manner, a long burlap strip or "collar" is wrapped around the edge of the entire block. In some cases as, for example, an extended burial—the block may be strengthened with sticks or with wire.

After the plaster has set and hardened, excavate below the level of the block and around and below the pedestal. Then carefully turn the specimen over on its plaster cap. Repeat the process on the newly exposed side after removing excess dirt to a few inches from the bone.

The specimen is now ready for transport. The plaster block will stand considerable abuse, but should nevertheless be handled carefully.

Antler Generally speaking, antler is like bone and the same treatments and precautions should be used in handling it (Leechman, 1931: 140). Wet artifacts of antler should be dried slowly and coated with a thin solution of celluloid when they are thoroughly dry. Specimens in a poor or decomposing condition may be immersed in a jar containing a thin solution of celluloid until the bubbles cease to rise, then dried and immersed again.

Shell   Shell artifacts and specimens in good dry condition may be packed immediately for transport to the museum. However, specimens that are delicate or flaking should be soaked in a thin celluloid solution after cleaning (Leechman, 1931: 146; Burns, 1940: 154–155; Johnson, 1941).

Shells taken from damp soil are likely to pulverize when they are dry. Whenever practical, these specimens should be sent to the museum in a container that will preserve their moisture. Otherwise, they may be treated as they would be in the museum by cleaning them with a soft brush while they are immersed in a five percent solution of clear gelatin. After this gelatin bath, they are placed directly in a formaldehyde bath. This treatment will form an insoluble protective coating.

Stone   Stone artifacts rarely need any treatment in the field. Should broken stone artifacts be found, it is preferable to pack them as carefully as necessary and to leave repair for the museum. Stone that is crumbling or badly weathered may be treated with "Lithiol" according to instructions on the container. Lewin (1966) has compiled a bibliography dealing with the techniques of preserving stone objects.

Textiles   Textiles from open prehistoric sites are usually found in carbonized fragments. Such specimens are delicate and must be treated with extreme care if the investigator hopes to identify the weave. A thin solution of celluloid and acetone may be applied (several layers) with a sprayer or an eye-dropper to one side of each specimen; when this dries, the other side should be treated in like manner. For fine-woven fabrics, Laudermilk (1937) recommends a solution of clear rosin and acetone rather than one containing celluloid because the celluloid solution tends to shrink the specimen upon drying.

No celluloid, acetone, or like solutions should be used if carbonized textile remains are to be subjected to radiocarbon dating. This applies to wood and to amorphous charcoal fragments as well. Preservative materials, even when apparently removed from the sample, can adversely affect the result of the dating technique. Keel (1963) has an excellent section dealing with the preservation, repair, cleaning, and care of textiles.

Ceramics   Unpainted pottery may safely be washed, with care. It is useful to include a tag with potsherds, warning the museum preparators to use care in soaking any salts from the sherds, particularly painted sherds. For details on care and preservation, see Leechman (1931: 156–157), Lucas (1932: 188–192), Burns (n.d.: 160–162), Keel (1963: 9–13), Plenderleith (1956: 326–339), Wolff (1960), Printup (1961), and Calhoun (1963). For *baked clay objects and artifacts,* follow the same instructions as for pottery.

Metal objects   Excellent guides to the cleaning and study of metal objects have been prepared by Plenderleith ((1956: Part II) and Biek (1963), and Dunton (1964) has authored a study on the conservation of metals in small laboratories. Methods of analyzing metals fall outside our subject here, but the reader may wish to consult on this subject the works of Coghlan (1951, 1956, 1960), Organ (1963), Caley (1951), Gettens and Usilton (1955: 113–155), and Hodges (1964: Chaps. 4–6). The usual materials are iron, copper, and brass. Occasionally silver, gold, and lead are encountered.

Metal objects, particularly those altered by rust or corrosion, must be treated with the utmost care. Under no circumstances should an attempt be made in the field to remove the rust or the corrosion. To do so may mean losing the specimen as an artifact and as a potential source of information. The corrosion products of metals may tell the metallurgical specialist a great deal about the age and history of a specimen (cf. Heizer, 1941b: App.). The so-called Drake Plate, a brass plate allegedly nailed to a post on the California coast in 1579 by the English explorer, was found in 1936. It was subjected to intensive chemical and microscopic analysis, but the conclusions on its authenticity would have been considerably strengthened had its discoverer not removed the precious patina from its face with abrasives.

The museum should also be warned against overzealous cleaning and reminded of the need for extreme care in handling corroded objects (Dunton, 1964).

If it is absolutely necessary to remove the corrosion from metal surfaces, this can be done by scraping, by soaking in a solution that dissolves the corroded surface, or by electrochemical means (Gettens, 1964; Nichols, 1930).

Iron objects have generally been subjected to rusting that may have carried deep into the metal. Treatment of specimens depends on the extent of rusting (Biek, Cripps, and Thacker, 1954; Folan, Rick, and Zacharchuk, 1968; Foley, 1965; Pelikan, 1964; South, 1962). Iron objects are often so badly rusted that little remains but a thin core of the iron encased in rust (ferric oxide). In such cases it is best to dry the object thoroughly and soak it immediately in a celluloid solution to preserve its shape.

Lightly corroded specimens of *copper, bronze,* and *lead* may be cleaned in the museum. Heavily corroded copper should be soaked in clean water to remove salts that may be present, then dried and coated with a thin solution of celluloid or dipped in a tarnish-removing solution (Brenner, 1953). Corrosion products on lead can be removed by methods outlined by Caley (1955), Organ (1953), and Garlake (1969a).

Wood   Wooden objects in a dry state usually need little preparation in the field other than brushing and cleaning. When wooden objects such as those found in dry caves are suspected of insect infestation, they should be coated with a solution of celluloid in acetone. This embalms any boring insects and eliminates the need for fumigation in the field. Alternatively the object can be soaked in pentachlorophenol (Carswell and Hatfield, 1939) or alum (Deaton, 1962). However, any wooden or other specimens of organic origin that may be infested or subject to infestation, should be appropriately labeled when they are sent to the museum. Special cases of preserving wood materials for dendrochronological purposes are treated by Hall (1939) and Hargrave (1936).

Wet wood, or wood excavated from damp soil, needs special preparation in the field. Damp or wet wood must be kept in this condition until it arrives at the museum. It should be packed in a watertight container, such as a coffee can or large tin, surrounded by wet crumpled paper, moss, or wet cloth. This will preserve the humid condition of the wood. A wood specimen that has lain in water may best be sent back in water to which a 10 percent solution of wood alcohol has been added as a temporary preservative (Leechman, 1931: 151). Polyethylene glycol applied to wet wood serves as a preservative (Albright, 1966; Seborg and Inverarity, 1962), and paraffin treatment has also been used successfully (Heizer, 1959: 43–49, quoting Shetelig and Falk; Wiertelak and Czarnecki, 1935), as has an alum process (Eaton, 1962). The rest of the careful preparation necessary for damp wooden objects can then be done in the museum (see Leechman, 1931: 151; Keel, 1963: 29–37; Gairola, 1961; and Purdy, 1974 for details of museum preparation). Further information on the treatment of wooden artifacts may be found in papers by Kostich (1965) and Reed (1966).

Materials from dry caves Problems confronting the archaeologist working in dry caves are caused chiefly by the fragility of perishable materials and by insects that may continue to eat away at the objects after excavation. In addition, materials such as baskets, skins, cordage, etc., will be found that need treatment in the museum. For such special problems see Leechman (1931), Laudermilk (1937), Burns (n.d.), Keel (1963: 48–53, 59–60), Cann (1937), Deschiens and Coste (1957), Gaussen (1950), and Nopitsch (1953).

CLASSIFICATION AND TYPOLOGY OF ARTIFACTS

Except in major excavation projects, the field analysis of excavated artifacts is seldom pushed beyond a preliminary assessment. Nevertheless, the classification and typology of artifacts obviously are intimately linked to field archaeology. For instance, the cultural and historical implications of artifacts recovered by surface reconnaissance at an archaeological site ordinarily constitute one of the rationales for excavating the site. And during the course of excavation, the kinds of artifacts discovered and their relationships will largely determine the form and direction of the continued program of excavation.

Artifacts have been classified according to material, color, shape, function, technology, and other features in attempts to bring order to a large and otherwise confusing body of chaotic data. According to a well-reasoned statement by Byers and Johnson (1940: 33):

> The purpose of a classification of archaeological material is to arrange the products of aboriginal industry in an order permitting the accurate description of everything found. From this order it should also be possible to determine with a minimum of effort the complete range of variation of all products of the industrial life of a community, region, or large area depending upon the scope of the particular problem under discussion. Furthermore, the various categories which are segregated in a classification should be so arranged that they can be studied separately or used for comparative purposes. In considering any category in a classification, one should never lose sight of the fact that it is really so closely related to the whole that it can be considered as a unit only in the most general terms.

Although the study of artifacts in itself might be an interesting pastime, the archaeologist's objective is to elucidate cultural process and reconstruct culture history. As a step or level in archaeological analysis, the classification of artifacts must further this objective, and any system of classification be ultimately judged according to how well it does so. Some archaeologists have been increasingly concerned to investigate and consider carefully the scientific meaningfulness of various systems of classification. In particular, these archaeologists have been concerned with the cultural and historical significance of their artifact categories. Thus Krieger (1945: 489) writes: "One of the fundamental precepts of archaeological thinking should be that specimens are not so much objects to be classified, but the concrete, overt expression of the mental and social world in which their makers live." This important concern marks a different direction in more recent archaeological classifications as compared to earlier research. As Ford (1954b: 43) notes:

> Initially archaeological classifications were made for the purpose of describing collections, and the smallest divisions of the items were frequently called types. These groupings were defined without reference to the temporal and spatial coordinates of culture history. Where chronological information is lacking such descriptive classifications are the only sort that can be made and are extremely useful. A good example of such a classification is S. K. Lothrop's (1926) analysis of pottery collections from Costa Rica and Nicaragua.

Reflecting the concern for the cultural meaning of artifact categories, and proposing what has come to be called the "typological method" of ordering artifacts, Krieger would draw an important distinction between classification and typology (1960: 143):

> The two terms have, of course, generally been regarded as synonyms, and probably few will agree that they can or need be distinguished. However, I prefer to think of *classification* as any act of sorting or designating, and of a *typology* as a more orderly system of actions, obeying certain laws or prin

ciples. Thus, anyone can classify in any manner of ways, but a typological (or taxonomic) system can only be attained in a limited number of ways, must have a clear aim, and requires knowledge of how the material occurs in space, time, and context.

In Krieger's view, artifact *types,* as he uses the term, should "approximate as closely as possible that combination of mechanical and aesthetic executions which formed a definite structural pattern in the minds of a number of workers, who attained this pattern with varying degrees of success and interpretation" (Krieger, 1944: 279). "Any group which may be labeled a 'type' must embrace material which can be shown to consist of individual variations in the execution of a definite constructional idea; likewise, the dividing lines between a series of types must be based upon demonstrable historical factors, not, as is often the case, upon the inclinations of the analyst or the niceties of descriptive orderliness" (Krieger, 1944: 272).

This view of types describes, it should be noted, not only a homogeneous group of artifacts but also a kind of ideal artifact, according to the criteria set up, that the actual implements approach. Thus Rouse (1939: 11) refers to a type artifact, "an abstract kind of artifact which symbolized the group." And Ford (1954b: 45) writes that "variation in actual artifacts tends to cluster about a mean" that can be visualized as "the central theme of the type."

The "typological method" thus establishes artifact categories, or types *sensu strictu,* that conform to "concrete human behaviors" and are therefore basic conceptual tools for cultural interpretation far beyond the level of "mere classifications." Spaulding (1953: 305) writes that "a properly established type is the result of sound inferences concerning the customary behavior of the makers of the artifacts and cannot fail to have historical meaning." The term "type" thus acquires a very special meaning not envisaged either in earlier archaeological usage or in its common wider currency. This is very unfortunate, but where confusion may result, "cultural type" may be used to signify the special meaning.

The typological method has been criticized as too artificial and arbitrary. Spaulding (1953), for instance, maintains that artifact types are "real," existing in societies as norms (the "right way") of manufacturing the objects being typed, and describes a statistical method for the "discovery" of such types in archaeological cultures. In contrast, Ford supports the arbitrary method of constructing types from a continuous stream of cultural development, considering that a type's "validity" depends solely on how well it serves its end purpose (Ford and Willey 1949: 40; Ford 1954a, 1954b). Thus types are "designed" rather than "discovered."

Although these two views have been characterized as diametrically opposed, we agree wholeheartedly with the observation of Willey and Phillips (1958: 13):

Our attitude is that these opposing views are not completely antagonistic. We maintain that all types are likely to possess some degree of correspondence to this kind of reality (i.e. behavioral reality) and that increase of such correspondence must be the constant aim of typology. The actual procedure of segregating types is therefore a more complex operation than is suggested simply by such words as "design" or "discovery," and is in effect a painstaking combination of both.

Other problems with the typological method lie not in its concepts but in their application. It should be remembered that because of the limitations of archaeological sampling (see Chapter 15), type definitions are always being refined. And because named types aim at specific historical meanings, they should not be used loosely. Unfortunately, some archaeologists use named historical types merely as convenient terms to describe morphologically similar specimens whose cultural relationship to the defined types is so remote, if existent at all, as to be meaningless (cf. Epstein, 1964). Finally, Krieger notes (1964b: 491) that whereas ceramics generally have been subjected to increasingly rigorous typological analysis, the typologies of other artifact categories are for the most part confused and inconsistent. As an outstanding example of careful typological classification, the student may consult the *Handbook of Texas Archeology* (Suhm, Krieger, and Jelks, 1954) where numerous ceramic types and projectile point types are defined and illustrated. For discussions and instructions on the actual sorting of artifacts into types, the student is referred to Ford (1962: 18–20), Krieger (1944: 279–283), Newell and Krieger (1949: 71–74), Phillips, Ford, and Griffin (1951: 66–68), Rouse (1960: 316), and Shepard (1956: 322–332).

Rouse (1960) proposes "analytic" classification as the logical basis for the "taxonomic" classification that formulates artifact cultural types. Analytic classification focuses upon those attributes of artifacts that reflect "any standard, concept, or custom which governs the behavior of the artisans of a community, which they hand down from generation to generation, and which may spread from community to community over considerable distances" (Rouse 1960: 313). Such a standard, concept, or custom is termed a "mode," and analytic classification aims to read such modes out of the artifacts. Types may then be formulated from two or more modes that have time-space significance or satisfy the specified objectives of the typology. Rouse concludes that modes may be more useful in analyzing one situation and types more useful in another, but that both are essential for the complete interpretation of archaeological remains.

The many aspects of artifact classification and typology, not to mention description, cannot be pursued at greater length within the framework of this guide. But lest students be unaware of the several aspects of the subject not mentioned or referred to here, they should study carefully the following papers: Binford (1963), Bresillon (1968), Chang (1967: 71–88), Deetz (1967:

43–52), Ford (1954b), Gardin (1958, 1967), Gifford (1960), Hole (1971), Hole and Heizer (1973: 201–206), Krieger (1944, 1960), Movius *et al.* (1968), Rouse (1939, 1944, 1960, 1970, 1972: 48ff.), Sears (1960), Spaulding (1973), and Thomas (1974: 6–14). Bibliographic citations in these works will provide a guide to further readings. Special attention might also be called to Wood-bury's (1954) impressive study of some 8,000 stone artifacts from northeastern Arizona, in which he aims at the same goals pursued in the typological method but without recourse to the naming of any actual types.

CERAMICS IN ARCHAEOLOGY

The study of prehistoric pottery is often a major part of archaeological research in areas with well-developed ceramic traditions. Indeed in some regions (portions of the eastern United States for instance), the great body of present archaeological knowledge derives almost entirely from the area's pottery. This predominance demands that we single out ceramics for special mention although the limits of this guide preclude any thorough survey of the subject. As a basic general reference and guide to the literature on ceramic technology for archaeological and analysis and classification students are referred to the manuals by Shepard (1956; see also Shepard, 1971), Colton (1953b), and Matson (1965).

There are several compelling reasons for archaeologists' great interest in this single artifactual category, the most obvious being simply that pottery survives. In the great majority of archaeological situations, only stone artifacts are more durable. Combined with this survival potential are other very attractive features for archaeological analysis. The variety of styles, techniques, and materials employed offers great opportunities for archaeological research. Finally, since pottery vessels were often broken (Foster, 1960), new ones were always having to be made—or acquired—and sherds were likely to be abundant and widely distributed through archaeological deposits.

Thus far, pottery studies have been overwhelmingly devoted to determining relative chronology. This emphasis has arisen largely because chronological control is the basic requirement for much of archaeological analysis and pottery is so useful an indicator of the passage of time. The seemingly disproportionate amount of archaeological literature devoted to ceramic chronology, however, should not be allowed to obscure the potential of pottery in other areas of archaeological interpretation. Continuity in ceramic style or tradition is commonly interpreted as one evidence of genetic continuity in populations and, conversely, a sudden change in style may indicate a shift in population. Similarities between the pottery of two cultures provide evidence of relationships and influences, sometimes of a very specific order. Intrusive (dissimilar) pottery is direct evidence of trade and other relations.

These are all common cultural interpretations deriving from ceramic studies.

There are, however, many less frequently exploited potentials of ceramic interpretation. Turner and Lofgren (1966), for example, try to estimate household size among the prehistoric Anasazi by comparing the capacities of individual serving bowls and cooking jars. An attempt to determine the social functions of different rooms through statistical analysis of sherds from the room floors is illustrated by Hill (1966) and Longacre (1964). Although it would be naive to assume that the potter's art necessarily mirrors political or social conditions, the freedom of expression that clay affords a potter undoubtedly holds many potentials not yet fully exploited by the archaeologist. Thus Deetz (1965) proposes that specific changes in Arikara social structure are reflected in changes in Arikara pottery; and regardless of how these conclusions are received, they suggest the possible scope of future exploitation of pottery.

Lest pottery be emphasized at the expense of other artifact categories or possibilities, however, a few cautionary notes may be in order. As Grahame Clark (1952: 205) observes:

> The significance of pottery for the understanding of prehistoric society can easily be overrated, though the variety in which it can be fashioned and its great durability, when compared with many other categories of material equipment, makes it peculiarly suitable for classification. It must always be remembered that pottery was only one of many substances used to make containers and that even when it had come into use it was not everywhere the most important of these.

And Shepard (1956: 353) writes:

> Anyone dealing with archaeological materials realizes that the near-indestructibility of potsherds gives a false impression of the importance of ceramics in the over-all picture of crafts and commerce. The circumstance makes it imperative to give due allowance for possible perishables such as foodstuffs, textiles, wooden objects, and feathers, and also to give the most careful attention to the less distinctive imperishables.

The point of these remarks is not to depreciate the value of pottery studies, but simply to emphasize that the importance of pottery should not lead to the neglect of other data or approaches. There is, of course, nothing in the study of any one aspect of a culture that precludes studying any other, and one of our basic aims is to understand the interrelations of the various aspects as fully as possible (Shepard, 1956: 334–335).

Ceramic sampling The general problems of archaeological sampling are considered in Chapter 15. At this point, we merely note that at some archaeological sites the enormous quantities of potsherds encountered in excavation present serious practical problems. As an example of how abundant pottery may be at an archaeological site, we cite the great ruin of Kaminaljuyu in the Guatemalan Highlands. Shook and Kidder (1952: 46), excavating an earthen mound 20 meters high, estimate that the structure contained the astonishing total of about 15 million potsherds. Borhegyi (1965: 13) suggests that these figures can be used to estimate the manufacture of about 50 million vessels over a period of about a thousand years at the site as a whole! Willey (1961) and Cowgill (1964) discuss the problems of dealing with large volumes of potsherds and offer some suggestions.

Egloff (1973) describes and illustrates a device used to determine the orifice radius of the original vessel from rim sherds; a count of the minimum number of vessels represented by a group of sherds can thus be obtained. In an earlier study, Krieger (in Newell and Krieger, 1949: 75 ff.) relates the problems of trying to obtain a vessel count in his analysis of 96,000 sherds from the Davis site in eastern Texas. The advantages of weighing sherds as well as counting them are discussed by Baumhoff and Heizer (1959), Solheim (1960), and Evans (1973).

Ceramic typology   The close attention typologists have given to pottery is evidenced in the various published handbooks of ceramic types (e.g., Hawley, 1936; Colton and Hargrave, 1937; Suhm, Krieger, and Jelks, 1954). A further refinement of ceramic typology, called the type-variety method, has been advocated by some archaeologists. In this approach, the ceramic variety is the basic unit of analysis, which, as ceramic knowledge increases, becomes synonymous with the type in the case of a single-variety type or becomes one of a number of varieties within a type. The pottery type is a particular class of pottery produced during a specific time interval within a specific region and expressed in one or several varieties (R. E. Smith and Gifford, 1965: 501). R. E. Smith, Willey, and Gifford (1960) provide a statement of the method, incorporating various changes from earlier papers by these and other authors.

Because of their time, space, and context dimensions, artifact types, especially pottery types, have become American archaeologists' most widely used tool for relative dating. According to Rowe (1959), however, these dimensions are far too elastic for adequate precision in research. He advocates the use of "significant features" of artifacts rather than the constellation of features or attributes subsumed in the type. Rowe believes that this approach in the study of Classical and Peruvian archaeological pottery demonstrates the possibility of defining time units on the order of twenty-five to thirty years, a considerably shorter period of time than spanned by the type. This concept is also incorporated into the type-variety method where such significant features or attributes are termed pottery modes and are studied apart from types and varieties (R. E. Smith and Gifford, 1965: 501).

To derive greater chronological precision from ceramic types than is afforded simply by noting their presence or absence, some archaeologists advocate using type frequencies. In this method the relative frequencies of various types are calculated for each of the successive levels of a stratigraphic column, which in turn allows the life-history of each type to be charted relative to the others. A pottery collection of unknown age but presumably representing a relatively brief interval of time is then fitted or dated to the stratigraphic column by matching the relative type frequencies in the undated collection against the master life-history chart. The classic example of the method is provided in the Ford and Willey (1949) study of the ceramic chronology of the Viru Valley, Peru. Bennyhoff (1952; see rejoinder by Ford, 1952) has been highly critical of the method. The seriation of surface collections on the basis of pottery type frequencies to construct a relative chronology is well discussed and illustrated by Tolstoy (1958) and Ford (1962).

Whallon (1972) has proposed yet another approach to pottery typology, based heavily on applied statistics. He describes the two main principles of his analysis: "hierarchy of importance of attributes which exist at any step in the classificatory procedure, and . . . a shifting of relevant criteria for type definition at any step" (p. 32).

A morphological classification scheme for ceramics has been proposed by Ericson and Stickel (1973). The major goal of their study is international standardization of ceramic data, thus allowing for cross-cultural comparisons of vessel morphology.

In closing, we remind the reader that artifacts are important in being clues to human action. How artifacts were made, used, valued, and disposed of and the part they played in the activity pattern of prehistoric people provide the key to their significance. Artifacts are among the most abundant documents of the unwritten, prehistoric past of humanity. Drawing every possible inference about them that can reasonably be drawn is one of the main duties of the archaeologist.

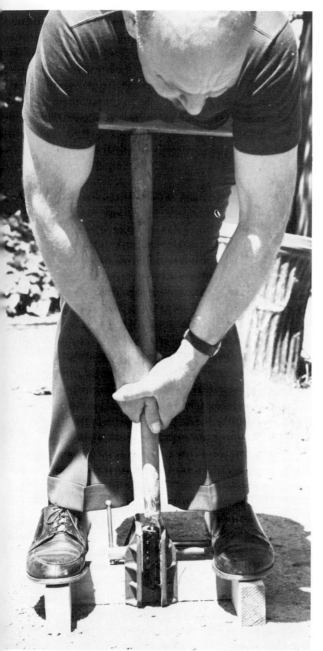

11-1. *Using a modern replica of a chest-punch described by Spanish writers, Don Crabtree successfully reproduces a Meso-american technique of striking blades from an obsidian core. Left: pressure is applied to a core held in a vise. Below: a detached blade falls from the core after the pressure is increased.* (Photographs courtesy of E. Prince.)

REPLICATION AND EXPERIMENT IN THE SERVICE OF ARCHAEOLOGY

11

The fact that for a long time Cubism has not been understood and that even today [ca. 1930] there are people who cannot see anything in it means nothing. I do not read English; an English book is a blank book to me. This does not mean that the English language does not exist. Why should I blame anyone but myself if I cannot understand what I know nothing about?

—PICASSO

 Because archaeologists deal so much with artifacts whose method of manufacture or manner of use is unknown, they often experiment to learn how an artifact may have been made or used (Ascher, 1961a; Coles, 1968; Hough, 1916; Proudfoot, 1965). The archaeologist who can successfully produce a flint implement by applying flaking techniques observed among living aboriginal craftsmen (cf. Coutier, 1929; Pond, 1930; Mewhinney, 1957; Knowles, 1944; Honea, 1965a, 1965b; Ellis, 1940; Bordes, 1947; Baden-Powell, 1949; Kragh, 1951; Neill, 1952; Crabtree, 1968, 1972) will gain a real appreciation for the prehistoric flint implements he or she recovers in the course of doing field work. That archaeologist will, for example, know more about how the flaked implements were made, realize that the flint had to be secured from some source, and thus begin to think about the flint tools in much the same way as did the people who originally made them. The flint tools, in other words, will be seen as things to be made and used rather than as objects for detached study.

Knowing the efficiency of prehistoric tools can impart a more realistic view of the ways in which prehistoric peoples used their cultural equipment to secure food, clothing, and shelter. The difficulty and time involved in drilling a hole through a stone, shaping a wooden implement with stone scrap-

225

ers, butchering a dead animal, or building a burial mound can be known for certain only by replicative experiments. Not every process, of course, can be replicated, but from the many that can, we often learn something useful (see Figs. 11-1 and 11-2). When the ecological (man-environment relationship) factor is added, human culture begins to come into focus (Sonnenfeld, 1962b; Helm, 1962; Hawley, 1944; Butzer, 1964).

On pages 228–32, we list, merely as a sample of a much larger number of experimental investigations, some of the kinds of efforts at replication in ar- by or in behalf of archaeologists. General discussions of experiment in archaeology can be found in Ascher (1961b), Coles (1968), Graham, Heizer, and Hester (1972), Hester and Heizer (1973b), Pfeiffer (1969), and Proudfoot (1967).

An important part of archaeological training is learning to determine with some confidence the functions of artifacts. The vast body of recorded data on tool use among primitive societies is the most common source of evidence for such identifications. This process of ethnographic analogy has been discussed most ably by Ascher (1961a). As modern technological civilization replaces more and more aboriginal (i. e., "primitive") techniques and tools, younger archaeologists will soon have to learn how simple or aboriginal societies operated from published accounts, motion picture records, and museum collections. Archaeologists must steep themselves as thoroughly as possible in the culture and working of primitive societies. They should read ethnographic and social anthropological accounts omnivorously; study (and, where possible, handle) museum collections of artifacts from simple societies; and absorb as much as possible from the several compendia or histories of technology (Daumas, 1962; Singer, Holmyard, and Hall, 1954; *Dictionnaire Archéologiques des Techniques*, 1963–64; Lucas, 1962).

In addition to the text sections in the works just cited, there are large numbers of illustrations of archaeological specimens as well as numerous reproductions of ancient technological activities taken from sculptures, wall paintings and reliefs, and painted ceramic designs. All in all, the beginner in archaeology could scarcely do better as a means of orienting herself or himself in the almost unlimited data of prehistoric material culture and technological methods than to read and absorb as much as possible of these encyclopedic surveys.

Finally, students of archaeology may find much satisfaction and insight in attempting to produce replicas of prehistoric objects. By going through the motions anciently employed they will not only gain a sympathetic understanding of manual processes, but begin to participate in that indefinable feeling of identification with the once-living people of the past.

11-2. *Top: unfired vessels in a pottery kiln that replicates a Romano-British type. Bottom: the kiln during firing. (After Mayes, 1961; photographs courtesy of Archaeometry, Cambridge University Press.)*

Subject	References
1. Cutting trees with stone axes	Evans, 1897: 162
	Iversen, 1956
	Jorgensen, 1953
	Leechman, 1950
	Morris, 1939: 137
	Nietsch, 1939: 70
	Klindt-Jensen, 1957: 38
	Aberg and Bowen, 1960: 146
	G. V. Smith, 1893
	Woodbury, 1954
2. Clearing forest with stone axes and planting grain (Denmark)	Proudfoot, 1965: 131
	Iversen, 1956
	Saraydar and Shimada, 1973
3. Incising with flint "gravers"	Nero, 1957
4. Notching atlatl dart and arrow foreshafts	Cosgrove, 1947: 52
	Sollberger, 1969
5. Woodworking with flint knife-scraper tools	Müller-Beck, 1965
	McEwen, 1946
	Moir, 1926
6. Cutting and scraping with chipped implements	Semenov, 1964
	Outwater, 1957
7. Cutting animal bones to evaluate evidence of cutting on archaeological specimens	Lartet, 1860
	Frison, 1973: 14, 85–86
8. Groove-and-splinter cutting of antler with flint burin	Clark and Thompson, 1954: 148
	Leakey, 1954: 140
9. Sculpting a stone statue by hammer-dressing	Heyerdahl, 1959
	Heyerdahl and Ferdon, 1961
10. Storing wheat in pits	Bowen and Wood, 1967
11. Skinning animals with Egyptian Paleolithic and Neolithic stone tools	Swauger and Wallace, 1964
12. Drilling stone	McGuire, 1892, 1896
	Rau, 1869, 1881
	Preston, 1973
	Steele, 1930
13. Drilling stone beads	Haury, 1931
14. Stone tool-blades for digging	Sonnenfeld, 1962a

Subject	References
15. Efficiency of animal scapula as a shovel	Curwen and Curwen, 1926 Pitt-Rivers, 1876 Jewell, 1963: 52
16. Efficiency of antler picks for chalk or flint digging	Pitt-Rivers, 1876 Jewell, 1963: 51–52
17. Hafting and using an ard	Aberg and Bowen, 1960: 144–147 Steensberg, 1964 Hansen, 1964: 118–121
18. Using a stone-bladed hoe	Sonnenfeld, 1962a
19. Straightening an arrowshaft	Cosner, 1951
20. Quarrying granite using plugs and heavy wedges	Clarke and Engelbach, 1930 Lucas and Harris, 1962: 499
21. Pre-heating flint for making flaked implements	Crabtree and Butler, 1964 Purdy and Brooks, 1971 Bordes, 1969 Sollberger and Hester, 1972
22. Natural production of stone objects sometimes interpreted as artifacts	Harner, 1956
23. Pottery-making, decoration, and firing	Griffin and Angell, 1935 Denninger and Ebinger, 1953 Bimson, 1956 MacIver, 1921 Noble, 1960 Thorneycroft, 1933 Hodges, 1962 Cornwall and Hodges, 1964 Mayes et al., 1961, 1962 Hansen, 1964: 115 Janzen, 1968: 42–43 Riegger, 1972
24. Egyptian pottery glazes	Lucas and Harris, 1962: 169–178
25. Roulette decoration of pottery	Quimby, 1949
26. Trepanning human skulls	Munro, 1897: 220
27. Building a Stone Age house	Hansen, 1962
28. Planned destruction of a mud-hut village	Gordon, 1953

Subject	References
29. Burning a model of a Plains earth lodge	C. S. Smith, 1953
30. Building a Danish Neolithic wattle-daub walled, turf-roofed house based upon archaeological data; splitting logs with wooden wedges; experimental burning of the house; making wooden utensils of Neolithic type	Hansen, 1964
31. Reconstructing (1956–58) Neolithic wattle-daub houses; time-study of their weather-induced decay; accidental burning of houses (1958); studying their features after incineration.	Hansen, 1961
32. Determining the pull of bows; flight distance and penetrating qualities of arrows	Pope, 1923
33. Reproducing a Neolithic bow from England	Grahame Clark, 1962, 1963
34. Weight range of chipped points on arrows	Evans, 1957
35. Cooking in earth ovens	Layard, 1922 O'Kelly, 1954
36. Stone-boiling meat	O'Kelly, 1954
37. Smelting copper ore	Coghlan, 1940
38. Smelting iron ore	Wynne and Tylecote, 1958
39. Hardening copper by hammering	Lucas and Harris, 1962: 213
40. Casting bronze in ancient molds	Voce, 1951
41. Using ancient harvesting implements	Steensberg, 1943 Curwen, 1930b, 1935 Harlan, 1967
42. Tropical milpa corn agriculture to determine yield and changes in soil fertility	Steggerda, 1941 Cowgill, 1961, 1962
43. Catching ocean fish with C-shaped shell fishhooks	Robinson, 1942

Subject	References
44. Making papyrus paper	Lucas and Harris, 1962: 138–139
45. Building and navigating a balsa sailing raft from South America to Polynesia	Heyerdahl, 1950
46. Transporting multi-ton stones	Heizer, 1966b Atkinson, 1956: 99–110 Heyerdahl, 1959: 132–134 Heyerdahl and Ferdon, 1961: 365–372, 511–512 Heyerdahl, 1952: 366–371
47. Erecting obelisks; Avebury and Stonehenge sarsens and lintels	Daniel, 1962b: 21 Engelbach, 1923 Stone, 1924 Daumas, 1962: 162 Thomsen, 1954
48. Carrying or dragging stones weighing one ton or more	Drucker, Heizer, and Squier 1959: 12h Lehmann, 1957 Roder, 1944–49
49. Building an Egyptian pyramid	Dunham, 1956 Petrie, 1930 Tellefsen, 1970
50. Time and labor required to build earth or rubble mounds, dig ditches, or build defense works	Ashbee and Cornwall, 1961 Jewell, 1963 Erasmus, 1965 U.N. Economic Commission, 1961 Wheeler, 1953, 1954
51. Cave painting to reproduce lines and surface color	Johnson, 1957
52. Acid-etching of shell	Haury, 1937c: 150–151
53. Extracting fibers with notched animal ribs or scapulae	Morris and Burgh, 1954: 61–62, 100
54. Egyptian oleo-resin wood varnishes	Lucas and Harris, 1962: 360–361
55. Efficiency of Bronze Age leather or metal-faced shields	Coles, 1962: 184–185
56. Ancient Egyptian methods for determining true North	Edwards, 1961: 255–261

Subject	References
57. Analyzing the musical range of Bronze Age trumpets	Coles, 1963
58. Burying human hair in different soils to determine preservation potential	Brothwell and Spearman, 1963: 429–430
59. Storage capabilities, and effects on grain, of basketry-lined beehive earth pits	Proudfoot, 1965: 132
60. Testing storage capability of Maya chultuns	Puleston, 1971
61. Rate of silting in ditches	Pitt-Rivers, 1898 Curwen, 1930a Pyddoke, 1961 Wheeler, 1954
62. Extracting animal from *Strombus gigas*	de Booy, 1915: 79–80
63. Using atlatl weights	Peets, 1960 Howard, 1974 Spencer, 1974
64. Making fluted points	Neill, 1952 Crabtree, 1966
65. Making serrated Hohokam points	Crabtree, 1973
66. Hardening wood by fire	Cosner, 1956 Evans, 1958
67. Cooking in animal skins	Ryder, 1966, 1969 Black, 1969
68. Using scraper planes for preparing *Agave* cordage	Hester and Heizer, 1972
69. Replicating petroglyphs	Sierts, 1968 Bock and Bock, 1972 Bard and Busby, 1974
70. Hafting stone saws	Hayden, 1957: 146
71. Making wooden pegs for rodent traps	Wylie, 1974
72. "Living archaeology"	Callahan, 1973, 1974

ARCHAEOLOGICAL FIELD PHOTOGRAPHY

12

There is something fascinating about science. One gets such wholesale returns of conjecture out of such a trifling investment of fact.

—MARK TWAIN

As I practised conjecture more, I learned to trust it less.

—SAMUEL JOHNSON

 We have stressed repeatedly that the full and accurate recording of an archaeological exploration is the *sine qua non* of archaeological analysis as well as the overriding moral and ethical responsibility of the excavator. Photography is of such primary importance in archaeological recording that it is discussed separately in this chapter.

The purpose and responsibility of archaeological field photography are to produce a comprehensive and precise pictorial record of an investigation. Since virtually never is it feasible to have a professional photographer at hand at all times during an archaeological exploration, responsibility for an adequate photographic record usually devolves upon the excavator. This is not entirely unfortunate. Unless accustomed to thinking in terms of scientific photography, the professional photographer will probably see subjects in terms of dramatic and artistic representation. The archaeologist must point out the significant details to be recorded and the manner in which they should be recorded for scientific purposes.

To adequately control photography as a tool of archaeological research, investigators must possess not merely the necessary technical equipment, but a thorough understanding, based on experience, of the potentials and limitations of field photography and equipment. They must have developed such a "feel" for both equipment and subjects that they need not "hope" for good results—but should be able to gauge results fairly accurately in advance.

The archaeologist must always bear in mind that photography is an interpretation of reality, not a means of duplicating reality. The photographic process reduces a three-dimensional subject to a two-dimensional depiction. In this process certain qualities will be enhanced while others are diminished. Furthermore, the properties of different films will result in various tonal alterations. Pictures may not lie, but photographic reproductions can be entirely misleading unless these points are borne in mind and adequately compensated for in the photographing.

SOME BASIC ELEMENTS OF PHOTOGRAPHY

Although many students have a working knowledge of fundamental photography, it may be helpful to review here some of the basic elements of photography as a preface to the remaining text of this chapter. It is not possible to pursue these fundamental aspects beyond the most elementary level, and students should familiarize themselves more fully with these and other points not discussed. The books by Cookson (1954), Feininger (1965), and Simmons (1969) all contribute useful details.

Aside from the qualities of the equipment used and similar considerations, successfully exposing (admitting the proper amount of light to) film depends upon the combination of film speed, diaphragm opening (aperture), and exposure time (shutter speed). The first refers to a film's measured response or sensitivity to light; the second and third define the control of the light to which the film is exposed, and they must be determined by the photographer.

In the United States film speed is expressed in terms of an ASA number. An ASA number of 25 or 40 describes a "slow" film, requiring relatively more light, and thus a longer exposure and/or a larger diaphragm opening. Slow films are generally fine-grained, grain being the tiny light-sensitive particles of metallic silver that form the negative. Grain is a basic quality of a film's definition, and finer grain contributes to higher definition, to more fine detail being distinguishable in a photograph. Fine-grain films are therefore of particular importance for scientific photography. Further, these films may be essential where negatives are small, since the process of magnification in enlargement will also increase the grain.

An ASA of 500 or above describes a "fast" film, requiring relatively less light, and thus a shorter exposure and/or smaller diaphragm opening. Since the faster films have a larger grain structure, their use in archaeological photography may be more restricted. Furthermore, fast films generally have somewhat lower contrast quality ("soft gradation") than the slower, fine-grained films ("hard gradation"). The gradation of black-and-white films, however, is also affected by exposure (underexposure increases contrast) and development (prolonging development increases contrast), other factors being equal. It has been concluded that the "best" film is the slowest film that is fast enough to do a perfect job (Feininger, 1965: 124).

Diaphragm opening and exposure time control the amount of light reaching the film and the duration of the film's exposure to the light. The diaphragm is a variable aperture built into the lens of the camera; it controls the amount of light reaching the film by varying the actual opening or aperture through which the light passes—the diaphragm itself. The sizes of the diaphragm openings are expressed in terms of "f-numbers" according to the following scale that reflects increasingly *smaller* openings: 1, 1.4, 2.8, 4, 5.6, 8, 11, 16, 22, 32, etc. Each larger f-number indicates a *decrease* of one half in light intensity. These diaphragm settings are commonly referred to as "f-stops," and the difference between successive settings is called a "full stop." An intermediate setting, for example f/3.5, is called a "half stop."

The duration of exposure at any of these settings is regulated by the shutter with its built-in timing device. Shutter speed is now measured for fractions of a second by the following series: 1/2, 1/4, 1/8, 1/15, 1/30, 1/60, 1/125, 1/250, 1/500, 1/1000, etc. Again, the difference between successive settings is termed a stop. Obviously, the amount of light reaching the film is a reciprocal result of shutter speed and diaphragm opening. When correct exposure data have been determined, an increase in one must be accompanied by a corresponding decrease (same number of stops) in the other. This strict reciprocity of speed to opening holds except for an extremely short or an extremely long exposure time. It should be noted also that when the aperture is changed to one with a number *twice* as high, a *four-fold* increase in exposure time is required rather than a two-fold one.

A light meter provides the objective basis for measuring light intensity in order to determine the correct exposure under existing light conditions. Set at the appropriate film speed, the meter will indicate the various combinations of shutter speed and diaphragm opening that may be used to obtain the correct exposure for the given film. Which combination of settings is selected will depend upon what is being photographed. Fast shutter speeds are employed to "capture" the split moment of action and will require correspondingly larger diaphragm openings (i.e., smaller f-numbers). With stationary subjects, slower shutter speeds can be used, resulting in smaller reciprocal diaphragm openings (i.e., larger f-numbers) to be set.

The f-numbers are used to describe the "speed" of a camera lens (or its "relative aperture," the measure of its transmission of light); its largest *effective* diameter is said to be its highest possible speed. Thus an f/2 lens is said to be a very "fast" lens while an f/8 lens is "slow." Because of certain optical properties, it is often not desirable to use the maximum speed of a lens. Smaller diaphragm openings provide greater depth of field, meaning greater sharpness of objects behind and forward of the object focused upon. For example, the large diaphragm opening of f/2 has very minimal depth of focus; in a photograph where the subject is close to the camera, objects not far behind or forward of the subject will be blurred at this setting. Depth of field increases, however, with increasing distance between subject and camera.

The size of the diaphragm opening also affects the sharpness of definition, and, generally, the faster the lens the greater the problem of controlling aberrations affecting sharpness. At full aperture, most lenses produce negatives with sharpness greatest in the center and decreasing toward the edges. Optimum sharpness is achieved with most lenses when the diaphragm is stopped down two to four stops beyond the maximum opening. Although depth of field continues to improve as the diaphragm is stopped down beyond this, sharpness remains about the same up to the last two or three stops, at which point it may begin to decline again. Finally, a slight improvement in contrast may be achieved with smaller aperture openings.

In archaeological photography, where subjects are stationary, it is almost always desirable to gain the increased depth of field and other advantages allowed by the smaller diaphragm settings. Since shutter speed must be slowed correspondingly, exposures will often have to be made on a tripod or the unsteadiness will be recorded by blurring in the photograph. Actually, it is desirable to use a steady tripod even at quite rapid shutter speeds. Professional photographers appear to agree that lack of sharpness in photographs results from camera movement or vibration more than any other single factor. There is usually a distinct and visible difference between hand-held and tripod-supported pictures even with quite high shutter speeds and careful holding.

EQUIPMENT

The perfect photographic equipment for any purpose would be technically versatile, simple to use, capable of making highest-quality photographs, and yet economical to buy and operate. Such ideal qualities do not combine naturally, but fairly adequate compromises can usually be made.

Discounting glass plates, the finest-quality photographs are obtained from large negative made from cut or sheet film. Since a large negative allows contact printing, the finished print suffers no loss in quality through enlargement. Contact printing further means the greatest freedom in film choice since film grain will not be increased through enlarging. Finally, the large negative allows maximum laboratory manipulation to enhance picture quality. Generally speaking, we are referring to a minimal negative size of 4 × 5 inches; smaller films will usually require enlargement.

Of the large cameras, the press cameras of the Graphic/Graflex type have been the most commonly used in archaeological field photography in the United States. Some 4 × 5 press cameras offer the optimum combination, among large cameras, of versatility, efficiency, and manageable size and consequently have been considered best suited to archaeological field work. Almost all of these cameras have been discontinued in recent years, however, and they are usually available today only as used equipment. The rather specialized, and very expensive, Lindhof line is a notable exception.

The view cameras, the other principal large-camera type, offer almost unparalleled photographic potentiality but are quite cumbersome and inefficient for general field use. Where there are no limits to photographic resources, however, it should be pointed out that the view cameras are the ultimate equipment for photographing archaeological architecture; their extreme adjustability allows perspective to be corrected and depth of field to be increased. With the decline of the press camera, the view camera has enjoyed more general use.

In contrast to the great advantages of their large negative size, the large cameras have several shortcomings for field work when compared to the best small cameras. Even in their best models, the large cameras are heavy, bulky, and somewhat cumbersome and inefficient to operate where time is at a premium and a large number of photographs are required. Film cost becomes a major operating expense where several hundred photographs may be desired. Processing expense, however, may be reduced slightly by the fact that contact printing will be done rather than enlarging. Greater film economy can be achieved by using a roll-film adapter and smaller film for routine record photographing, although the advantages of the large negatives will of course be lost. It should be mentioned also that in using the large cameras great attention must be given to depth of field; the longer lens focal length of these cameras greatly reduces the effective depth of field.

Among the smaller cameras used in field work, the twin-lens reflex cameras of the Rolleicord/Rolleiflex type have been very popular among archaeologists. In these cameras viewing is done from the top on a ground glass the same size as the actual picture made. The ground-glass image is reflected by a mirror from a view lens (the "twin lens") placed directly above the lens that actually exposes the film. The viewing lens is coupled to the lower lens so that focusing the ground-glass image also focuses the photographing lens. These cameras generally use 120-mm.-size roll film to make a 2¼-inch-square negative, so that enlargement is almost always required for illustration purposes. Because of the separate positions of the twin lenses and the consequent problem of parallax, these cameras are quite poorly suited for close-up work. Furthermore, they have very limited versatility in terms of interchangeable lenses and other accessories. If the 2¼-inch negative is desired, there are several very fine single-lens reflex cameras of this size offering great versatility and many advantages.

Aside from sub-miniature cameras that have few qualities to offer the archaeological photographer, the opposite extreme in negative size from the large cameras is offered by the numerous 35-mm. film cameras. Of these cameras only the high-quality single-lens reflex models offer enough advantages to make them serious competitors to the best of the large cameras. In the single-lens reflex cameras, viewing and focusing are done by means of mirrors and prisms through the actual lens exposing the film. Precise framing of the picture is, accordingly, quite accurate and in some models is absolutely so. This is always advantageous, but it is supremely so in close-up work where the single-lens reflex is precise, efficient, and very speedy in operation. Furthermore, this quality is retained in using the many interchangeable lenses available in the best models. Since 35-mm. film is commonly available in 36-exposure rolls—compared to the usual 12-exposure rolls or film packs for the other cameras discussed—it increases the speed and convenience of making a large number of exposures. The use of interchangeable backs on the best models also allows rapid shifting from one film type to another, as from color to black-and-white, an advantage shared by the film packs of the larger cameras.

The high-quality 35-mm., single-lens reflex camera offers great technical versatility, extreme mobility, very efficient and rapid operation, and great film economy. Its single but substantial disadvantage is the small negative size, usually 24 × 36-mm. To preserve maximum definition and clarity of detail with this negative size, it is necessary to control film grain as much as possible. With the great improvement in film quality during recent years, this is no longer so difficult as it once was. Maximum grain control can be obtained by using a very fine-grained film, small diaphragm openings, and fine-grain developing. This last is easily done in a home laboratory but is also available on request at any good-quality photographic plant. Although grain does not present the problems it once did in 35-mm. photography, it must be remembered that with a negative of this format a tiny particle of dust or a pin prick can mar a print. Naturally, enlarging should be done only with the highest-quality professional enlarging lens.

We have tried to summarize the most important advantages and disadvantages of the principal types of cameras that might be used in field work. No one of these cameras can be said to offer all the advantages that the archaeologist might desire; in the final analysis, the choice of field cameras depends upon which qualities are the most important for a particular project. Finally, we may point out that as *supplementary* camera equipment, the Polaroid Land camera can be very useful in an excavation project. Its instant prints of features can be glued into the field notebook at the time of excavation and recording, frequently facilitating and improving the written description. Although not desirable as final photographic recording, the Polaroid prints in the field notebook do provide a minimal record in the event that the primary record is lost.

If the camera equipment includes a 4 × 5 camera, it will probably not be necessary to include a Polaroid Land camera. Polaroid Land film holders are available to fit most 4 × 5 cameras and even some 2¼ × 2¼ cameras. Actually, such a combination is highly desirable since most Polaroid Land cameras are not at all versatile.

A good exposure meter is an essential item in the list of photographic equipment. A good-quality cadmium-sulphide meter is particularly recommended because of its great accuracy and remarkable range of sensitivity. Although the miniature versions of some of these meters are very handy—not to say of high quality—the larger models frequently have advantages offsetting the small increase in bulk. The scale, for example, may be easier to read accurately, allowing full opportunity to be taken of the meter's capabilities. Also, many of the larger models have a viewer or even a focusing device allowing the user to read precisely the light reflection from a particular object or small area. Since these meters are battery-activated, it is desirable to obtain a meter with a built-in means of testing battery strength. Although the battery is very long-lasting, it is a good idea to carry a spare; the minute size of the battery makes this no inconvenience. Finally, as these meters can be quite delicate, it is desirable to obtain a durable model for field work. A second, back-up meter is strongly recommended.

A flash unit can be extremely useful under special field conditions. Although somewhat expensive, the most efficient for field use are the compact electronic units. These eliminate the need for carrying flash bulbs and provide a far superior light source. Either the rechargeable cadmium-sulphide units or the C-cell battery units may be used in the field. The latter will probably be desirable for a long field season in an area without electricity since some models will allow 400 and more flashes from one set of C-cells. It should be noted that flash photography requires practical experience for its successful use for scientific purposes. As in the case of the other equipment, the student should experiment fully with the equipment under different lighting conditions before going into the field. A flash extension cord will be useful if the flash is to be used for side lighting.

The results of flash-illuminated photography are very difficult to predict precisely, particularly in cases such as side lighting used to emphasize relief. Furthermore, "hot spots" (reflections or glare) can appear when a shiny surface is photographed with flash. Reflecting natural sunlight into shaded or dark areas can often be an excellent solution to illumination problems. Suitable reflectors can easily be made by taping aluminum foil to Bristol board or some similar lightweight backing. The reflector's size will depend upon the amount of light needed and convenience in handling.

A tripod is essential for long exposures and may be used advantageously, as mentioned above, even with fairly rapid shutter speeds. Adequate attention is seldom given to the selection of tripods, but a carelessly selected tripod can cause many headaches in the field. Tripods must be sturdy; many are not. Careful attention should be given to the locking devices used on the extending legs; many locking mechanisms begin to jam, fail to hold securely, or simply are troublesome to use after prolonged field work. A universal or swivel-type head is usually very convenient, but one may be added to a tripod not so equipped; several models are available. An air-bulb shutter release should be used with the camera when it is mounted on the tripod. Alternatively but less conveniently, the delayed-action shutter-release mechanism present on some cameras can be set for a few seconds ahead to ensure that the camera will be motionless when the exposure is made.

The usefulness of other pieces of equipment will depend upon special circumstances and the preferences and habits of the photographer. In conclusion, it should be noted that although the purchase price must often determine the choice of equipment, good equipment carefully selected will provide so many advantages in the long run as to justify the greater investment many times over. The best way to save money on photographic equipment is not to buy lower-quality items, but to buy used ones. Purchased from a known and reputable dealer, quality equipment can often be obtained at a savings of as much as half of the original price. Lenses in particular do not wear out; unless scratched or otherwise damaged, many older lenses are superior to newer ones costing much more. Similarly, a 35-mm. camera equipped with an f/2.8 lens will be considerably cheaper than one that goes all the way to f/1.4, a lens speed that the archaeologist will seldom use in any case.

SOME ASPECTS OF FIELD PHOTOGRAPHY

During the excavation of a site certain photographs will have to be made without delay and perhaps with no choice of time of day or natural lighting conditions. Nothing can be done in these instances but to try to make the best of the circumstances, using one's ingenuity to overcome adverse conditions and to capitalize on whatever advantages may be present. Other photographs, however, can be made at any moment over a period of time. In these cases, the subject should be observed at different times of day to see when the lighting is most favorable and effective. When this is ascertained, the photograph should be made without further delay as needless waiting is frequently disastrous. It should be considered also that in a site to be excavated over a period of several months, the sun's shifting path may significantly affect the lighting of certain subjects at the site.

Where photographs are of extreme importance, make several exposures at different settings of the same view as a safety precaution. How much the settings should vary depends upon the latitude of the film. Color film has a restricted latitude and "safety" exposures should be made at one stop above and below the exposure meter's reading. Most black-and-white films have considerably greater latitude, and two stops' difference from the meter's reading is usually called for.

If 35-mm. photography is being used, film expense is a minor aspect of the total cost of the field work, and exceptionally full photographic recording is to be expected. No one has ever taken too many photographs. When developing is done, inexpensive proof sheets will serve as a guide, to be checked against the negative, of course, as to which views will be enlarged. In making color transparencies, it is worth bearing in mind that if duplicates are desired they are best shot in the field rather than having the laboratory duplicate them from an original. Color quality will be far superior and the cost will be less.

Great care must be given to both film and equipment while in the field. Heat and dampness are the principal sources of damage to film. A metal tin with a vacuum-push lid is a good film container so long as it is kept in the shade. In humid areas a desiccating agent such as silica gel should be kept in the tin and regularly checked for moisture absorption; combined with the slight vacuum effect, the air within the tin will be kept dry and slightly cooler than that outside so long as the tin is carefully kept in the shade. Color film is particularly subject to deterioration; Eastman Kodak Company advises that Kodak color films will keep for two months at temperatures up to 70 degrees Fahrenheit and six months up to 60 degrees.

It may be desirable to store film under refrigeration in a moisture-proof container. If film is so stored, it must be remembered that in order to prevent moisture from condensing upon the cold film surface, the film must be removed from refrigeration well in advance of its use to allow it to warm up before it can be removed from its container. When the exposed film is again stored, humidity should first be removed with a desiccating agent. In areas of extremely high temperature, it may very well be unwise to entrust the film to the local postal service.

Camera equipment should also be kept out of the sun except when making a photograph. Dust and dirt are the greatest sources of damage to the equipment, and they often foul delicate camera mechanisms unless carefully guarded against. Plastic bags are often useful to protect the camera and other equipment from this danger. Dust frequently settles on the camera lens during the photographing of excavations, and great care must be exercised in removing it. Optical glass is extremely soft and can be cleaned only with utmost care. Using a handkerchief to clean a lens may permanently scratch it. Only a camel's-hair brush, air bulb, photographic lens tissue, and lens-cleaning fluid should ever be employed.

General site views   Every effort should be made to obtain good overall views of the site at all stages of the investigation: before and after clearing of brush or vegetative cover, at the beginning of excavations and during all stages thereof, and at the conclusion of the work. The photographer should attempt to bring out the shape and height of the site in addition to any special features. Placing a person at various effective points for the photographs will frequently emphasize aspects of the site's configuration. The person serves as a convenient approximate scale and probably should be included in most or all views. Make certain that the figure does not detract from the central interest of the photograph—the view of the site. Have the person engage in some activity rather than facing blankly into the camera.* Hammond (1973) describes a useful giant scale for long-distance photography.

Views that bring out the relationship of the site to the various features of the adjoining landscape are frequently very useful. Make certain that the views are taken at a series of distances; carefully judge the most effective distances to emphasize the various features of the site's configuration and relationship to the countryside. Careful thinking out of each photographic view is the only way of obtaining a useful photographic record.

A wide-angle lens is often very useful for panoramic views of the site. A moderate length wide-angle lens is much to be preferred. Lenses taking in an extremely wide view may distort perspective so drastically that the photographs will have little value. Simply climbing a tree may give an excellent perspective while special devices such as balloons (Guy, 1932; Bascom, 1941; Whittlesey, 1967), tripod ladders (Merrill, 1941a, 1941b; Piggott and Murray, 1966), the "Swedish turret" (Straffin, 1971), and poles (Schwarz, 1964) have been valuable in making photographs from varying heights above the ground. Although the excavator rarely has the opportunity of making aerial photographs of the site, the remains may show up on existing aerial photographs, and these may be useful as part of the site records as well as for publication purposes. Chapter 3 above lists several series of aerial photographs covering most of the United States.

---

*The following quotation dealing with the use of human scales in photographing archaeological monuments is by Maxine Du Camp, and was recorded during his travels with Gustave Flaubert in Egypt in 1850 (see F. Steegmuller, *Flaubert in Egypt: A Sensibility on Tour,* Little, Brown and Company, 1972; by permission of Little, Brown and Company, Boston):

> Every time I visited a monument I had my photographic apparatus carried along and took with me one of my sailors, Hadji Ismael . . . whom I had climb up onto the ruins which I wanted to photograph. In this way, I was always able to include a uniform scale or proportions. The great difficulty was to get Hadji Ismael to stand perfectly motionless while I performed my operations, and I finally succeeded by means of a trick whose success will convey the depth of the naivete of these poor Arabs. I told him that the brass tube of the lens jutting from the camera was a cannon, which would vomit a hail of shot if he had the misfortune to move—a story which immobilized him completely, as can be seen from my plates.

Features and burials Photographing smaller features and burials usually involves making moderate close-ups, at a distance of ten feet or less. In such photographs it is usually desirable to have as much as possible of the picture in clear focus and hence particular attention must be paid to the depth of field. Usually it is effective to focus upon an important central item and use a small diaphragm opening to achieve maximum depth of field from this point. The range of sharp focus can be checked by using the depth-of-field scale present on most cameras, and any necessary adjustments can then be made.

Various accessories are usually required in these pictures. These should include a northward pointing arrow, a scale (for example, a six-inch ruler painted black and white in alternate inches), and a feature or burial number with the site designation. For the last a small blackboard or other sign can be used. These accessories must be arranged so as not to distract from the main center of interest and yet be legible in the picture. Care should be taken to see that the sign board is relatively parallel to the plane of the film. It is essential that the scale be parallel to the film plane or it will be foreshortened and useless; it should also be placed near the main object of the picture and in the same plane as this object.

Photographs must show clearly the exact relationship of artifacts to the feature or burial. Care should be taken to minimize distortion of perspective in the photographing; views from directly above are most satisfactory in this respect, but they may be difficult to make. The use of high tripods, ladders, or other devices may be called for (Merrill, 1941a, 1941b; Straffin, 1971; Schwarz, 1964). In other general views it will usually be advisable to have the film plane parallel to the longest dimension of the burial or feature. Detailed close-ups of important aspects of the burial or feature are also frequently of great value.

Burial photographs on black-and-white film are often best made in shade under a supported tarpaulin, or on overcast days, since the contrast between shade and lighted areas under bright sunlight may be too great. For features partially in open sunlight and partially in shade, it frequently will be desirable to expose for the sunlit area, using flash to fill in the shaded portion.

Photogrammetric recording of archaeological excavations has not been widely employed in the past, but it will undoubtedly become a standard procedure in the future as more archaeologists become familiar with it. Long a standard procedure in map-making and other exacting jobs with similar problems of precise measurement, photogrammetry has made extraordinary advances in recent years in connection with problems of lunar mapping. Utilizing a precisely made stereo photographic pair of an archaeological feature, photogrammetry can measure the size and relationships of all visible objects more accurately than the tape in hand. Hallert (1971) describes the basic principles of photogrammetry and provides illustrations of some applications; Whittlesey (1966; cf. Schwarz, 1964) discusses its employment in the detailed measurement and recording of excavations at Sardis. McFadgen (1971) provides an exceptionally full account of a photogrammetric mapping method developed for use with a 35-mm. camera.

Excavation techniques   A series of photographs illustrating the various techniques used in excavating the site will often prove valuable for illustrations in the site report. Although excavation techniques will probably be apparent in the general views of the site, it is usually desirable to make special photographs to illustrate these techniques. Cole (1972) has suggested using time-lapse photography to document the process of excavating a site and to aid in laboratory "reconstruction" of site evidence.

Soil profiles   Photographic recording of soil profiles is a particularly important and especially difficult aspect of field photography. If color and texture differences between strata are difficult to distinguish with the eye, they may be even more difficult to bring out in photographs, while the cramped space of a trench may make photographing at the proper position difficult if not impossible. For purposes of greatest utility and scientific value, the camera should be centered on the profile with the film plane precisely parallel to the profile wall. For important profiles, it may be worthwhile enlarging the trench somewhat in order to secure an adequate photographic view.

Several techniques are available to bring out differences between strata and emphasize stratification, none entirely satisfactory. During excavation dust will settle on the profile so that scraping clean the profile is usually the first step. Slightly grooving the soil boundary between strata with the tip of a trowel is frequently effective, particularly when the sun is almost directly overhead so as to create a thin shadow in the groove. Utmost care must be exercised, however, only to groove *certain* lines of stratification. Frequently, color differences in strata will be more prominent when the whole profile is in the shade. If the strata are not too irregular, it may be desirable and practical to trace the stratum boundaries with a white string lightly pressed into the soil or held with staples. A slight dampening of the soil with a spray gun filled with water is sometimes quite effective in bringing out contrasts.

Other techniques depend on the special use of films and filters. In black-and-white photography various contrasts can be heightened by using various color filters. The effect of these filters can be gauged easily after a little practice by simply viewing through each filter and observing the contrast that results. In judging the effect it is important to concentrate solely upon the contrast produced and to disregard entirely the color effects produced. Usually, it will be desirable to try several filters and lighting angles in addition to making regular unfiltered photographs. Colored photographs should also be made, although the basic record must be preserved in black and white (Wood, 1945). In order to control color recording, it may be desirable to include a Kodak Color Correction Panel or Kodak Color Bar in the color photographs.

Infrared film can often be used to obtain greater contrast than can be secured with regular panchromatic film. Buettner-Janusch (1954), Brose (1964), and Gillio (1970) illustrate and discuss the use of infrared photography in recording soil profiles. Since experimentation is required in its use and the effects cannot be surely predicted, infrared photography must be viewed as a supplement to ordinary panchromatic recording. Detailed technical specifications for infrared film and instructions for its use are to be found in the current edition of the *Eastmen Kodak Infrared and Ultraviolet Data Book* available at larger photographic shops.

At the other end of the color spectrum, ultraviolet photography has also been used successfully to record soil profiles (Dorwin, 1967). In the same report, Dorwin describes the use of iodine gas to stain organic compounds in soil deposits.

Petroglyphs and pictographs   Petroglyphs are made by pecking shallow grooves into a stone surface. They usually appear clearest in photographs made when the light conditions produce shadows in the pecked grooves, which then contrast with the unmodified stone surface (see Fig. 12-1). When these lighting conditions are not obtainable naturally, side lighting by flash to "rake over" the surface of the stone may provide clear contrast (cf. Knight, 1966: 63). Colored filters, particularly red, can often be used to increase the contrast.

Chalk has often been used to outline or fill in the pecked grooves and thus further emphasizing the petroglyphs (see Fig. 6-6). Aluminum powder is an alternative (Swartz, 1963). The legend attached to the Petroglyph Record (see page 137) lists references to photographic and other techniques of petroglyph recording.

Pictographs are "rock paintings," and because of their fragile and perishable nature they require especially thorough recording. Unfortunately, since pictographs are often faded or faint in color, adequate photographic records may be very difficult to make. In black-and-white photography the pictograph will often show up better when the exposures are made in shaded light. Panchromatic film must be used; the old orthochromatic films were not sensitive to red, one of the more common colors found in pictographs. The use of color filters can often produce very much enhanced photographs. With panchromatic film a color is emphasized by a filter of its complementary color; thus a green filter would be used to bring out red (cf. Webster, 1962: Pl. V). Dampening pictographs with a water spray may also intensify the colors. The use of reflected ultraviolet light to bring out faded red ocher and

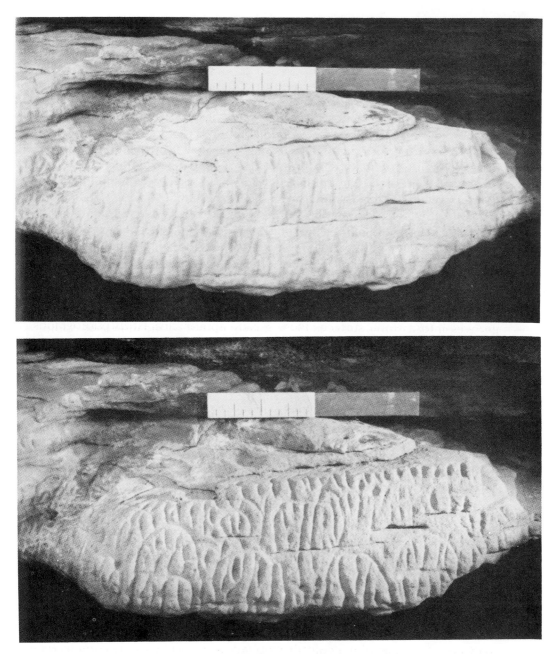

12-1. *Top: a badly eroded rock engraving photographed by normal daylight. Bottom: the same rock photographed under light provided by an obliquely held flashlight. (From Webster, 1962; Pl. III.)*

palimpsests of red and white ochers has been described by Webster (1966).

Color photographs or transparencies should also be made of rock paintings. Care should be given to proper lighting conditions in order to minimize color distortion, and a Kodak Color Bar should be employed as a color standard. Sun reflectors are often effective. Sketches should also be made, and watercolor copies are desirable. Gebhard (1960) discusses methods of pictograph recording, and the references cited in the legend of the Petroglyph Record (see page 137) should also be consulted.

As in similar photographic recording, the film plane should be kept as nearly parallel as possible to that of the carved or painted surface. A small scale and identifying legend board are essential accessories in petroglyph and pictograph photographs.

Photographic recording with grids   In photographically recording features, burials, profiles, etc., it may be desirable to set up a coordinate grid system with string or wire in order to provide greater precision of spatial control in the photographs. Portable grids, wires, or strings stretched over a frame are time-saving when this type of recording is done. Again, particular care must be taken to align the film plane parallel to that of the grid; otherwise such recording is pointless. Merrill (1941a, 1941b) describes and illustrates photography with coordinate grid systems; see also Cole and Deuel (1937: 271) and Chapter 6 of this guide.

ARTIFACT AND SPECIMEN PHOTOGRAPHY

The photography of artifacts and excavated specimens, usually for purposes of publication, is a considerably different task from field photography. Laboratory conditions can be controlled precisely, and various photographic devices can be used to facilitate the job. Furthermore, it is usually possible to obtain advice and consultation from professional photographers, if not their services. In the absence of the latter, the excellent handbook by Blaker (1965) should be carefully studied. Useful suggestions on general aspects of artifact photography are made by Dodge (1968) and Dafoe (1969). Problems in photographing obsidian and other translucent and glossy silicate specimens are discussed by Weide and Webster (1967), Wilkinson (1968), and Lutz and Slaby (1972). Kelemen (1946) ably discusses additional problems encountered in photographing archaeological art objects. A method of reversing intaglio to relief and increasing the relief, contrast, and detail of a cut surface is described by Erskine (1965) for use in photographing archaeological seals. Where attempts are made to photograph artifacts in the field, local circumstances and resources will dictate the extent to which these laboratory methods can be used.

FILM RECORDS AND FILES

It is essential to keep a field record of the photographs taken. Rolls or packs should be assigned a number as they are loaded into the camera and each shot must be recorded individually. The photographic field record should note, for each photograph, the subject and any special feature or reason motivating the view. The viewing direction is also frequently important as part of the record.

When the film is commercially processed, it should be specified that the rolls are not to be cut unless the film itself carries a serial numbering. If the rolls are cut, they must be kept separated until properly catalogued and filed. Film packs in particular must be kept separated since the negatives of each pack are precut.

Great attention must be paid to the safe and efficient filing of the photographic records. Various filing systems for negatives, transparencies, and photographs are available from the Negafile Company, Furlong, Pennsylvania, from whom a catalog may be obtained.

CLASSIFICATION OF ARCHAEOLOGICAL CULTURES

13

Our scientific men are rather too fond of details. They count out to us the whole consistency of earth in separate lots, and are so happy as to have a separate name for every lot. That is argilaceous earth; that is quartz; that is this, and this is that. But what am I the better if I am ever so perfect in all these names?

—GOETHE, In a conversation with Falk

Change is not in itself a value, nor is it an automatic producer of values. . . . As for the notion that technological innovations have been the main source of all human development, this is a disreputable anthropological fable.

—LEWIS MUMFORD, *The Myth of the Machine*

The classification of archaeological cultures is not a field procedure but results from the analysis and interpretation of the data gathered in archaeological field explorations. In fact, cultural classification is based upon the classifications worked out for the artifacts recovered and for the patterns of behavior discovered. It follows, then, that the reliability of cultural classification will depend to a considerable degree upon the reliability and appropriateness of the classification of archaeological materials into types characteristic and diagnostic of cultures.

Although cultural classification is not a field technique, field explorations are most successful when cultural units can be recognized during the course of the investigations, thereby allowing a better formulation of the exploration program. It will therefore be useful to briefly survey some of the terminology and concepts that have been used in classifying cultures, concentrating more on practice than on theory. A recent painstaking analysis of the problem of cultural classification can be found in Rouse (1972: 61–101); earlier but still useful discussions of the general problem of cultural classification and the synthesis of culture history can be found in Brew (1946: 32–66), Taylor (1948: 132–151), MacWhite (1956), and Rouse (1965). Dunnell

(1971) has contributed a detailed consideration of the general problem of systematics.

Effectively classifying excavated archaeological materials into cultures is often a difficult task, as witnessed by the variety of classificatory schemes devised and the constant revisions undergone by already established archaeological cultures and their sequences. Since the people studied are by definition extinct, it is impossible to discover where they drew the boundaries between themselves and their neighbors. Generally, one cannot be certain even of the language spoken, much less the dialect, usually an important criterion in the anthropological classification of peoples (Naroll, 1964). Anthropologists' classifications of living peoples, however, do not always accord with the people's own views on this matter, since anthropologists are often considering them from very different and expanded perspectives; and, in fact, anthropologists do not even agree among themselves on recognizing and defining basic "culture-bearing units" (cf. Naroll, 1964, and accompanying comments; see also Kroeber, 1962).

Although archaeologists study the remains left by extinct peoples, they are not primarily concerned with the remains themselves unless they are strictly technicians. The remains may indeed be of great intrinsic interest and fully worthy of study in their own right, as in the case of works of art. But archaeologists, or prehistorians as some scholars (Rouse, 1972: 6-11; Dunnell, 1971: 2-3) call them to distinguish them from technicians, are concerned with the remains as tools to use in reconstructing the life patterns of the peoples who produced them. Further, a number of archaeologists, often styling themselves as "new archaeologists," largely eschew the reconstruction of content in ancient cultures in order to study social processes that they believe can be discovered in, or postulated from, the archaeological record; their interests are thus more allied to social anthropology and sociology than to traditional and classical archaeologies with their varying degrees of humanistic orientation.

So many attempts have been made by anthropologists to define culture that some years ago an entire monograph was devoted to a survey of these definitions (Kroeber and Kluckhohn, 1952). The concept of an archaeological culture has also been defined in a great variety of ways and to suit many differing purposes. As we are not here concerned with systematics theory (cf. Dunnell, 1971), Childe's definition (1950: 2) will satisfy our needs: "an assemblage of artifacts that recur repeatedly associated together in dwellings of the same kind and with burials of the same rite. The arbitrary peculiarities of the implements, weapons, ornaments, houses, burial rites and ritual objects are assumed to be the concrete expressions of the common social traditions that bind together a people." The "arbitrary peculiarities" of the artifacts comprise the *cultural types* from which the archaeologist defines each culture.

It hardly seems necessary to emphasize that any archaeological reconstruction of a prehistoric culture will always be incomplete in contrast to a definitive ethnographic study since the archaeologists' data are limited to material objects, usually only the nonperishable artifacts, and the relations that may be inferred between these objects. Further, archaeological cultures are often, initially at least, based upon excavations at a single site, and it is seldom that a single community can embody the whole of its cultural tradition. Though many inferences can be made as to some of the intangibles that were associated with the objects found in an archaeological site, there will always remain a very large portion of past human behavior and accomplishment that cannot be reconstructed for any specific archaeological culture. Unfortunately, these elusive aspects of past culture generally include some of the most significant ones from the humanistic standpoint: philosophy, religion, song, dance, and the other more fragile advanced achievements of the human mind.

Systematic attempts to organize assemblages of prehistoric artifacts into useful and meaningful units have proceeded at varying rates and along remarkably different lines in various parts of the world. Distinctive assemblages and complexes, ranging in completeness from a few stone implements to entire cities, have been assigned names as cultures. These names have often been derived from the name of the site or locality where the complex was first recognized or is best recognized, but cultures have also been named after the numbered strata within a site, historic ethnic or linguistic groups (often falsely identified), mythological predecessors, subsistence patterns, characteristic artifacts or customs, etc. Early antiquarians apparently attributed artifacts to their immediate predecessors, whether real or imaginary, usually not appreciating that most areas have been occupied by a variety of past peoples.

As the foundations of a discipline of archaeology gradually began to grow firmer in the nineteenth century, one of the earliest and most significant systems of classifications came into extensive use, although it had actually been anticipated by some writers as early as the first millennium B.C.: the three ages of stone, bronze, and iron, first proposed for Denmark and then widely disseminated after 1836. The system was purely temporal and at first avoided naming specific cultures. The inception and subsequent revisions of this basic Old World classification have been chronicled in detail by Daniel (1943, 1950). It is interesting to compare this Old World system to the Pecos Classification, a classic New World example of a local temporal system developed for the American Southwest a century later (Kidder, 1927; Brew, 1946: 34–40; and Rouse, 1962: 1–53, summarize the history of subsequent modification).

Using archaeological assemblages to define specific cultures or prehistoric peoples gradually began to develop into more systematic classifications toward the end of the nineteenth century, and investigators began to

be interested in the distribution of cultures in space as well as their placement in time. Finally, in both hemispheres various generalized classifications
of cultures and periods were worked out on the basis of the comparative
method, stratigraphy, seriation, and, more recently, independent dating techniques such as radiocarbon age measurement (cf. Daniel, 1943; Braidwood,
1946b; typical applications will be found in Childe, 1958; Ehrich, 1965; Martin,
Quimby, and Collier, 1947; and Ford and Willey, 1941). These analytical tools
were also used in the "direct-historical approach" (Steward, 1942) followed
in some areas; in this method the archaeologist began from the earliest historic period in a region and worked from the cultural group or groups of that
period backward in time, defining a succession of cultural "periods" or
"phases" (Strong, 1935; Heizer, 1941c). This direct-historical method is thus
as much a chronological approach to the archaeology of an area as it is a
study of cultural classification. An important aspect of culture classification
problems was investigated by a 1955 seminar that defined eight types of
culture contact situation (Wauchope, 1956: 1–30).

Very early cultural remains (Paleolithic, Early Man or Paleo-Indian)
have always posed a distinct problem because of their very limited range of
artifact classes. Recent work has had considerable success in the definition
and chronological placement of stone-working "industries" or "traditions"
in the Old World (Bordaz, 1970; Bordes, 1968; Braidwood, 1967: 30–80; J. D.
Clark, 1970: 46–186; Grahame Clark, 1967; Howell, 1970; Oakley, 1965), and
of projectile point "complexes" in the New World (Haynes, 1964, 1969; Mac-
Neish, 1973; Shutler, 1971; Wormington, 1957; see Wheat, 1972, for an outstanding reconstruction of a Paleo-Indian kill site; note remarks of Rouse,
1960: 320, on "Folsom culture"); but the very broad geographical distribution
and lengthy chronological duration of many of these units raise considerable
doubt about the homogeneity and persistence of the cultures involved. Similarly, a very considerable controversy has raged over identifying the earliest
or initial New World occupations in the absence of universally acceptable
implements (Graham and Heizer, 1967; Martin, 1973).

For a number of years many New World archaeologists devoted much
attention to fairly elaborate classificatory systems that incorporated the distribution of cultures in time and space. For example, Gladwin and Gladwin
(1934) presented a "family-tree" classification system for the Southwestern
cultures that sought to illustrate temporal changes in the cultures of the different areas. The fundamental unit was the *phase,* comparable to Childe's
definition of a culture given above. Related phases were grouped together
as *branches,* similar branches composed a *stem,* and related stems formed a
root. The Gladwins recognized four roots, which, as subsequently modified
by Colton (1939), became Anasazi, Hohokam, Mogollon, and Patayan. Under
the influence of the McKern classification (1934, 1939), Colton also added
the term *component,* the expression of a certain phase at a single site, and

changed the term *phase* to *focus*. The Gladwin system was severely criticized for its genetic implications as well as for its failure to reflect relationships between contemporaneous phases in different "trees" (Brew, 1946: 41, 42, 47; Ford, 1962: 11–13; Reed, 1940, discuss Colton's modifications). Tello (1942) proposed for Peru a system using similar terminology—a system of geographic areas correlated with basic cultures or *trees* divided into *branches*—but extreme adherence to organic analogy and lack of actual stratigraphic support precluded any following for his classification.

The Midwestern Taxonomic Method, or McKern System, mentioned above, was presented by W. C. McKern (1934, 1939) and was widely used both in its original form and subsequently in modified versions in the Midwest and in the eastern United States. Griffin (1943: 327–341) has provided an excellent historical summary and methodological analysis of this important classificatory system (cf. Steward, 1944; Guthe, 1952: 9–11; Brew, 1946: 51–52; Rouse, 1972: 73–76). The basic unit is the *focus*, a complex of significant cultural traits, or "determinants," which recurs repeatedly in similar form at several sites. The expression of a specific focus at a single site is termed a *component*. Related foci are grouped into *aspects*, similar aspects determine a *phase*, and like phases constitute a *pattern*. Examples of the latter are the Archaic, Woodland, and Mississippi Patterns. The system ignores time, as McKern intended, for when he was developing the classification, chronologies were almost totally lacking from the regions in question. However, since the basic unit, the focus, was made up of components recognized from definite points in space (sites), a spatial dimension was inherent in the system from the beginning. An example of a spatial study without time dimensions is Drucker's (1943a: 123–128) areal analysis in terms of aspects for the northern Northwest Coast, where temporal relationships were also largely unknown. Soon, with the development of rudimentary chronological controls, most archaeologists began to use the McKern classification, or at least its basic units, for temporal studies as well (cf. Ritchie, 1944; Krieger, 1946; Griffin, 1952). Disagreement on the definition of phases in the McKern sense led most classifiers to drop this conceptual unit, and in practice only foci and aspects continued in wide usage.

In more recent years the problems of archaeological unit concepts have received thoughtful consideration by Willey and Phillips (1958) in an interesting study of method and theory in American archaeology. These authors proposed four spatial divisions: the *site* (a single unit of settlement, the minimal operational unit of geographic space), the *locality* (a district occupied by a single community or local group), the *region* (comparable in a general way to the territory held by an ethnographic tribe or society), and the *area* (equivalent to the culture area of ethnography).

They further define two basic units of content, the *component* (synonymous with McKern's component) and the *phase* (roughly equivalent to the common use, but not to the original definition, of McKern's *focus;* cf. Olson, 1962). They define a phase as "an archaeological unit possessing traits sufficiently characteristic to distinguish it from other units similarly conceived, whether of the same or other cultures or civilizations, spatially limited to the order of magnitude of a locality or region and chronologically limited to a relatively brief interval of time" (*ibid.,* p. 22).

To deal with cultural configurations within or beyond an area and over longer periods than a phase, these authors suggest two large-scale unit concepts, the *horizon* and the *tradition.* A horizon is defined as "a primarily spatial continuity represented by cultural traits and assemblages whose nature and mode of occurrence permit the assumption of a broad and rapid spread" (*ibid.,* p. 33). Horizons, or "horizon styles," are of value to synchronize sequences of culture units from area to area; thus archaeological units linked by a horizon style are assumed to be approximately contemporaneous, since by definition the spread is rapid with relatively little time lag from its appearance in one area to another. Horizon styles are usually distinguished by design motifs and specific artifact forms, sometimes termed "horizon markers," which are often thought to have a religious significance; many horizon markers are believed to have spread as parts of religious cults (Rouse, 1972: 130; cf. Willey, 1948).

In contrast to the horizontal distribution of horizon styles, Willey and Phillips (1958: 37) define an archaeological tradition as "a (primarily) temporal continuity represented by persistent configurations in single technologies or other systems of related forms." This definition of *tradition* is much narrower than its common usage to refer to the long-term cultural continuum constituted by the successive phases of a single culture's development (cf. Caldwell, 1958; Willey, 1966: 4–5).

A related concept, *area co-tradition,* in which tradition is defined even more broadly, was first proposed by Bennett (1948: 1–7) to characterize a culture area with time depth in which a series of cultural traditions (here, entire cultures with time depth) have interacted over a long period of time. Martin and Rinaldo (1951) have sought to apply the concept to the American Southwest, and other authors have occasionally used the term in other areas whose culture history meets the requirements of the definition. The concept has been critically explored at some length by Rouse (1954, 1957). Although Willey and Phillips (1958: 35–36, 39–40) did not incorporate the notion in the scheme of units, they did adopt Kroeber's concept of *climax* with respect both to horizon and tradition ("the type or types of maximum intensity and individuality of an archaeological horizon or tradition") as well as in whole cultural terms ("the phase or phases of maximum intensity and individuality of a culture or civilization").

As noted by Willey and Sabloff (1974: 176), a concept that partakes of some of the properties of both the tradition and the horizon is the *interaction sphere* proposed by Caldwell (1964). This term refers not to the interactions of individuals within a society, but to the regional interactions of a series of separate societies "resulting in what appears to be a distinctive set of phenomena." Thus a series of regional cultures are linked by a common participation in some elements of culture but not in others. The sharing of mortuary ritual and paraphernalia among otherwise distinct cultures may constitute an interaction sphere. Caldwell (1964: 135–136) believes that inter-action spheres are associated with increased rates of innovation; and further that "the interactions among separate societies, providing both cultural dif-ferences and exchange of experience, are . . . the primary opportunities for those vast results of innovation we call civilization."

During most of prehistory, people were fairly simply and homogeneous in culture. By late prehistoric times, however, some peoples had reached the culturally complex state we now describe as civilization, and Rouse (1972: 94–96) has proposed special classificatory concepts to deal with this situation. Although constituents of the same civilization, a farming peasantry and an urban elite will obviously be characterized by differing archaeological as-semblages; Rouse suggests speaking of *co-peoples* possessing *co-cultures* to describe this more complex cultural development. A civilization, therefore, is composed of two or more co-cultures.

An approach toward broad archaeological synthesis that has interested many archaeologists has been the formulation of "cultural-historical" or "his-torical-developmental" classifications in terms of eras, epochs, or stages. The general concept of stages has long been used in various forms, appearing in the Danish three ages; the Proto-literate, Early Dynastic, etc. of the Near East; the Preclassic (Formative), Classic, and Postclassic of Mesoamerica; and even to a certain extent in the Pecos Classification of the southwestern United States, to cite a few examples. Beginning in the late 1940's, however, a myriad of integrated functional systems proposed to define trait complexes shared by groups of cultures on the same developmental level. The nomenclatures and characteristics of the stages are quite variable. Strong (1948: Table 4) defined the following "epochs" for Peru: Pre-agricultural, Developmental, Formative, Florescent, Fusion, Imperial, and Colonial. Bennett and Bird (1949: Fig. 19) make the followng "time divisions" for the same Peruvian cultures: Hunters, Early Farmers, Cultists, Experimenters, Master Craftsmen, Expan-sionists, City Builders, Imperialists, and Conquest (cf. Bushnell, 1956; Kidder, 1964). Two variant systems for American high cultures and (by Armillas) for Mesoamerica will be found in Bennett (1948: 103–104, 105–111). Steward (1949) defined nine "eras" for cradles of civilization in the Old and New Worlds.

Perhaps the most sophisticated presentation of such developmental schemes is to be found in Willey and Phillips (1958a, revision of Willey and Phillips, 1955; revised still again in Willey, 1966: 476–478) where all of New

World cultural history is organized in terms of five stages: (1) Lithic (Paleo-Indian and other Early Man beginnings in the Americas); (2) Archaic (Post-Pleistocene hunting-collecting adaptations); (3) Formative (the village agricultural threshold and/or sedentary life); (4) Classic (beginnings of urban development); and (5) Postclassic (the imperialistic states). (For further reference to the history of culture stage formulations in American archaeology, see Willey and Sabloff, 1974: 117.) Willey and Phillips (1955: 725–727; 1958: 61–72) cite other examples of developmental classifications as well (see also Steward *et al.*, 1955; Adams, 1956; Wauchope, 1950; Borhegyi, 1956; Caldwell, 1958; Hester, 1962). One variant classification distinguishes seven primary community patterns and three nomadic variations, arranged in a developmental sequence and correlated with the total culture (Wauchope, 1956: 129–157).

Some of these developmental schemes were received with considerable enthusiasm as well as extreme criticism at their introduction, but none of them appears to be much used today. Most of the schemes were based upon unproved notions of cultural evolution, and have turned out to be premature when regional sequences and their chronologies were better understood. In Mesoamerica, for instance, although the developmental stage labels continue to be widely used, few scholars now view the terms as anything more than convenient tags for specific periods or units of time defined by other means. Willey (1966), in the most ambitious effort yet undertaken to synthesize New World prehistory, has organized his material largely in terms of major cultural traditions although his concluding summary uses both developmental stages and chronological periods.

Rowe (1962) has suggested that developmental schemes reflect early steps in archaeological interpretation where one sequence is reasonably well understood and an effort is made to understand the history of neighboring but less well-known regions in its terms. He further makes a strong case for the use of chronological periods (units of contemporaneity) rather than stages (units of similarity) for archaeological synthesis (cf. Daniel, 1943). It is absolutely essential that periods and stages be clearly distinguished; they have often been confused.

Aside from their synthesizing function, developmental stage schemes have reflected the desire of many of their creators to understand the processes of cultural development. The evolutionary bias of such schemes has been objectionable to many scholars, although most "new archaeologists" may be said to be enthusiastic evolutionists of one kind or another. Thus far, however, "new archaeologists" have devoted very little effort toward processual definitions of culture-unit concepts (Binford, 1965).

To conclude this limited survey of cultural classification in archaeology, a few brief practical points may be made. In defining cultures, whatever classificatory system is being followed, it is important to avoid mixed occupations where the remains of more than one culture are present. As Rouse (1972: 80–83) points out, cultural classification is best done from single-component sites or at least from sites where the multiple components are physically separated as by sterile deposits. Similarly, since archaeological assemblages often blend into each other along their spatial as well as their temporal dimensions, it is desirable to select assemblages from the central portion of a people's distribution, i.e., to select typical rather than transitional determinants, a procedure admittedly easier to specify than to follow in actual practice. Finally, with respect to naming new culture units, historic ethnic and linguistic terms should be firmly rejected in favor of neutral, noncommittal names; numerical labels are also to be avoided, since later research may revise the culture sequence.

CHRONOLOGICAL METHODS

14

*Time is like a river made up of the events which happen, and a violent stream;
for as soon as a thing has been seen, it is carried away, and another comes in
its place, and this will be carried away, too.*

—MARCUS AURELIUS

 As we have already pointed out, the study of the past concerns the sequence of human activity and events through time, and to understand the past we must know what prehistoric cultural evidence is earlier and what is later. Chronology, the temporal ordering of data, is not an end in itself, but the necessary prerequisite to understanding the sequence of events in prehistory.

We have set down some observations and references to pertinent literature on certain generally used techniques for determining chronology. Most methods are applicable only to certain types of sites or kinds of materials. Dry-cave or shelter sites, deposits formed in swampy areas, deeply buried finds of geologic antiquity, and pottery-producing sites will each offer certain possible avenues of determining their relative or absolute chronologic position. Techniques that yield exact dating in years are few, but many methods will reveal changes in the natural environment that can indirectly indicate the age of the associated cultural remains. The quantitative estimate of this age (i.e., in terms of years ago) will then depend upon the opinion of experts who are familiar with the causes for and the tempo of such environmental changes.

Movius (1949: 1445) says, "Prehistoric archaeology can be regarded as

259

ethnology projected backward in time until it is forced into intimate contact with the natural sciences, on which it must rely entirely both for chronological purposes and for establishing the environmental conditions that obtained during the particular stage of the [Quaternary] under consideration."

Zeuner (1958: v) defines geochronology as the "science which draws its methods from geology, botany, zoology, and physics. Its chief objective, the development of time scales in years which extend back into the distant past beyond the historical calendar, binds the different methods together . . . which . . . have been developed by specialists in their respective fields." The important point here is that prehistoric chronology is often the result of several scientific disciplines working in concert on a single problem. Notable examples of this cooperative approach are the reports on the Boylston Street fishweir (Johnson, 1942, 1949); Champe's (1946) report on Ash Hollow Cave; Cressman's (1942) report on the prehistory of the northern Great Basin, and the Tehuacan Valley project (Byers, 1967).

The reader is referred to the following publications for surveys of methods in archaeological and geological chronology: Aitken (1961), Allibone *et al.* (1970), Antevs (1953b), Bowen (1958), Brothwell and Higgs (1963: Section I), Butzer (1971), Griffin (1955), Heizer (1953), Michael and Ralph (1971a, 1971b), Michels (1973), Oakley (1964a, 1964b), Shapley (1953), Smiley (1955), Tilton and Hart (1963), and Zeuner (1958).

Refinements of old methods, new applications, and the development of new dating techniques, taken together with the large and growing literature on chronological methods, all help to make this subject one of the largest and most difficult in archaeology. Most archaeologists, especially beginners, will be content to know the basic operational principles of the most widely used methods and what kinds of prehistoric materials are used for dating. The dozen or so books dealing with chronological methods, the journal *Archaeometry*, and articles appearing from time to time in *Science, Nature, Antiquity,* and *American Antiquity* will help keep the student abreast of current research. Some universities (e.g., Pennsylvania, Arizona, UCLA, and UC Berkeley) are offering survey courses on chronological techniques. Despite all the means of determining sequence or absolute age, we are still very far from possessing adequate techniques for dating human beings' presence at particular spots and under special or unique conditions. Our inability to assign ages to so much of archaeology is a challenge for every archaeologist to help perfect, or invent, new methods of dating.

METHODS FOR ABSOLUTE (CHRONOMETRIC) CHRONOLOGY

A few methods will yield an exact dating for prehistoric remains. In the eastern

Mediterranean (Edwards, 1970; Sachs, 1970; Berger, 1970) and in Yucatan and Guatemala (Thompson, 1950; Caso, 1971), calendar systems were devised and dates were inscribed on stone monuments. These methods are employed for direct dating only locally, but the dated horizons can sometimes be extended into regions where such calendar systems were not used or known. Only rarely do artifacts such as pottery bear inscribed dates, and the archaeologist dealing with remains of ancient calendar-using peoples must proceed cautiously in assigning dates inscribed on monuments and buildings to the simpler items recovered. The absolute chronology for the Andean area based upon durations of Inca rulers' reigns is difficult to correlate with the materials recovered from refuse heaps; the same situation obtains in the Yucatan-Guatemala area, where dated monuments are of limited use in assigning dates to pottery types (R. Smith, 1955: 3–4, 105–108).

In ancient times many groups used time-reckoning systems for ritual or agricultural purposes. Most of these early systems have disappeared completely or are known to us by the merest chance. Thus Marshack (1964) and Vértes (1965) have proposed that certain Upper Paleolithic European peoples had devised accurate lunar calendars, probably for cultic purposes. Hawkins (1963, 1965a, 1965b) has proposed that the megalithic sites of Stonehenge in southern England and Callanish in Scotland were used to mark seasons and predict eclipses (see critical review by Atkinson, 1966). If true, this is evidence of complex and sophisticated calendrical systems among peoples who would ordinarily not have been thought to possess such knowledge. American Indians—both food-producers and collectors—are known to have used simple systems of time reckoning (Mallery, 1877; Cope, 1919; Dangel, 1928; Spier, 1955: 16–30), but these are of little significance to archaeology since no long-term record of their operation exists and they cannot be applied to archaeological data for dating purposes. The earliest astronomically based calendar in the New World may be that of the Olmecs of southeastern Mexico (Hatch, 1971). The famous Wyoming Medicine Wheel is interpreted as a device for determining the solstices, created by a Plains Indian tribe about 1700 A.D. (Eddy, 1974). Where permanent records are available of calendrical dates associated with archaeological materials, and where the calendar can be correlated with the Christian calendar, the age of archaeological sites can be determined. In the New World the best example is that of the Mayan calendar (Thompson, 1950; Satterthwaite, 1965), and efforts have been made to coordinate the Mayan dates with ceramic sequences in central Mexico (Thompson, 1941).

At times, pictorial records that were intended to be historical chronicles may be of aid to archaeology, as in the case of some of the surviving Mexican Codices (Bernal, 1960). An amusing case of documentary dating is the mummy purchased by A. Bandelier in 1894 from Caleta Vitor in Chile, which, when opened, was found to have folded against its chest a printed Proclamation of Indulgence signed by the Licentiate Pedro de Valarde and dated 1578 (Bird, 1943: 250).

Still another kind of recovery, which might be called quasi-documentary, is that of folklore and legend (Vansina, 1961; Lowie, 1915, 1917; Gifford, 1951). Several archaeologists have suggested that legendary accounts may derive from actual events in the past. It is impossible to generalize about this, but Daniel (1956) discusses twelve instances. Gifford (1951) investigated Fijian legends and archaeology and found probable cases of actual events in the legendary accounts. Jacobsen and Lloyd (1935: vii, 28–30) mention local Yezidi legends about the use and route of an aqueduct built by the Assyrian king Sennacherib, legends that have "survived the actual functioning of the [water-conducting] system for more than two thousand years."

Finally, we refer to historic or historical archaeology—the investigation of documented archaeological sites (Fontana, 1965; Cotter, 1968; Noël-Hume, 1969)—where (in North America at least) datable items of Caucasian manufacture found with aboriginal materials provide a means of determining the age of the deposit. For a discussion of the various situations in which cultures are definable as "historic," see Hole and Heizer (1973: 55–58) and Jones (1967).

Dendrochronology   Tree-ring dating, in which annual growth layers of trees are counted and matched with known environmental changes, can give the date when a tree was cut. Development of a reliable tree-ring chronology is attributable to the astronomer A. E. Douglass in about 1913. The potential of the method was appreciated much earlier, in the eighteenth and nineteenth centuries (Heizer, 1959: 53–58; Campbell, 1949; Neuman, 1962), but the technique was not developed until the time of Douglass' research. Only certain woods are reliable for dendrochronological analysis, and only well-preserved wood or sizable pieces of charcoal can be used. Champe (1946: 23–33) describes how the careful collecting of charcoal bits was richly rewarded by a dendrochronology established for his site. Charcoal may be saved by wrapping it carefully in Kleenex, toilet paper, or cotton. Experts disagree on the best ways to treat charcoal with preservatives, but the archaeologist who has recovered charred wood should nevertheless take immediate steps to secure expert advice (see Hall, 1939). Glock (1937) and Douglass (1929) have outlined the essential method of dendrochronology. Further published works of value are those of Douglass (1933), Gladwin (1940a, 1940b), Glock (1941), Hawley (1938, 1941), O'Bryan (1949), Schulman (1940, 1941), Stallings (1939), Bannister and Smiley (1955), Giddings (1962), Bell (1951), Fritts (1965), Ferguson (1970), and Bannister (1963).

Bannister (1963) summarizes the various attempts made in different parts of the world to develop tree-ring chronologies of significance to archaeological dating.

Bannister and Smiley (1955: 179) list the four basic requirements for dendrochronological research:

1. there must be trees that produce clearly defined annual rings as result of a definite growing season;
2. tree growth must be principally dependent upon one controlling factor;
3. there must have been an indigenous prehistoric population that made extensive use of wood;
4. the wood must be well enough preserved so that it still retains its cellular structure.

Lists of tree-ring dates for the American Southwest have been published by Agerter and Glock (1965), Smiley (1951), and Bannister et al. (1966a, 1966b).

The world's oldest living tree is not the redwood (Sequoia) but the bristle cone pine (Pinus aristata) that grows in the White Mountains in eastern California. A continuous sequence of annual rings going back slightly over 7,300 years has been recovered (Schulman, 1958). This sequence cannot be used for direct dating of archaeological materials because wood of the bristlecone pine has not been found directly associated with archaeological materials. At the same time, this tree, through its seventy-three-century year-by-year record of growth, has been extremely important in the calibration of the radiocarbon chronology (discussed below) with true time as represented in its annual rings.

Radiocarbon (Carbon 14) analysis There exists in the atmosphere a radioactive isotope of carbon (Carbon 14) that enters the life cycle of plants and animals after reacting with atmospheric oxygen to form carbon dioxide (CO_2). It is possible to determine the age of an organic sample by ascertaining its specific Carbon 14 activity. The physical nature of C-14 and the method for using it to date remains up to 50,000 years old are detailed in readily available publications. Excellent general treatments are by Aitken (1961: Chap. 6), Briggs and Weaver (1958), Broecker and Kulp (1956), Carr and Kulp (1955), Kulp (1952, 1953), Libby (1955, 1956, 1961, 1970a, 1970b), Michael and Ralph (1971a), Willis (1963), and Wise (1955). This radioactive carbon has a half-life of 5750 ± 40 years. At the Fifth Radiocarbon Dating Conference, Cambridge University, 1962, the half-life just cited was accepted as the best value presently obtainable, supplanting the formerly accepted half-life of 5570 ± 30 years. To convert dates calculated on the basis of the old figure, multiply them by 1.03 (Radiocarbon, Vol. 5, 1963).

Many laboratories have been established for dating. The following materials, listed in approximate order of preference, can be used for radiocarbon dating (see also Libby, 1955: 43ff.; Broecker and Kulp, 1956: 6): wood charcoal (or other charred organic material such as bone), well-preserved wood (as from a dry tomb, building, or cave), paper, parchment, grasses, cloth, peat, well-preserved antler or tusk, chemically unaltered shell (freshwater or marine species), guano or dung. Amounts of these materials necessary for securing a reliable date are given by the Teledyne Isotopes laboratory, Polach and Golson (1966), and Geochron Laboratories, Cambridge, Massachusetts, as follows: charcoal, 8 to 12 gr.; wood, 10 to 30 gr.; shell, 30 to 100 gr.; peat, 10 to 25 gr.; bone, 100–500 gr. Approximately 80 percent of the carbon in bone is contained in the collagen, which can be extracted for dating (Sinex and Faris, 1959; Taylor and Berger, 1967; Berger, Horney, and Libby, 1964). With regard to freshwater and marine mollusk shells, a difference of opinion exists as to their dating reliability. The reader is referred to papers by Weber and La Rocque (1963), Rubin and Taylor (1963), Keith and Anderson (1963, 1964), Berger, Taylor, and Libby (1966), Sellstedt, Engstrand, and Gejvall (1967), and Broecker (1964) for discussions of the problem.

Contamination of samples may cause errors in dating. Although wood charcoal is ordinarily assumed to be the best material for dating, it may become contaminated in various ways and have to be decontaminated. Furthermore, all that appears to be wood charcoal may not in fact be wood converted to elementary carbon by the action of fire. Cook (1964) has investigated several kinds of charcoal and charcoal-like samples from geological and archaeological deposits (cf. Haynes, 1966b).

A question that has been under investigation for the last two decades is the constancy of the rate of C-14 production by cosmic rays in the upper atmosphere. If the rate has been stable, all C-14 dates are consistent in being directly convertible from age in terms of elapsed years to age in terms of the Christian calendar. If the rate has varied, on the other hand, the C-14 and calendar chronometrics cannot be so simply correlated. Suess's work (1965) on long-term variations in atmospheric production of C-14 shows deviations over the last 2,000 years of as much as ±250 years when C-14 datings and known true ages of tree-ring dated wood are compared. Thus the true age of a wood sample may be 250 years greater or less than its C-14 age. Since C-14 age determinations ("dates") are always subject to some degree of analytical error (give as ±n years), the compounding of the inexactness of age determinations from several causes should at least be recognized as a fact. The actual number of elapsed years and the calculated age in radiocarbon years have been correlated by the radiocarbon dating of ring-wood of the bristlecone pine. Suess (1967, 1970), Switsur (1973), Renfrew and Clark (1974), Stuiver and Suess (1966), and Renfrew (1970) discuss the calibration of the radiocarbon calendar.

No single source records all of the radiocarbon dates of archaeological interest. The best single list is Jelinek's (1961), with about 3,000 dates; Movius' earlier Paleolithic date list (1960) is also important. Since 1959 the *American Journal of Science* has published annually a single volume, *Radiocarbon,* edited by R. F. Flint and E. S. Deevey. This volume lists dates determined by the several score of laboratories during the previous year. Also useful is the Radiocarbon Punch Card File published and distributed by Radiocarbon Dates Association, Inc., of Andover, Massachusetts, under the direction of Dr. Frederick Johnson (see Fig. 14-1). A comprehensive index of several thousand radiocarbon dates determined by 57 laboratories between 1950 and 1965 has been published by Deevey, Flint, and Rouse (1967). Useful bibliographies of earlier date lists have been published by Levi (1955), Griffin (1955: 141–147), and Wise (1955: 176).

Evaluating the accuracy of radiocarbon dates is a complex matter, and the reader is referred to Libby (1963), Barker (1970), Waterbolk (1971), and Spaulding (1958) for discussions. Not all radiocarbon dates are accurate within the stated variation. Errors may occur at the time of collection or during laboratory analysis mistakes or because of incorrect interpretations by archaeologists. Good discussions of these difficulties have been provided by Meighan (1956) and Stuckenrath (1965).

All materials known or thought to be suitable for radiocarbon analysis should be collected in screw-top glass jars, labeled, and stored until needed. The samples must not be contaminated by mold (wet specimens should be *thoroughly* dried before bottling) or any other organic material of more recent derivation. Thus they should not be kept in cloth bags or paper bags or boxes. Full notes should be made at the time the materials are collected. Included in this on-the-spot record should be the date, names of persons

Nevada, Pershing County   Guano   Chicago Laboratory   C-281   Av. 8660±300 yrs.
Lat. 40°16'N x Long. 118°30'W   Archaeology   Solid carbon

Leonard Rock Shelter, Nevada (Leonard Rock): Unburned guano from layer containing wooden artifacts in Leonard Rock Shelter, Nevada (LRS2). Submitted by R. F. Heizer.

Separate Runs   8443±510 yrs.
8820±400 yrs.

Arnold, J. R. and Libby, W. F., 1951, Radiocarbon Dates: Science, 113, p. 117
Libby, W. F., 1955, Radiocarbon Dating: 2nd ed., University Chicago Press; p. 118

®   1958   Radiocarbon Dates Association, Inc.   Serial no. 71

14-1. *An example of the edge-punched cards issued by Radiocarbon Dates Association, Inc., of Andover, Massachusetts, under the direction of Dr. Frederick Johnson*

present, exact position and depth of specimens, site, location at the site, cultural horizon, associated materials, method of collecting sample, any preservative treatment to which sample is subjected, a statement as to the significance of the date if one should be determined, citations to the pertinent literature referring to the site or culture horizon, and the like. These data should be kept with the sample, and a copy submitted to the analyst for his use.

Association of dated historic materials or identifiable sites   When early historic documents—such as journals of explorers, fur traders, missionaries, military reconnaissance parties, and the like—attest to the fact that certain sites were occupied at one time and more recent sources deny or remain silent on their occupation, one can assign the terminal occupation of the sites and the latest cultural manifestation to the time of the documentary record. In this way, using all available records, some definite knowledge of the particular culture type in operation on a certain date or within a definite time span can be determined (cf. Collier, Hudson, and Ford, 1942: 113; Kidd, 1954). Strong (1940a: 595) summarizes this approach by saying, "Of recent years numerous archaeologists have temporarily shifted their attention from prehistoric horizons of unknown age and affiliations to early historic and documented sites. These have been excavated in order to proceed from the known into the hitherto unknown. Such excavations objectively link history with prehistory and anchor archaeology to meaningful social science." This method, sometimes called the "direct historical approach," has been discussed by Steward (1942). Its utility has been demonstrated by Wedel (1936, 1938, 1959, 1961), Strong (1935, 1940b), Will and Spinden (1906), Heizer (1941c), Kelly (1945b: 4–21), H. G. Smith (1948), Swanton (1939), Vaillant (1938), Quimby (1960), Baerreis (1971), and Harrington (1955).

The occurrence of datable historic objects of metal or glass in refuse deposits or graves may also lead to the absolute dating of a culture phase. The two Norse settlements on the Greenland coast introduced European objects to the Eskimo—whose culture (Inugsuk) was thereby dated—and furnished a lead for the chronological duration of the various Eskimo archaeological cultures (cf. Mathiassen, 1931).

Quimby (1939, 1941) has discussed this matter, using materials from Michigan and Louisiana. For California, see Heizer (1941b, 1941c), Heizer and Mills (1952), and Walker (1947); for a Texas Gulf Coast site, see Campbell (1958); and for two west Alaskan sites, see Van Stone and Townsend (1970). The journal *Ethnohistory*, published by Indiana University, contains many articles of interest to archaeologists concerned with the period of early Indian-White contact. Not much serious effort has been made to publish detailed surveys of dated types of glass trade beads, metal objects, buttons, medals, bottles, etc., which, if they occur in archaeological sites, can be useful for dating the contact. On glass beads see De Jarnette and Hansen (1960: 54–55, 57–59), Orchard (1929), Woodward (1965), and Pratt (1961). The large but scattered literature on historic archaeological materials cannot be cited here.

Glacial varve sequences   Baron Gerard de Geer is credited with discovering that the thin clay laminae of certain deposits were annual layers (varves) deposited in melt-water basins by retreating glacial ice. Glacial ice-retreat stages back to about 20,000 years can be dated with absolute exactness by varve counts. This method was first applied in the Baltic region by de Geer, and in eastern North America by Ernst Antevs. Although the varve counts are exact, human and cultural remains are rarely found in the ancient melt-water basins, so that these counts are seldom directly useful in archaeological dating. However, an archaeological deposit may be shown by its associated diatoms or pollen to have occurred when the climate was of a particular nature. The climate substage may then be cross-correlated with the varve chronology, and an indirect varve dating for the site determined. All of Antevs' age determinations for remains of early man in North America are ultimately based on the results of his varve counts. The fact that there are several gaps in the New World varve sequence that must be filled by estimates makes this dating method less reliable here than in the Old World (cf. Bryan and Ray, 1940: 58–67). For expositions of the varve analysis method, see de Geer (1937, 1940), Antevs (1925, 1931, 1935), and Zeuner (1948, 1958: Chaps. 2, 3).

METHODS FOR RELATIVE CHRONOLOGY

In the majority of archaeological investigations, excavators must be content with the relative dating of cultures, where, for example, they can show that culture A is older than cultures B and C, and culture C is younger than culture B. They may be able to estimate the relative duration of each culture, and point out that culture B endured for approximately twice as long as culture A. The latest culture (C) may terminate at the historic period and thus be datable, but the *actual* dating of cultures B and A and the absolute duration of culture A will be a mystery.

There always remains the possibility that some method, whether known but not yet applied or still awaiting discovery, will allow the relative sequence to be made absolute. Dendrochronology was such a method for the American Southwest, and Carbon-14 dating promises to allow absolute dating for some of the local sequences based upon imprecise ceramic sequences, obsidian-hydration curves, bone-fossilization, etc., elsewhere in the New World.

Some of the more widely used or potentially useful techniques for achieving relative chronology are listed below.

Stratigraphy   Vertical stratification, revealed by the excavation of occupation sites is the surest method of determining the order of succession of cultures (see Chapter 6 above). It is a method borrowed directly from geology (cf. Grabau, 1924), and its regular use by American archaeologists dates from as recently as 1916, when Nelson determined the pottery sequence at the Tano ruins (Nelson, 1916; cf. Woodbury, 1960). About the same time, Kidder used the stratigraphic method at Pecos, and Spier was testing the Trenton argillite culture with vertical sequence in mind (Spier, 1916; Wissler, 1916). Willey and Sabloff (1974) mention a number of earlier uses of stratigraphy that failed to stimulate other workers to adopt it as part of excavation technique and archaeological interpretation. Petrie used the stratigraphic method at Lachish, Palestine, in 1891 (Woolley, 1954: 47–48).

The beginnings of archaeological chronology in the American Southwest predate 1916, although this early work was neither appreciated nor exploited. Before 1900 Fewkes saw the connection between Sitkyatki and modern Hopi pottery and interpreted the differences as changes over time (Fewkes, 1896). F. H. Cushing, on the other hand, when he excavated the Los Muertos site in the 1890's, noted two different methods of disposing of the dead (cremations and inhumations), each associated with characteristic types of pottery (Gila Polychrome and Red-on-yellow). He suggested that the two modes of burial, which he assumed to be contemporaneous, reflected different social positions, interment being a mark of the "priestly class." It was not until 1925, with Schmidt's stratigraphic study of the area, that cremation was shown to be earlier than burial (Schmidt, 1927: 297–298; 1928: 281).

Stratification may be visible, as in the case of some Mississippi Valley mounds that were built and rebuilt successively (Setzler and Jennings, 1941: Fig. 4), or the stratigraphic sequence may have to be worked out by statistical methods (Strong and Corbett, 1943; Ford and Willey, 1949: 44–57; Beals, Brainerd, and Smith, 1945: 56 ff., App. III; Schmidt, 1928; Kroeber, 1940; Olson, 1930).

Rouse (1939: 80–92) points out that most archaeologists assume continuous occupancy of sites, and therefore attribute different frequencies of artifact types to temporal changes of fashion. However, the worker should ever be aware of the possibility of intermittent or discontinuous occupation, in itself a feature in which time is an important factor. Such interrupted occupation may be indicated in many ways—intrusive graves or storage pits, superimposed house floors, and the like—and the individual worker must judge the evidence in each case.

Stratigraphy may be reversed—i.e., older layers may lie atop newer ones—as evidenced by the examples presented by Hawley (1934: 31–35,

51-61), Crabtree (1939), Coon (1951: 33), Colton (1946: 297-299), Crowfoot (1935: 191-192), and Hole and Heizer (1973: 147).

Chemical analysis of bone   As has often been pointed out, buried bone is subject to varying conditions of moisture and soil minerals in different parts of the same site. As a result, fossilization (replacement of the bone by minerals from the soil, or loss of organic matter, and addition of mineral material) may take place at very different rates and a heavily mineralized bone from one location in a site is not necessarily older than an almost unmineralized bone from another.

However, since fresh or living bone is unfossilized, and most ancient bone is fossilized, the general axiom that fossilization is a correlate of time holds true (Cook, Brooks, and Ezra, 1961). Theoretically, therefore, if one were able to secure enough bone samples from an area where the bone was subject to similar soil-moisture-temperature conditions over a sufficiently long time span, it should be possible to make quantitative and qualitative chemical tests to determine whether mineralization of bone was random and accidental or proceeded at an orderly pace relative to increasing age. This actually has been done, and the orderly pace does seem on the whole to prevail. Because the curve of fossilization does not invariably conform to the attribution of age as deduced from archaeological evidence, however, it should still be used with caution (Bayle and de Noyer, 1939). For the Central California area see the articles by Cook (1951a, 1951b), Cook and Heizer (1947, 1952, 1953a, 1953b, 1959), and Heizer and Cook (1949). It is hoped that the anomalies encountered in correlating age and degree of mineralization in Central California may yet be explained, and that some *tertium quid* may be invoked to establish the absolute dating of two or more points on the curve of mineralization.

It may be added here that chemical analysis of bone to achieve relative dating is probably best applied to open sites, is expensive because a laboratory is needed, and has not yet been fully worked out. The several factors (e.g., soil minerals, ground water, and temperature) that cause variability (deceleration or acceleration of the fossilization process) cannot at this time be put into a formula because their individual or joint effects are not fully understood (Barber, 1939; Cook, 1951b, 1960).

An allied but different technique of bone analysis that may demonstrate relative (not absolute) age differences is called the fluorine method. Most ground waters contain small amounts of fluorine (F). Fluorine ions combine with the hydroxyapatite crystals of the bone to form fluorapatite, a stable mineral resistant to weathering and leaching and having almost no affinity for other materials. A bone buried for a long time will contain more fluorapatite than one buried for a short time. This fact of increasing F-content with age, together with its application for dating bones, was first announced by

Middleton (1844), carried further by Carnot (1892a, 1892b, 1892c, 1893), and recently revived by Oakley (1948, 1951, 1953, 1963a, 1964a). See also Montagu and Oakley (1949: 367–369) and Heizer (1950). The F-content method, because of the variability of fluorine content in ground waters and the relative slowness of uptake of fluorine in bone, cannot be expected to yield an absolute time curve (McConnell, 1962). As pointed out by Carnot (1893: 192–193) and Heizer (1950), and as demonstrated by Oakley (citations *supra*), the F-content method will chiefly be of value in determining whether bone implements or human skeletal remains found in association with bones were actually buried at the same time or not.

The fluorine method has been applied to some supposedly ancient New World human remains in California (Heizer and Cook, 1952), Mexico (Heizer and Cook, 1959), and Texas (Oakley and Howells, 1961). A dating method advanced by Gangl (1936) based upon the fat content of prehistoric bone produced discouraging results when applied to prehistoric California bones.

Other methods of age differentiation in bone, involving use of the electron microscope and radiological and optical techniques, are cited in Heizer and Cook (1956), Escalon de Fonton, Michaud, and Perinet (1951), and Baud (1960).

The amount of nitrogen in buried bones tends to decrease with age, and good relative datings have been secured based upon nitrogen determination (Oakley, 1963b; Ezra and Cook, 1957; Ortner, Vonendt, and Robinson, 1972; Cook and Heizer, 1952: 3–5). A similar dating method based on the rate of disappearance of conchiolin in buried shells (Schoute–Vanneck, 1960) seems promising but has not been extensively applied.

The collagen fraction in bone can be extracted and dated by the radiocarbon method (Protsch, 1970; Tamers and Pearson, 1965; Longin, 1971). Some ages for human skeletal material from California sites have been published by Berger *et al.* (1971). The collagen method promises to throw new light on the time of earliest animal domestication in the Old World (Protsch and Berger, 1973; Berger and Protsch, 1974), though the significance of these dates has been challenged (Bokonyi, Braidwood, and Reed, 1973) on the grounds that the bones so dated may have been those of wild rather than domesticated animals.

Another and more recent dating method uses the rate of "racemization" (change of L-amino acid to D-amino acid) in fossil bone. Some results using human skeletal material from California (Bada, Schroeder, and Carter, 1974) and human and animal bone from Olduvai Gorge (Bada and Protsch, 1973) have been secured.

Patination analysis   The surface oxidation of artifacts, as often pointed out (e.g., Service, 1941), is a tricky kind of evidence for assigning age to the implements. Nevertheless, Renaud (1936: 5–7), Kelly (1938: 3–6), and Rogers

(1939: 19–20) argue convincingly for the limited and objective use of this feature to infer relative dating of artifacts. Rogers (1939: 19) says:

> Although the processes of patination and oxidation are understood only to a certain degree, and practically nothing is known about the rate of progress, the phenomena, when properly used, can be of aid in establishing an implement sequence in localized fields. When types are suspected of being common to two or more industries, or when an age relation between different types is being sought, the procedure leading to a solution must be conducted with certain controls. Only artifacts of the same lithologic composition which have been subjected to the same natural agencies over varying lengths of time should be used for comparative study. The weakness of the system, of course, lies in the fact that the last-named factors can only be roughly estimated. However, I cannot agree with the many who believe patination and oxidation to be worthless diagnostic factors. The investigator who knows both the causative and tempering factors, and is thoroughly familiar with his field, should certainly make an attempt to employ this methodology.

Desert varnish (surface alteration, usually a polish, that accrues on stone tools after long exposure in a desert environment) is adequately discussed by Engel and Sharp (1959). The best general discussion of patination with reference to archaeology is the paper by Goodwin (1960).

Further investigations of the lithic patina and attempts to use differences in surface oxidation to place stone tools in chronological series are published by Hunt (1954), Hue (1929), Gehrcke (1933), Kelly (1938: 3–8), De Terra and Paterson (1939: 328, 333–334), Renaud (1936: 5–7), Kelly and Hurst (1956), Hurst and Kelly (1961), Schmalz (1960), and Curwen (1940).

Patination of metals is a similar process of surface chemical alteration. Because of the near absence of metal objects in prehistoric sites in North America, no effort is made here to cite references to the literature beyond the bibliographies contained in the works of Fink and Polushkin (1936), Gettens and Usilton (1955), and Biek (1963).

Obsidian hydration analysis So much has been written on the subject of archaeological dating by calculating the time required to produce a given thickness of the "hydration layer" (depth to which water absorbed through the surface has penetrated) on obsidian artifacts or debitage that a detailed explanation here is not necessary. Suffice it to say that the thickness of this hydration layer depends upon how long the article has been buried, the temperature conditions to which it has been subject since burial, and the petrographic nature of the obsidian itself. Variable hydration rates have been devised depending upon climatic conditions within latitudinal range, and by applying these appropriate rates, the age of an obsidian implement can be calculated. Obsidian implements exposed on the surface and subject to strong diurnal and seasonal temperature and moisture changes are not suitable for dating. General accounts of the theory, the techniques employed, and the results secured have been published by Friedman *et al.* (1960), D. L. Clark (1961), Friedman, Smith, and Clark (1963), and Katsui and Kondo (1965).

Early efforts to calculate the age of obsidian implements from Central California sites (D. L. Clark, 1964) and from Ecuador (Meggers, Evans, and Estrada, 1965) have not been very successful, but current efforts to refine the analytic technique promise to yield much more reliable results (Michels, 1967; Michels and Berbrich, 1971; Michels, 1973: 201–215).

Artifacts of glass (unknown in the New World before the advent of Caucasians, but attested for Egypt and Mesopotamia at least as early as 1600 B.C.) often acquire annual weathering layers that can be counted in the same way as tree rings (Brill, 1961, 1963). For American archaeologists the usefulness of this dating technique would probably be limited to historic sites.

Seriation   This term, variously used by American archaeologists, is here defined as the determination of the chronological sequence of styles, types, or assemblages of types (cultures) by any method or combination of methods. Stratigraphy may be employed, or the materials may be from surface sites. These several methods of seriation may be judged by investigating the publications by Kroeber (1916), Spier (1917), Ford (1938), Dunnell (1970), Michels (1973: 66–82), Lothrop (1942: 183–199), Petrie (1899, 1901), Rogers (1939: 1–2), Ford and Willey (1949: *passim,* esp. pp. 38 ff.), Kidder (1931), Spier (1931), and Holmes (1894). Spier (1931: 283) describes the seriation method: "Remains of a stylistic variable (such as pottery) occurring in varying proportions in a series of sites are ranged, by some auxiliary suggestion, according to the seriation of one element (one pottery type). Its validity is established if the other elements (two or more other pottery types) fall in smooth sequences (e.g., the Zuñi ruin series obtained by Kroeber and Spier)." An instructive example of seriation compared with a stratigraphic sequence is contained in Ford and Willey (1949: 52). Ford (1962) has provided us with an extremely clear and useful manual outlining procedures for developing archaeological chronologies based upon surface collections of pottery. His discussion of seriation (pp. 41–44) is excellent.

Classification and typology are important in seriation, and the student can read what Brew (1946), Ford and Willey (1949), Kluckhohn (1960), Steward (1954), Rouse (1939, 1944), Taylor (1948), Krieger (1944, 1960), Spaulding (1953), Movius (1944: 102, 106–108), and Ford (1952a, 1952b, 1962: 14–17) have to say on this matter. See also Chapter 13 just above.

A mathematical technique of seriation has been proposed by Brainerd (1951a) and Robinson (1951), and tested on a California example by Belous (1953). A second re-examination of the Central California culture sequence by Dempsey and Baumhoff (1963) uses "a more appropriate statistical method for establishing chronology" termed "contextual analysis" (cf. Lipe,

1964). Dempsey and Baumhoff's results conform much more closely to previous chronological conclusions based on stratigraphy (Heizer, 1949) than Belous' statistical manipulation of the same data, using the Brainerd-Robinson method.

Statistical methods applicable to archaeological data are varied. Some are suited to time ordering data to derive sequence; others are aimed at ordering data in ways that permit inferences to be drawn about cultural processes (Clarke, 1968; Higgs, 1970; Tugby, 1965; Cowgill, 1968; Hole and Shaw, 1967; Kuzara, Mead, and Dixon, 1966; Craytor and Johnson, 1968; Gelfand, 1971).

Additional discussions of interest are by Spaulding (1953), Brainerd (1951b), Myers (1950), Driver and Kroeber (1932), Kroeber (1940), Orr (1951), Troike (1957), and Tugby (1958). The reader is also referred to the discussions of statistical analysis of artifacts by Moberg (1961), Ascher and Ascher (1963), Sackett (1966), Bohmers (1963), and Spaulding (1960).

Typology Artifact types may be distinguished and their relative antiquity assigned on the *presumption* that change or variation measurable by the chosen criterion (from simple to elaborate, poorly preserved to well preserved, crude to refined, etc.) is correlated with age. The evolution of types may be revealing, but so long as it continues to be a presumption, unsupported by concrete facts of relative (or absolute) time dating, it can be nothing more than a logical scheme. Atkinson (1946: 172–173) and Grahame Clark (1947: 115–118) point out that the evidence of associated finds (assemblages, aggregates, industries, find-complexes) may either verify or deny the presumed evolution of a type. Childe (1948: 51; 1956), Braidwood (1946a), Ford (1954b, 1962: 14–17), Tugby (1958), and Rouse (1960) provide useful discussions of typology.

Judicious use of the typological approach may yield indications of temporal sequence. No student of archaeology will be wasting time by reading the works of Petrie (1899, 1901, 1904), Uhle (1903), Willey (1945), Grahame Clark (1947: Chap. 5), and Lothrop (1942: 183–199).

Analysis of the rate of refuse accumulation Where no other method suggests itself, some estimate of the rate at which a refuse deposit accumulates may yield a date figure for a site. Provided that all of the variable factors (number of houses and occupants, amount of food eaten, firewood burned, etc., etc.) could be exactly controlled, the time required to amass a specified amount of midden could be calculated (cf. Cosgrove and Cosgrove, 1932: 100–103). But because these variables can never be raised even to the rank of probabilities, any age estimate derived from this method must be considered to be of extremely limited value.

R. Pumpelly used this method at Anau and cited data from Egypt;

Nelson (1909: 345–356), Gifford (1916), Schenck (1926: 205–212), and Cook (1946) have tried to calculate the antiquity of the San Francisco Bay shell-mounds by this method; Harrington (1933: 171) used the rate-of-increment techniques at Gypsum Cave (see also critique by Kroeber, 1948: 681); Loud and Harrington (1929: 120–123) used this method as supporting evidence for their estimate of the antiquity of Lovelock Cave; Vaillant (1935: 166–167, 257–258) compares the rate of refuse accumulation at Pecos and certain Valley of Mexico sites; Milne (1881) applied the rate of alluvial soil accumulation in Tokyo Bay to shellmounds; Bird (1948: 21, 27–28) suggests the time involved in the building of an artifact-bearing soil profile at Viru; and Braidwood and Howe (1960: 159) use the life expectancy of and debris from dwellings to calculate that the site of Jarmo was probably occupied for about 200 years. Kubler (1948) determined that the guano composing the "stacks" off the Peruvian coast—stacks that have yielded artifacts of known cultural affiliation from precisely recorded depths—was deposited in annual layers that could be counted, but which were of such uniform thickness that depth measurements could be substituted for layer counts. Thus the age of an artifact found at a depth of so many feet could easily be calculated. The parallel with the glacial-varve-counting method (cf. Bryan and Ray, 1940: 57 ff.) is striking. Kubler's guano dating and Allison's (1926) measurement of the growth rate of stalagmites at Jacob's Cavern might reasonably be included in the preceding section on methods for absolute chronology. Champe (1964: 32–33) dates some levels of Ash Hollow Cave by dendrochronology and uses the depth of dated levels to estimate the time required for nondated levels to accumulate. Lothrop (1928: 197) estimates the population of each district and the total volume of middens to compute the rate at which deposits accumulate in Tierra del Fuego. Strong (1935: 236–239) estimates the antiquity of the Signal Butte site by calculating the rate of dune migration. These may be taken as special examples of the rate-of-accumulation method. Morrison (1942: 380), Schenck (1926: 208–212), Grahame Clark (1947: 139), and Woolley (1954: 79) have called attention to the difficulties of making and relying upon such age estimates.

The clearest demonstration known to us of variable rates of deposition in a single site is Fowler's at Modoc Shelter, Illinois (Fowler, 1959: 19–20). Fowler showed that between 8000 and 5000 B.C. the rate was constant at about one foot per 500 years, between 5000 and 3600 B.C. the rate increased markedly to 1.7 feet per 100 years, and between 3300 and 2700 B.C. the rate was reduced to one foot per 400 years.

This chronological method is the same as that used by geologists in estimating the age of the oceans from the annual increment of sodium or estimating the rate of formation of sedimentary rocks (cf. Zeuner, 1958: Part IV) or estimating the age of North American glacial periods by the rate of leaching of soils.

Distributional method   A common though hazardous method of inferring the antiquity of two artifact types is by comparing their distribution; the more widespread being assumed to be the more ancient. Distribution maps can serve, of course, a separately useful purpose in indicating the geographical spread of a trait or culture complex, thus providing a body of data that can be matched with geomorphological, climatological, and geochronological facts (cf. J. D. Clark, 1957).

Kroeber (1923), in an avowedly hypothetical historical reconstruction of the history of native culture in California, illustrates this technique. Grahame Clark (1947: 131–133) discusses the method in archaeology. Workers in the field of Eskimo ethnology and prehistory have used the distributional method (though not invariably or exclusively for chronological purposes) to advantage, as attested by the works of Collins (1937), Dixon (1963), de Laguna (1934), Larsen and Rainey (1948), Lister (1955), and Birket-Smith (1929). Kroeber (1931) gives a general survey of the distributional method. Sapir's classic *Time Perspective* (1916) can still be read by all American archaeologists with considerable profit. The distributional method must be employed critically, and some precautions are outlined by Linton (1936: 374–381), Dixon (1928), and Wallis (1945).

Cross-dating   An artifact type absolutely or relatively dated in one area may provide the lead for pegging down the chronology of material it occurs with elsewhere. Grahame Clark (1947: 133–136) discusses this source of dating under "synchronisms." American archaeologists are well aware of this method and the rich results it often brings. It is the basic technique in Krieger's monumental Texas volume (Krieger, 1946); it was employed at Snaketown (Heizer, 1959: 368–374); it has assisted Middle American archaeologists (cf. Kidder, Jennings, and Shook, 1946: 250); and has long been used in Old World prehistory (Ehrich, 1965).

Trade objects, which are the clearest evidence of actual contemporaneity between two geographically separated cultures, may permit an absolute chronology to be extended to a region whose materials have hitherto been only relatively datable. Trait *resemblances* between two distant cultures may be so unmistakably due to diffusion that no reasonable doubt may be entertained. But these similarities are usually to be taken as evidencing not exact synchronisms, but *general* contemporaneity. Thus Kidder, Jennings, and Shook (1964: 251) and Kidder and Thompson (1938) suggest that the temporally floating Maya Long Count may some day, through the discovery of a chain of cross-finds, be equated and synchronized with the Southwestern dendrochronological time sequence (cf. Davis, 1937). In California, where much of the archaeology is poorly dated, there is hope of ultimately synchronizing local culture phases with tree-ring dated cultures of the Southwest by means of shell beads and pottery trade objects (Heizer, 1941a, 1946;

Gifford, 1949). Patterson (1963) has written a useful survey of methodological principles and precautions to be observed in using archaeological data for cross-dating, and Michels (1973: 83–111) discusses paleontological, geomorphological, and cultural cross-dating.

Synchronisms may also be determined from the evidence of natural phenomena. If a fall of volcanic ash covers a wide area, for example, cultural remains can be assigned to periods before and after a given volcanic eruption, according to whether they occur above or below the ash layer (Cressman, 1942; Colton, 1945; Vaillant, 1935: 165–166; Fernald, 1962; Fryxell, 1965; Wilcox, 1965; Rapp, Cooke, and Henrickson, 1973).

As already noted in Chapter 3, archaeologists must be aware that pieces much older than the general run of artifacts at a site—prehistoric antiques or heirlooms—may be recovered. Any conclusion that these isolated pieces were contemporaneous with the rest could lead to errors in cross-dating (Patterson, 1963; Heizer, 1959: 367–368). The re-using of ancient pieces by modern native groups is a well-documented practice: Poor people in Brazil collect ancient funerary urns and use them to store maize or manioc flour (Laming-Emperaire, 1963: 70); Persian pilgrims visiting Moslem shrines collect ancient Babylonian cuneiform cylinders and use them as good-luck charms (Rich, 1819: 58); and the Maidu Indians of California re-use ancient stone mortars for grinding acorns (Dixon, 1905: 136). That similar acts were performed in prehistoric times is indicated by prehistoric stone projectile points recovered from historic Seneca graves in New York (Ritchie, 1954: 67–68); older Nazca-type pots in Middle Inca-period graves in Peru (Kroeber and Strong, 1924: 116); and carved stelae and monuments re-used by the people of the Piedras Negras site in Guatemala (Coe, 1959: 155).

Important information for cross-dating can often be derived from knowledge about artifact origins. As noted in an earlier chapter, the precise composition of many kinds of stone can be determined (by x-ray fluorescence, neutron-activation analysis, and standard petrographic methods), and an artifact made from one of these kinds of stone can be compared with stone from a known geological source to test whether it is different in composition. If it is identical, its source may be established. Pottery is also analyzed in this way to learn where the clay came from (Winter, 1971; Perlman and Asaro, 1969, 1970). Obsidian can also be analyzed for trace elements, and work has been done in associating Mediterranean obsidian sources and artifacts (Wright, 1969; Dixon, Cann, and Renfrew, 1968). Similar work has been done in Mesoamerica (Hester, Heizer, and Jack, 1971), New Zealand (Ward, 1974), and California (Stevenson, Stross, and Heizer, 1971; Kowalski, Schatzki, and Stross, 1972; Bowman, Asaro, and Perlman, 1973). Flint can be similarly analyzed (de Sieveking et al., 1972), as can quartzite (Heizer et al., 1973) and metal ores (Friedman et al., 1966).

An excellent survey of petrography in the service of archaeology is by

Stelcl and Malina (1970). A bibliography of petrography and its archaeological application is presented by Hester and Heizer (1973b: 48–56). Still valuable is the pioneering work of H. Fischer (1878). Wallis (1955) has a useful survey of petrology with special reference to locating geologic sources of materials used to make axes in prehistoric Britain. Ponce Sanginés and Mogrovejo Terrazas (1970) have thoroughly studied the provenience of lithic materials used at the site of Tiahuanaco, Bolivia. Williams and Heizer (1965a) have done likewise for the stones used in Olmec sculpture. Greek marbles can readily be distinguished by their varying ratios of oxygen-18 and oxygen-16 isotopes, and through these variations the quarry sources can be identified (Craig and Craig, 1972).

On the basis of such data, ancient trade routes and the items exchanged along them can be reconstructed (cf. Wright, 1974; Hammond, 1972). The field archaeologist who is aware of the potentialities in laboratory study of stones used in prehistoric times will collect samples of all stone types used at a site, and will try to locate and sample their geological sources.

Geological methods   Under this general heading will come those archaeological finds that have some relationship with geological features. For example, sites located in positions now unfavorable to occupancy, sites covered by alluvial deposition, and eroded sites furnish a *priori* evidence that the occupants lived there before the changes occurred, and the geologist may be asked to offer some opinion about the length of time involved and to explain the depositional history of the spot since the evidence of human presence was laid down.

Former occupation sites may be considered to have become unfavorable if they are too far from drinking water, too poor in economic resources, etc. In such cases, one should investigate the possibility that climatic changes have occurred since the site was occupied. Schenck (1926) and Nelson (1909), who dealt with the Emeryville and Ellis Landing shellmounds on San Francisco Bay, concluded that subsidence of the shore was evidenced by the sub-sea-level base of the midden deposits. Geologists were unable to suggest a subsidence rate, and this observation was therefore unusable as a means for determining the age of the cultural deposits. However, since radiocarbon dating has been available, the basal occupation layers of several San Francisco Bay shellmounds have been age-dated, and a geological age estimate is no longer needed. The archaeological radiocarbon dates are, on the other hand, of interest to geologists studying the elevational history of the shoreline of San Francisco Bay (Wright, 1971; Nichols and Wright, 1971).

Bird (1938, 1946: 21) found that some Patagonian shell middens had risen about fifteen feet. He was able to estimate the minimum rate of shore elevation to determine the total age of the cultural deposits. Mathiassen (1927: 6–10, 129–130) showed that a rising shoreline and a progressively shallow sea at Naujan account for the abandonment of that area by whales and thus by the Thule Eskimo who depended so heavily upon this animal for food. The house pits of the former Thule settlements are now five to fifteen meters higher than when they were built some centuries ago. Shore subsidence or sea-level rise in connection with archaeological sites is also discussed by Goldthwait (1935), Bird (1943), Johnson and Raup (1947), Grahame Clark (1947: 129–131), Hopkins (1959), Vinton (1962), Shepard (1964), and Deevey (1948).

The presence of human beings on the borders of pluvial or postglacial lakes in what is now desert Southern California has been proposed by E. W. C. and W. H. Campbell (1935) and E. Campbell *et al.* (1937). Geologists estimate dates for the time when the lakes were full. Provided the evidence of human presence there when the now-dry basins were full is sufficiently strong, the cultures are datable.* Greenman and Stanley (1943) cite a similar situation at George Lake, Ontario.

The soil overburden or mass of an archaeological deposit may be studied by a geologist who can interpret it as, to quote Kirk Bryan, an "alluvial chronology." The sequence, time, and causes of erosion or deposition may be ascribed to glacial, pluvial, or arid conditions. The following works are offered as examples of the method: Antevs (1949), Bryan (1941, 1948), Bryan and Ray (1940), Bryan and McCann (1943), Cook (1949: 8–10, 16–18, 20–21, 23–24, 35–36, 41–42, 45–48, 51–52, 84–86), Hack (1942, 1945), Judson (1949), Kelley, Campbell, and Lehmer (1940), Leighton (1936), MacClintock *et al.* (1936), Schultz (1938), Carter (1956), Cornwall (1954, 1960), Carter and Pendleton (1956), Phillips, Ford, and Griffin (1951: 23–25), Péwé (1954), Lais (1941), Cailleux (1946), Martin (1963), Haynes (1966a), and Williams (1952).

The postglacial period of the last 11,000 years is important since most New World archaeological remains occur within this time span. The derivation of a fairly exact chronology of climatic changes and its application to archaeology has been due largely to the efforts of Antevs (1948, 1950, 1953a, 1953b, 1954, 1955). See also Lougee (1953) and Wright and Frey (1965).

At times, progressive changes in geomorphology can be linked with archaeological sites of different ages. Examples of this are the beach ridges at Cape Krusenstern (Giddings, 1966) and the meander pattern of the lower Mississippi River (Phillips, Ford, and Griffin, 1951: 295–308; Ford and Webb, 1956: 116).

Soil profiles and surface soil chemistry *per se* may yield some indication of age. The most specific claim advanced for dating soils is that of Siniaguin (1943). Additional attempts along this line are described by Li (1943) and

---

*Actually, in Southern California the evidence of association is *not* very strong, despite the confident assertions of certain workers. Opposing opinions, each supported by a different array of evidence, have been proposed by Antevs (1952), Brainerd (1953), Rogers (1939), and Heizer (1965).

Sokoloff and Lorenzo (1953). Other works treating this matter are by Bryan and Albritton (1943), Hack (1943), Leighton (1934, 1936, 1937), Thorp (1949), Zeuner (1958: 349), Sokoloff and Carter (1952), Hunt and Sokoloff (1950), Schultz and Frankfurter (1948), and Simonson (1954). Further aspects of soil analysis such as phosphate concentration indicating intensive human occupancy are discussed by Arrhenius (1963), Firtion (1947), Koby (1946), Dauncey (1952), Gundlach (1961), Lorch (1939), Louis (1946), Solecki (1951), Cook and Heizer (1965b), Parsons (1962), Eddy and Dregne (1964), and Lotspeich (1961).

Botanical methods   Under this heading we include the study of all plant remains or botanical evidence associated with sites. The affinity of certain plants for archaeological sites has repeatedly been observed (Griffin, 1948: 3–4; Drucker, 1943a: 114–115; Hrdlicka, 1937). Because particular plants find particular microenvironments favorable for reasons of soil chemistry, drainage, or other factors, it is reasonable to suppose that surface sites of different time periods will support somewhat different floras (Larsen, 1950: 177; Heizer, 1959: 207–213; Yarnell, 1964, 1965). This is certainly the case in Central California where Early, Middle, and Late Horizon sites each favor the growth of distinctive plant species. The whole question of floral associations of sites is much in need of investigation since it promises to produce a rough technique for relative chronology.

Paleobotanists can deduce much about the climate and flora of the past from pollen preserved in soils. The collection and preservation of archaeological botanical materials are treated by Barghoorn (1944) and Faegri and Iversen (1965). The method and results of pollen analysis are illustrated in the works by Cain (1939), Cooper (1942), Deevey (1944, 1949), Erdtman (1943), Faegri and Iversen (1950), Godwin (1934), Hansen (1942, 1946), Johnson (1942: 96–129), Sears (1932, 1937), Wilson (1949), Knox (1942), Grahame Clark (1947: 123–127), Sears and Roosma (1961), Mehringer (1965), Zeuner (1958: Chap. 3), Wendorf (1961), and Anderson (1955). Jelinek (1966) has provided a particularly useful example of correlating archaeological materials (artifacts) and palynological data.

The botanical identification of wood, charcoal, or fruits may also be of ultimate chronological significance. For examples see Barghoorn (1949), Chaney (1935a, 1935b, 1941), Bailey and Barghoorn (1942), and Western (1963).

A special application of botanical identification arises when material from a dry cave or shelter is analyzed. Here, in addition to being a possible aid to chronology, the identification of seeds, leaves, stems, and other parts of plants may contribute importantly to determining the ecologic adaptation of the occupants. Intensive studies of plant remains deposited and preserved under dry conditions are reported in Jones (1936, 1945), Jones and Fonner (1954), Cutler (1952), Harrington (1933: 194–195), Wells (1966), C. E. Smith

(1966), and Wells and Jorgensen (1964). Plant remains present in carbonized form may not be readily apparent to the excavator. Flotation (Struever, 1968a; Helbaek, 1969) is often an effective means of recovering carbonized plant remains from midden soils. Much of the important record of ancient cultigens for the area east of the Rockies (Cutler and Blake, 1973) consists of carbonized seeds from refuse deposits.

Zoological-paleontological methods   The discovery of remains of extinct animals along with evidences of man in both the Old and New Worlds has now become commonplace (cf. Stock, 1936; Jelinek, 1957; Hester, 1960). Any definite association between human bones or artifacts and the bones of extinct animals, however, should be carefully recorded and, if possible, the whole kept *in situ* until one or more paleontologists can study the find. Such discoveries are still rare and, because of their probable antiquity, highly important. Environmental reconstructions through vertebrate animal remains are possible; see Harris (1963) and Heizer (1960: 122–123).

Microfossils contained in soil or peat may yield, to expert study, indications of chronological value. For diatom analyses, see Conger (1942, 1949) and Linder (1942). For studies of foraminifera, see Stetson and Parker (1942), Phleger (1949), and Wendorf (1961).

Mollusks are also sensitive indicators of climate, and their remains (shells) in association with artifacts often furnish excellent information for erecting an archaeological chronology (Lambert, 1960). See the works of Baker (1920, 1930, 1937, 1942), Germain (1923), Evans (1969), Burchell (1961), Boekelman (1936), Eiseley (1937), Greengo (1951), Sears (1952), Lais (1937, 1938), Griffin (1948), Richards (1936, 1937), Clench (1942), Goggin (1949: 23), Reed (1962), Cunnington (1933), Geyer (1923), Petrbok (1931), Allen and Cheatum (1961), and Matteson (1959, 1960). The remarkable papers by Morse (1882) present a method of chronology based upon metrical analysis of mollusk shells that could yield not only relative chronologies but, theoretically at least, absolute chronologies as well. It is to be hoped that further work will be carried out in this direction (cf. Doki, 1934; Suzuki, 1935).

Paleomagnetism   Changes in the earth's magnetic fields over time have long been known. The rates of change have varied from time to time and place to place, but enough data have been accumulated since the sixteenth century—when magnetic observatories began to make systematic records—or have been gained from study of volcanic rocks to yield both ancient geological dates and more recent archaeological ones.

Lavas, baked earth fireplaces, pottery kilns, and bricks that have been fired to a temperature of 600 to 700 Curie points may be dated by this method.

The reader may consult the journal *Archaeometry*, Aitken (1960, 1961, 1970a, 1970b), Cook (1963), Heizer (1953), Watanabe (1959), Cox, Doell, and Dalrymple (1965), Michels (1973: 130–145), Bucha (1971), and Thellier and

Thellier (1959) for an introduction to the methods and principles of dating by paleomagnetism (also known as archaeomagnetism or thermoremanent magnetism or, to use Watanabe's term, geomagnetochronology).

Thermoluminescence For the last fifteen years investigators have been trying to perfect laboratory methods for applying the known principles of thermoluminescence (TL) to dating ceramics or cave fills (see Dort et al., 1965).

The basic principle of TL dating is outlined in the following quotation taken from Mazess and Zimmerman (1966); their article may be consulted for details:

> Thermolumescence (TL) is the release in the form of light of stored energy from a substance when it is heated. The phenomenon occurs in many crystalline nonconducting solids, and has been suggested as the basis of a dating technique for rocks and minerals. Naturally occurring radioactive elements in these materials are a nearly constant source of ionizing radiation. It is assumed that [as] some of the electrons excited by this radiation become trapped in metastable states, a few electrons work above the ground state. Released from their traps by heating, the electrons return to the ground state, emitting light.
>
> Pottery accumulates . . . trapped electrons, with time, and the amount of natural TL produced by a sherd, therefore, depends on the time elapsed since its last firing. The amount of natural TL also depends on the amount of ionizing radiation present, and on the nature and number of electron traps in the material (which determines the material's sensitivity to radiation-induced TL). By taking these factors into account, natural TL has been used for dating limestones, lava flows, ice, and pottery.

Mazess and Zimmerman (1966) and Ralph and Han (1966) have secured good dating results, and in the future we may expect special laboratories to be established and a veritable flood of TL dates to appear. Enormous amounts of pottery have been collected and stored in museums. The fairly precise dates of ceramic phases that could be established by TL dating of this material would be critical to the development of accurate chronologies in many areas of the world. They would eliminate the need, for example, of stylistic and type seriation analysis of ceramics. It is to be hoped, however, that the developers and practitioners of the TL dating method will learn from the radiocarbon experience, and not rush into an incompletely thought-out system of date lists, laboratory references, indications of plus-or-minus ranges (possible error), etc.

The oldest TL-dated fired clay, from the Upper Paleolithic site of Dolni Vestonice, Czechoslovakia, has been assigned an age of 33,000 years. This TL age agrees fairly well with C-14 ages of 28,300 and 29,000 years (Zimmerman and Huxtable, 1971). TL dates have also been determined for baked clay balls and burned flint from the Poverty Point (Louisiana) culture (Huxtable, Aitken, and Weber, 1972; Goksu et al., 1974).

The journal *Archaeometry* carries papers on this subject in nearly every issue, and there are good summaries of the method in Zimmerman (1971), Aitken and Alldred (1972), and Aitken (1970a, 1970c).

Fission-track dating   This method is most applicable to materials one to two million or more years old, although it can be applied to much younger materials. The method applies to uranium-bearing glass, of either human or natural origin (e.g., obsidian). For details see Fleischer and Price (1964), Fleischer, Price, and Walker (1965), Rainey (1966), Suzuki and Watanabe (1968), Watanabe and Suzuki (1969), Nishimura (1971), Michels (1973: 181–187), and Faul and Wagner (1971).

Lexicostatistic dating   A technique for estimating the age of languages, called glottochronology (a method for determining the date of divergence between two languages by examining the changes in them) has been under development since about 1945. A very large literature concerning methodology and results has accumulated. For statements of the method, see Hymes (1960), Hoijer (1956), Bergsland and Vogt (1962), Kroeber (1955), and Swadesh (1960). Swadesh has tried (1959) to set forth the principles involved in applying linguistic time depths to the data of prehistory, and Swadesh and others have tried to apply it to European archaeology (Hencken, 1955; Swadesh, 1953) and American Indians (Swadesh, 1962; Taylor and Rouse, 1955; Baumhoff and Olmsted, 1963; Hopkins, 1965; Taylor, 1961).

CONCLUDING OBSERVATIONS

No part of archaeology is more difficult, generally speaking, than the determination of chronology. Archaeologists must ever be aware of the need for dating their sites and cultures, and must collect the materials and make the necessary observations during excavation to assist them in making time determinations. Since no two archaeological deposits are ever exactly the same, each excavation will pose a unique problem. Beyond the routine collecting of charcoal, wood, molluscan remains, vertebrate and invertebrate remains, and soil samples, the cultural materials themselves and the stratigraphy will also be essential elements in age determination. Stimulating ideas and fresh approaches to a problem will often result from consultation with specialists in certain disciplines in the biological and physical sciences. The large and ever-growing literature on scientific techniques applied to archaeological dating cannot be cited here. As a beginning, the student of archaeology may consult Aitken (1961), Butzer (1964), Biek (1963), Brothwell and Higgs (1963), Pyddoke (1963), Oakley (1963a, 1964a), Jelinek and Fitting (1963, 1965), Michels (1973), Michael and Ralph (1971), Berger (1970), Allibone et al. (1970), Heizer and Cook (1960), and the journal Archaeometry.

A REVIEW OF TECHNIQUES FOR ARCHAEOLOGICAL SAMPLING*

Sonia Ragir

15

I emphasize the point that our only exact data as to the physical world are our sensible perceptions. We must not slip into the fallacy of assuming that we are comparing a given world with given perceptions of it. The physical world is, in some general sense of the term, a deduced concept.

Our problem is, in fact, to fit the world to our perceptions, and not our perceptions to the world.

—ALFRED NORTH WHITEHEAD

 An archaeological site is an accumulation of materials that are the residues of cultural activity. These accumulations can provide both qualitative and quantitative information about the activities, ecology, and cultural and chronological relationships of the human occupants of the site. Qualitative analysis identifies the constituents of a material (or archaeological site) irrespective of their amount (or archaeological site) irrespective of their amount. Quantitative analysis determines the amounts in which the various constituents of a material (or site) are present (*Chamber's Technical Dictionary*, 1962: 692). Both types of analysis are basic to archaeology: the qualitative aspect is typological and takes the form of setting up categories of countable units without which there can be no quantitative analysis. Quantitative analysis is prerequisite to any comparison between: 1) components of a site (either vertical strata or horizontal facies); 2) individual sites; or 3) constellations of sites or regions. In other words, such an analysis is necessary for any kind of cultural interpretation based on comparisons between the proportion and distribution of cultural and natural elements.

The introduction of quantitative techniques, because they demand greater precision in the definition of categories, usually modifies the existing

---

*This chapter has not been revised, but remains, except for minor editing, a new epigraph, and the addition of some new references, in the form originally published in 1967.

descriptive framework to a greater or lesser extent. In archaeology these techniques have been important in greatly expanding and modifying the field of study. The discussion of quantitative methods during recent years was stimulated by the expansion of goals to include reconstruction of group activity (behavior) from archaeological evidence (Taylor, 1948; Spaulding, 1960; Binford, 1962; Hole and Heizer, 1973; Watson, LeBlanc, and Redman, 1971). Moreover, the increasing cooperation between archaeologists and other natural scientists (physiologists, geologists, botanists, paleontologists, etc.) has made archaeologists aware of a long neglect or misuse of quantitative techniques borrowed from the natural sciences in the collection of samples and in subsequent laboratory analysis (Brothwell and Higgs, 1963; Stanton, 1965). This chapter will briefly review the literature of field sampling techniques and discuss collecting techniques and sampling designs (see also Chapter 3).

HISTORICAL BACKGROUND

Early attempts at systematic sampling designed to obtain "representative samples" of surface archaeological materials were made by American archaeologists in response to questions raised by the development of seriation analysis of pottery (Kroeber, 1916). The interpretation of surface materials was and is still limited in scope. Three traditional problems have been attacked: 1) cultural identification; 2) ceramic chronology or seriation (temporal sequences of ceramic style changes); and 3) the use of associated ceramic and other material for dating various site features or assigning them to cultural context (Cowgill, 1964).

Spier's early work on seriation in the American Southwest (1917) largely ignores the sampling problem, although Spier did some test excavation to check similarity between ceramic collections at the surface and those below ground (Spier, 1917) (see Chapter 3). The "representative sampling" technique, a method intended to eliminate bias, was first described by Gladwin (1928: 1) (italics added).

> When a ruin is found, a collection of sherds is made *at random*, care being taken that all pottery types in evidence are gathered . . . . Occasionally, at large sites, two collections are made, one in which every sherd within a given area is taken, in order to obtain the percentages of types; the other covering, the whole area in which only those sherds are picked up which are regarded as significant.

As with Spier, the word "random" simply meant an effort not to collect predominantly painted or pretty sherds (cf. Kroeber, 1916: 384, 387). The concept of unconscious selective bias for particular sizes, shapes, colors, materials, densities, and known function is not explicitly discussed. However,

Gladwin was aware that the sherds collected by the method described above would not yield significant percentages—a fact not recognized or admitted by many later archaeologists.

In the Viru Valley survey (Ford and Willey, 1949) and in the survey of the Lower Mississippi River Valley (Phillips, Ford, and Griffin, 1951) the misunderstanding of random sampling procedures reaches absurdity. Ford (1949: 34–35) writes:

> Two workmen who accompanied Willey and me gathered most of the collections. These usually were made from a small section of each site, not more than 10 meters in diameter. The workmen were instructed not to select sherds when collecting and were watched to see that they did not. Their goal at each place was to fill the required number of bags so that they might rest until Willey had finished writing notes. The men were also repeatedly cautioned and watched to see that they did not gather all material from one spot for at some sites they might have made a collection of the required size without moving . . .

And as late as 1951 Ford (1951: 43) wrote:

> Generally speaking, our only concern was to get as large a sample as possible and a reasonably honest one . . . The only sure way to eliminate this difficulty is to hire local people to pick sherds up at so much per sack.

These methods were succinctly characterized and evaluated by Alcock (1951: 75):

> The American technique of surface collecting makes use of random samples— so random that they are best collected by untrained and uncomprehending laborers.

This, he argues, is not science. Furthermore, it is not "random." Alcock's criticism and reappraisal of surface surveying techniques includes discussion of the kinds of inferences one might make from surface collections other than the traditional typological ones. He specifically mentions the utility of such techniques in planning excavations (Alcock, 1951: 76):

> What is required is not a random sample, but one selected on rational principles, so that each sherd may be significant. Decorated sherds we must have, but we must balance them with plain wares, endeavoring to preserve the proportion between them as they appear on the surface. But is it enough to collect indiscriminately from the entire site and lump all our finds together in one bag? Different parts of a large complex may have been occupied at different times, and there may even be a contouring of cultures, an archaeological treeline above which sherds of the earlier occupations are not found. This evidence could, and should, be obtained when making a surface collection, the more so since sherds are not autogenous, and there is a real danger of completely denuding popular sites.

Alcock's thoughtful article is marred, however, by the continued misunderstanding of what random samples really are. The techniques he proposes will not necessarily provide a systematically collected sample approaching a representative selection of all the materials from the surface of the site.

With the refinement of ceramic chronologies, investigators began to doubt that surface sherds could be relied on to represent an isolated temporal unit. Controlled excavations such as Spier's (1917) were made to test the assumed temporal reliability of surface collections (see also Ford and Willey, 1949; Tolstoy, 1958). It was concluded that "a representative collection of surface sherds does not represent a cultural unit in time" (Bennyhoff, 1952: 232). This conclusion, right or wrong, is unfounded when reached without examining a single truly random (much less representative) sample. In a stratified site there is little doubt that the surface contains some degree of mixture of later and earlier materials. A representative sample will reflect this mixture and indicate the duration of occupation. Short-term, single-period occupation sites result in temporally homogeneous deposits above and below ground, and any kind of sample will contain sherds only from the single temporal unit of the occupation.

One field solution devised by some investigators interested mainly in ceramic chronology was "spot sampling," in which "most of the visible sherds of reasonable size in and around the point selected for sampling were gathered until a bagful, generally between 200–800 sherds—about 300 in most cases—was obtained" (Tolstoy, 1958: 9). Specifically aimed at obtaining pottery samples for seriation, "spot sampling" improved upon other haphazard collecting methods in the increased homogeneity of its sample. Its major weakness is that one can have no idea how representative the collection is of the rest of the site.

Surface surveys and descriptions of collecting techniques in the literature exemplify the existing confusion about the definition of "an adequate sample." Even more evident is the outright misunderstanding of the phrase "random sample," often incorrectly considered synonymous with "representative sample." Many archaeologists assume that selected or haphazard collections are truly representative of an artifact population. Such an assumption is unjustified. Grab samples can yield only small amounts of qualitative information (e.g., that the elements collected exist on the site); they cannot be made to yield "demonstrably sound quantitative information" (Vescelius, 1960: 461).

RANDOM SAMPLING

All statistical treatment of archaeological material assumes a random sample (i.e., any one item or element of the population is as likely to be drawn as any other element and so the collection is free from conscious or unconscious bias). Certainly this is an ideal condition more to be striven for than achieved. In surface collecting and excavation some device must be utilized to minimize selective bias, personal preference, and convenience in collecting as exhibited in the tendency to pick up painted sherds, worked flints, whole items, and conveniently sized pieces, to name only a few. One such device is the randomly chosen sampling unit. The size and shape of the unit can be arbitrarily defined according to the archaeological problem, the physical condition of the surface to be collected (i.e., density of artifact scatter, topography), and obvious cultural differences (cf. Fig. 15-1).

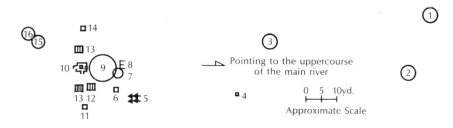

15.1 *The plan of an Ainu village. The scattered activity pattern indicated has important applications for the distribution of artifacts and kinds of refuse. The numbered locations are: 1, skinning spot; 2, skin dump; 3, bone dump; 4, tool storehouse; 5, wooden racks for drying meat and skins; 6, cage for bear cub; 7, ash dump; 8, outdoor altar; 9, area for bear ceremony; 10, living house; 11, meat storehouse; 12, meat drying frames; 13, fish drying frames; 14, fish storehouse; 15, spring for drinking water; 16, fish preparation place. (After Watanabe, 1964: Fig. 30.)*

The essential problem in comparing artifact populations is that of evaluating the chances that differences in frequencies of artifact categories in two or more sampling units reflect accidents of sampling rather than real differences in the artifact populations. Sampling, as used here, does not mean merely substituting a partial collection of a population for the total population. It is a technique by which one can control and measure the reliability of information through statistical tools based on the theory of probability (Binford, 1964: 427). Basically the archaeologist's task is to insure that: 1) the sample is selected from the population in such a way that statistical theory is applicable, and 2) the absolute size of the sample is large enough to permit satisfactory conclusions concerning the problems being studied (Cowgill, 1964: 467). The first problem, that of sample selection, is treated by Vescelius (1960), Binford (1964), Cowgill (1964), and Rootenberg (1964). Their definitions and techniques are in substantial agreement.

A truly representative sample is a selection of individual elements from a population in the exact proportion that they exist in the original population. In order to obtain a representative sample the original population must be known. Simple random sampling is a method of selection in which every member of the population has exactly the same chance of being included in the sample as does every other member. A random sample is used to *estimate* a representative sample of a population of unknown constitution. The larger the random sample is, the greater is the probability that it resembles a truly representative sample.

A population is defined (Binford, 1964: 427) as an aggregate of analytical units within an isolated field of study. It is imperative that both the analytical units and the field within which they are chosen be clearly defined in a sampling design. Sample units are the subdivision of the universe (the field of study—a geographical region, or an archaeological site) into distinct and identifiable units (natural or arbitrary) approximately equal in size. The descriptive categories in the sample unit may or may not be identical to those that make up the population. When partial coverage of a population within a universe is attempted, the sample units are selected from a frame (list of all units in the universe) so that all units of the frame have an equal chance of being chosen for investigation. A frame composed of many small units is preferable to one composed of only a few large units because small sampling units are a safeguard against including an unrepresentative amount of heterogeneity in any given sample (Binford, 1964: 428).

VARIETIES OF RANDOM SAMPLING TECHNIQUES

Several basic works such as those of Cochran (1963) and Slonim (1960) contain chapters on each of the sampling techniques mentioned in this section. The sampling of mineral deposits, and indeed of all materials in field sciences, poses similar to those encountered in archaeology (cf. Jackson and Knaebel, 1934).

Krumbein's chapter in the *Handbook of Paleontological Techniques* (Kummel and Raup, 1965: 137–150), called "Sampling in Paleontology," is an extremely clear and complete description of the various kinds of statistical sampling. I have revised some of it in the following pages to fit an archaeological rather than a geologic or paleontological context. Archaeological situations and problems are substituted for paleontological ones; brackets indicate revisions. Similarly, my paraphrasing of Krumbein uses an archaeological rather than a paleontological context.

> A principal attribute of statistical sampling is its element randomization, which assures each individual in the population some chance of being included in the sample. . . . Complexities in obtaining statistical samples from [an archaeological] population are mentioned later; nevertheless, on any one [site] it is possible to collect various kinds of statistical samples (p. 139).

Sampling techniques are discussed here in terms of a single site. For this purpose the site may be considered as a subpopulation within some larger population representing, let us say, the distribution of the refuse from an extinct people's activity in a particular geographical region.

> The first step in choosing a sampling plan is to define the subpopulation being sampled, in terms of its physical limits and of the individuals that make it up (p. 139).

In the example mentioned the objects of direct interest are cultural debris of all sorts, and the population to be sampled may be defined in any of several ways. One way is to define the population of artifacts or features directly, and the other is to define a population of unit volumes of earth or equal areas of surface of a site.

Setting up a population, defining its units, devising a problem of archaeological interest with relation to the material at hand, and deciding on a sampling plan all involve a number of purely archaeological decisions.

> Once these have been made . . . the statistical model that is to be used in analyzing the data is in turn evident, and this model controls to some extent the kind[s] of samples that are to be collected. There is no assurance that an arbitrarily selected sampling plan will be equally appropriate for different kinds of arbitrarily chosen statistical models (p. 139)

Since the kind of samples to be collected depends on what is to be done with them, and this in turn depends on the purpose of the archaeological study, four main sampling variants are described: 1) simple random sampling; 2) systematic sampling; 3) stratified sampling; and 4) cluster sampling.

Exactly the same plans are applicable to sampling in both the horizontal and the vertical section.

> [Areal sampling] requires mainly a modification of the randomization procedure to permit location of points on a map or on an outcrop face. Thus, for simple random sampling, two random numbers are taken, one representing the horizontal distance from some origin, and the other representing the vertical distance from that origin (pp. 145–146).

Simple random sampling   Suppose a large site has 100 roughly circular depressions exposed on its surface. The problem is to obtain a random sample of these features in order that their varied functions and the differences in their use and chronology can be determined. Simple random sampling requires numbering all sampling units (in this case the depressions) and randomizing a sample from these numbered individuals. Define the features as the sampling unit. Call the first feature 00, and number the depressions serially to 99. Let us take a sample of 10, although in the case of feature units a larger sample is probably necessary to be confident that all variation is included in the sample and that a representative sample is approached. A sample as large as 60 out of 100 units could be called for if the variance of the variable in question was very large. In archaeological sampling of artifact and multiple variable populations (especially in cluster and feature sampling) this is often the case. A table of random numbers is used to select 10 or more two-digit numbers lying between 00 and 99, omitting duplicates. An alternative to the table of random numbers is the random-number generator (icosahedral polyhedrons with faces numbered in pairs) as suggested by Rowlett (1970). The corresponding depressions are carefully excavated. In this plan each feature is an individual in a subpopulation of 100, but within each feature is a cluster sample (see below) of the subpopulations of the archaeological refuse characteristic of the site and of the particular feature being excavated. The population sampled satisfies the condition that each feature has an equal chance of being included in the sample, but there is no randomization of items within the feature.

The laboratory analysis of this sample may involve: 1) segregating the artifacts into types or classes in order to facilitate counting and measurement; 2) analyzing the soil samples as to physical-chemical composition (animal and fish bone, shell, seeds, pollen and other vegetal remains; organic carbon, charcoal, calcium carbonate, phosphates, acidity, and soil color have all been used to enhance the archaeologist's idea of the activities that took place in any one part of an archaeological site); 3) identifying animal and vegetable food debris as to genera and species (if possible); and 4) comparing vertical and horizontal floor plans in order to group the features at last into functionally differentiated classes. The depressions mentioned above might be classed as house depressions possibly belonging to persons of different status or occupation, storage pits, hearths or fire pits, religious or community structures, or sweat houses, on the basis of the analysis of the materials sampled.

In the process of analysis new types of populations have been generated: the depression is an individual in a population of features, but the artifacts and food debris are individuals of pottery sherds, worked stone, animal- and fish-bone fragments, shells, seeds, and pollen; and each may in turn be sampled by a randomization procedure if the number of specimens referred to any category is very large in each feature. Soil samples, for example, should be randomly selected from the three-dimensional plan of the feature (either systematic or stratified cluster sampling is a possible procedure; see below).

In archaeology this procedure of simple random sampling is applicable to large features exposed on the surface of a site such as hearths, buildings, pit depressions, and rooms of a large structure, or to arbitrarily defined sampling units. The method involves numbering all occurrences and randomizing a sample from these numbered individuals.

In simple random sampling some samples are taken in clusters and others are widely spaced. As long as the population is homogeneous, showing no trends or gradients, and as long as all individuals in the subpopulation are equally accessible, simple random sampling is a standard procedure for estimating the population mean and variance of measured attributes (p. 141).

Systematic sampling   Systematic sampling provides a plan in which the sampling units are spread fairly evenly over the area to be sampled. Let us assume the site to cover an area of 2,500 square feet. This area is divided into ten 250-square-foot nonoverlapping segments, each of which contains ten 25-square-foot nonoverlapping grid units. Number the grid squares of each segment from zero to nine. One number in the range zero to nine is chosen at random to locate the individual sample unit in the first segment. Then, from each segment, the grid square bearing this number is collected to obtain a systematic sample of each segment.

> Systematic samples satisfy the condition of equal spacing, but statistical models related to systematic sampling may differ from those based on simple random samples. Regression models for detecting trends are conveniently used with systematic samples, whereas estimates of population means and variances and of statistical correlation among variates are commonly based on simple random samples. . . . systematic samples may give better estimates of mean values (because the whole [site] is involved) than simple random samples will; but estimates of population variances may be larger for systematic than for simple random samples. This arises because . . . random samples allow some clustering, and thus include in the variance estimate the balancing influence of greater resemblance between neighbors, and less between individuals farther away (p. 142).

Homogeneity of debris is assumed in the systematic samples. Such samples furnish, however, an opportunity for testing this point, in that if the subpopulation does have a gradient or trend, regression analysis can commonly detect it.

This method might be particularly applicable to detecting dietary or ecological shifts through the successive deposits of a shell midden or habitation mound. The segments in a midden mound would be vertically stratified through the depth of the deposit and the sample could be a column subdivided according to the arbitrarily or naturally defined levels of the segments. In general, systematic sampling is not recommended for archaeological problems. The usual statistical procedures for calculating estimated sampling error are not applicable to this type of sampling procedure.

Stratified sampling   Again quoting Krumbein, "In this method of statistical sampling, some control can be exerted on the spacing of the samples by setting up two or more *sampling strata*" (p. 142). These may be selected arbitrarily, or they may be selected on the basis of depositional or cultural criteria. A common cultural criterion is the division of a deposit into living floors (the material on and above one geologically and culturally defined floor is considered one unit).

> The appropriate sampling procedure may be to collect simple random [cluster] samples from each stratum, to obtain a set of *stratified samples.*
>   The word *stratum* as used in statistical sampling is similar to its use in geology. . . . the population is "sliced" into categories or subpopulations much as geological strata "slice" a stratigraphic section into parts. Stratified sampling permits the variability in each sampling stratum to be evaluated separately, in contrast to evaluation of the overall variability in the whole population (p. 143).

The archaeologist may decide to use arbitrary sampling strata even on a single surface. Thus, as in the surface-collecting example of systematic sampling, the site can be divided into ten 250-square-foot nonoverlapping segments, each of which contains ten 25-square-foot units. Ten separately randomized samples are drawn from the segments. As Krumbein states, ". . . this tends to spread the samples over the outcrop [or site] more regularly than in simple random sampling, but less so than in systematic sampling" (p. 143). Stratified sampling, especially when more than a single sample is collected per archaeologically relevant surface area or depositional stratum, "yields a better estimate of the overall population mean than simple random samples collected over the [horizontal surface or vertical profile] without regard to strata, because the variability in each sampling stratum is taken into account in setting confidence limits on the population mean" (p. 143). A variant of stratified sampling, termed "stratified unaligned systematic" sampling, has been developed by geographers (Berry, 1962; Haggett, 1965), and an example of its use on an archaeological site in Turkey has been provided by Redman and Watson (1970: 281–282).

Cluster sampling   In Krumbein's definition, "Cluster sampling is a procedure by which more than one individual in the population being sampled is taken at each randomized position" (p. 143). In terms of a gridded archaeological site a number of randomized grid units are chosen and every item within that unit is collected. This procedure yields clusters of various kinds of cultural debris, in which the spacing between major positions is random but the spacing within the cluster (of pottery, stone, bone, etc.) is not random. This type of sampling is often used inititially in collecting and excavating material to be subjected to other sampling techniques in the field and in the laboratory.

> Cluster sampling can be extended to more than two levels, and can be designed as *nested sampling,* in which each sampling level is nested within a higher level (p. 144).

This system can be illustrated in areal sampling where, for example, the study area may include several townships as the top level, a random sample of square-mile sections within the townships as the second level, a sample of archaeological sites located within the sections as the third level, and cluster samples of grid units on the sites as the fourth level. This kind of sampling is very useful when questions of regional scales of variability are part of the archaeological study.

It is necessary to consider what restraint is imposed upon statistical sampling by the absence of sites in positions that happen to be selected by randomization.

> These restraints give rise to the concept of a *target population* that is the object of interest, as against a *sampled population* that represents the accessible portion of the target population. (p. 146)
> Limitations on statistical sampling imposed by inaccessible parts of the target population add up to this: the [archaeologist] may derive valid statistical inferences about the sampled population from his samples, but any extension of these generalizations to the target population is substantive (p. 148).

The archaeologist must draw from his or her knowledge of variation among archaeological sites from other regions in evaluating the possibilities of differences between the sample and target populations.

> There is no direct statistical method by which this comparison can be made, unless the entire target population ultimately becomes available for study (p. 148).

Thus, "statistical analysis provides a safeguard at various stages of a study," by assuring the archaeologist that his sample is "free of unintentional bias; and that his substantive assumptions, judgments, and decisions are supported by the objectively derived statistical inferences that arise from his sample data" (p. 149).

The most important point emerging from the preceding discussion is that although there is a close relationship between archaeological objectives and the statistical model with its sampling plan, it is the archaeologist who decides what to study. This decision involves evaluating sources of variability that may enter the data and the choice of sources to be taken into account in reaching generalizations. The archaeologist can be greatly aided in problems of sampling and statistical design by a professional statistician.

Vescelius (1960) was the first archaeologist to recommend and adapt cluster sampling to the archaeological problem of surface sampling. The method is complex and time-consuming compared to nonrandom sampling; nevertheless, the quality of the returns in information and precision far outweighs the cost in extra effort and time required. The technique of cluster sampling in an archaeological context as described by Vescelius, Binford, Cowgill, and Rootenberg is practically identical to that described by Krumbein. The technique is used for surface collecting as described in the Aschers' article on "Recognizing the Emergence of Man" (1965).

SAMPLE SIZE

The concept of "adequate sample size" is often mentioned but rarely explored in detail. The consensus in the earlier archaeological literature is that a sample of somewhat over 100 sherds is an adequate sample of surface materials. Ford, in the Viru Valley Report (Ford and Willey, 1949: 36), states:

> It seems to be indicated that when a type appears in a strength of over 5 percent the chances are excellent that it will be represented in a collection of over 100 sherds. . . . Further, fairly substantial variation from the theoretical actual percentage conditions on the site is to be expected in types that approach 50 percent popularity, even in collections of 300 to 500 sherds. Variation between the substantial (over 10 percent) type pairs . . . ranges from 3 to 20 percent. . . .
> As a result of experience in analyzing classification results, rather than from any basis demonstrated here, I have come to regard a random collection of over 100 sherds as fairly dependable, and anything over 50 sherds as usable for rough dating.

Tolstoy (1958: 10) considers a sample size of less than 100 "definitely suspect." These estimates are for samples to be used only for seriation, which is a descriptive, not a quantitative, method of analysis as used in the reports published before 1960.

Vescelius (1960: 462) briefly discusses sample size with reference to functional analysis of a surface collection.

> The problems of sample size are discussed in many elementary textbooks. . . . Suffice it to say that while there is no single optimum, a sample consisting of 5 to 10 percent of all the clusters (grid squares) in the population should yield results of adequate reliability for most archaeological purposes.

An adequate sample is a fraction of the surface elements of the entire site. The size of the fraction depends largely on the size of the site, the density of the surface scatter, the type of archaeological problem (functional or chronological) to be solved, and, finally and most important, the degree of statistical reliability desired by the investigator. The more powerful statistical tools require a larger, more rigorously controlled sample. In any kind of matrix analysis (i.e., grid sampling and analysis), each grid unit must contain a minimum number of units to be reliable.

Sample size can be calculated for any given degree of accuracy. The estimated size may be different for each variable sampled in the site, depending on the variability within the item or estimated variance. When sampling for more than one variable (more than one kind of information) as is usually the case in archaeological work, the archaeologists may take the maximum sample size if they have unlimited resources, or they may calculate an adequate sample size for most of the variables and sacrifice accuracy in certain areas for convenience. The statistical procedure followed in calculating sample size can be found in either of the statistical texts mentioned previously (Cochran, 1963; Slonim, 1960) and many others. Cowgill (1964: 470) discusses sample size:

> Adequacy of the sample is far more a matter of its absolute size than of the proportion it constitutes of the total population; the frequencies of very common attributes and common combinations can be estimated satisfactorily by a properly drawn sample that includes only a small proportion of all examples in the total collection. On the other hand very rare attributes, or combinations using every example found in the collections, will probably provide none too good a basis for making inferences about this occurrence in target populations.

In analyzing ceramics, a much smaller proportion of the material in common categories is required to reduce the risk of sampling error to any specific level than in rare categories. Cowgill (1964: 471) suggests a subdivision of categories into first- and second-rank classes, that is, into one class of numerous and another class of rare elements.

> One can then determine roughly what proportion of the lots from these units will be needed to give a large enough sample of the most common categories to permit inferences of the desired precision about their proportions in the target population, on the basis of formulas appropriate for cluster sampling. Enough lots or stratigraphic columns are then drawn at random to provide a sample of this size, and all material from these provenience units is described in detail and saved in some single institution.

This procedure is one of "first-order" sampling. "Second-rank" categories are included in first-order sample lots, but there are not enough to permit satisfactory conclusions to be drawn.

> We can increase our sample of these second-rank categories by drawing a number of additional lots at random (from the list of provenience units relevant to whatever population we are interested in) and thus forming a second-order sample. The size of the second-order sample should be such that when we take both first- and second-order sample data, we have enough information on second-rank categories to permit us to draw satisfactory conclusions. However, all the very common specimens of first-rank categories in this second-order sample do not provide us with any worthwhile additional information. After being cleaned, broadly identified and counted, they may be discarded or distributed.

If there is a third rank in scarcity one goes through the same procedures as for the second-rank sample. Both first- and second-rank categories in the third-order sample may be discarded or distributed.

A major advantage of this procedure is that the whole range of material is preserved for future reference. It can then be restudied or reclassified according to any new dimension or attribute.

SURFACE COLLECTING

Horizontal distribution of artifacts and other cultural debris may be affected by natural and human activity both during and after the original occupation of a site. However, statistically valid associations are possible despite the disturbance of original artifact scatter. Areas of intensive prehistoric activity, where a specialized tool kit was employed, will retain a character distinct from the remainder of the site if the factors acting to disturb the area are relatively uniform over the entire site (e.g., plowing) and/or not so intense as to destroy part or all of the site. In dealing with surface collecting, the surveyor may be able to obtain some control information about disrupting agents. He is at leisure to observe the topography of the site and delineate areas of differential erosion or postoccupational deposition. Local inhabitants or recorded information may be able to provide information on previous surface collecting or excavation. Disruptions that have been differentially destructive may be detectible. If these disruptive factors are taken into consideration, artifact clustering can tentatively be interpreted in terms of specialized cultural activity and temporal change. The surveyor or excavator can then proceed to salvage, through proper collecting techniques, significant cultural information.

Random samples taken from archaeological sites can yield information on numerous important questions such as the density of debris per unit area; the range of artifact types; the proportion of specific artifact types in the population; and the distribution or patterned spacing of amount and kinds of cultural debris within the site. Knowing the relative density of artifacts or food debris per unit area may enable one to make a rough estimate of intensity of occupation (i.e., number of people living on the site during the period in question), length of occupation, seasonal inhabitation, or type and intensity of ecological exploitation. An idea of distribution (or dispersion) of elements within the site may help one to distinguish among: 1) a large group occupying the site for a short time; 2) a small group living on the site for a long time; and 3) a large population occupying the site for a long time. The interpretation of length and/or intensity of occupation, however, depends on *a priori* assumptions or documented correlations between cultural activity and the material remains of that activity (Heizer, 1960: 112–115; Cook and Heizer, 1965a; Meighan, 1958: 2–3). Clustering of particular tools or artifact configurations can reveal sections of the site where special activities were performed. The range of tool types and their proportional frequencies may give information on specific activities conducted within the site as well as on the relative importance of these activities.

The proper sampling design can isolate not only activity foci within a site but differences in activity between sites in a single area. Regional studies have made it possible to combine what were considered separate cultures into a single multi-facies culture, the variations being a function of different activities that may or may not have been seasonally determined.

Three factors contribute to differences between archaeological samples taken from undisturbed archaeological strata: 1) sampling error; 2) functional differences; and 3) temporal differences between the parent populations from which the samples were drawn. Many archaeologists have concentrated on temporal variations between parent populations, ignoring sampling error and relegating functional specificity to a minor role (Brown and Freeman, 1964: 162). In a UNIVAC analysis of the pottery from Carter Ranch Pueblo, Brown and Freeman (1964: 166) were able to delineate four functional differences from the pottery distribution of the pueblo: 1) there were four constellations of pottery types that may have been used for functionally diverse purposes, among them a possible mortuary complex; 2) four room types established on the basis of floor features were distinguishable through frequencies of pottery found on their floors, and this suggested that different cultural activities were taking place in each type of room; 3) functional differences were discovered in the deposition of midden materials in five discrete areas, though there were no consistent demonstrable temporal differences between painted and unpainted pottery in the five trenches through the midden; and 4) the largest frequencies of painted pottery were found in the kiva and the four rooms closest to it, leading the investigators to suspect involvement with a mortuary complex. Further, they were able to explain differences between floor and fill debris that would otherwise have gone unnoticed.

Statistical techniques describe associations among elements of a site and/or constellations of sites. It is clear from Brown and Freeman's UNIVAC analysis (1964) that such an analysis merely describes a body of material. The relationships discovered were associations of the same validity but of a different nature from the more common "visible associations," such as the association of grave goods, skeletal material, and burial pits. Explaining such associations in cultural terms is not the job of the machine or of the statistical techniques, but of the prehistorian himself. However, the very complete descriptions of the data made possible by statistical tools will not only help the prehistorian to see pertinent factors involved in that explanation, but may also give insights into other problems and ease their solution (Brown and Freeman, 1964: 163). Hill's discussion (1966: 9–30) of prehistoric communities in eastern Arizona summarizes some of the recent contributions to archaeology that have resulted from using statistical techniques in excavation and data processing. The method presents "an example of some of the kinds of inferences which may be made concerning the internal structure and social organization of a prehistoric Pueblo site. It has also examined some of the evidence related to an ultimate explanation of changes in site structure through time" (Hill, 1966: 27).

Binford (1964: 432–435) outlines procedures for a regional site survey that might serve to exemply the kind of research design proper to statistical analysis. This design allows for the description of the environment as well as the archaeological sites. Culture is considered an adaptive system. In such a system, the operations and the modifications that culture undergoes can only be understood within the context of "the adaptive milieu." "All those elements which represent or inform about the ways and means by which groups have exploited or adjusted to the natural and cultural environment form this milieu" (Binford, 1964). Thus, both the ecological and the cultural aspects of a region must be investigated, and ecological as well as archaeological components are broken down into subclasses representing different populations (pollen, soil, and animal bone) that may be sampled for information about the natural environment.

In Binford's research design, two sampling universes are defined: 1) the region; and 2) the site. The region is divided into "strata"—natural areas (river frontage, forest, plateau, etc.) and/or arbitrary ones (e.g., square-mile grids)—and a combination of stratified and cluster sampling techniques can be used to obtain a random sample of sites from all segments of the area. Thus the surveyor is able to cover a randomly chosen proportion of the area and, perhaps, to recognize functional differences between sites associated with specific natural strata. The surfaces of the sites located in the course of the survey are mapped in detail and sampled. The populations of cultural items (artifacts and debris) present at each of the sites are evaluated in terms of a formal characterization of the sites. The ultimate aim is to classify activity loci as to their degree of similarity and difference—in other words, a taxonomy of sites. From this frame of sites as many from each of the several categories may be excavated as interest, time, and money will allow. The student is referred to the work of Judge (1973) for an excellent example of the regional site survey in practice.

SAMPLING IN EXCAVATION

The major emphasis thus far in this discussion has been on surface sampling rather than sampling techniques used during excavation. Random sampling of midden areas for information on subsistence and ecology has been worked out with some precision (cf. Cook and Heizer, 1951, 1962; Cook and Treganza, 1947, 1950; Gifford, 1916; Greengo, 1951). This kind of sampling uses basically the same assumptions and techniques as the kinds previously described. There are, however, three important differences: 1) the grid or matrix is extended vertically as well as horizontally, with arbitrary or natural stratification serving to demarcate vertical boundaries; 2) in shell-refuse middens horizontal homogeneity is assumed (Cook and Heizer, 1951); and 3) the elements of the samples (bone, shell, and organic material) are often minute if not microscopic. These differences demand some change in technique. The systematically sampled grid units are excavated as free-standing columns, as vertical walls of the deposit, or with augers, and the samples are bagged separately by levels. This process allows control over vertical as well as horizontal trends within the deposit. Furthermore, an adequate sample may consist of fewer units of a much smaller size. There is not space to review here the large volume of literature on midden analysis and sampling, but since the principles are basically those of systematic cluster sampling, a reference is made to some of the details of sample collection that differ according to the nature of the deposit being sampled.

Column sampling was originally inspired by A. L. Kroeber (Gifford, 1916: 1), pioneered in practice by Gifford (ibid.), later extensively applied by Cook, Heizer, Treganza, and Greengo, and discussed as a method by Meighan et al. (1958) and Cook and Heizer (1965a). It has been used principally in Northern and Central California, although any shell or habitation midden is amenable to it. Much of the work on California habitation and shellmounds in the late 1940's and early 1950's is still methodologically sound. Changes have been primarily in the direction of refinement and speed of data recovery, for example, in adopting standard screen and sample sizes (Ascher, 1959; Greenwood, 1961; Cook and Heizer, 1962: 3-4).

The work is based on the one major assumption: ". . . in order to reconstruct the life of extinct peoples all material residues must be studied, and concomitantly, no tangible material is too crude or insignificant to tell us something about the conditions in which aboriginal populations lived" (Cook and Heizer, 1951: 281).

Treganza and Cook established the methodological principles by completely excavating a single small habitation mound. From this site all the earth was weighed and screened, and every artifact, bone, and shell was counted. This enabled the investigators to devise a general formula for sampling other sites and comparing sampling results. The method assured adequate statistical treatment of the content and at the same time reduced excavation at these other sites to a minimum. Cook and Heizer (1951: 281) report sampling a series of sites:

> It was then possible to point out how these areas differed, both qualitatively and quantitatively, in certain aspects of material culture and to correlate these differences with variations in the physiography and ecology of the corresponding regions. In this particular instance many of our conclusions could have

been reached equally well by the use of ethnographic data. However, our results demonstrated that physical analysis leads to essentially correct deductions even in the total absence of any ethnographic knowledge.

Cook and Heizer's standard procedure for physical analysis entailed taking a series of column samples. Each sample was then transported to the laboratory and passed through a ⅛-inch or 2-mm. screen. Comparisons were based upon the material retained by the screen. Screening a column sample in the field can be accomplished most efficiently with a ¼-inch screen. A few samples sent to the lab and screened through a ⅛- or ¹⁄₁₆-inch screen establish the ratio of components in the field sample to those in the more accurate laboratory sample (Cook and Heizer, 1962; Ascher, 1959). Field identification of mound components has also been proved possible and helpful in guiding the progress of the excavation. "Any mound component occurring in pieces smaller than ½-inch in diameter should be sampled by the column method or its equivalent, with the single exception of artifacts" (Cook and Heizer, 1951: 291). In the sampling of artifacts many large refuse samples are necessary because artifacts are rare and unevenly distributed. When properly handled, this method of screening large samples is capable of yielding information on the occurrence and distribution of artifacts in one site as well as on the differences between sites.

Greenwood (1961: 416–417) designed a shell-refuse study to test and perfect methods of quantitative analysis.

> Experiments were performed to determine the optimum size of sample, dimension of screen, number of samples, and the practicability of rapid analysis in the field to guide the progress of excavation. . . . The methodological experiments demonstrated that a 500gm. sample produces as accurate a measure of the shell in a level as the total sample from the level, that a ¼th inch screen is adequate when brittle types such as *Mytilus* and abalone which break into very small fragments are absent or present in only very small quantities, that rough field sorting produces results which correlate well with those based on closely controlled laboratory analysis. . . . Field identification, weighing, tabulating and interpreting of shell remains could be used to advise the digging crew about horizontal and columnar distributions in time to modify the excavation schedule if that seemed advisable.

The principles for sampling at an archaeological site remain the same, whether the sampling is done on the surface, during excavation (treating each level of excavation as a surface), in the deposit, or when soil, carbon, or pollen samples are taken. As representative a sample as possible is sought by a random sampling technique. Some of the techniques outlined above require time and a number of workers not always available to the weekend student crew or to a lone archaeologist looking over a new site. Infinite modifications are possible in the systems described to adjust for lack of time, labor, and/or money. If a random sample is not possible, then an intelligently selected sample in which biases are relatively explicit is preferable to a haphazard one. Marking the areas collected on a site map then becomes a prerequisite. Preferably all items collected in the small area should be bagged together. If two small segments of the site are sampled, each sample should go into a separate bag or container; large areas can be broken up into smaller units in which everything is collected and each segment is bagged separately.

In the method described by Alcock (1951: 25–26) the entire site is paced off into "zones" that are collected separately. Particular materials are explicitly selected, such as all pottery or all flint, leav)ng out animal remains, fire-cracked rock, or flint waste (in the case of a largely ceramic site). This type of collection will, of course, tell one only about the distribution within the site of the material collected and nothing about the numerical relations of one component to another or to the total surface population. A sketch map with bags designated according to area, a notebook description of the selective bias (i.e., what was collected entirely, partially, or not at all), and the rationale behind the bias are, as always, imperative.

In the final analysis, cluster or stratified cluster sampling is the most reliable, giving more information on more aspects of the population than any other. Vescelius' article (1960: 463–464) contains a description of the statistical methods involved in analyzing cluster samples. Other, rougher methods are useful only when previous work (i.e., excavation) at similar sites has given the archaeologist an added basis for interpretation. At sites unlikely to be excavated (the majority of sites), a random cluster sample from the surface can provide valuable information to support the cultural evaluation of an entire region. Prehistory is best understood, however, through the excavation of a carefully planned sample of a total range of sites in a region. The sampling of an entire region is invaluable in making an intelligent selection of key sites to be excavated. Surface collections at the sites yield clues for excavation strategy. And random testing of the areas of a site that are not to be excavated can give investigators some assurance that they have not missed an important feature.

This chapter has not developed new statistical strategies for the preliminary survey or excavation of an archaeological deposit; it has merely summarized statistical techniques already adapted to archaeological problems. Perhaps a more useful and exciting approach to the discussion of statistical techniques would be to create new statistical designs specifically for the analysis of archaeological field and laboratory problems. This task is beyond our scope here, but must eventually be done in order that particular field problems can be approached more rationally than is now customary. Work by Brown, Freeman, Longacre, and Hill in the Southwest does explore various research designs and techniques "that can be used in recovering and analysing data . . . useful in making more complete descriptions of prehistoric sociocultural systems and more complete explanations of their change in time and space" (Hill, 1966: 28).

Full development of these techniques will require some time, considering present ignorance about statistical methods as applied to archaeology. More preliminary field analysis from an archaeological viewpoint is required because each archaeological deposit may be approached with numerous problems in mind, and the research design applicable to their solution is modified by the unique constitution of the individual site. A more detailed discussion of basic statistical methods and their possible uses in archaeology is imperative. Students of prehistory cannot understand published material, much less hope to contribute creatively to the theoretical growth of the subject, without a working knowledge of statistical techniques.*

Addendum

Since 1967 archaeologists have become increasingly concerned with developing better methods of sampling, and the reader is here referred to a selection of these: Mueller (1974, especially pp. 26–47 and bibliography), Redman (1974), Redman and Watson (1970), Thomas (1969b), Martin, Longacre, and Hill (1967: 145–157), and Cowgill (1970).

---

*The student may find useful Woodall's (1968) bibliography of the use of statistics in archaeology.

APPENDIX I

THE WRITING OF ARCHAEOLOGICAL REPORTS

He who gives quickly gives twice, and he who publishes fully and soon discovers double.

—SIR W. M. F. PETRIE

It would be presumptuous if the present authors attempted to advise students on the proper methods of writing archaeological reports. There are as many proper methods as there are good reports, and our experience certainly does not encompass them all.

Most beginning students will probably not try to write an archaeological report for submission to a technical journal. Usually, a student's writing is first published during graduate study. Some years of study and experience are required in order to ensure that what they are doing is professionally adequate. By the time archaeologists begin to write and publish reports, they will have read scores or even hundreds of articles, monographs, and books and should, in this process, have a good idea of the way in which data are properly presented to their colleagues.

In other words, writing reports is something that gradually takes care of itself with experience. One cannot be taught how to write reports—like excavation, this can be learned only by actual practice. However, the student can consult a variety of sources regarding the technical aspect of report preparation, including Harrison (1945) and Grinsell, Rahtz, and Warhurst (1966). Some textbooks and guides have brief sections offering advice on preparing archaeological reports (see Atkinson, 1953: 173–206; Hole and Heizer, 1973: 416 ff.; Webster, 1963: 131–166; and, Wheeler, 1954: 182–199). Map drafting is treated by Bryant and Holtz (1965), Livingston (1967), and Piggott and Hope-Taylor (1965). Preparation of illustrations is discussed by Brodribb (1970), Combes (1964), Isham (1965), Ives (1948), Kenrick (1971), Kobayashi and Bleed (1971), Platz (1971), Ridgway (1938), Rivard (1964), Smith (1970), Staniland (1953), Van Riet Lowe (1954), Vinnicombe (1963), and Young (1970).

Furthermore, the student should always keep in mind that a report is not enhanced by verbiage or by the coinage of new terms. Reports should be concise and, above all, clear. As Osborne (1968: 383) has cogently observed: "Muddy writing equals muddy thinking and equally muddy comprehension."

Every published archaeological paper or site report becomes part of the total body of fact and opinion regarding human beings and their past activities. It is available to all students, and makes its own small contribution to the history of mankind, the complete reconstruction of which is the grand aim of archaeology. Thus each writer will want to make the very best record of which he or she is capable, and to report all observations and thoughts of any possible significance as items bearing upon the life of earlier peoples.

In concluding, we call attention to the remarks that introduce this appendix. Although Petrie's comments date from around the turn of the century, they are still good advice today. Indeed, at a time when sites are being pillaged, and are being destroyed by urban expansion at a rapidly increasing rate, it becomes ever more crucial that excavation results be quickly and fully published. To allow field notes and artifacts to sit unattended for years is a dereliction of archaeological responsibility. Persons wishing to merit the title of archaeologist must promptly communicate to their colleagues, through publication, what they have found and how they view the data in terms of current archaeological knowledge. Pallis (1956: 307) puts the matter in proper light: "An excavation without a final, detailed, scientific publication must be said to mean to science the same as if it had not been made."

APPENDIX II

CHOOSING ARCHAEOLOGY AS A PROFESSION

If you go buzzing about between right and wrong, vibrating and fluctuating, you come out nowhere; but if you are absolutely and thoroughly and persistently wrong, you must, some of these days, have the extreme good fortune of knocking your head against a fact, and that sets you all straight again.

—T. H. HUXLEY

As university professors the authors of this book are asked perhaps thirty times a year by students to inform or advise them about their opportunities if they should decide to make a career of archaeology.

Students who take up archaeology as a career will first have to go through the four-year drill of undergraduate studies. During these college years, they will probably participate in both field and laboratory research in archaeology, either as enrolled students in a summer-session training course, as unpaid volunteers on a research dig, or as paid workers doing salvage excavations. Provided their undergraduate grades are good enough, they will be admitted to graduate studies leading to the doctor's (Ph.D.) degree. There is usually little point in putting in two years to earn the master's (M.A.) degree, since the degree is often not very highly regarded and will, at most, allow one to teach in a local college or community college. However, given recent federal legislation, there is the likelihood that persons terminating their studies with a M.A. degree and trained in field archaeology can find continuing employment doing contract investigations, particularly field studies designed to assess the environmental impact of proposed construction activities. Some graduate students, for various reasons, will take an M.A. degree at one university and transfer to some other institution to complete their work for the Ph.D. degree.

Many college students who opt for undergraduate majors in anthropology and whose special interests during college revolve around archaeology will not become career archaeologists. They will find, or be forced by circumstances to select, more lucrative means of making a living; but many of them will retain a deep interest in prehistoric societies and their archaeological evidences. Many of the most promising undergraduate students whom we have had in courses and who have participated in field work have not gone on to make archaeology a profession.

Students who succeed in surmounting all the hurdles of graduate training—e.g., keeping up their grades; demonstrating a satisfactory reading knowledge of two foreign languages, usually French or Spanish and German; passing the university oral examination(s) that are administered by five professors; writing a dissertation (thesis), 150 to 200 pages (or more) in length and based upon original research—and receiving their Ph.D. degrees can be said to have their "union card." They will now probably accept appointments as beginning assistant professors at a university, where, for several years, they will feel even greater pressures imposed by: 1) low salary; 2) teaching responsibilities; 3) the need to do research and publish results in order to demonstrate to their tenured colleagues and to their dean that they are serious and productive intellectuals. Probably they will have married while graduate students and begun to accumulate a family. If so, they will feel the pinch of too little money and the conflict of family demands during the whole of the four to six (or even eight) years of apprenticeship as an assistant professor. During these years, they will probably teach courses in summer session to earn a little extra pay and spend the rest of the vacation period in the field. Assistant professors are usually very tired. Beyond this point (i.e., when they become associate professors), there is somewhat better pay, and the feeling of being on probation is somewhat alleviated.

Most archaeologists have the option of selecting the area and kind of problems with which they wanted to become involved. Possibly they started, while college students, working in local sites. They may continue this interest and become authorities on the prehistory of the region in which they live or, as they find more opportunities to branch out during graduate study, they may manage to join an expedition working in Mexico, Alaska, Nubia, Chile, or some other outland area.

There are alternatives to going into the college or university teaching-research system, although these may be less rewarding both economically and intellectually. One of these is to secure a position in a museum, but such jobs can become rather routine, eight-hour-a-day grinds, and co-workers may be unstimulating. Museum employees are not paid to follow their own research interests, but must catalogue specimens, arrange exhibits, and answer questions put by the visiting public. A few museums are primarily research organizations, but most such institutions are public-service oriented, and therefore museum workers' activities are devoted to this end.

Another alternative is to become a free-lance archaeologist. Federal- and state-supported salvage archaeology programs have operated continuously in the United States, except during World War II, since about 1930. Archaeology has, however unobtrusively, become a regular item in the tax-supported public-works program, and recent legislation (the Moss-Bennett bill) suggests that federal support will greatly increase in coming years. Archaeologists can make a career of this work in the sense that once they become part of the system, they can probably gain employment in salvage archaeology in one or another of the 50 states at any time. A good deal of uncertainty is involved in this way of making a living, but if people can adjust to this and really want to do archaeology, it can be managed. This public-service-oriented category includes not only prehistoric archaeological sites (Stephenson, 1954; Johnson, 1966), but also sites of historic interest (Hudson, 1963; Green, 1960; Harrington, 1952, 1955; Fontana, 1965), and sites that yield paleontological remains.

Still another career for would-be archaeologists lies in federal or state civil service positions. Rangers or guides at a national monument that is an archaeological site will have to deal with the tourist public, but they will be close to archaeology, and may occasionally be allowed to do archaeological surveys or excavations as part of their duties. There are some desk jobs in state or federal archaeological agencies, but these are often awarded to persons who have come up through the ranks.

All the job possibilities mentioned should give the person who is genuinely interested in archaeology a satisfying way of life. There is enough variety of need for people with real archaeological interests so that most individuals' special inclinations can be satisfied. In addition, various employments can be adjusted to individual abilities.

Kenyon (1961: 167–222) and Rowe (1954) have provided discussions of archaeology as a career. Since archaeologists are also anthropologists, the excellent surveys of Sturtevant (1958) and Mandelbaum (1964) are recommended.

But, if you really want to become an archaeologist, you are going to have to be prepared to work hard at it, both in field work and in absorbing a significant proportion of the enormous amount of information that is already known. Not only will you be a teacher (regardless of what kind of job you secure), but it is incumbent upon you to discover new facts, assess their significance in terms of what we already know, and make this new knowledge available to whoever is interested in it in the form of publication. To claim to be an archaeologist and only talk about, but not practice, archaeology is taking a free ride on the work of others. To learn and to communicate your findings is a rewarding activity in personal as well as professional terms.

We have deliberately avoided giving advice on what kinds of courses to take and what kinds of special knowledge to acquire. As a college student, you will of course have the guidance of trained professors and a carefully planned program of study. An occasional half hour of discussion with one of your professors will help you see directions to take and ways to explore a new aspect of archaeology that interests you; and through these talks, you will begin to get the "professional feel" for your subject. Even though archaeology as a formal discipline is barely a century old, many archaeologists have been very busy writing during that period, and one of your big jobs will be to keep reading and absorbing as much of that large literature as you can. It is obviously impossible to learn everything that is known about archaeology, and that is one reason why archaeologists become regional specialists. But becoming too specialized may hinder you from working with a broad perspective of human prehistory.

Assuming that students who find this volume useful will devote some or all of their research efforts to American prehistory, the following broad treatments of North American archaeology and archaeological theory can be recommended for background reading: S. R. and L. R. Binford, *New Perspectives in Archeology* (Aldine, 1968); J. M. Campbell, ed., *Prehistoric Cultural Relations Between the Arctic and Temperate Zones of North America* (Arctic Institute of North America, 1962); R. C. Dunnell, *Systematics in Prehistory* (Free Press, 1971); J. B. Griffin, ed., *Archaeology of Eastern United States* (University of Chicago Press, 1952); J. E. Fitting, ed., *The Development of North American Archaeology* (Anchor Books, 1973); J. D. Jennings, *Prehistory of North America* (McGraw-Hill, 1968); J. D. Jennings and E. Norbeck, eds., *Prehistoric Man in the New World* (University of Chicago Press, 1964); F. Johnson, ed., *Man in Northeastern North America* (Papers of the R. S. Peabody Foundation for Archaeology, Vol. 3, 1946); A. D. Krieger, "New World Culture History: Anglo-America" (*Anthropology Today,* ed. by A. L. Kroeber, pp. 238–264, 1953); M. P. Leone, *Contemporary Archaeology* (Southern Illinios University Press, 1972); P. S. Martin, G. Quimby, and D. Collier, *Indians Before Columbus* (University of Chicago Press, 1947); B. J. Meggers, *Prehistoric America* (Aldine, 1972); B. Meggers and C. Evans, eds., *New Interpretations of Aboriginal American Culture History* (Anthropological Society of Washington, 1955;) T. C. Patterson, *America's Past: A New World Archaeology* (Scott, Foresman and Company, 1973); W. T. Sanders and J. Marino, *New World Prehistory* (Prentice-Hall, 1970); E. H. Sellards, *Early Man in America* (University of Texas Press, 1952); J. H. Steward, ed., *Essays in Historical Anthropology of North America* (Smithsonian Miscellaneous Collections, Vol. 100, 1940); D. H. Thomas, *Predicting the Past* (Holt, Rinehart and Winston, 1974) P. J. Watson, S. A. Leblanc and C. L. Redman, *Explanation in Archaeology* (Columbia University Press, 1971); W. R. Wedel, *Prehistoric Man on the Great Plains* (University of Oklahoma Press, 1961); G. R. Willey, ed., *Archaeological Research in Retrospect* (Winthrop, 1974); G. R. Willey, *An Introduction to American Archaeology* (Prentice-Hall, 1966); G. R. Willey and P. Phillips, *Method and Theory in New World Archaeology* (University of Chicago Press,

1958); G. R. Willey and J. A. Sabloff, *A History of American Archaeology* (Thames and Hudson, 1973); H. M. Wormington, *Ancient Man in North America* (Denver Museum of Natural History, 1957).

Since World War II, not only have a very large number of new nations come into existence, but old countries as well as newly founded ones have acted on the basis of intense nationalism in foreign relations. This nationalism is reaching more and more levels of activity, and American researchers in botany, zoology, geology, and archaeology are experiencing increasing difficulty in many countries in securing official permits to carry out their investigations. As both new and long-established nations develop a corps of trained scientific workers, these countries become eager to do their own work, and thus discourage entry of workers from outside. Also foreign research is often taken to be a form, however mild, of exploitation.

We believe that more and more areas of the world will be closed or accessible only under very limited and rigidly defined conditions to American archaeologists. The trend in this direction will take different forms, proceed at variable rates, and therefore affect some kinds of archaeological research more than others. It seems possible that in the future, foreign archaeological permits or contracts will carry a clause forbidding large-scale excavation and will limit research to surface exploration. Such restrictions will not necessarily mean the end to effective and productive work overseas. For example, as our colleague Robert Rodden has pointed out to us, an approach that is essentially what the British call "field archaeology" (Crawford, 1953) may have to be learned and applied by Americans, who now tend to be intensive excavators rather than observers of surface remains. A great deal can be learned by using sub-surface detection apparatus (resistivity and magnetometer surveys), by exploiting collections of surface materials more fully, (i.e., using proper sampling methods, seriation techniques, etc.), and by using augers to collect stratigraphic soil samples to be analyzed by pedologists, palynologists, etc. Further, the host of nondestructive physical and chemical methods of analyzing artifacts that are now available (such as trace-element analysis), when applied to materials already collected and stored in museums, provide a vast field of inquiry that is virtually untouched (Rainey, 1966; Biek, 1963; Rainey and Ralph, 1966; Tite, 1972).

If the prognosis just given is even partly true, students of archaeology will find a grounding in physics, chemistry, and other "hard sciences" increasingly useful, and they will find it important to learn as much as they can about laboratory methods and the application of analytical instruments to archaeological materials. We are not trying to say that the nations of the world are going to exclude all American archaeologists or that American prehistorians are going to have to become scientific gadgeteers, but what we see as present trends may eventually make both of these propositions true in some degree.

APPENDIX III

STATE AND FEDERAL REGULATIONS CONCERNING ARCHAEOLOGICAL SITES

Let's not get lost in archeology—a widespread and fatal tendency, I think, of the coming generation.

—GUSTAVE FLAUBERT, *in Cairo, June, 1850*

As of 1974, 43 states had laws or regulations protecting sites of archaeological, historical, or paleontological interest on state-owned lands. Antiquities on federal lands are covered by the Antiquities Act (Public Law 34–209, 34th Congress, S. L. 225, June 8, 1906); the Historic Sites Act (Public Law 74–292, 74th Congress, S. 2073, August 21, 1935); and the Salvage Archaeology Act (Public Law 86–523, 85th Congress, S. 1185, June 27, 1960). These federal acts are all printed in full in Wendorf (1962: 83–93) and McGimsey (1972). C. R. McGimsey's book *Public Archaeology* (Seminar Press, 1972) is an in-depth study of state and federal legislation and funding practices regarding archaeology. It contains full texts of recent federal acts pertaining to archaeological remains. State laws are summarized by Agogino and Sachs (1960a, 1960b) and McNeil (1969) and the problems of vandalism ("pot hunting") in American archaeology are discussed by H. Davis (1971) and Nickerson (1962a, 1962b).

Anyone applying for permission to excavate on private lands in the United States should make every effort to get this permission in writing. For official university excavations, written permission is mandatory. It is important that this permission be obtained from the bona fide owner of the land as well as from the tenant or lessee.

All lands controlled by the federal government are protected by the Antiquities Act of June 1906, cited above. It is a misdemeanor to "appropriate,

311

excavate, injure or destroy any historic or prehistoric ruin or monument or object of antiquity situated on lands owned or controlled by the United States. . . ."

Permits to excavate may be secured from the secretary of the department having jurisdiction over the land, i.e., the Secretary of the Interior, Agriculture, or Defense. With the application must be sent an outline of the intended work, the name of the public institution in which the materials are to be deposited, etc. Full information concerning this procedure may be found in "The Uniform Rules and Regulations . . . to carry out the provisions for the Act for the Preservation of American Antiquities" (34 Stat. L., June 8, 1906). The background and development of federal site protection laws is amply covered by R. F. Lee (1970).

Historically, it is interesting to note that the American Association for the Advancement of Science, in 1888, appointed a Committee for the Preservation of Archaeologic Remains, and a year later (*Popular Science Monthly,* 34: 136, 1889) the committee (consisting of Alice C. Fletcher and T. E. Stevenson) recommended that measures be taken to preserve a number of sites in the Southwest, Dakota, and Alaska. It is not known to us what connection, if any, this activity had with the passage of the federal act of 1906.

In 1887, Daniel G. Brinton, M.D. (no Ph.D. in Anthropology had yet been granted in the United States), in the vice-presidential address to Section H of the American Association for the Advancement of Science, wrote:

> As Americans of adoption, it should be our first interest and duty to study the Americans by race, in both their present and past development. The task is long and the opportunity is fleeting. A century more, and the anthropologist will scarcely find a native of pure blood; the sites and languages of today will have been extinguished or corrupted. Nor will the archaeologist be in better case. Every day the progress of civilization, ruthless of the monuments of barbarism, is destroying the fabled vestiges of the ancient race; mounds are levelled, embankments disappear, the stones of temples are built into factories, the holy places desecrated. We have assembled here to aid in recovering something from this wreck of a race and its monuments; let me urge upon you all the need of prompt action and earnest work, inasmuch as the opportunities we enjoy will never again present themselves in such fullness.

APPENDIX IV

TABLES OF EQUIVALENTS AND CONVERSION FACTORS

LENGTH, DISTANCE

1 meter	= 1.09361 yards
1 meter	= 39.37 inches
1 meter	= 3.28 feet
1 centimeter	= .3937 inches
1 kilometer	= .62137 miles
1 kilometer	— 1093.61 yards
1 yard	— .9144 meters
1 foot	= .3048 meters
1 inch	= 2.54 centimeters
1 mile	= 1609.35 meters

WEIGHT

1 kilogram	= 2.20462 pounds
1 gram	= .0353 ounces
1 ounce	= .02835 kilograms
1 pound	= .45359 kilograms
1 metric ton	= 1000 kilograms
1 short ton	= 907.185 kilograms
1 long ton	= 1016.05 kilograms

AREA

1 hectare	= 2.47104 acres
1 square meter	= 1.19598 square yards
1 square yard	= .836131 square meters
1 square foot	= .09290 square meters
1 square inch	= .0006452 square meters
1 acre	= 4046.9 square meters
1 square mile	= 2.59 square kilometers

VOLUME

1 liter	= 1.05668 quarts
1 liter	= .26417 gallons
1 cubic inch	= .1639 liters
1 cubic foot	= 28.3170 liters
1 cubic yard	= 764.559 liters
1 quart	= .94636 liters
1 gallon	= 3.78543 liters
1 pint	= .95 liters

Conversion of compass points to degrees

	Points	Angular measure °	′		Points	Angular measure °	′
North to East:				South to West:			
North	0	0		South	16	180	
N. by E.	1	11	15	S. by W.	17	191	15
NNE.	2	22	30	SSW.	18	202	30
NE. by N.	3	33	45	SW. by S.	19	213	45
NE.	4	45		SW.	20	225	
NE. by E.	5	56	15	SW. by W.	21	236	15
ENE.	6	67	30	WSW.	22	247	30
E. by N.	7	78	45	W. by S.	23	258	45
East to South:				West to North:			
East	8	90	0	West	24	270	
E. by S.	9	101	15	W. by N.	25	281	15
ESE.	10	112	30	WNW.	26	292	30
SE. by E.	11	123	45	NW. by W.	27	303	45
SE.	12	135		NW.	28	315	
SE. by S.	13	146	15	NW. by N.	29	326	15
SSE.	14	157	30	NNW.	30	337	30
S. by E.	15	168	45	N. by W.	31	348	45
				North	32	360	

Conversion factors

Multiply	By	To obtain
cubic centimeters	3.531×10^{-5}	cubic feet
″	6.102×10^{-2}	cubic inches
″	10^{-6}	cubic meters
″	1.308×10^{-6}	cubic yards
″	2.642×10^{-4}	gallons
″	10^{-3}	liters
cubic feet	2.832×10^{4}	cubic centimeters
″	1728	cubic inches
″	.02832	cubic meters
″	.03704	cubic yards
″	7.48052	gallons
″	28.32	liters
gallons	3785	cubic centimeters
″	.1337	cubic feet
″	231	cubic inches
″	3.785×10^{-3}	cubic meters
″	4.951×10^{-3}	cubic yards
″ (water)	8.3453	pounds of water

Conversion factors

Multiply	By	To obtain
temperature (°C) +273	1	absolute temperature (°C)
" (°C) +17.78	1.8	temperature (°F)
" (°F) +460	1	absolute temperature (°F)
" (°F) −32	5/9	temperature (°C)
long tons	2240	pounds
"	1016	kilograms
"	1.12000	short tons
metric tons	10^3	kilograms
"	2205	pounds
short tons	2000	pounds
"	32,000	ounces
"	907.18486	kilograms
"	.89287	long tons
"	.90718	metric tons
centimeters	.3937	inches
cubic inches	16.39	cubic centimeters
"	5.787×10^{-4}	cubic feet
"	1.639×10^{-5}	cubic meters
"	2.143×10^{-5}	cubic yards
cubic meters	10^6	cubic centimeters
"	35.31	cubic feet
"	61,023	cubic inches
"	1.308	cubic yards
cubic yards	7.646×10^5	cubic centimeters
"	27	cubic feet
"	46,656	cubic inches
"	.7646	cubic meters
feet	30.48	centimeters
"	.3048	meters
"	.36	varas
gallons	3785	cubic centimeters
"	.1337	cubic feet
"	231	cubic inches
"	3.785×10^{-3}	cubic meters
"	4.951×10^{-3}	cubic yards
grams	15.43	grains (Troy)
"	10^{-3}	kilograms
"	10^3	milligrams
"	.03527	ounces
"	2.205×10^{-3}	pounds
hectares	1.076×10^5	square feet
inches	2.540	centimeters
kilograms	10^3	grams
"	2.2046	pounds
"	1.102×10^{-3}	tons (short)

Conversion factors

Multiply	By	To obtain
kilometers	3281	feet
"	10^3	meters
"	.6214	statute miles
"	1093.6	yards
meters	3.2808	feet
"	39.37	inches
"	10^{-3}	kilometers
"	1.0936	yards
millimeters	.03937	inches
miles	1609.35	meters
"	1.6093	kilometers
ounces	28.35	grams
"	.0625	pounds
pounds of water	.01602	cubic feet
"	27.68	cubic inches
"	.1198	gallons
quarts (dry)	67.20	cubic inches
" (liquid)	57.75	cubic inches
rods	16.5	feet
square centimeters	1.076×10^{-3}	square feet
"	.1550	square inches
"	10^{-6}	square meters
square feet	929	square centimeters
"	144	square inches
"	.09290	square meters
"	1/9	square yards
square inches	6.452	square centimeters
"	6.944×10^{-3}	square feet
square meters	10.764	square feet
"	3.861×10^{-7}	square miles
"	1.196	square yards
square miles	27.88×10^6	square feet
"	2.590	square kilometers
"	3.098×10^6	square yards
square kilometers	.3861	square miles
square yards	9	square feet
"	.8361	square meters
"	3.228×10^{-7}	square miles
varas	2.7777	feet
yards	.9144	meters
hectares	2.471	acres
acres	.4047	hectares

Map scale equivalents

Map scale	Inches to mile	Statute miles to an inch	Feet to an inch	Kilometers to an inch
1:600	105.6	.0095	50.	.0153
1:1,200	52.8	.0189	100,	.0305
1:2,400	26.4	.0379	200.	.061
1:2,500	25.34	.0394	208.3	.0635
1:3,600	17.6	.0568	300.	.0914
1:4,800	13.2	.0758	400.	.1219
1:6,000	10.56	.0947	500.	.1524
1:7,200	8.8	.1136	600.	.1829
1:7,920	8.	.125 (i.e., 1/8 mi.)	660.	.2012
1:10,000	6.34	.1578	833.3	.254
1:10,560	6.	.167 (i.e., 1/6 mi.)	880.	.268
1:12,000	5.28	.1894	1,000.	.305
1:15,840	4.	.250 (i.e., 1/4 mi.)	1,320.	.402
1:20,000	3.17	.3156	1,666.	.508
1:21,120	3.	.3333 (i.e., 1/3 mi.)	1,760.	.536
1:25,000	2.53	.3945	2,083.	.635
1:31,680	2.	.5 (i.e., 1/2 mi.)	2,640.	.804
1:62,500	1.01	.986	5,208.	1.587
1:63,360	1.	1.	5,280.	1.609
1:100,000	.634	1.578	8,333.	2.54
1:125,000	.507	1.972	10,416.	3.175
1:316,800	.2	5.	26,400.	8.05
1:500,000	.1267	7.891	41,666.	12.7
1:1,000,000	.063	15.783	83,333.3	25.40

Bibliography abbreviations

AA		American Anthropologist
AAA-M		American Anthropological Association, Memoirs
A Ant		American Antiquity
AJPA		American Journal of Physical Anthropology
AMNH		American Museum of Natural History
	-AP	Anthropological Papers
	-B	Bulletin
	-M	Memoirs
BAE		Bureau of American Ethnology
	-B	Bulletin
	-R	(Annual) Report
CIW-P		Carnegie Institution of Washington, Publications
FMNH-PAS		Field Museum of Natural History, Publications, Anthropological Series
GP-MP		Gila Pueblo, Medallion Papers
JRAI		Journal of the Royal Anthropological Institute
MAIHF-INM		Museum of the American Indian, Heye Foundation, Indian Notes and Monographs
PM		Peabody Museum, Harvard University
	-M	Memoirs
	-P	Papers
PPS		Proceedings of the Prehistoric Society
SAA		Society of American Archaeology
	-M	Memoirs
	-N	Notebook
SDM		San Diego Museum
	-B	Bulletin
	-P	Papers
SI		Smithsonian Institution
	-AR	Annual Report
	-MC	Miscellaneous Collections
SM		Southwest Museum
	-M	Masterkey
	-P	Papers
SWJA		Southwestern Journal of Anthropology
TAS		Texas Archeological Society
	-B	Bulletin
	-N	Newsletter (Texas Archeology)
TASP		Texas Archeological Salvage Project
	-P	Papers
UC		University of California
	-AR	Anthropological Records
	-CARF	Contributions, Archaeological Research Facility
	-IA	Ibero-Americana
	-PAAE	Publications in American Archaeology and Ethnology
UCAS-R		University of California Archaeological Survey, Reports
USGS		United States Geological Survey
USNM		United States National Museum
	-P	Proceedings
	-R	Reports
VFPA		Viking Fund Publications in Anthropology
YU-PA		Yale University, Publications in Anthropology

BIBLIOGRAPHY

Aberg, F. A., and Bowen, H. C.
   1960   Ploughing experiments with a reconstructed Donneruplund ard. Antiquity 34: 144–147

Acsádi, G., and Nemeskéri, J.
   1970   History of human life span and mortality (trans. by K. Balas). Akadémiai Kiadó, Budapest.

Adams, R. E. W.
   1971   The ceramics of Altar de Sacrificios. PM-P 63(1).

Adams, R. M.
   1956   Some hypotheses on the development of early civilization. A Ant 21: 227–232.

Agerter. S. R., and Glock, W. S.
   1965   An annotated bibliography of tree growth and growth rings (1950–1962). Univ. of Arizona Press, Tucson.

Agogino, G. A., and Sachs, S.
   1960a   Criticism of the museum orientation of existing antiquity laws. Plains Anthropologist 5: 31–35.
   1960b   The failure of state and federal legislation to protect archaeological resources. Tebiwa 3: 43–46.

Ahler, S. A.
   1973   Chemical analysis of deposits at Rodgers Shelter, Missouri. Plains Anthropologist 18(60): 116–131.

Ahlfeld, F.
   1946   Estudios sobre la procedencia semipreciosas y las rocas encontradas en las ruinas preincaicos de
            Tiahuanacu. Boletin de la Sociedad Geologia del Peru 19: 33–34.

Aikens, C. M.
   1970   Hogup Cave. Univ. of Utah Anthro. Papers 93.

Aitken, M. J.
   1960   Magnetic dating. Archaeometry 3: 41–44.
   1961   Physics and archaeology. Interscience Publishers, New York.
   1970a   Dating by archaeomagnetic and thermoluminescent methods. In T. F. Allibone et al., The impact of
            the natural sciences on archaeology (pp. 77–88). Oxford Univ. Press.
   1970b   Magnetic prospecting. In R. Berger (ed.), Scientific methods in medieval archaeology (pp. 423–434).
            Univ. of California Press, Berkeley
   1970c   Thermoluminescence dating of ancient pottery. In R. Berger (ed.), Scientific methods in medieval
            archaeology (pp. 271–279) Univ. of California Press, Berkeley.

319

————, and Alldred, J. C.
 1972   The assessment of error limits in thermolumiscent dating. Archaeometry 14: 257–268.
Albright, A. B.
 1966   The preservation of small water-logged wood specimens with polyethylene glycol. Curator 9(3): 228–234.
Albright, W. F.
 1957   From the Stone Age to Christianity (2nd ed.). Doubleday Anchor Books (A100), Garden City, N.Y.
Alcock, L.
 1951   A technique for surface collecting. Antiquity 25: 75–98.
Alexander, R. K.
 1970   Archeological investigations at Parida Cave, Val Verde County, Texas. TASP-P 19.
Alford, J. J., Bundschuh, J. E., and Caspall, F. C.
 1971   A simple field test for the detection of manganese in Quaternary deposits. A Ant 36(4): 476–477.
Allen, Don, and Cheatum, E. P.
 1961   Ecological implications of fresh water and land gastropods in Texas archaeological studies. TAS-B 31: 291–316.
Allen, W. L., and Richardson, J. B., III
 1971   The reconstruction of kinship from archaeological data: the concepts, methods and feasibility. A Ant 36(1): 41–53.
Allibone, T. E., et al.
 1970   The impact of the natural sciences on archaeology. Oxford Univ. Press.
Allison, V. C
 1926   The antiquity of the deposits in Jacob's Cavern. AMNH-AP 19, Pt. 6.
Althin, C. A.
 1954   Man and environment: a view of the Mesolithic material in southern Scandinavia. K. G. L. Hum. Vetenskap, Lund Arsberrattesle 6: 269–293.
Ambro, R.
 1967   Dietary-technological-ecological aspects of Lovelock Cave coprolites. UCAS-R 70: 37–48.
Anati, E.
 1960   La civilisation du Val Camonica. Mondes Anciens, No. 4. Paris.
Andersen, J.
 1969   A new technique for archaeological field measuring. Norwegian Arch. Review 2: 68–77.
Anderson, J. E.
 1962   The human skeleton: a manual for archaeologists. National Mus. of Canada, Ottawa.
Anderson, K. M.
 1969   Ethnographic analogy and archaeological interpretation. Science 163: 133–138.
 1973   Prehistoric settlement of the Upper Neches River. TAS-B 43: 121–197.
Anderson, R. V.
 1955   Pollen analysis, a research tool for the study of cave deposits. A Ant 21: 84–85.
Angel, J. L.
 1946   Social biology of Greek culture growth. AA 48(4), Pt. 1: 493–533.
 1947   The length of life in ancient Greece. Journal of Gerontology 2: 18–24.
 1969   The bases of paleodemography. AJPA 30: 427–438.
Anonymous
 1936   Note on the use of polymerised vinylacetate and related compounds in the presentation and hardening of bone. AJPA 21: 449–450.
Antevs, E.
 1925   Retreat of the last ice-sheet in eastern Canada. Canada Dept. of Mines, Geol. Survey Memoir 146. Ottawa.
 1931   Late-glacial correlations and ice recession in Manitoba. Canada Dept. of Mines, Geol. Survey Memoir 168. Ottawa.

1935   Telecorrelations of varve curves. Geol. Fören, Stockholm Förh. 51: 47–58.

1948   Climatic changes and pre-white men. Univ. of Utah Bull. 38: 168–191. (Reprinted in part in UCAS-R 22.)

1949   Age of Cochise artifacts on the Wet Leggett. *In* Cochise and Mogollon sites. FMNH-Fieldiana 38(1).

1950   Postglacial climatic history of the Great Plains and dating the records of man. Proc. of Sixth Plains Arch. Conference, Univ. of Utah Anthro. Papers, No. 11: 45–50.

1952   Climatic history and the antiquity of man in California. UCAS-R 16: 23–31.

1953a   On division of the last 20,000 years. UCAS-R 22: 5–8.

1953b   Geochronology of the deglacial and neothermal ages. Journal of Geol. 61: 195–230.

1954   Telecorrelation of varves, radiocarbon chronology, and geology. Journal of Geol. 62: 516–521.

1955   Geologic-climatic dating in the West. A Ant 20: 317–335.

Antle, H. R.
1940   Some points in bone preservation. SAA-N 1: 188–125.

Armelagos, G. J., Mielke, J. A., and Winter, J.
1971   Bibliography of human paleopathology. Dept. of Anthro., Univ. of Massachusetts, Research Reports, No. 8.

Arnold, J. B., III
1974   A magnetometer survey of the steamboat Black Cloud. TAS-B 45: 225–230.

———, and Kegley, G. B., III
1974   A magnetometer survey of the prehistoric village in western Texas. Paper distributed at the annual meeting of the Soc. for Amer. Arch., Washington, D. C.

Arrhenius, O.
1963   Investigation of soil from old Indian sites. Ethnos, Nos. 2–4. 122–136.

Arroyo de Anda, L. A., Maldonado-Koerdell, M., and Martínez del Rio, P.
1953   Cueva de la Candelaria. Memorias del Instituto Nacional de Antropología e Historia 5. Mexico City.

Ascher, M., and Ascher, R.
1963   Chronological ordering by computer. AA 65: 1045–1052.

Ascher, R.
1959   A prehistoric population estimate using midden analysis and two population models. SWJA 15: 168–178.

1961a   Analogy in archaeological interpretation. SWJA 17: 317–325.

1961b   Experimental archaeology. AA 63: 793–816.

1968   Time's arrow and the archaeology of a contemporary community. In K. C. Chang (ed.), Settlement archaeology (pp. 43–52). National Press, Palo Alto.

———, and Ascher, M.
1965   Recognizing the emergence of man. Science 147: 243–250.

Ashbee, P., and Cornwall, I.
1961   An experiment in field archaeology. Antiquity 35: 129–134.

Ashworth, M. J., and Abeles, T. A.
1966   Neutron activation analysis and archaeology. Nature 210: 9–11.

Aspinall, A.
1968   Induced polarization as a technique for archaeological surveying. Prospezioni Archeologiche 3: 91–93.

———, and Feather, S. W.
1972   Neutron activation analysis of flint mine products. Archaeometry 14(1): 41–53.

Aten, L. E.
1971   Archaeological excavations at the Dow-Cleaver Site, Brazoria County, Texas. TASP-Technical Bull. 1.

———, and Bollich, C. N.
1969   A preliminary report on the development of a ceramic chronology for the Sabine Lake area of Texas and Louisiana. TAS-B 40: 241–258.

Atkins, H.
1972   Spying on the past. The Sciences 12(6): 22–24.

Atkinson, R. J. C.
1946   Field archaeology. Methuen, London.

1953   Field archaeology (2nd ed.). Methuen, London.
1956   Stonehenge. H. Hamilton, London.
1963   Resistivity surveying in archaeology. *In* E. Pyddoke (ed.), The scientist and archaeology (pp. 1–30). Phoenix House, London.

———, Piggott, C. M., and Sanders, N. K.
1951   Excavations at Dorchester, Oxon. Ashmolean Mus., Oxford.
1966   Moonshine on Stonehenge. Antiquity 40: 212–216.

Aveni, A. F., and Linsley, R. M.
1972   Mound J. Monte Alban: possible astronomical orientation. A Ant 37(4): 528–531.

Ayres, F. D.
1961   Rubbings from Chavín de Huantar, Peru. A Ant 27: 239–245.

Baby, R. S.
1954   Hopewell cremation practices. Ohio Hist. Soc., Papers in Arch., No. 1.

Bada, J. L., and Protsch, R.
1973   Racemization reaction of aspartic acid and its use in dating fossil bones. Proc. of National Acad. of Sciences 70: 1331–1334.

———, Schroeder, R. A., and Carter, G. F.
1974   New evidence for the antiquity of man in North America deduced from aspartic acid racemization. Science 184: 791–793.

Baden-Powell, D. W. F.
1949   Experimental Clactonian technique. PPS, n.s., 15: 38–41.

Baerreis, D. A.
1971   The ethnohistoric approach and archaeology. Ethnohistory 8: 49–77.

Bagnold, A. H.
1888   Account of the manner in which two colossal statues of Rameses II at Memphis were raised. Proc. of Soc. of Biblical Arch., 18th Session, 1887–88, pp. 452–463.

Bailey, I. W., and Barghoorn, E. S., Jr.
1942   Identification and physical condition of the stakes and wattles from the fishweir. *In* F. Johnson (ed.), The Boylston Street fishweir (pp. 82–95). Papers of R. S. Peabody Foundation for Arch. 2.

Baity, E. C.
1973   Archaeoastronomy and ethnoastronomy so far. Current Anthro. 14(4): 389–431.

Baker, F. C.
1920   The life of the Pleistocene or glacial period. Bull. of Univ. of Illinois 17: 195–370.
1930   Influence of the glacial period in changing the character of the molluscan fauna of North America. Ecology 11: 469–480.
1937   Pleistocene land and fresh-water mollusca as indicators of time and ecological conditions. *In* G. G. MacCurdy (ed.), Early man (pp. 67–74). Lippincott, Philadelphia.
1942   Mollusca contained in the test pit deposits. *In* L. S. Cressman, Archaeological researches in the northern Great Basin (pp. 117–119). CIW-P 538.

Bannister, B.
1963   Dendrochronology. *In* D. R. Brothwell and E. S. Higgs (eds.), Science in archaeology (pp. 162–176). Thames and Hudson, London.

———, and Smiley, T. L.
1955   Dendrochronology. *In* T. L. Smiley (ed.), Geochronology (pp. 177–195). Univ. of Arizona Bull. Ser. 26.

———, Dean, J. S., and Gall, E. A. M.
1966a   Tree-ring dates from Arizona E: Chinle–de Chelly–Red Rock Area. Laboratory of Tree-Ring Research, Univ. of Arizona, Tucson.

———, Hannah, J. W., and Robinson, W. J.
1966b   Tree-ring dates from Arizona K: Puerco–Wide-Run–Ganado Area. Laboratory of Tree-Ring Research, Univ. of Arizona, Tucson.

Barber, H.
1939   Untersuchungen über die chemische Veränderung von Knochen bei der Fossilization. Paleobiol. 7: 217–235.

Bard, J. C., and Busby, C. I.
1974   The manufacture of a petroglyph: a replicative experiment. UC-CARF 20: 83–102.

Barghoorn, E. S.
1944   Collecting and preserving botanical materials of archaeological interest. A Ant 9: 289–294.
1949   Paleobotanical studies of the Boylston Street fishweir. In F. Johnson (ed.), The Boylston Street fishweir II (pp. 49–83). Papers of R. S. Peabody Foundation for Arch. 4(1).

Barker, H.
1970   Critical assessment of radiocarbon dating. In T. E. Allibone et al., The impact of the natural sciences on archaeology (pp. 37–46). Oxford Univ. Press.

Barker, R. M.
1960   Constituency and origins of cyclic growth layers in pelecypod shells. UC, Space Sciences Laboratory, Ser. II, Issue 43. Berkeley.

Barnes, A. S.
1939   The difference between natural and human flaking in prehistoric flint implements. AA 41: 99–112.

Bartlett, J. R.
1854   Personal narrative of explorations. 2 vols. Appleton, New York.

Bascom, W. R.
1941   Possible application of kite photography to archaeology and ethnology. Illinois Acad. of Sci. Trans. 34(2).

Bass, G. F.
1963   Underwater archaeology: key to history's warehouse. National Geog. Magazine 124: 138–156.
1964   Methods of wreck excavation in clear water. In Diving into the past (pp. 20–27). St. Paul.

Bass, W. M.
1971   Human osteology: a laboratory and field manual of the human skeleton. Missouri Arch. Soc., Special Publ., Columbia.

Bastian, T.
1961   Trace element and metallographic studies of prehistoric copper artifacts in North America. Mus. of Anthro., Univ. of Michigan, Anthro. Papers, No. 17: 150–175.

Baud, C. E.
1960   Dating of prehistoric bones by radiological and optical methods. VFPA No. 28: 246–264.

Baumhoff, M. A.
1955   Excavation of site Teh-1 (Kinsley Cave). UCAS-R 30: 40–73.
1963   Ecological determinants of aboriginal California populations. UC-PAAE 49: 155–236.

———, and Heizer, R. F.
1959   Some unexploited possibilities in ceramic analysis. SWJA 15: 308–316.

———, and Olmsted, D. L.
1963   Palaihnihan: radiocarbon support for glottochronology. AA 65: 278–284.

Bayard, D. T.
1969   Science, theory, and reality in the "new archaeology." A Ant 34(3): 376–384.

Bayle, A. and de Noyer, R.
1939   Contribution à l'étude des os en cours de fossilisation: essai de détermination de leur âge. Bull. Soc. Chimique de France, Ser. 5, Vol. 6: 1011–1024.

Beals, R. L., Brainerd, G. W., and Smith, W.
1945   Archaeological studies in northeast Arizona. UC-PAAE 44: 1–236.

Bell, E. H. (ed.)
1936   Chapters in Nebraska archaeology. Univ. of Nebraska 1: 1–6.

Bell, R. E.
1951   Dendrochronology at the Kincaid site. *In* F. C. Cole, Kincaid, a prehistoric Illinois metropolis (App. I, pp. 233–292). Univ. of Chicago Press.
1965   Investigaciones arqueologicas en el sitio El Inga, Ecuador. Quito.

Belous, R. E.
1953   The central California chronological sequence re-examined. A Ant 18: 341–353.

Belshé, J. C.
1965   Archaeo-magnetic techniques. 6th International Congress of Prehistoric and Protohistoric Sciences, Atti 2: 44.

Bennett, W. C.
1946   Excavations in the Cuenca region, Ecuador. YU-PA No. 35.

——— (assembler)
1948   The Peruvian co-tradition. *In* A reappraisal of Peruvian archaeology (pp. 1–7). SAA-M 4.

———, and Bird, J. B.
1949   Andean culture history. AMNH-Handbook Ser., No. 15.

Bennyhoff, J. A.
1952   The Viru Valley sequence: a critical review. A Ant 17: 231–249.
1956   An appraisal of the archaeological resources of Yosemite National Park. UCAS-R 34.

———, and Heizer, R. F.
1958   Cross-dating Great Basin sites by Californian shell beads. UCAS-R 42: 60–92.

Bentzen, C. B.
1942   An inexpensive method of recovering skeletal material for museum display. A Ant 8: 176–178.

Berger, R.
1970   Ancient Egyptian radiocarbon chronology. *In* T. E. Allibone *et al.*, The impact of the natural sciences on archaeology (pp. 23–36). Oxford Univ. Press.

———, and Protsch, R.
1974   Radiocarbon dates for earliest domesticated animals from Europe and the Near East. Science 183: 1100–1102.

———, Horney, A. G., and Libby, W. F.
1964   Radiocarbon dating of bone and shell from their organic components. Science 144: 999–1001.

———, Taylor, R. E., and Libby, W. F.
1966   Radiocarbon content of marine shells from the California and Mexican West Coast. Science 153: 864–866.

———, *et al.*
1971   New radiocarbon dates based on bone collagen of California Paleo-Indians. UC-CARF 12: 43–49.

Bergsland, K., and Vogt, H.
1962   On the validity of glottochronology. Current Anthro. 3: 115–153.

Bernal, I.
1952   Introducción a la arqueologia. Fondo de Cultura Económica, Mexico City.
1960   Archaeology and written sources. Akten des 34. Internationalen Amerikanistenkongresses (pp. 219–225). Vienna.
1963   Teotihuacán. Instituto Nacional de Antropología e Historia. Mexico City.

Berry, B. L.
1962   Sampling, coding, and storing flood plain data. Farm Economics Division, U.S. Dept. of Agriculture, Agriculture Handbook 237.

Biddle, M.
1974   The archaeology of Winchester. Scientific American 230(5): 32–43.

———, and Kjølbye-Biddle, B.
1969   Metres, areas and robbing. World Archaeology 1(2): 208–219.

Biek, L. E.
1963   Archaeology and the miscroscope. Lutterworth Press, London.

————, Cripps, E. S., and Thacker, D. M. D.
1954   Some methods for protecting cleaned iron objects. Museums Journal 54: 32–36.

Bimson, M.
1956   The technique of Greek Black and *Terra Sigillata* Red. Antiquaries Journal 36: 200–204.

Binford, L. R.
1962   Archaeology as anthropology. A Ant 28: 217–225.
1963   A proposed attribute list for the description and classification of projectile points. Mus. of Anthro., Univ. of Michigan, Anthro. Papers 19: 193–221.
1964   A consideration of archaeological research design. A Ant 29: 425–441.
1965   Archaeological systematics and the study of culture process. A Ant 31: 203–210.
1968   Archeological perspectives. *In* S. R. Binford and L. R. Binford (eds.), New perspectives in archeology (pp. 5–32). Aldine, Chicago.
1971   Mortuary practices: their study and their potential. *In* J. A. Brown (ed.), Approaches to the social dimensions of mortuary practices (pp. 6–29). SAA-M 25.

————, et al.
1970   Archaeology at Hatchery West. SAA-M 24.

Binford, S. R., and Binford, L. R.
1968   New perspectives in archeology. Aldine, Chicago.

Bird, J. B.
1938   Antiquity and migrations of the early inhabitants of Patagonia. Geog. Review 28: 250–275.
1943   Excavations in northern Chile. AMNH-AP 38, Pt. 4.
1946   The archaeology of Patagonia. *In* J. Steward (ed.), Handbook of South American Indians (pp. 17–74). BAE-B 143, Vol. 1.
1948   Preceramic cultures in Chicama and Viru. SAA-M 4: 21–28.
1968   More about earth-shaking equipment. A Ant 33(4): 507–509.

————, and Ford, J. A.
1956   A new earth-shaking machine. A Ant 21: 399–401.

Birket-Smith, K.
1929   The Caribou Eskimos. Reports of the Fifth Thule Expedition, 1921–24, Vol. 5, Pt. 2.

Black, E. C.
1969   Can one cook in a skin? Antiquity 43: 217–218.

Black, G. A.
1944   Angel site, Vanderburgh County, Indiana. Indiana Hist. Soc., Prehist. Research Ser. 2, No. 5.
1967   Angel site: an archeological, historical, and ethnological study. Indiana Hist. Soc., Indianapolis.

————, and Johnston, R. B.
1962   A test of magnetometry as an aid to archaeology. A Ant 28: 199–205.

Blaker, A. A.
1965   Photography for scientific publication: a handbook. Freeman, San Francisco.

Bock, F., and Bock, A. J.
1972   The signs that man was here. SM-M 46: 47–60.

Boekelman, H. J.
1936   Report on the mollusks of St. Lawrence Island. *In* O. W. Geist and F. G. Rainey, Archaeological excavations at Kukulik, St. Lawrence Island, Alaska; preliminary report (App. VI, pp. 379–386). Misc. Publs. of Univ. of Alaska 2. Govt. Printing Office, Washington, D.C.

Bohmers, A.
1963   A statistical analysis of flint artifacts. *In* D. R. Brothwell and E. S. Higgs (eds.), Science in archaeology (pp. 469–481). Thames and Hudson, London.

Bokonyi, S., Braidwood, R. J., and Reed, C. A.
1973   Earliest animal domestication dated? Science 182: 1161.

Bonnichsen, R.
1973a   Millie's camp: an experiment in archaeology. World Archaeology 4(3): 277–291.

1973b   Some operational aspects of human and animal bone alteration. *In* B. M. Gilbert, Mammalian osteo-archaeology: North America (pp. 9–24). Missouri Arch. Soc., Special Publ., Columbia.

Bordaz, J.
1970   Tools of the Old and New Stone Age. Natural History Press, Garden City, N.Y.

Borden, C.E.
1950   A translucent shelter for field work in regions with high precipitation. A Ant 15: 252–253.
1952   A uniform site designation scheme for Canada. British Columbia Provincial Mus., Anthro. in British Columbia, No. 3: 44–48. Victoria.

Bordes, F.
1947   Etude comparative des différentes techniques de taille du silex et des roches dures. L'Anthropologie 51: 1–29.
1968   The Old Stone Age. McGraw-Hill, New York.
1969   Reflections on typology and techniques in the Paleolithic. Arctic Anthropology 6(1): 1–29.

Borhegyi, S. F.
1956   The development of folk and complex cultures in the southern Maya area. A Ant 21: 343–356.
1958   Underwater archaeology in Guatemala. Actas del XXXIII Congreso Internacional de Americanistas (Vol. 2, pp. 229–240). San José, Costa Rica.
1965   Archaeological synthesis of the Guatemalan Highlands. *In* G. R. Willey (ed.), Handbook of Middle American Indians (Vol. 2, pp. 3–58). Univ. of Texas Press, Austin.

Bothmer, D. von, and Noble, J. V.
1965   An inquiry into the forgery of the Etruscan terracotta warriors in the Metropolitan Museum of Art. Metropolitan Mus. of Art, Occasional Papers, No. 11.

Bouchard, A.
1966   De l'emploi des méthodes chimiques et spectrographiques pour l'étude des porteries antiques. Geologische Rundschau 55: 113–118. Stuttgart.

Bouchard, H., and Moffitt, F. H.
1960   Surveying. International Textbook Co., Scranton, Pa.

Bourdier, F.
1953   Pseudo-industries humaines sur galets de quartzite glaciares. Bull. de la Soc. Préhist. Française 50: 436. Paris.

Bowen, H. C., and Wood, P.
1967   Experimental storage of corn underground and its implications for Iron Age settlements. Bull. of Inst. of Arch. 7: 1–14. London.

Bowen, R. N. C.
1958   The exploration of time. Lewnes, London.

Bowman, H. R., Asaro, F., and Perlman, I.
1973   Composition variations in obsidian sources and the archaeological implications. Archaeometry 15: 123–127.

Braidwood, R. J.
1937   Mounds in the Plain of Antioch. Univ. of Chicago, Oriental Inst. Publs. 48.
1946a   The order of incompleteness of the archaeological record. *In* Human origins (2nd ed.), Selected Readings Series II (article No. 11, pp. 108–112). Univ. of Chicago Press.
1946b   Terminology in prehistory. *In* Human origins (2nd ed.), Selected Readings Series II (article No. 14, pp. 127–144). Univ. of Chicago Press.
1963   Prehistoric men (6th ed.). Chicago Nat. Hist. Mus., Popular Ser., Anthro., No. 37.
1967   Prehistoric men (7th ed.). Scott, Foresman, Chicago.
1974   The Iraq Jarmo project. *In* G. R. Willey (ed.), Archaeological researches in retrospect (pp. 61–83). Winthrop, Cambridge, Mass.

———, and Howe, B.
1960   Prehistoric investigations in Iraq Kurdistan. Oriental Inst. of Univ. of Chicago, Studies in Oriental Civilization, No. 31.

Brain, C. K.
  1967   Bone weathering and the problem of bone pseudo-tools. South African Journal of Science 63: 97–99.

Brainerd, G. W.
  1951a   The place of chronological ordering in archaeological analysis. A Ant 16: 301–313.
  1951b   The use of mathematical formulations in archaeolocal analysis. In J. B. Griffin (ed.), Essays on archaeological methods (pp. 117–127). Univ. of Michigan Press, Ann Arbor.
  1953   A re-examination of the dating evidence for the Lake Mojave artifact assemblage. A Ant 18: 270–271.

Bray, W.
  1971   Ancient American metal-smiths. Proc. of Royal Anthro. Inst. of Great Britain and Ireland for 1971: 25–43.

Breiner, S.
  1965   The rubidium magnetometer in archaeological exploration. Science 150: 185–193.
  1973   Applications manual for portable magnetometers, Geometrics, Palo Alto.

——, and Coe, M. D.
  1972   Magnetic exploration of the Olmec civilization. Amer. Scientist 60: 566–575.

Brennan, L. A.
  1973   Beginner's guide to archaeology. Stackpole Books, Harrisburg, Pa.

Brenner, H.
  1953   Tarnish-removing dips for silver, gold, and copper. Electroplating and Metal Finishing 6: 371–376.

Bresillon, M. N.
  1968   La dénomination des objets de pierre taillée: matériaux pour un vocabulaire des préhistoriens de langue française. Gallia Préhistoire, Suppl. IV: 413 pp.

Brew, J. O.
  1946   Archaeology of Alkali Ridge, southeastern Utah. PM-P 21.
  1964   Report on the advisability of drawing up international regulations concerning the preservation of cultural property endangered by public and private works. General Conference, 13th Session, Programme Commission, UNESCO, PRG, 13C/PRG/16. Paris, July 24.

Briggs, L. J., and Weaver, K. F.
  1958   How old is it? National Geog. Magazine 114: 234–255.

Brill, R. H.
  1961   The record of time in weathered glass. Archaeology 14: 18–22.
  1963   Ancient glass. Scientific American 209: 120–130.

—— (ed.)
  1971   Science and archaeology. Mass. Inst. of Technology Press, Cambridge.

Brinker, R. C., and Taylor, W. C.
  1955   Elementary surveying (3rd ed.). International Textbook Co., Scranton, Pa.

Brinton, D. G.
  1887   A review of the data for the study of the prehistoric chronology of America. Proc. of Amer. Assoc. for Advancement of Science 36: 283–301.

Brodribb, C.
  1970   Drawing archaeological finds for publication. J. Baker, London.

Broecker, W. S.
  1964   Radiocarbon dating: a case against the proposed link between river mollusks and soil humus. Science 143: 596–597.

——, and Kulp, J. L.
  1956   The radiocarbon method of age determination. A Ant 22: 1–11.

Brooks, R. H.
  1965   The feasibility of microanalysis in Southwestern archaeological sites. In D. Osborne (ed.), Contributions of the Wetherill Mesa Archeological Project. SAA-M 19: 182–185.

Brooks, S. T
  1955   Skeletal age at death: the reliability of cranial and pubic age indicators. AJPA 13: 567–598.

Brose, D.
  1964   Infra-red photography: an aid to stratigraphic interpretation. Michigan Archaeologist 10(4): 69–73.
Brothwell, D. R.
  1963   Digging up bones. British Mus., London.
  1968   The skeletal biology of earlier human populations. Pergamon Press, New York.
  1970   The palaeopathology of Pleistocene and more recent mammals. In D. R. Brothwell and E. S. Higgs (eds.), Science in archaeology (rev. and enl. ed.) (pp. 310–314). Praeger, New York.
  1971   Paleodemography. In W. Brass (ed.), Biological aspects of demography (pp. 111–130). Taylor and Francis, London.
———, and Higgs, E. S. (eds.)
  1963   Science in archaeology. Thames and Hudson, London.
  1970   Science in archaeology (rev. and enl. ed.). Praeger, New York.
———, and Spearman, R.
  1963   The hair of earlier peoples. In D. R. Brothwell and E. S. Higgs (eds.), Science in archaeology (pp. 427–436). Thames and Hudson, London.
Brown, J. A. (ed.)
  1971   Approaches to the social dimensions of mortuary practices. SAA-M 25
———, and Freeman, J. L. G.
  1964   A UNIVAC analysis of sherd frequencies from the Carter Ranch Pueblo, eastern Arizona (with comments by Paul S. Martin). A Ant 30: 162–167.
Brown, M. K.
  1974   A preservative compound for archaeological materials. A Ant 39(2): 469–473.
Bruce-Mitford, R. L. S. (ed.)
  1956   Recent archaeological excavations in Britain. Routledge and Kegan Paul, London.
Bruhns, K. O.
  1972   The methods of huaqueria: illicit tomb looting in Colombia. Archaeology 25(2): 140–143.
Bryan, K.
  1941   Correlation of the deposits of Sandia Cave, New Mexico, with the glacial chronology. SI-MC 99(23).
  1948   Los suelos complejos y fosiles de las altiplanicie de México, en relacion a los cambios climaticos. Bol. Soc. Geol. Mejicana 13: 1–20.
  1950   Flint quarries. PM-P 17(3).
———, and Albritton, C. C., Jr.
  1943   Soil phenomena as evidence of climatic changes. Amer. Journal of Science 241: 469–490.
———, and McCann, F. T.
  1943   Sand dunes and alluvium near Grants, New Mexico. A Ant 8: 281–290.
———, and Ray, L. R.
  1940   Geologic antiquity of the Lindenmeier site in Colorado. SI-MC 99(2).
Bryant, V. M., Jr.
  1974   The role of coprolite analysis in archaeology. TAS-B 45: 1–28.
———, and Holtz, R. K.
  1965   A guide to the drafting of archaeological maps. TAS-B 36: 269–285.
  1968   The role of pollen in the reconstruction of past environments. Pennsylvania Geographer 6(1): 1–8.
Bucha, V.
  1971   Archaeomagnetic dating. In H. N. Michael and E. K. Ralph (eds.), Dating techniques for the archaeologist (pp. 57–117). Mass. Inst. of Technology Press, Cambridge.
Bucy, D. R.
  1974   A technological analysis of a basalt quarry in western Idaho. Tebiwa 16(2): 1–45.
Buettner-Janusch, J.
  1954   Use of infrared photography in archaeological field work. A Ant 20: 84–87.
Bullard, W. R., Jr.
  1960   Maya settlement pattern in northeastern Petén. A Ant 25: 355–372.

1965 Stratigraphic excavations at San Estevan, northern British Honduras. Royal Ontario Mus., Art and Archaeology Occasional Paper No. 9. Toronto.

Bullen, R. P.
1949 Excavations in northeastern Massachusetts. Papers of R. S. Peabody Foundation for Arch 1(3).

Burchell, J. P. T.
1957 Land-shells as a critical factor in the dating of post-Pleistocene deposits. PPS 23: 236–238.
1961 Land shells and their role in dating deposits of postglacial time in southeast England. Arch. Newsletter, No. 7: 34–38. London.

Burkitt, M. C.
1956 The Old Stone Age. Bowes and Bowes, London.

Burns, G. E.
1940 A practical method for mending bone. SAA-N 1: 98.

Burns, N. J.
n.d. Field manual for museums. National Park Service, Washington, D.C.

Burton, D.
1969 Aluminum foil as a recording technique of incised rock art. Archaeology in Montana 10(3): 67–68.

Bushnell, G. H. S.
1956 Peru. Praeger, New York.

Butler, B. R.
1966 A guide to understanding Idaho archaeology. Idaho State Univ. Mus., Special Publs.

Butler, J. J., and Van der Walls, J. D.
1964 Metal analysis, Sam I, and European prehistory. Helinium 4: 3–39.

Butzer, K. W.
1964 Environment and archaeology: an introduction to Pleistocene geography. Aldine, Chicago.
1971 Environment and archeology: an ecological approach to prehistory. Aldine-Atherton, Chicago.

Byers, D. S.
1967 The prehistory of the Tehuacan Valley, Vol. 1: Environment and subsistence. Univ. of Texas Press, Austin.
——, and Johnson, F.
1939 Some methods used in excavating eastern shell heaps. A Ant 4: 189–212.
1940 Two sites on Martha's Vineyard. Papers of R. S. Peabody Foundation for Arch. 1: 1–104.

Cailleux, A.
1946 Application de la pétrographie sedimentaire aux recherches préhistoriques. Bull. de la Soc. Préhist. Francaise 43: 182–191. Paris.

Cain, H. T.
1950 Petroglyphs of central Washington. Univ. of Washington Press, Seattle.

Cain, S. A.
1939 Pollen analysis as a paleo-ecological research method. Botanical Review 5: 627–654.

Calabrese, F. A.
1972 Cross Ranch: a study of variability in a stable cultural tradition. Plains Anthropologist, Memoir 9

Caldwell, J. R.
1958 Trend and tradition in the prehistory of the Eastern United States. AAA-M No. 88.
1964 Interaction spheres in prehistory. In J. R. Caldwell and R. L. Hall (eds.), Hopewellian studies (pp. 135–143). Illinois State Mus., Scientific Papers 12. Springfield.

Caley, E. R.
1951 Symposium on archaeological chemistry. Journal of Chemical Engineering 28: 63–96.
1955 Coatings and incrustations on lead objects from the Agora and the method used for their removal. Studies in Conservation 2: 49–54. Aberdeen.

Calhoun, C. A.
1963 The use of casein glue in mending artifacts. TAS-N 7(4): 4–5.

Callahan, E. (ed.)
1973 The Old Rag report: a practical guide to living archeology. Dept. of Sociology and Anthro., Virginia Commonwealth Univ., Richmond.
1974 The Ape: experimental archeology papers, No. 3. Student papers from Dept. of Sociology and Anthro., Virginia Commonwealth Univ., Richmond.

Callen, E. O.
1963 Diet as revealed by coprolites. In D. R. Brothwell and E. S. Higgs (eds.), Science in archaeology (pp. 186-194). Thames and Hudson, London.
1965 Food habits of some pre-Columbian Mexican Indians. Economic Botany 19(4): 335-343.

———, and Cameron, T. W. M.
1960 A prehistoric diet revealed by coprolites. New Scientist (July 7): 35-40.

Camp, C. L., and Hanna, G. D.
1937 Methods in paleontology. Univ. of California Press, Berkeley.

Campbell, E. W. C., and Campbell, W. H.
1935 The Pinto Basin site. SM-P 9.

———, et al.
1937 The archaeology of Pleistocene Lake Mohave: a symposium. SM-P 11.

Campbell, T. N.
1949 The pioneer tree-ring work of Jacob Kuechler. Tree Ring Bull. 15(3). Tucson.
1958 Archaeological remains from the Live Oak Point site, Arkansas County, Texas. Texas Journal of Science 10: 423-442.

Cann, F. R.
1937 Insect damage in timber and wooden exhibits in museums. Museums Journal 37: 281-291.

Cann, J. R., and Renfrew, C.
1964 The characterization of obsidian and its application to the Mediterranean region. PPS 30: 11-133.

Carabelli, E.
1966 A new tool for archaeological prospecting: the sonic spectroscope for the detection of cavities. Prospezioni Archeologiche 1: 25-35.

Carneiro, R. L., and Hilse, D. F.
1966 On determining the probable rate of population growth during the Neolithic. AA 68: 177-181.

Carnot, M. A.
1892a Recherche du fluor dans les os modernes et les os fossiles. Comptes Rendus de l'Acad. des Sciences 114: 1189-1192. Paris.
1892b Sur une application de l'analyse chimique pour fixer l'âge d'ossements humains préhistoriques. Comptes Rendus de l'Acad. des Sciences 115: 243-246. Paris.
1892c Sur la composition des ossements fossiles et la variation de leur teneur en fluor dans les différents étages géologiques. Comptes Rendus de l'Acad. des Sciences 115: 243-246. Paris.
1893 Recherches sur la composition générale et la teneur en fluor des os modernes et des os fossiles des différents âges. Ann. Mines 3, Ser. 9 (Mem.): 115-195. Paris.

Carr, D. R., and Kulp, J. L.
1955 Dating with natural radioactive carbon. Trans. of New York Acad. of Science, Ser. 2, Vol. 16: 175-181.

Carr, R. F., and Hazard, J. E.
1961 Tikal report No. 11: map of the ruins of Tikal, El Petén, Guatemala. Univ. of Pennsylvania Mus., Mus. Monographs. Philadelphia.

Carswell, T. S., and Hatfield, I.
1939 Pentachlorophenol for wood preservation. Industrial Engineering Chemistry 31: 1431-1435.

Carter, G. F.
1950 Evidence for Pleistocene man in southern California. Geog. Review 40: 84-102.
1956 On soil color and time. SWJA 12: 295-324.
1957 Pleistocene man at San Diego. Johns Hopkins Press, Baltimore.

———, and Pendleton, R. L.
1956 The humid soil: process and time. Geog. Review 46: 488-507.

Caso, A.
1971   Calendrical systems of central Mexico. *In* Handbook of Middle American Indians Vol. 10, Pt. 1: 333–348. Univ. of Texas Press, Austin.

Casteel, R. W.
1970   Core and column sampling. A Ant 35(4): 465–467.
1972   Some archaeological uses of fish remains. A Ant 37: 404–419.
1974   On the remains of fish scales from archaeological sites. A Ant 39: 557–581.

Ceram, C. W.
1958   The march of archaeology. Knopf, New York.
1971   The first American: a story of North American archaeology. Harcourt Brace Jovanovich, New York.

Chamber's technical dictionary
1962   3rd ed. rev., with suppl. Macmillan, New York.

Champe, J. L.
1946   Ash Hollow Cave. Univ. of Nebraska Studies, n.s., No. 1.

Chaney, R.
1935a   The food of "Peking Man." Carnegie Inst. of Washington, News Service Bull. 3(25): 197–202.
1935b   The occurrence of endocarps of *Celtis barbouri* at Choukoutien. Bull. of Geol. Soc. of China 14: 99–113. Peking. (See also 12: 323–328 [1933].)
1941   Charcoal from the Double Adobe site. *In* E. B. Sayles and E. Antevs, The Cochise culture (p. 68). GP-MP 29.

Chang, K. C.
1967   Rethinking archaeology. Random House, New York.
1972   Settlement patterns in archaeology. Addison-Wesley Module in Anthro. 24. Reading, Mass.

Chaplin, R. E.
1971   The study of animal bones from archaeological sites. Seminar Press, London and New York.

Chenhall, R. G.
1967   The description of archaeological data in computer language. A Ant 32(2): 149–160.
1971   Positivism and the collection of data. A Ant 36: 372–373.

Chevallier, R.
1964   L'avion à la découverte du passé. Fayard, Paris.

Childe, V. G.
1948   Archaeology as a social science: an inaugural lecture. *In* Inst. of Arch., Univ of London, 3rd report (pp. 49–60).
1950   Prehistoric migrations in Europe. Harvard Univ. Press, Cambridge.
1951   Social evolution. Watts, London.
1956   Piecing together the past. Praeger, New York.
1958   The dawn of European civilization (6th ed.). Knopf, New York.
1962   A short introduction to archaeology. Collier Books (AS240Y), New York.

Christensen, A. E., Jr.
1969   The significance and practical value of the 3-point method. Norwegian Arch. Review 2: 76–77.

Clark, D. L.
1961   The obsidian dating method. Current Anthro. 2: 11–114.
1964   Archaeological chronology in California and the obsidian hydration method, Pt. I. UCAS-Los Angeles, Annual Report 1963–64: 139–228.

Clark, G. R., II
1968   Mollusk shell: daily growth lines. Science 161: 800–802.

Clark, Grahame (J. G. D.)
1947   Archaeology and society (rev. ed.). (Later editions 1952, 1957, 1960.) Methuen, London.
1952   Prehistoric Europe. Methuen, London; Philosophical Library, New York.
1954   Excavations at Star Carr. Cambridge Univ. Press.
1961   World prehistory: an outline. Cambridge Univ. Press.

1962   Prehistoric ancestors of the weapons which brought England victory at Crecy . . . : Neolithic long bows of 4500 years ago, found in the Somersetshire peat. Illustrated London News 10 (Feb.): 219–221.

1963   Neolithic bows from Somerset, England, and the prehistory of archery in North-West Europe. PPS 29: 50–98.

1967   The Stone Age hunters. Thames and Hudson, London.

1972   Star Carr: a case study in bioarchaeology. Addison-Wesley Module in Anthro. 10. Reading, Mass.

1974   Prehistoric Europe: the economic basis. *In* G. R. Willey (ed.), Archaeological researches in restrospect (pp. 33–57). Winthrop, Cambridge, Mass.

————, and Piggott, S.

1965   Prehistoric societies. Knopf, New York.

————, and Thompson, M. W.

1954   The groove and splinter technique of working antler in Upper Paleolithic and Mesolithic Europe, with special reference to the material from Star Carr. PPS 19: 148–160.

Clark, J. Desmond

1957   The importance of distribution maps in the study of prehistoric cultures. South African Museums Assoc. Bull. 6: 314–320.

1958   The natural fracture of pebbles from the Batoka Gorge, Northern Rhodesia, and its bearing on the Kafuan industries of Africa. PPS 24: 64–77.

1961   Fractured chert specimens from the Lower Pleistocene Bethlehem Beds, Israel. British Mus. of Nat. Hist., Bull. (Geol.) 5(4).

1969   The Middle Acheulian occupation site at Latamne, northern Syria (second paper); further excavations (1965): general results, definition and interpretation. Quaternaria 10: 1–71.

1970   The prehistory of Africa. Praeger, New York.

Clark, J. W., Jr.

1967   Three pictograph sites in the Central Pecos Valley of Texas. Texas Journal of Science 19(3): 245–257.

Clarke, D. L.

1968   Analytical archaeology. Methuen, London.

1973   Archaeology: the loss of innocence. Antiquity 47: 6–18.

Clarke, S.

1916   Cutting granite. Ancient Egypt 1916, Pt. 3: 110–113.

————, and Engelbach, R.

1930   Ancient Egyptian masonry. Oxford Univ. Press.

Clausen, C. J.

1966   The proton magnetometer: its use in plotting the distribution of the ferrous components of a shipwreck site as an aid to archeological interpretation. Florida Anthropologist 19(2): 77–84.

1967   A new underwater excavating system for the archaeologist. Conference on Historic Site Archaeology, Papers 2(1): 98–106. Raleigh.

Cleator, P. E.

1973   Underwater archaeology. St. Martin's Press, New York.

Cleland, C. E.

1966   The prehistoric animal ecology and ethno-zoology of the Upper Great Lakes Region. Univ. of Michigan Anthro. Papers, No. 29.

Clements, F. E.

1936   Notes on archaeological methods. A Ant 1: 193–196.

Clench, W. J.

1942   The mollusks. *In* F. Johnson (ed.), The Boylston Street fishweir (pp. 45–66). Papers of R. S. Peabody Foundation for Arch. 2.

Clewlow, C. W., Jr.

1968   Surface archaeology of the Black Rock Desert, Nevada. UCAS-R 73: 1–94.

1970   Some thoughts on the background of early man, Hrdlicka, and Folsom. Kroeber Anthro. Soc., Papers 42: 26–46.

Clutton-Brock, J.
    1970   The origins of the dog. *In* D. R. Brothwell and E. S. Higgs (eds.), Science in archaeology (rev. and enl. ed.) (pp. 303–309). Praeger, New York.

Cobean, R. H., *et al.*
    1971   Obsidian trade at San Lorenzo Tenochtitlan, Mexico. Science 174: 666–671.

Cochran, W. G.
    1963   Sampling techniques. Wiley, New York; Chapman and Hall, London.

Coe, W. R.
    1959   Piedras Negras archaeology: artifacts, caches, and burials. Univ. of Pennsylvania Mus. Monographs.
    1962   A summary of excavation and research at Tikal, Guatemala: 1956-61. A Ant 27: 479–507.

———, and McGinn, J. J.
    1963   Tikal: the North Acropolis and an early tomb. Expedition 5(2): 24–32.

Coggins, C.
    1969   Illicit traffic in pre-Columbian antiquities. Art Journal 39: 1.

Coghlan, J. J.
    1940   Prehistoric copper and some experiments in smelting. Trans. of Newcomen Soc. 20: 49–65.
    1951   Notes on the prehistoric metallurgy of copper and bronze in the Old World. Pitt Rivers Mus., Oxford Univ., Occasional Papers on Technology, No. 4.
    1956   Notes on prehistoric and early iron in the Old World. Pitt Rivers Mus., Oxford Univ., Occasional Papers on Technology, No. 8.
    1960   Metallurgical analysis of archaeological materials: 1. VPFA No. 28: 21–23.

———, Butler, J. R., and Parker G.
    1963   Ores and metals. Royal Anthro. Inst. of Great Britain and Ireland, London.

Cole, F. C.
    1951   Kincaid, a prehistoric Illinois metropolis. Univ. of Chicago Press.

———, and Deuel, T.
    1937   Rediscovering Illinois. Univ. of Chicago Press.

———, *et al.*
    1930   Guide leaflet for amateur archaeologists. Reprint and circular ser. National Research Council, Washington, D.C.

Cole, J. P., and King, C. A. M.
    1968   Quantitative geography. Wiley, London.

Cole, J. R.
    1972   Time-lapse photography in archaeological data recording. Plains Anthropologist 17(58), Pt. 1: 347–349.

Coles, J. M.
    1962   European Bronze Age shields. PPS 28: 156–190.
    1963   Irish Bronze Age horns and their relations with northern Europe. PPS 29: 326–356.
    1968   Experimental archaeology. Proc. of Soc. of Antiquaries of Scotland 99: 1–21.

Collier, D., Hudson, A. E., and Ford, A.
    1942   Archaeology of the Upper Columbia region. Univ. of Washington Publs. in Anthro. 9: 1–178.

Collins, H. B.
    1937   Archaeology of St. Lawrence Island, Alaska. SI MC 96(1).

Collins, M. B.
    1969   Test excavations at Amistad International Reservoir, Fall, 1967. TASP-P 16.

———, and Fenwick, J. M.
    1974   Population growth rate estimates, Grasshopper Pueblo. *In* W. A. Longacre (ed.), Multi-disciplinary research at Grasshopper. Univ. of Arizona, Anthro. Papers. In press.

———, Hester, T. R., and Weir, F. A.
    1969   The Floyd Morris site (41 CF 2): a prehistoric cemetery site in Cameron County, Texas, *In* Two prehistoric cemetery sites in the Lower Rio Grande Valley of Texas (pp. 119–146). TAS-B 40.

Colton, H. S.
1932   A survey of prehistoric sites in the region of Flagstaff, Arizona. BAE-B 104.
1939   Prehistoric culture units and their relationships in northern Arizona. Mus. of Northern Arizona, Bull. 17. Flagstaff.
1945   A revision of the date of the eruption of Sunset Crater. SWJA 1: 345–355.
1946   The Sinagua: a summary of the archaeology of the region of Flagstaff, Arizona. Northern Arizona Soc. of Science and Art, Flagstaff.
1953a   Field methods in archaeology. Mus. of Northern Arizona, Technical Ser. No. 1. Flagstaff.
1953b   Potsherds: an introduction to the study of prehistoric Southwestern ceramics and their use in historic reconstruction. Mus. of Northern Arizona, Bull. 25. Flagstaff.

————, and Hargrave, L. L.
1937   Handbook of northern Arizona pottery wares. Mus. of Northern Arizona, Bull. 11. Flagstaff.

Combes, J. D.
1964   A graphic method for recording and illustrating burials. A Ant 30(2): 216–218.

Compton, R. R.
1962   Manual of field geology (pp. 135–153). Wiley, New York.

Conger, P. S.
1942   Diatoms from Lower Klamath Lake. In L. S. Cressman, Archaeological researches in the northern Great Basin (pp. 115–116). CIW-P No. 538.
1949   The diatoms. In F. Johnson (ed.), The Boylston Street fishweir II (pp. 109–123). R. S. Peabody Foundation for Arch. 4(1).

Cook, R. M.
1963   Archaeomagnetism. In D. R. Brothwell and E. S. Higgs (eds.), Science in archaeology (pp. 59–71). Thames and Hudson, London.

Cook, S. F.
1946   A reconsideration of shell mounds with respect to population and nutrition. A Ant 12: 51–53.
1947   Survivorship in aboriginal populations. Human Biology 19: 83–89.
1949   Soil erosion and population in central Mexico. UC-IA 34.
1950   Physical analysis as a method for investigating prehistoric habitation sites. UCAS-R 7: 2–5.
1951a   Chemical analysis of fossil bone. Univ. of Michigan Anthro. Papers, No. 8: 73–84.
1951b   The fossilization of human bone: calcium, phosphate, and carbonate. UC-PAAE 40: 263–280.
1960   Dating prehistoric bone by chemical analysis. VFPA No. 28: 223–245.
1964   The nature of charcoal excavated at archaeological sites. A Ant 29: 514–517.
1972   Prehistoric demography. Addison-Wesley Module in Anthro. 16. Reading, Mass.

————, Brooks, S. T., and Ezra, H. C.
1961   The process of fossilization. SWJA 17: 355–364.

————, and Heizer, R. F.
1947   The quantitative investigation of aboriginal sites: analyses of human bone. AJPA, n.s., 5: 201–220.
1951   The physical analysis of nine Indian mounds of the Lower Sacramento Valley. UC-PAAE 40: 281–312.
1952   The fossilization of bone: organic components and water. UCAS-R 17.
1953a   Archaeological dating by chemical analysis of bone. SWJA 9: 213–238.
1953b   The present status of chemical methods for dating prehistoric bone. A Ant 18: 354–358.
1959   The chemical analysis of fossil bone: individual variation. AJPA 17: 109–115.
1962   Chemical analysis of the Hotchkiss site (CCo-138). UCAS-R 57, Pt. 1: 1–24.
1965a   The quantitative approach to the relation between population and settlement size. UCAS-R 64.
1965b   Studies on the chemical analysis of archaeological sites. Univ. of California Publs. in Anthro. 2.

————, and Treganza, A. E.
1947   The quantitative investigation of aboriginal sites: comparative physical and chemical analysis of two California Indian mounds. A Ant 13: 135–141.
1950   The quantitative investigation of Indian mounds. UC-PAAE 40: 223–262.

Cooke, C. K.
1961   The copying and recording of rock-paintings. South African Arch. Bull. 16(62): 61–65.
1963   Report on excavations at Pomongwe and Tshangula caves, Matopo Hills, Southern Rhodesia. South African Arch. Bull. 18, Pt. 3: 73–151.

Cookson, M. B.
    1954   Photography for archaeologists. Parrish, London.

Coon, C. S.
    1951   Cave explorations in Iran, 1949. Univ. of Pennsylvania Mus. Monographs.

Cooney, J. F.
    1963   Assorted errors in art collecting. Expedition 6(1): 20–27.

Cooper, W. S
    1942   Contributions of botanical science to the knowledge of postglacial climates. Journal of Geol. 50: 981–984.

Cope, L.
    1919   Calendars of the Indians north of Mexico. UC-PAAE 16(4).

Copley, G. J.
    1958   Going into the past. Puffin Books (PS117), Harmondsworth.

Corbyn, R. C.
    1973   Basic steps in archeological plane table mapping. Oklahoma Anthro. Soc., Newsletter 21(3).

Corcoran, J.
    1966   The young field archaeologist's guide. Bell, London.

Cornwall, I. W.
    1954   Soil science and archaeology with illustration from some British Bronze Age monuments. PPS for 1953: 129–147.
    1956   Bones for the archaeologist. Macmillan, New York.
    1958   Soils for the archaeologist. Phoenix House, London.
    1960   Soil investigations in the service of archaeology. VFPA No. 28: 265–299.
——, and Hodges, H. W. M.
    1964   Thin sections of British Neolithic pottery: Windmill Hill—a test site. Bull. of Univ. of London Inst. of Arch. 4: 29–33.

Cosgrove, C. B.
    1947   Caves of the Upper Gila and Hueco areas of New Mexico and Texas. PM-P 4(2).

Cosgrove, H. S., and Cosgrove, C. B.
    1932   The Swarts Ruin. PM-P 15(1).

Cosner, A. J.
    1951   Arrowshaft straightening with a grooved stone. A Ant 17: 147–148.
    1956   Fire-hardening of wood. A Ant 22: 179–180.

Cotter, J. L.
    1968   Handbook for historical archaeology, Privately printed, Wynecote, Pa.
——, and Corbett, J. M.
    1951   Archaeology of the Bynum Mounds, Mississippi. National Park Service, Arch. Research Ser., No. 1.

Coutier, L.
    1929   Expériences de taille pour rechercher les anciennes techniques paléolithiques. Bull. de la Soc. Préhist. Française 26: 172–174. Paris.

Cowgill, G. L.
    1964   The selection of samples from large sherd collections. A Ant 29: 467–473.
    1968   Archaeological applications of factor, cluster, and proximity analysis. A Ant 33: 367–375.
    1970   Some sampling and reliability problems in archaeology. In Archéologie et calculateurs (pp. 161–175). Editions du Centre National de la Recherche Scientifique, Paris.

Cowgill, U. M.
    1961   Soil fertility and the ancient Maya. Trans. of Connecticut Acad. of Arts and Sciences 42: 1–56.
    1962   An agricultural study of the Southern Maya lowlands. AA 64: 273–286.

Cox, A., Doell, R. R., and Dalrymple, G. B.
    1965   Quaternary paleomagnetic stratigraphy. In H. E. Wright and D. G. Frey (eds.). The Quaternary of the United States (pp. 817–830). Princeton Univ. Press.

Cox, G. H., Dake, C. L., and Muilenburg, G. A.
1921   Field methods in petroleum geology. McGraw-Hill, New York.

Crabtree, D. E.
1939   Mastodon bone with artifacts in California. A Ant 5: 148–149.
1966   A stoneworker's approach to analyzing and replicating the Lindenmeier Folsom. Tebiwa 9: 3–39.
1968   Mesoamerican polyhedral cores and prismatic blades. A Ant 33: 446–478.
1972   An introduction to flint-working. Idaho State Univ. Mus., Occasional Papers 28.
1973   Experiments in replicating Hohokam points. Tebiwa 16: 10–45.

———, and Butler, B. R.
1964   Notes on experiments in flint knapping: I, heat treatment of silica minerals. Tebiwa 7: 1–6.

Craig, H., and Craig, V.
1972   Creek marbles: determination of provenance by isotopic analysis. Science 176: 401–403.

Crawford, O. G. S.
1953   Archaeology in the field. Praeger, New York.

Craytor, W. B., and Johnson, L.
1968   Refinements in computerized item seriation. Mus. of Nat. Hist., Univ. of Oregon, Bull. No. 10.

Cressman, L. S.
1937   Petroglyphs of Oregon. Univ. of Oregon Publ. in Anthro. No. 2.
1942   Archaeological researches in the northern Great Basin. CIW-P No. 538.

———, Williams, H., and Krieger, A. D.
1940   Early man in Oregon. Univ. of Oregon Monographs, Studies in Anthro., No. 3.

Crowfoot, J. W.
1935   Report on the 1935 Samaria excavations. Palestine Exploration Fund, Quarterly Statement for 1935. London.

Culbert, T. P. (ed.)
1973   The Classic Maya collapse. Univ. of New Mexico Press, Albuquerque.

Cunnington, M. E.
1933   Evidence of climate derived from snail shells and its bearing on the date of Stonehenge. Wilshire Arch. Magazine 46: 350–355.

Curwen, E., and Curwen, E. C.
1926   The efficiency of the scapula as a shovel. Sussex Arch. Collections 67: 139–145.

Curwen, E. C.
1930a   The silting of ditches in chalk. Antiquity 4: 97–100.
1930b   Prehistoric flint sickles. Antiquity 4: 179–186.
1935   Argiculture and the flint sickle in Palestine. Antiquity 9: 62–66.
1940   The white patination of black flint. Antiquity 14: 435–437.

Cutler, H. C.
1952   A preliminary study of the plant remains of Tularosa Cave. FMNH-PAS 40: 461–480.

———, and Blake, L. W.
1973   Plants from archeological sites east of the Rockies. Missiouri Botanical Garden, St. Louis.

Dafoe, T.
1969   Artifact photography. Arch. Soc. of Alberta, Newsletter No. 19: 1–17.

Dangel, R.
1928   Die Zeitrechnung der kalifornischen Indianer. Anthropos 23: 110–134.

Daniel, G. E.
1943   The three ages. Cambridge Univ. Press.
1950   A hundred years of archaeology. Duckworth, London.
1962a   The idea of prehistory. Watts, London.
1962b   The megalith builders of Western Europe. Penguin Books (A-633), Baltimore.
1966   Man discovers his past. Crowell, New York.

———— (ed.)
    1956   Myth or legend? Bell, London.

Daugherty, R. D.
    1956   Archaeology of the Lind Coulee site, Washington. Amer. Philos. Soc., Proc. 100(3). Philadelphia.

Daumas, M. (ed.)
    1962   Histoire générale des techniques, Vol. 1: Les origines de la civilisation technique. Presses Universitaires de France, Paris.

Dauncey, K. D. M.
    1952   Phosphate content of soils in archaeological sites. Advancement of Science 9: 33–36.

Davies, R. G.
    1971   Computer programming in quantitative biology. Academic Press, London.

Davis, E. C.
    1937   Tree rings and the Mayan calendar. Science, n.s., 86(10), Suppl. (Nov. 26).

Davis, E. M., Srdoc, D., and Valastro, S., Jr.
    1973   Radiocarbon dates from Stobi: 1971 season. Studies in the Antiquity of Stobi 1: 23–36. Belgrade.

Davis, H. A.
    1971   Is there a future for the past? Archaeology 24(4): 300–306.

Davis, J. T., and Treganza, A. E.
    1959   The Patterson Mound: a comparative analysis of the archaeology of site Ala-328. UCAS-R 47.

Deaton, J. W.
    1962   The preservation of wood by the alum process. Florida Anthropologist 15: 115–117.

Debenham, F.
    1955   Map making. Blackie, London and Glasgow.

de Booy, T.
    1915   Pottery from certain caves in eastern Santo Domingo, West Indies. AA 17: 69–97.

Deetz, J. F.
    1965   The dynamics of stylistic change in Arikara ceramics. Illinois Studies in Anthro., No. 4. Urbana.
    1967   Invitation to archaeology. Natural History Press, Garden City, N.Y.
    1970   Archeology as a social science. In A. Fischer (ed.), Current directions in anthropology (pp. 115–125). AAA-Bull. 3(3), Pt. 2.

Deevey, E. S.
    1944   Pollen analysis and history. Amer. Scientist 32: 39–53.
    1948   On the date of the last rise of sea level in southern New England, with remarks on the Grassy Island site. Amer. Journal of Science 246: 329–352.
    1949   Biogeography of the Pleistocene. Bull. of Geol. Soc. of Amer. 60: 1315–1416.
    1958   The equilibrium problem. In R. G. Francis (ed.), The population ahead (pp. 64–86). Univ. of Minnesota Press, Minneapolis.

————, Flint, R. F., and Rouse, I.
    1967   Radiocarbon measurements: comprehensive index, 1950–1965. Yale Univ., New Haven.

De Jarnette, D. L., and Hansen, A. T.
    1960   The archaeology of the Childersburg site, Alabama. Florida State Univ., Notes in Anthro., No. 6. Tallahassee.

Deming, O. V.
    1952   Tooth development of the Nelson bighorn sheep. California Fish and Game 38: 523–529.

Dempsey, P., and Baumhoff, M. A.
    1963   The statistical use of artifact distributions to establish chronological sequence. A Ant 28: 496–509.

Denninger, E., and Ebinger, H.
    1953   Versuche über die Rekonstruktion der "Terra Nigra." Germania 31: 67–68.

Deschiens, R., and Coste, C.
    1957   The protection of works of art in wood from the attacks of wood-eating insects. Museum 10: 56–59.

De Terra, H., and Paterson. T. T.
1939   Studies on the Ice Age of India and associated human cultures. CIW-P No. 493.

———, Romero, J., and Stewart, T. D.
1949   Tepexpan man. VFPA No. 11.

Detweiler, A. H.
1948   Manual of archaeological surveying. Amer. Schools of Oriental Research, Publs. of Jerusalem School, Arch. 2. New Haven.

Deuel, L.
1969   Flights into yesterday: the story of aerial archaeology. St. Martin's Press, New York.

Dibble, D. S.
1971   Archeological survey. The Record, Dallas Arch. Soc. 27(3): 8–11.

———, and Lorrain, D.
1968   Bonfire Shelter: a stratified bison kill site, Val Verde County, Texas. Texas Memorial Mus., Misc. Papers 1.

Dickinson, W. R., and Shutler, R., Jr.
1971   Temper sands in prehistoric pottery of the Pacific Islands. Arch. and Physical Anthro. in Oceania 6(3): 191–203.

Dictionnaire archéologique des techniques
1963–64 2 vols. Editions de l'Accueil, Paris.

Diehl, R. A.
1970   A site designation system for Latin America. A Ant 35(4): 491–492.

Dills, C. E.
1970   Coordinate location of archaeological sites. A Ant 35(3): 389–390.

Dittert, A. E., and Eddy, F. W.
1963   Pueblo period sites in the Piedra River section, Navajo Reservoir district. Mus. of New Mexico, Papers in Anthro., No. 10. Santa Fe.

———, and Wendorf, F.
1963   Procedural manual for archaeological field research projects of the Museum of New Mexico. Mus. of New Mexico, Papers in Anthro., No. 12. Santa Fe.

———, Hester, J. J., and Eddy, F. W.
1961   An archaeological survey of the Navajo Reservoir district, northwestern New Mexico. School of Amer. Research and Mus. of New Mexico Monograph 23. Santa Fe.

Dixon, J. E., Cann, J. R., and Renfrew, C.
1968   Obsidian and the origins of trade. Scientific American 218: 38–46.

Dixon, K. A.
1963   The interamerican diffusion of a cooking technique: the culinary shoe-pot. AA 65: 593–619.

Dixon, R. B.
1905   The Northern Maidu. AMNH-B 17: 119–346.
1928   The building of cultures. Scribner's, New York.

Dobie, J. L.
1971   Reproduction and growth in the alligator snapping turtle, *Macroclemys temminicki* (Troost). Copeia 1971(4): 645–658.

Dobyns, H. F.
1966   Estimating aboriginal American population I: an apprasial of techniques with a new hemispheric estimate. Current Anthro. 7: 395–415.

Dobzhansky, T.
1962   Mankind evolving. Yale Univ. Press, New Haven.
1965   Evolution, genetics, and man. Wiley, New York.

Dodge, D.
1968   Laboratory artifact photography. Archaeology in Montana 9(1): 17–23.

Doki, N.
1934   On the relationship between the number of radial costae of prehistoric *Anadara* shells and the stratigraphy of shell-mounds in the Kanto District. Shizengaku Zasshi 6: 321–348. (In Japanese.)

Dort, W., *et al.*
1965   Paleotemperatures and chronology at archaeological cave sites revealed by thermoluminescence. Science 150: 480–482.

Dorwin, J. T.
1967   Iodine staining and ultraviolet photography field techniques. A Ant 32: 105–107.
1971   The Bowen site: an archaeological study of culture process in the late prehistory of central Indiana. Indiana Hist. Soc., Prehistory Research Series 4(4).

Douglass, A. E.
1929   The secret of the Southwest solved by talkative tree rings. National Geog. Magazine 56 (Dec.): 737–770.
1933   Tree growth and climatic cycles. Scientific Monthly 37: 481–495.

Downan, E. A.
1970   Conservation in field archaeology. Methuen, London.

Dragoo, D. W.
1963   Mounds for the dead. Annals of Carnegie Mus. 37. Pittsburgh.

Driver, H. E., and Kroeber, A. L.
1932   Quantitative expression of cultural relationships. UC-PAAE 31: 211–256.

Drucker, P.
1943a   Archaeological survey of the northern Northwest Coast. BAE-B 113: 17–142.
1943b   Ceramic sequences at Tres Zapotes, Veracruz, Mexico. BAE-B 140.
1952   La Venta, Tabasco: a study of Olmec ceramics and art. BAE-B 153.
1953   Site patterns in the eastern part of Olmec territory. Journal of Washington Acad. of Sciences 43(12): 389–391.

————, Heizer, R. F., and Squier, R.
1959   Excavations at La Venta, Tabasco, 1955. BAE-B 170.

Duffield. L. F.
1970   Vertisols and their implications for archeological research. AA 72(5): 1055–1062.

Duma, G.
1972   Phosphate content of ancient pots as indication of use. Current Anthro. 13(1): 127–130.

Dumas F.
1962   Deepwater archaeology. Routledge and Kegan Paul, London.

Dunham, D.
1956   Building an Egyptian pyramid. Archaeology 9: 159–165.

Dunnell, R. C.
1970   Seriation method and its evaluation. A Ant 35: 305–319.
1971   Systematics in prehistory. Free Press, New York.

Dunton, J. V.
1964   The conservation of excavated metals in the small laboratory. Florida Anthropologist 17(2): 37–43.

Easby, D. T.
1965   Pre-Hispanic metallurgy and metalworkings in the New World. Amer. Philos. Soc., Proc. 109(2): 89–98.
1966   Early metallurgy in the New World. Scientific American 214(4): 73–81.

————, and Dockstader, F.
1964   Requiem for Tizoc. Archaeology 17: 85–90.

Eaton, J. W.
1962   The preservation of wood by the alum process. Florida Anthropologist 15(4): 115–117.

Eddy, F. W., and Dregne, H. E.
1964   Soil tests on alluvial and archaeological deposits, Navajo Reservoir district. El Palacio 71: 5–21.

Eddy, J. A.
1974   Astronomical alignment of the Big Horn medicine wheel. Science 184: 1035–1043.

Edwards, I. E. S.
1961   The pyramids of Egypt. Penguin Books, Baltimore.
1970   Absolute dating from Egyptian records and comparison with carbon-14 dating. In T. E. Allibone et al., The impact of the natural sciences on archaeology (pp. 11–18). Oxford Univ. Press.

Edwards, R. L.
1969   Archaeological use of the Universal Transverse Mercator Grid. A Ant 34(2): 180–182.

Egloff, B. J.
1973   A method for counting ceramic rim sherds. A Ant 38(3): 351–353.

Ehrich, R. W. (ed.)
1965   Chronologies of Old World archaeology. Univ. of Chicago Press.

Eidt, R. C.
1973   A rapid chemical field test for archaeological site surveying. A Ant 38(2): 206–210.

Eiseley, L. C.
1937   Index mollusca and their bearing on certain problems of prehistory: a critique. In Twenty-fifth anniversary studies, Philadelphia Anthro. Soc. (pp. 77–93). Philadelphia.

Ekholm, G. F.
1964   The problems of fakes in pre-Columbian art. Curator 7: 19–32.

Ellis, H. H.
1940   Flint-working techniques of the American Indians: an experimental study. Lithic Laboratory, Dept. of Anthro., Ohio State Univ., Columbus.
1965   Flint-working techniques of the American Indians: an experimental study (reprinted ed.). Ohio Hist. Soc., Columbus.

Emery, K. O.
1966   Early man may have roamed the Atlantic shelf. Oceanus 12: 3–4.

Engel, C. G., and Sharp, R. P.
1959   Chemical data on desert varnish. Bull. of Geol. Soc. of Amer. 69: 487–518.

Engelbach, R.
1923   The problem of the obelisks. T. Fisher Unwin, London.

Engerrand, G.
1912   L'état actuel de la question des éolithes. Revue Générale des Sciences, 23ème Année: 541–548.

Epstein, J. F.
1964   Towards the systematic description of chipped stone. Actas y Memorias, XXXV Congreso Internacional de Americanistas 1: 155–169.
1969   The San Isidro site: an early man campsite in Nuevo Leon, Mexico. Dept. of Anthro., Univ. of Texas, Anthro. Series 7.

Erasmus, C.
1965   Monument building: some field experiments. SWJA 21: 277–301.

Erdtman, G.
1943   An introduction to pollen analysis. Ronald Press, New York.

Ericson, J. E., and Stickel, E. G.
1973   A proposed classification system for ceramics. World Archaeology 4(3): 357–367.

Erskine, C. A.
1965   Photographic documentation in archaeological research: increasing the information content. Science 148: 1089–1090.

Escalon de Fonton, M., Michaud, R., and Perinet, G.
1951   Etude par diffraction des rayons X de la fossilisation d'ossements préhistoriques. Comptes Rendus de l'Acad. des Sciences 233:706–707. Paris.

Evans, C., and Meggers, B.
1959   Archaeological investigations at the mouth of the Amazon. BAE-B 167.

Evans, J.
1897   Ancient stone implements, weapons and ornaments of Great Britain (2nd ed.). Longmans, London.

Evans, J. D.
　1973　Sherd weights and sherd counts: a contribution to the problem of quantifying pottery. *In* D. E. Strong (ed.), Archaeological theory and practice (pp. 131–149). Academic Press, New York.

Evans, J. G.
　1969　Land and freshwater mollusca in archaeology: chronological aspects. World Archaeology 1: 170–181.

Evans, J. W.
　1972　Tidal growth increments in the cockle *Clinocardium nuttalli*. Science 176 (4033): 416–417.

Evans, O. F.
　1957　Probable uses of stone projectile points. A Ant 23: 83–84.
　1958　More on wood hardening by fire. A Ant 23: 312.

Eydoux, H.-P.
　1968　History of archaeological discoveries. Leisure Arts, London.

Eyman, C. E.
　1965　Ultraviolet fluorescence as a method of skeletal identification. A Ant 31: 109–112.

Ezra, H. C., and Cook, S. F.
　1957　Amino acids in fossil human bone. Science 126: 80.

Faegri, K., and Iversen, J.
　1950　Textbook of modern pollen analysis. Munksgaard, Copenhagen.
　1965　Field techniques (for collecting pollen-bearing samples). *In* B. Kummel and D. Raup (eds.), Handbook of paleontological techniques (pp. 482–494). Freeman, San Francisco.

Fagan, B.
　1972　In the beginning: an introduction to archaeology. Little, Brown, Boston.
　1973　Belzoni the plunderer. Archaeology 26(1). 40–51.

Fahkry, A.
　1947　A report on the inspectorate of Upper Egypt. Annales du Service des Antiquités de l'Egypte 46: 25–54.

Fairbridge, R. W.
　1958　Dating the latest movements of the Quaternary sea level. Trans. of New York Acad. of Sciences, Ser. 2, Vol. 20: 471–482.

Falconer, D. S.
　1964　Introduction to quantitative genetics. Edinburgh.

Fant, J. F., and Loy, W. G.
　1972　Surveying and mapping. *In* W. A. MacDonald and G. R. Rapp (eds.), The Minnesota Messenia Expedition: reconstructing a Bronze Age regional environment (Chap. 2). Univ. of Minnesota Press, Minneapolis.

Faul, J., and Wagner, G. A.
　1971　Fission track dating. *In* H. N. Michael and E. K. Ralph (eds.), Dating techniques for the archaeologist (pp. 152–156). Mass. Inst. of Technology Press, Cambridge.

Feininger, A.
　1965　The complete photographer. Prentice-Hall, Englewood Cliffs, N.J.

Fenega, F.
　1949　Methods of recording and present status of knowledge concerning petrolglyphs in California. UCAS-R 3.

Ferguson, C. W.
　1970　Concepts and techniques of dendrochronology. *In* R. Berger (ed.), Scientific methods in medieval archeology (pp. 183–200). Univ. of California Press, Berkeley and Los Angeles.

Fernald, A. T.
　1962　Radiocarbon dates relating to widespread volcanic ash deposit, eastern Alaska. USGS Professional Papers, No. 450B.

Fewkes, J. W.
　1896　A contribution to ethnobotany. AA 9: 16–21.

Fink, C. F., and Polushkin, E. P.
  1936   Microsopic study of ancient bronze and copper. Trans. of Amer. Inst. of Mineral and Metallurgical Engineering 122: 90–120.
Firtion, F.
  1947   Les organismes siliceux et leur importance dans l'étude des sédiments quaternaires. Session des Sociétés Belges de Géologie (pp. 186–189). Brussels.
Fischer, H.
  1878   Die Mineralogie als Hilfswissenschaft für Archaeologie, Ethnographie u.s.w., mit specieller Berücksichtigung mexicanischer Sculpturen. Anthropos 19: 177–214, 345–357.
Fisher, R. D.
  1930   The archaeological survey of the Pueblo plateau. Univ. of New Mexico Bull. 177, Arch. Ser., Vol. 1, No. 1.
Fitting, J. E.
  1973a   An early Mogollon community: a preliminary report on the Winn Canyon site. The Artifact 11(1/2). El Paso.
——— (ed.)
  1973b   The development of North American archaeology. Anchor Press/Doubleday, Garden City, N.Y.
Flannery, K. V.
  1967   Culture history vs. cultural process: a debate in American archaeology. Scientific American 217: 119–122.
  1968   Archeological systems theory and early Mesoamerica. In Anthropological archeology in the Americas (pp. 67–87). Anthro. Soc. of Washington.
  1973   Archeology with a capital "S." In C. L. Redman (ed.), Research and theory in current archeology (pp. 47–58). Wiley-Interscience, New York.
Fleischer, R. L., and Price, P. B.
  1964   Glass dating by fission fragment tracks. Journal of Geophysical Research 69: 331–339.
———, and Walker, R. M.
  1965   Fission-track dating of Bed I, Olduvai Gorge. Science 148: 72–74.
Folan, W. J., Rick, J. H., and Zacharchuk, W.
  1968   The mechanization of artifact processing. A Ant 33(1): 86–89.
Foley, V. P.
  1965   Another method for the treatment of ferrous artifacts. Florida Anthropologist 18(3): 65–68.
Fontana, B. L.
  1965   On the meaning of historic sites archaeology. A Ant 31: 61–65.
Forbes, R. A.
  1955   Forestry handbook. Ronald Press, New York.
Ford, J. A.
  1936   Analysis of Indian village site collections from Louisiana and Mississippi. Dept. of Conservation, State of Louisiana, Anthro. Study No. 2.
  1938   A chronological method applicable to the Southeast. A Ant 3: 260–264.
  1951   Greenhouse: A Troyville-Coles Creek period site in Avoyelles Parish, Louisiana. AMNH-AP 44, Pt. 1.
  1952a   Measurements of some prehistoric design developments in the Southeastern states. AMNH-AP 44(3).
  1952b   Reply to "The Viru Valley sequence: a critical review." A Ant 17: 250.
  1954a   Comment on A. C. Spaulding, "Statistical techniques for the discovery of artifact types." A Ant 19: 390–391.
  1954b   On the concept of types. AA 56: 42–54.
  1962   A quantitative method of deriving cultural chronology. Pan Amer. Union, Technical Manual No. 1. Washington, D.C.
  1963   Hopewell culture burial mounds near Helena, Arkansas. AMNH-AP 50, Pt. 1.
———, and Webb, C. H.
  1956   Poverty Point, a late archaic site in Louisiana. AMNH-AP 46: 5–136.
———, and Willey, G. R.
  1941   An interpretation of the prehistory of the Eastern United States. AA 43: 325–363.
  1949   Surface survey of the Viru Valley, Peru. AMNH-AP 43, Pt. 1.

Ford, J. L., Rolingson, M. A., and Medford, L. D.
1972   Site destruction due to agricultural practices in southeast Arkansas [and] in northeast Arkansas. Arkansas Arch. Survey, Research Ser. 3.

Forde, C. D.
1931   Ethnography of the Yuma Indians. UC-PAAE 28(4).

Foster, G. M.
1960   Life-expectancy of utilitarian pottery in Tzintzuntzan, Michoacan, Mexico. A Ant 25: 606–609.

Fowler, M. I.
1959   Summary report of Modoc Rock Shelter: 1952, 1953, 1955, and 1956. Illinois State Mus., Report of Investigations No. 8. Springfield.

Fraikor, A. L., Hester, J. J., and Fraikor, F. J.
1971   Metallurgical analysis of a Hopewell copper earspool. A Ant 36(3): 358–361.

Fraser, F. C., and King, J. E.
1954   Faunal remains. In J. G. D. Clark, Excavations at Star Carr (pp. 70–95). Cambridge Univ. Press.

Freeman, L. G.
1973   The significance of mammalian faunas from Paleolithic occupations in Cantabrian Spain. A Ant 38(1): 3–44.

French, D. H.
1971   An experiment in water-sieving. Anatolian Studies 21: 59–64.

Friedman, A. M., et al.
1966   Copper artifacts: correlation with source types of copper ores. Science 152: 1504–1506.

Friedman, I., Smith, R. L., and Clark, D. L.
1963   Obsidian dating In D. R. Brothwell and E. S. Higgs (eds.), Science in archaeology (pp. 35–46). Thames and Hudson, London.

———, et al.
1960   A new dating method using obsidian. A Ant 25: 476–537.

Frison, G.
1968   A functional analysis of certain chipped stone tools. A Ant 33: 149–155.
1973   The Wardell Buffalo trap 48 SU 301: communal procurement in the Upper Green River, Wyoming. Mus. of Anthro., Univ. of Michigan, Anthro. Papers, No. 48.

Fritts, H. C.
1965   Dendrochronology. In H. E. Wright and D. G. Frey (eds.), The Quaternary of the United States (pp. 871–879). Princeton Univ. Press.

Fritz, J. M., and Plog, F. T.
1970   The nature of archaeological explanation. A Ant 35(4): 405–412.

Frost, H.
1963   Under the Mediterranean. Prentice-Hall, Englewood Cliffs, N.J.

Fry, E. I.
1965   The skeleton in the physical anthropology closet. Plains Anthropologist 10(27): 1–6.

Fry, R. E.
1972   Manually operated post hole diggers as sampling instruments. A Ant 37(2): 259–260.

Fryxell, R.
1965   Mazama and Glacier Peak volcanic ash layers: relative ages. Science 147: 1288–1290.

Furusho, T.
1968   On the manifestation of genotypes responsible for stature. Human Biology 40(4): 437–455.

Gairola, T. R.
1961   Preservation of wooden antiquities. Journal of Indian Museums 7: 25–35. Calcutta.

Gangl, I.
1936   Alterbestimmung fossiler Knochenfunde auf chemischen Wege. Oester. Chem. Zeitschrift 39: 79–82.

Gannett, H.
1906   Manual of topographic methods. USGS Ser. F, Geog. 56, Bull. 307.

Gardin, I.-C.
1958   Four codes for the description of artifacts: an essay in archaeological technique and theory. AA 60: 335–357.
1967   Methods for the descriptive analysis of archaeological material. A Ant 32(1): 13–30.

Garlake, M.
1969a   Cleaning corroded copper. South African Arch. Bull. 24(93): 30–31.
1969b   Recovery and treatment of fragile artefacts from an excavation. South African Arch. Bull. 24(94): 61–62.

Garn, S.
1962   The newer physical anthropology. AA 64: 917–918.

Gaussen, A.
1950   Preservation of skins and leather. Ciba Review 7: 2960–2962.

Gebhard, D.
1960   Prehistoric paintings of the Diablo region of western Texas. Roswell Mus. and Art Center Publs. in Art and Science, No. 3.

Geer, G. de
1937   Early man and geochronology. In G. G. MacCurdy (ed.), Early man (pp. 323–326). Lippincott, Philadelphia.
1940   Geochronology suecica principles. Kon. Svensk. Vet. Akad. Handl. 18. Stockholm.

Gehrcke, E.
1933   Ueber Zeitbestimmungen an Gesteinen jüngerer geologischer Epochen. Gerlands Beiträge zu Geophysik 38: 147–166.

Gejvall, N. G.
1963   Cremations. In D. R. Brothwell and E. S. Higgs (eds.), Science in archaeology (pp. 379–390). Thames and Hudson, London.

Gelfand, A. E.
1971   Seriation methods for archaeological materials. A Ant 36: 263–274.

Genoves, S. T.
1963a   Sex determination in earlier man. In D. R. Brothwell and E. S. Higgs (eds.), Science in archaeology (pp. 343–350). Thames and Hudson, London.
1963b   Estimation of age and mortality. In D. R. Brothwell and E. S. Higgs (eds.), Science in archaeology (pp. 353–364). Thames and Hudson, London.

Germain, L.
1923   Les climats des temps quaternaires d'après les mollusques terrestres at fluviatiles. L'Anthropologie 33: 301–322.

Gettens, R. J.
1964   The corrosion products of metal antiquities. SI-AR for 1963: 547–568.

———, and Usilton, B. M.
1955   Abstracts of technical studies in art and archaeology 1943–52. Freer Gallery of Art, Occasional Papers 2(2). Washington, D.C.

Geyer, D.
1923   Die Quartärmollusken und die Klimafrage. Paleontologisches Zeitschrift 5: 72–94.

Giddings, J. L.
1962   Development of tree-ring dating as an archaeological aid. In T. T. Kozlowski (ed.), Tree growth (pp. 119–132). Ronald Press, New York. .
1966   Cross-dating the archaeology of northwestern Alaska. Science 153: 127–135.

Gifford, E. W.
1916   Composition of California shellmounds. UC-PAAE 12: 1–29.
1949   Early central California and Anasazi shell artifact types. A Ant 15: 156–157.
1951   Fijian mythology, legends and archaeology. Univ. of California Publs. in Semitic Philology 11: 167–177.

Gifford, J. C.
1960   The type-variety method of ceramic classification as an indicator of cultural phenomena. A Ant 25: 341–347.

Gilbert, B. M.
1973   Mammalian osteo-archaeology: North America. Missouri Arch. Soc., Special Publ., Columbia.

Gilbert, F. F.
1966   Aging white-tailed deer by annuli in the cementum of the first incisor. Journal of Wildlife Management 30(1): 200–202.

Gillio, D. A.
1970   Uses of infrared photography in archaeology. Colorado Anthropologist 2(2): 13–19.

Gladwin, H. S.
1940a   Methods and instruments for use in measuring tree-rings. GP-MP 27.
1940b   Tree ring analysis: methods of correlation. GP-MP 28.

Gladwin, W., and Gladwin, H. S.
1928   A method for the designation of ruins in the Southwest. GP-MP 1.
1934   A method for the designation of cultures and their variations. GP-MP 15.

Glob, P. V.
1969   The bog people, Iron Age man preserved. Ballantine Books, New York.

Glock, W. S.
1937   Principles and methods of tree analysis. CIW-P No. 486.
1941   [Tree] growth rings and climate. Botany Review 7: 649–713.

Godwin, H.
1934   Pollen analysis, an outline of the problems and potentialities of the method. New Phytologist 33: 278–305, 325–358.

Goggin, J. M.
1949   Cultural traditions in Florida prehistory. In The Florida Indian and his neighbors (pp. 13–44). Inter-Amer. Center, Rollins College, Winter Park, Fla.
1960   Underwater archaeology: its nature and limitation. A Ant 25: 348–354.

Goksu, H. Y., et al.
1974   Age determination of burned flint by a thermoluminescent method. Science 183: 651–653.

Goldstein, M. S.
1953   Some vital statistics based on skeletal material. Human Biology 25: 3–10.
1957   Skeletal pathology of early Indians in Texas. APJA 15: 299–311.

Goldthwait, R. P.
1935   The Damariscotta shell heaps and coastal stability. Amer. Journal of Science 30: 1–13.

Goodman, M. E.
1944   The physical properties of stone tool materials. A Ant 9. 415–433.

Goodwin, A. J. H.
1953   Method in prehistory (2nd ed.). South African Arch. Soc. Handbook Ser., No. 1. Capetown.
1960   Chemical alteration (patination) of stone. VFPA No. 28: 300–324.

Gordon, D. H.
1953   Fire and the sword: the technique of destruction. Antiquity 27: 149–153.

Gorenstein, S.
1965   Introduction to archaeology. Basic Books, New York.

Gorsline, E. P.
1959   Artist to the rescue. Desert Magazine 22: 23–24.

Gould, R. A.
1963   Aboriginal California burial and cremation practices. UCAS-R 60: 149–168.
1968a   Chipping stones in the outback. Nat. Hist. 77(2): 42–49.
1968b   Living archaeology: the Ngatatjara of western Australia. SWJA 24(2): 101–122.

Grabau, A. W.
  1924   Principles of stratigraphy (2nd ed.). Seiler, New York.

Graham, J. A., and Davis, W. A.
  1958   Appraisal of the archeological resources of Diablo Reservoir, Val Verde County, Texas. Archeological Salvage Program Field Office, National Park Service, Austin.

———, and Heizer, R. F.
  1967   Man's antiquity in North America: views and facts. Quaternaria. 9: 225–235. Rome.

———, Heizer, R. F., and Hester, T. R.
  1972   A bibliography of replicative experiments in archaeology. Arch. Research Facility, Univ. of California, Berkeley.

———, Hester, T. R., and Jack, R. N.
  1972   Sources for the obsidian at the ruins of Seibal, Guatemala. UC-CARF 16: 11–116.

Graham, R., and Wray, C. F.
  1962   The percentage of recovery in salvaging beads from disturbed burials. Arkansas Archeologist 3(1): 14–17.

Gramly, R. M.
  1970   Use of a magnetic balance to detect pits and postmolds. A Ant 35(2): 217–220.

Grant, C.
  1965   The rock paintings of the Chumash. Univ. of California Press, Berkeley and Los Angeles.

Gray, C.
  1961   Geologic maps of the fifty states. California State Division of Mines, Mineral Information Service 14(11): 14–15.

Grebinger, P.
  1971   The Potrero Creek site: activity structure. Kiva 37(1): 30–52.

Green, E. L.
  1973   In search of man: readings in archaeology. Little, Brown, Boston.

Green, E. R. R.
  1960   Industrial archaeology. Antiquity 34: 43–48.

Green, J. N., et al.
  1971   Simple underwater photogrammetric techniques. Archaeometry 13(2): 221–232.

Greene, J. C.
  1959   The death of Adam. Iowa State Univ. Press, Iowa City.

Greengo, R. E.
  1951   Molluscan species in California shell middens. UCAS-R 13.
  1964   Issaquena: an archaeological phase in the Yazoo Basin of the Lower Mississippi Valley. SAA-M No. 18.

Greenhood, D.
  1964   Mapping. Univ. of Chicago Press.

Greenman, E. F.
  1957   An American eolithic? A Ant 22: 298.

———, and Stanley, G. M.
  1943   The archaeology and geology of two early sites near Killarney, Ontario. Papers of Michigan Acad. of Science, Arts and Letters 28: 505–530.

Greenwood, R. S.
  1961   Quantitative analysis of shells from a site in Goleta, California. A Ant 26: 416–420.

Griffin, J. B.
  1943   The Fort Ancient aspect. Univ. of Michigan Press, Ann Arbor.
  1955   Chronology and dating processes. Yearbook of Anthro., 1955: 133–147. Chicago.
  1959   The pursuit of archaeology in the United States. AA 61: 379–388.

——— (ed.)
  1952   Archaeology of Eastern United States. Univ. of Chicago Press.

————, and Angell, C. W.
   1935   An experimental study of the techniques of pottery making. Papers of Michigan Acad. of Science, Arts and Letters 20: 1-6.

————, Gordus, A. A., and Wright, G. A.
   1969   Identification of the sources of Hopewellian obsidian in the Middle West. A Ant 34: 1-14.

Griffin, J. W.
   1948   Green Mound, a chronological yardstick. Florida Naturalist 22: 1-8.

Griffiths, D. W.
   1973   Local archaeomagnetic research. Bull. of New York State Arch. Assoc. 58: 24-25.

Griggs, K.
   1973   Toxic metal fumes from mantle-type camp lanterns. Science 181: 842-843.

Grinsell, L., Rahtz, P., and Warhurst, A.
   1966   The preparation of archaeological reports. J. Baker, London.

Guerreschi, A.
   1973   A mechanical sieve for archaeological excavations. Antiquity 47(187): 234-235.

Guilday, J. E., Parmalee, P. W., and Tanner, D. P.
   1962   Aboriginal butchering techniques at the Eschelman site (36 La 12), Lancaster County, Pennsylvania. Pennsylvania Archaeologist 32: 59-83.

Gumerman, G. J.
   1971   (ed.), The distribution of prehistoric population aggregates. Prescott College Anthro. Reports 1.

————, and Lyons, T. R.
   1971   Archaeological methodology and remote sensing. Science 172: 126-132.

————, and Neely, J. A.
   1972   An archaeological survey of the Tehuacan Valley, Mexico: a test of color infrared photography. A Ant 37(4): 520-527.

Gundlach, H.
   1961   Tüpfelmethode auf Phosphat angewandt in prähistorischer Forschung (als Feldmethode). Mikrochimica et Ichnoanalytica Acta 5: 735-737.

Guthe, C. E.
   1952   Twenty-five years of archaeology in the Eastern United States. In J. B. Griffin (ed.), Archaeology of Eastern United States (pp. 1-12). Univ. of Chicago Press.

Guy, P. L. O.
   1932   Balloon photography and archaeological excavation. Antiquity 6: 148-155.

Hack, J. T.
   1942   The changing physical environment of the Hopi Indians of Arizona. PM-P 35(1).
   1943   Antiquity of the Finley site. A Ant 8: 235-241.
   1945   Recent geology of the Tsegi Canyon. In R. L. Beals, G. W. Brainerd, and W. Smith, Archaeological studies in northeast Arizona (pp. 151-158). UC-PAAE 44.

Hadleigh-West, F.
   1967   A system of archaeological site designation for Alaska. A Ant 32(1): 107-108.

Haggett, P.
   1965   Locational analysis in human geography. E. Arnold, London.

Hainline, J.
   1965   Culture and biological adaptation. AA 67: 1174-1197.

Hall, C. A., Jr., Dollase, W. A., and Corbato, C. E.
   1974   Shell growth in Tivela stultorum and Callista chione: annual periodicity, latitudinal differences, and diminution with age. Palaeography, Palaeoclimatology, Palaeoecology 15: 33-61.

Hall, E. R.
   1946   Mammals of Nevada. Univ. of California Press, Berkeley.

Hall, E. T.
   1939   Dendrochronology. SAA-N 1: 32-41.

1966   The use of the proton magnetometer in underwater archaeology. Archaeometry 9: 32–44.
1970   Survey techniques in underwater archaeology. Royal Soc. of London, Philos. Trans., Ser. A, 269(1193): 121–124.

Hallert, B.
1971   Photogrammetry and culture history. Norwegian Arch. Review 4: 28–36.

Hammond, A.
1971   Tools for archaeology: aids to studying the past. Science 173: 511–512.

Hammond, N.
1972   Obsidian trade routes in the Mayan area. Science 178: 1092–1093.
1973   A giant scale for long-distance photography. Antiquity 47: 144.

Hammond, P. C.
1963   Archaeological techniques for amateurs. Van Nostrand, Princeton, N.J.

Hanna, R. E., and Washburn, S. L.
1953   The determination of the sex of skeletons as illustrated by a study of the Eskimo pelvis. Human Biology 25: 21–27.

Hansen, H. O.
1961   Ungdommelige Oldtidshuse. Kuml 1961: 128–145.
1962   I built a Stone Age house. Phoenix House, London.
1964   Mand og Hus. Rhodus, Copenhagen.

Hansen, H. P.
1942   A pollen study of peat profiles from Lower Klamath Lake of Oregon and California. In L. S. Cressman, Archaeological researches in the northern Great Basin (pp. 103–114). CIW-P No. 538.
1946   Early man in Oregon: pollen analysis and postglacial climate and chronology. Science Monthly 42: 52–65.

Harbottle, G.
1970   Neutron activation analysis of potsherds from Knossos and Mycenae. Archaeometry 12: 23–24.

Hargrave, L. L.
1936   The field collection of beam material. Tree Ring Bull. 2(3).

Harlan, J. R.
1967   A wild wheat harvest in Turkey. Archaeology 20: 197–201.

Harner, M. J.
1956   Thermo-facts vs. artifacts: an experimental study of the Malpais industry. UCAS-R 33: 39–43.

Harrington, J. C.
1952   Historic site archaeology in the United States. In J. B. Griffin (ed.), Archaeology of Eastern United States (pp. 335–344). Univ. of Chicago Press.
1955   Archaeology as an auxiliary science to American history. AA 57: 1121–1130.

Harrington, M. R.
1933   Gypsum Cave, Nevada. SM-P 8.

Harris, A. H.
1963   Vertebrate remains and past environmental reconstruction in the Navajo Reservoir district. Mus. of New Mexico, Papers in Anthro., No. 11. Santa Fe.

Harrison, G. A.
1964   Human genetics. In G. Harrison et al., Human biology (pp. 101–186). Oxford Univ. Press.

Harrison, M. W.
1945   The writing of American archaeology. A Ant 10: 331–339.

Harriss, J. C.
1971   Explanations in prehistory. PPS 37: 38–55.

Hatch, M. P.
1971   An hypothesis on Olmec astronomy, with special reference to the La Venta site. UC-CARF 13: 1–64.

Hatt, G.
1957   Nørte Fjand, an early Iron Age village site in West Jutland. Arkeologisk Danske Videnskabernes Selskab 2(2). Copenhagen.

Haury, E. W.
1931   Minute beads from prehistoric pueblos. AA 33: 80–87.
1937a   Stratigraphy. *In* Excavations at Snaketown (Chap. 4). GP-MP 25.
1937b   The Snaketown Canal. *In* Excavations at Snaketown (Chap. 6). GP-MP 25.
1937c   Shell. *In* Excavations at Snaketown (Chap. 11). GP-MP 25.
1959   Review of G. F. Carter, "Pleistocene man at San Diego." Amer. Journal of Arch. 63: 116–117.

———, Sayles, E. B., and Wasley, W. W.
1959   The Lehner Mammoth site, southeastern Arizona. A Ant 25: 2–30.

Hawkes, J.
1968   The proper-study of mankind. Antiquity 42: 255–262.

Hawkins, G.
1963   Stonehenge decoded. Nature 200: 306–308.
1965a   Callanish, a Scottish Stonehenge. Science 147: 127–130.
1965b   Stonehenge decoded. Doubleday, Garden City, N.Y.

Hawley, A.
1944   Ecology and human ecology. Social Forces 22: 398–405.

Hawley, F. M.
1934   The significance and the dated prehistory of Chetro Ketl. Univ. of New Mexico Monograph Ser., Vol. 1, No. 1.
1936   Field manual of Southwestern pottery types. Univ. of New Mexico Bull., Anthro. Ser., Vol. 1, No. 4. (Rev. ed., 1950.)
1938   Tree ring dating for Southeastern (United States) mounds. BAE-B 118: 359–362.
1941   Tree-ring analysis and dating in the Mississippi drainage. Univ. of Chicago, Occasional Papers in Anthro., No. 2.

Hayden, J. D.
1957   Excavations, 1940, at University Indian Ruin. Southwestern Monuments Assoc., Technical Ser. No. 5. Globe, Ariz.
1965   Fragile-pattern areas. A Ant 31(2): 272–276.

Hayes, A. C.
1964   The archeological survey of Wetherill Mesa, Mesa Verde National Park, Colorado. National Park Service, Arch. Research Ser. 7-A.

———, and Osborne, D.
1961   Fixing site location with radio-direction finder at Mesa Verde. A Ant 27(1): 110–112.

Haynes, C. V.
1964   Fluted projectile points: their age and dispersion. Science 145(3639): 1408–1413.
1966a   Geochronology of Late Quaternary alluvium. Geochronology Laboratories, Univ. of Arizona, Interim Research Report No. 10. Tucson.
1966b   Radiocarbon samples: chemical removal of plant contaminants. Science 151: 1391–1392.
1969   The earliest Americans. Science 166(3906): 709–715.

Haynes, V.
1973   The Calico site: artifacts or geofacts? Science 181: 305–310.

Hedden, M.
1958   "Surface printing" as a means of recording petroglyphs. A Ant 23: 435–439.

Hederström, H.
1959   Observations on the age of fishes. Drottningholm Statens Undersoknings och Forsaksanstalt for Sotvattensfisket 40: 161–164. (Original 1759.)

Heizer, R. F.
1937   Baked-clay objects of the Lower Sacramento Valley, California. A Ant 3: 34–50.
1941a   Aboriginal trade between the Southwest and California.
1941b   Archaeological evidence of Sebastian Rodriguez Cermeno's California visit in 1595. California Hist. Soc. Quarterly 20(4). (Reprinted separately with contributions by A. L. Kroeber and C. G. Fink.)
1941c   The direct-historical approach in California archaeology. A Ant 7: 98–122.
1946   The occurrence and significance of Southwestern grooved axes in California. A Ant 11: 187–193.

1949   The archaeology of central California: I, The Early Horizon. UC-AR 12: 1–84.
1950   On the methods of chemical analysis of bone as an aid to prehistoric culture chronology. UCAS-R 7.
1953   Long range dating in archaeology. *In* A. L. Kroeber (ed.), Anthropology today (pp. 1–42). Univ. of Chicago Press.
1960   Physical analysis of habitation residues. VFPA No. 28: 93–157.
1962   Man's discovery of his past: literary landmarks in archaeology. Spectrum Books (S-46), Prentice-Hall, Englewood Cliffs, N.J.
1965   Problems in dating Lake Mojave artifacts. SM-M 39: 125–134.
1966a   Methods and achievements of ancient heavy transport. Science 153: 821–830.
1966b   Salvage and other archaeology. SM-M 40: 54–60.
1967   Analysis of human coprolites from a dry Nevada cave. UCAS-R 70: 1–20.
1968a   Migratory animals as dispersal agents of cultural materials. Science 161: 914–915.
1968b   Suggested change in system of site designations. A Ant 33(2): 254.

——— (ed.)
1959   The archaeologist at work. Harper, New York.

———, and Baumhoff, M. A.
1959   Great Basin petroglyphs and prehistoric game trails. Science 129: 904–905.
1962   Prehistoric rock art of Nevada and eastern California. Univ. of California Press, Berkeley.

———, and Brooks, R.
1965   Lewisville—ancient campsite or wood rat houses? SWJA 21: 155–165.

———, and Cook, S. F.
1949   The archaeology of central California: a comparative analysis of human bone from nine sites. UC-AR 12: 85–112.
1952   Fluorine and other chemical tests of some North American human and animal bones. AJPA 10: 289–304.
1956   Some aspects of the quantitative approach in archaeology. SWJA 12: 229–248.
1959   New evidence of the antiquity of Tepexpan and other human remains from the Valley of Mexico. SWJA 15: 36–42.
1960   The application of quantitative methods in archaeology. VFPA No. 28.

———, and Hester, T. R.
1973   The archaeology of Bamert Cave, Amador County, California. Univ. of California Arch. Research Facility, Berkeley.

———, and Hewes, G. W.
1940   Animal ceremonialism in central California in the light of archaeology. AA 42: 587–603.

———, and Krieger, A. D.
1956   The archaeology of Humboldt Cave, Churchill County, Nevada. UC-PAAE 47: 1–190.

———, and Mills, J. E.
1952   The four ages of Tsurai. Univ. of California Press, Berkeley.

———, and Napton, L. K.
1969   Biological and cultural evidence from prehistoric human coprolites. Science 165(3893): 563–568.
1970   Archaeology and the prehistoric Great Basin lacustrine subsistence regime as seen from Lovelock Cave, Nevada. UC-CARF 10.

———, and Squier, R. J.
1953   Excavations at site Nap-32 in July, 1951. *In* R. F. Heizer (ed.), Archaeology of the Napa region (App. 4). UC-PAAE 12(6).

———, and Williams, H.
1965   Stones used for colossal sculpture at or near Teotihuacan. UC-CARF 1: 55–77.

———, Stross, F. H., and Hester, T. R.
1973   New light on the Colossi of Memnon. SM-M 47(3): 94–105.

———, Williams, H., and Graham, J.
1965   Notes on Mesoamerican obsidians and their significance in archaeological studies. UC-CARF 1: 94–103.

———, et al.
1973   The Colossi of Memnon revisited. Science 182: 1219–1225.

Helbaek, H.
    1953   Archaeology and agricultural botany. Inst. of Arch., Univ. of London, Ninth Annual Report: 44–59.
    1969   Plant collecting, dry-farming, and irrigation agriculture in prehistoric Deh Luran. *In* F. Hole, K. V. Flannery, and J. A. Neely, Prehistory and human ecology of the Deh Luran Plain (pp. 383–426). Mus. of Anthro. Univ. of Michigan, Memoirs, No. 1.

Helm, J.
    1962   The ecological approach in anthropology. Amer. Journal of Sociology 47: 630–639.

Hencken, H. C.
    1955   Indo-European languages and archaeology. AAA-M 84.

Hertzog, K. P.
    1967   Shortened fifth medial phalanges. AJPA 27: 113–118.

Hesse, A.
    1966   Prospections géophysiques à faible profondeur: applications a l'archéologie. Dunod, Paris.

Hester, J. J.
    1960   Late Pleistocene extinction and radiocarbon dating. A Ant 26: 58–77.
    1962   A comparative typology of New World cultures. AA 64: 1001–1015.
——, and Conover, K. J.
    1970   Ecological sampling of middens on the Northwest Coast. Northwest Anthro. Research Notes 4(2): 137–152.
——, and Hobler, P. M.
    1969   Prehistoric settlement patterns in the Libyan desert. Univ. of Utah Anthro. Papers 92.

Hester, T. R.
    1968   Paleo-Indian artifacts from sites along San Miguel Creek: Frio, Atascosa, and McMullen counties, Texas TAS-B 39: 147–166.
    1970   A study of wear patterns on hafted and unhafted bifaces from two Nevada caves. UC-CARF 7: 44 54.
    1973   Chronological ordering of Great Basin prehistory. UC-CARF 17.
    1974   Archaeological remains from site NV Wa 197, western Nevada: atlatl and animal skin pouches. UC-CARF 21: 1–36.
——, and Heizer, R. F.
    1972   Problems in the functional interpretation of artifacts: scraper planes from Mitla and Yagul, Oaxaca. UC-CARF 14: 107–123.
    1973a   Arrow points or knives? Comments on the proposed function of "Stockton Points." A Ant 38(2): 220–221.
    1973b   Bibliography of archaeology I: experiments, lithic technology, and petrography. Addison-Wesley Module in Anthro. 29. Reading, Mass.
——, Gilbow, D., and Albee, A. D.
    1973   A functional analysis of "Clear Fork" artifacts from the Rio Grande Plain of Texas. A Ant 38(1): 90–96.
——, Heizer, R. F., and Jack, R. N.
    1971   Technology and geologic sources of obsidian from Cerro de las Mesas, Veracruz, Mexico, with observations on Olmec trade. UC-CARF 13: 133–142.
——, Jack, R. N., and Benfer, A.
    1973   Trace element analysis of obsidian from Michoacan, Mexico: preliminary results. UC-CARF 18: 167–176.
——, Jack, R. N., and Heizer, R. F.
    1971   The obsidian of Tres Zapotes, Veracruz, Mexico. UC CARF 13: 65–131.

Hewer, H. R.
    1964   The determination of age, sexual maturity, longevity and a life table in the grey seal (*Halichoerus grypus*). Proc. of Zoological Soc. of London 142: 523–624.

Heye, G. G.
    1919   Certain aboriginal pottery from southern California. MAIHF-INM 7(1).

Heyerdahl, T.
    1950   The Kon Tiki expedition by raft across the South Seas (trans. by F. H. Lyon). G. Allen and Unwin, London.

1952   American Indians in the Pacific. G. Allen and Unwin, London.
1959   Aku-aku. Cardinal (Giant Pocket Book No. GC-758), New York.

————, and Ferdon, E.
1961   Archaeology of Easter Island. Monographs of School of Amer. Research and Mus. of New Mexico, No. 24. Sante Fe.

Heyn, A. N. J.
1954   Fiber microscopy. Interscience Publishers, New York.

Heyns, O. S.
1947   Sexual differences in the pelvis. South African Journal of Medical Science 12: 17–29. (Reprinted in Yearbook of Physical Anthro. 2: 267–270. Viking Fund, 1948.)

Higgs, E. S.
1970   Review of D. L. Clarke, "Analytical archaeology." PPS 36: 396–399.

Hill, A. T., and Kivett, M.
1940   Woodland-like manifestations in Nebraska. Nebraska Hist. Magazine 21: 143–243.

Hill, J. N.
1966   A prehistoric community in eastern Arizona. SWJA 22: 9–30.
1967   Sampling at Broken K Pueblo: chapters in the prehistory of eastern Arizona, III. FMNH-Fieldiana 57: 151–157.
1968   Broken K Pueblo, patterns of form and function. In S. R. Binford and L. R. Binford (eds.), New perspectives in archeology (pp. 103–142). Aldine, Chicago.
1970   Broken K Pueblo, prehistorical social organization in the American Southwest. Anthro. Papers of Univ. of Arizona, No. 18.

Hodge, F. W.
1920   Hawikuh bonework. MAIHF-INM 31(3): 65–151.

Hodges, H. W. M.
1962   Thin sections of prehistoric pottery: an empirical study. Bull. of Univ. of London Inst. of Arch. 3: 58–68.
1964   Artifacts: an introduction to early materials and technology. J. Baker, London.

Hodgkiss, A. G.
1970   Maps for books and theses. Universe Books, New York.

Hoijer, H.
1956   Lexicostatistics: a critique. Language 32: 49–60.

Hole, F.
1971   Approaching typology rationally. The Record, Dallas Arch. Soc. 27(3): 11–16.

————, and Heizer, R. F.
1965   An introduction to prehistoric archeology. Holt, Rinehart and Winston, New York.
1973   An introduction of prehistoric archeology (3rd ed.). Holt, Rinehart and Winston, New York.

————, and Shaw, M.
1967   Computer analysis of chronological seriation. Rice Univ. Studies 53(3).

————, Flannery, K. W., and Neely, J. A.
1969   Prehistory and human ecology of the Deh Luran Plain. Mus. of Anthro., Univ. of Michigan, Memoirs, No. 1.

Holmes, W. H.
1894   Natural history of flaked stone implements. In C. S. Wake (ed.), International Congress of Anthro. memoirs (pp. 120–139). Chicago.
1919   Handbook of aboriginal American antiquities: Part I, The lithic industries. BAE-B60.

Honea, K. H.
1965a   The bipolar flaking technique in Texas and New Mexico. TAS-B 36: 259–267.
1965b   A morphology of scrapers and their methods of production. Southwestern Lore 31(2).

Hooton, E. A.
1930   The Indians of Pecos Pueblo: a study of their skeletal remains. Yale Univ. Press, New Haven.
1946   Up from the ape (rev. ed.). Macmillan, New York.

Hopkins, D. M.
    1959   Cenozoic history of the Bering land bridge. Science 129: 1519–1528.

Hopkins, N. A.
    1965   Great Basin prehistory and Uto-Aztecan. A Ant 31: 48–60.

Hough, W.
    1916   Experimental work in American archaeology and ethnology. In Holmes anniversary volume (pp. 194–197). Washington, D.C.

Howard, C. D.
    1974   The atlatl: function and performance. A Ant 39(1): 102–104.

Howard, H.
    1929   The avifauna of Emeryville shellmound. Univ. of California Publ. in Zoology 32: 301–394.

Howell, F. C.
    1970   Early man. Time-Life Books, New York.

Howell, M. I.
    1968   The soil conductivity anomaly detector (SCM) in archaeological prospection. Prospezioni Archeologiche 3: 101–104.

Howells, W. W.
    1960   Estimating population numbers through archaeological and skeletal remains. VFPA No. 28: 158–180.

Hranicky, W. J.
    1972   Application of resistivity surveying to American archaeology. The Chesopiean 10(2): 43–50.
    1973   Archaeology: a means to the past. The Artifact 11(3). El Paso.

Hrdlicka, A.
    1937   Man and plants in Alaska. Science 86: 559–560.
    1948   Practical anthropometry (3rd ed; rev. by T. D. Stewart). Wistar Inst., Philadelphia.

Hudson, K.
    1963   Industrial archaeology: an introduction. J. Baker, London.

Hue, E.
    1929   Recherches sur la patine des silex. Bull., Soc. Préhist. Française 26: 461–468. Paris.

Hunt, C. B.
    1954   Desert varnish. Science 126: 183–184.

———, and Sokoloff, V. P.
    1950   Pre-Wisconsin soil in the Rocky Mountain region: a progress report. USGS Professional Paper 221-G.

Hurst, V. J., and Kelly, A. R.
    1961   Patination of cultural flints. Science 134: 251–256.

Hurt, W. R.
    1953a   A comparative study of the preceramic occupations of North America. A Ant 15: 204–222.
    1953b   Report of the investigation of the Thomas Riggs site, 39HU1, Hughes County, South Dakota. South Dakota Arch. Commission. Arch. Studies Circular 5. Pierre.
    1970   A report on the investigations of the New Heart Creek site, 39AR2, Dewey County, South Dakota, 1960. Plains Anthropologist 15(49): 169–215.

Huxtable, J., Aitken, M. J., and Weber, J. C.
    1972   Thermoluminiscent dating of baked clay balls of the Poverty Point culture. Archaeometry 14: 269–276.

Hymes, D. H.
    1960   Lexicostatistics so far. Current Anthro. 1: 3–44.

Isaac, G. L.
    1971   The diet of early man: aspects of archaeological evidence from Lower and Middle Pleistocene sites in Africa. World Archaeology 2(3): 278–299.

Isham, L. B.
    1965   Preparation of drawings for paleontologic publications. In B. Kummel and D. Raup (eds.), Handbook of paleontological techniques (pp. 459–468). Freeman, San Francisco.

Iversen, J.
    1956   Forest clearance in the Stone Age. Scientific American 194: 36–41.
Ives, R. L.
    1948   Line drawings from unsatisfactory photographs. A Ant 13: 323.
Jack, R. N., Hester, T. R., and Heizer, R. F.
    1972   Geologic sources of archaeological obsidian from sites in northern and central Veracruz, Mexico. UC-CARF 16: 117–122.
Jackson, A. T.
    1938   Picture-writing of Texas Indians. Univ. of Texas Publ. 3809, Anthro. Papers 2. Austin.
Jackson, C. F., and Knaebel, J. B.
    1934   Sampling and estimation of ore deposits. U.S. Bureau of Mines, Bull. 365.
Jacobsen, T., and Lloyd, S.
    1935   Sennacherib's aqueduct at Jerwan. Oriental Inst. Publs. 24.
Janzen, D. E.
    1968   The Naomikong Point site and the dimensions of Laurel in the Lake Superior region. Mus. of Anthro., Univ. of Michigan, Anthro. Papers, No. 36.
Jarman, H. N., Legge, A. J., and Charles, J. A.
    1972   Retrieval of plant remains from archaeological sites by froth flotation. In E. S. Higgs (ed.), Problems in economic prehistory (pp. 39–48). Cambridge Univ. Press.
Jehle, A. J.
    1957   Removing a fragile burial. Arch. Soc. of New Jersey, Bull. 14: 21–22.
Jelinek, A. J.
    1957   Pleistocene faunas and early man. Papers of Michigan Acad. of Science, Arts and Letters 42: 225–237.
    1961   An index of radiocarbon dates associated with cultural materials. Current Anthro. 3: 451–480.
    1966   Correlation of archaeological and palynological data. Science 152: 1507–1509.
———, and Fitting, J. E.
    1963   Some studies of natural radioactivity in archaeological and paleontological materials. Papers of Michigan Acad. of Science, Arts and Letters 48: 531–540.
    1965   Studies in the natural radioactivity of prehistoric materials. Mus. of Anthro., Univ. of Michigan, Anthro. Papers, No. 25.
Jelks, E. B., and Tunnell, C. D.
    1959   The Harroun site. Dept. of Anthro., Univ. of Texas, Archaeology Ser., No. 2.
Jennings, J. D.
    1957   Danger Cave. SAA-M No. 14.
Jewell, P. A.
    1963   The experimental earthwork on Overton Down, Wiltshire, 1960. British Assoc. for Advancement of Science. London.
Johnson, E. N.
    1941   Preservation and cleaning of shell material. SAA-N 2: 9–10.
Johnson, F.
    1966   Archaeology in an emergency. Science 152: 1592–1597.
——— (ed.)
    1942   The Boylston Street fishweir. Papers of R. S. Peabody Foundation for Arch. 2.
    1949   The Boylston Street fishweir II. Papers of R. S. Peabody Foundation for Arch. 4(1).
———, and Miller, J.
    1958   Review of G. F. Carter, "Pleistocene man at San Diego." A Ant 24: 206–210.
———, and Raup, H. M.
    1947   Grassy Island. Papers of R. S. Peabody Foundation for Arch. 1(2).
Johnson, L., Jr.
    1963   A guide to archaeological reconnaissance. TAS-B 34: 203–217.
    1964   The Devil's Mouth site. Dept. of Anthro., Univ. of Texas, Archaeology Ser., No. 6.
    1972   Problems in "avant-garde" archaeology. AA 74(3): 365–377.

Johnson, R. A., and Stross, F. H.
  1965   Laboratory-scale instrumental neutron activation for archaeological analysis. A Ant 30: 345–347.

Johnson, R. T.
  1957   An experiment with cave-painting media. South African Arch. Bull. 12(47): 98–101.
  1958   Facsimile tracing and redrawing of rock-paintings. South African Arch. Bull. 13(50): 67–69.

Johnston, R. B.
  1964   Proton magnetometry and its application to archaeology. Indiana Hist. Soc., Prehist. Research Ser., Vol. 4, No. 2.
  1965   Trails of the ELSEC proton magnetometer at two sites on Wetherill Mesa. In D. Osborne (ed.), Contributions of the Wetherill Mesa Archeological Project (pp. 180–181). SAA-M 19.

Jones, T. B.
  1967   Paths to the ancient past. Free Press, New York.

Jones, V. H.
  1936   The vegetal remains of Newt Kash Hollow Shelter. In W. S. Webb and W. D. Funkhouser, Rock shelters in Menifee County, Kentucky (pp. 147–165). Univ. of Kentucky Reports in Arch. and Anthro. 3(4).
  1945   Plant materials. In R. L. Beals, G. W. Brainerd, and W. Smith (eds.), Archaeological studies in northeast Arizona (App. II, pp. 159–163). UC-PAAE 44.

———, and Fonner, R. L.
  1954   Plant materials from sites in the Durango and La Plata areas, Colorado. In E. H. Morris and R. F. Burgh, Basket Maker II sites near Durango (App. C, pp. 93–115). CIW-P No. 604.

Jonsgard, A.
  1969   Age determination of marine mammals. In H. T. Andersen (ed.), The biology of marine mammals (pp. 1–30). Academic Press, New York.

Jope, E. M.
  1953   History, archaeology, and petrology. Advancement of Science 9: 432–435.

Jorgensen, S.
  1953   Skovryoning med flintokse (Forest clearance with flint axes). Nationalmuseets Arbejdsmark 1953: 34–43, 109–110.

Judge, W. J.
  1973   Paleoindian occupation of the Central Rio Grande Valley in New Mexico. Univ. of New Mexico Press, Albuquerque.

Judson, S.
  1949   Pleistocene stratigraphy of Boston, Massachusetts, and its relation to Boylston Street fishweir. In F. Johnson (ed.), The Boylston Street fishweir II (pp. 7–48). Papers of R. S. Peabody Foundation for Arch. 4(1).

Kapitan, G.
  1966   A bibliography of underwater archaeology. Argonaut, Chicago.

Karklins, K.
  1970   The Fire Cloud site (39BF237), Buffalo County, South Dakota. Plains Anthropologist 15(48): 135–142.

Katsui, Y., and Kondo, J.
  1965   Dating of stone implements by using hydration layer of obsidian. Japanese Journal of Geol. and Geog. 36: 45–60. (In English.)

Kautz, R. R., and Thomas, D. H.
  1972   Palynological investigations of two prehistoric cave middens in central Nevada. Tebiwa 15(2): 43–54.

Keel, B. C.
  1963   The conservation and preservation of archaeological and ethnological specimens. Southern Indian Studies 15.

Keeley, L.
  1974   Techniques and methodology in microwear studies: a critical review. World Archaeology 5(3): 323–336.

Kehoe, T. F.
  1967   The Boarding School Bison Drive site. Plains Anthropologist, Memoir 4.

Keith, M. L., and Anderson, G. M.
1963   Radiocarbon dating: fictitious results with mollusk shells. Science 141: 634–636.
1964   Radiocarbon dating of mollusk shells: a reply [to Broecker, 1964]. Science 144: 890.

Kelemen, P.
1946   Pre-Columbian art and art history. A Ant 11: 145–154.

Keller, C. M.
1973   Montagu Cave in prehistory: a descriptive analysis. UC-AR 28.

Kelley, J. C., Campbell, T. N., and Lehmer, D. J.
1940   The association of archaeological materials with geological deposits in the Big Bend region of Texas. Sul Ross State Teachers College Bull. 21(3).

Kelly, A. R.
1938   A preliminary report on archaeological explorations at Macon, Georgia. BAE-B 119, Anthro. Papers 1: 1–68.

———, and Hurst, V. J.
1956   Patination and age relationship in south Georgia flint. A Ant 22: 193–194.

Kelly, I. T.
1945a   Excavations at Culiacan, Sinaloa. UC-IA 25.
1945b   The archaeology of the Autlan-Tuxacacuesco area of Jalisco, I: The Autlan Zone. UC-IA 26.
1947   Excavations at Apatzingan, Michoacan. VFPA No. 7.

Kenrick, P.
1971   Aids to the drawing of finds. Antiquity 45(179): 205–209.

Kenyon, K. M.
1957   Digging up Jericho. Praeger, New York.
1961   Beginning in archaeology. Praeger, New York.

Kidd, K. E.
1954   Trade goods research techniques. A Ant 20: 1–8.

Kidder, A. V.
1927   Southwestern archaeological conference. Science 66: 489–491.
1931   The pottery of Pecos. Papers of R. S. Peabody Foundation for Arch. 1(5).
1932   The artifacts of Pecos. New Haven.

———, and Guernsey, S. J.
1921   Basket Maker caves of northeastern Arizona. PM-P 8(2).

———, and Thompson, J. E.
1938   The correlation of Maya and Christian chronologies. In Cooperation in research (pp. 493–510). CIW-P No. 501.

———, Jennings, J. D., and Shook, E. M.
1946   Excavations at Kaminaljuyú, Guatemala. CIW-P No. 561.

Kidder, A. V., II
1964   South American high culture. In J. D. Jennings and E. Norbeck (eds.), Prehistoric man in the New World (pp. 451–486). Univ. of Chicago Press.

Kirkbride, D.
1960   Excavation of a Neolithic village at Seyl Aqlat, Beidha, near Petra. Palestine Exploration Quarterly, July–Dec. 1960. London.

Kirkland, F., and Newcomb, W. W., Jr.
1967   Rock art of Texas Indians. Univ. of Texas Press, Austin.

Kjellstrom, B.
1967   Be expert with map and compass. Amer. Orienteering Service, La Porte, Ind.

Klindt-Jensen, O.
1957   Denmark before the Vikings. Praeger, New York.

Kluckhohn, C.
1960   The use of typology in anthropological theory. *In* A. F. C. Wallace (ed.), Men and cultures (pp. 134–140). Univ. of Pennsylvania Press, Philadelphia.

Knight, H.
1966   The photography of petroglyphs and pictographs. New Zealand Arch. Assoc. Newsletter 19(2).

Knowles, F. H. S.
1944   The manufacture of a flint arrowhead by a quartzite hammer stone. Pitt River Mus., Oxford Univ., Occasional Papers on Technology, No. 1.

Knox, A. S.
1942   The pollen analysis of the silt and the tentative dating of the deposits. *In* F. Johnson (ed.), The Boylston Street fishweir (pp. 96–129). Papers of R. S. Peabody Foundation for Arch. 2.

Kobayashi, T., and Bleed, P.
1971   Recording and illustrating ceramic surfaces with Iahukon rubbings. Plains Anthropologist 16(53): 219–221.

Koby, F. E.
1943   Les soi disant instruments osseux du paléolithique alpin et le charriage à sec des os d'ours des cavernes. Verhandlungen der Naturforschenden Gesellschaft in Basel 54: 59–95.
1946   La chronologie du sol des cavernes. Arch. Suisse d'Anthro. Générale 12: 22–38.

Kostich, J. L.
1965   Problems in conservation: a Maya sculpture in wood. Museum News 44(3): 31–32.

Kowalski, B., Schatzki, T. F., and Stross, F. H.
1972   Classification of archaeological artifacts by applying pattern recognition to trace element data. Analytical Chemistry 44: 2176–2180.

Kragh, A.
1951   Stenalderens flinttknik. Kuml 1951: 49–64.

Krieger, A. D.
1944   The typological concept. A Ant 9: 271–288.
1945   An inquiry into supposed Mexican influence on a prehistoric "cult" in the Southern United States. A Ant 47: 483–515.
1946   Culture complexes and chronology in northern Texas with extension of Puebloan datings to the Mississippi Valley. Univ. of Texas Publs. 4640.
1958   Review of George F. Carter, "Pleistocene man at San Diego." AA 60: 974–978.
1959   Comment on George F. Carter, "Man, time and change in the far Southwest." Assoc. of Amer. Geog. Annals 49: 31–33. Washington, D.C.
1960   Archaeological typology in theory and practice. *In* A. F. C. Wallace (ed.), Men and cultures (pp. 141–151). Univ. of Pennsylvania Press, Philadelphia.
1964a   Early man in the New World. *In* J. Jennings and E. Norbeck (eds.), Prehistoric man in the New World (pp. 23–84). Univ. of Chicago Press.
1964b   New World lithic typology project: Part II. A Ant 29: 489–493.

Kroeber, A. L.
1916   Zuni potsherds. AMNH-AP 28, Pt. 1.
1923   The history of native culture in California. UC-PAAE 20: 123–142.
1925   Archaic culture horizons in the Valley of Mexico. UC-PAAE 17: 373–408.
1927   Disposal of the dead. AA 29: 308–315.
1931   The culture-area and age-area concepts of Clark Wissler. *In* S. A. Rice (ed.), Methods in social science (pp. 248–265). Univ. of Chicago Press.
1940   Statistical classification. A Ant 6: 29–44.
1948   Anthropology. Harcourt, Brace, New York.
1955   Linguistic time depth results so far and their meaning. International Journal of Amer. Linguistics 21: 91–104.
1962   A roster of civilizations and culture. VFPA No. 33.
————, and Kluckhohn, C.
1952   Culture: a critical review of concepts and definitions. PM-P 47(1).

————, and Strong, W. D.
   1924   The Uhle pottery collection from Ica. UC-PAAE 21: 95–133.

Krogman, W. M.
   1939   A guide to the identification of human skeletal material. F.B.I. Law Enforcement Bull. 8(8).
   1940   The skeletal and dental pathology of an early Iranian site. Bull. of Hist. of Medicine 8: 28–48.
   1962   The human skeleton in forensic medicine. C. C. Thomas, Springfield.

Krumbein, W. C.
   1965   Sampling in paleontology. In B. Kummel and D. Raup (eds.), Handbook of paleontological techniques (pp. 137–149). Freeman, San Francisco.

Kubler, G.
   1948   Towards absolute time: guano archaeology. SAA-M 4: 29–50.

Kühn, H.
   1956   The rock pictures of Europe. Sidgwick and Jackson, London.

Kulp, J. L.
   1952   The Carbon-14 method of age determination. Scientific Monthly 75: 259–267.
   1953   Dating with radioactive carbon. Journal of Chemical Education 30: 432–435.

Kummel, B., and Raup, D. (eds.)
   1965   Handbook of paleontological techniques. Freeman, San Francisco.

Kushner, G.
   1970   A consideration of some processual designs for archaeology as anthropology. A Ant 35(2): 125–132.

Kuzara, R. S., Mead, G. R., and Dixon, K. A.
   1966   Seriation of anthropological data: a computer program for matrix-ordering. AA 68: 1442–1455.

Lacaille, A. D.
   1931   Aspects of intentional fracture. Trans. of Glasgow Arch. Soc. 9: 313–341.

Laguna, F. de
   1934   The archaeology of Cook Inlet, Alaska. Univ. of Pennsylvania Press, Philadelphia.

Lahee, F. H.
   1952   Field geology. McGraw-Hill, New York.

Lais, R.
   1938   Molluskenkunde und Vorgeschichte. Deutsches Archäol. Inst., Römisch-Germanische Kommission, Ber. 26 (1936): 5–23.
   1941   Ueber Höhlensedimente. Quartär 3: 56–108. (See also L'Anthropologie 53 [1949]: 159–167.)

Lamberg-Karlovsky, C. C.
   1970   Operations problems in archeology. In A. Fischer (ed.), Current directions in anthropology (pp. 11–114). AAA-Bull. 3(3), Pt. 2.
   1974   Excavations at Tepe Yahya. In G. R. Willey (ed.), Archaeological researches in retrospect (pp. 269–292). Winthrop, Cambridge, Mass.

Lambert, R. J.
   1960   Review of the literature of ethno-conchology pertinent to archaeology. Sterkiana 2: 1–8.

Laming-Emperaire, A.
   1963   L'archéologie préhistorique. Editions du Seuil, Paris.
   1964   Origines de l'archéologie préhistorique en France. Picard, Paris.

Lancaster, J. A., et al.
   1954   Archaeological investigations in Mesa Verde National Park, Colorado, 1950. National Park Service, Arch. Research Ser., No. 2.

Langan, L.
   1966   Use of new atomic magnetometers in archaeology. Prospezioni Archeologiche 1: 61–66.

Laplace-Jauretche, G.
   1954   Application des coordonnées cartesiennes à la fouille d'un gisement. Bull. de la Soc. Préhist. Française 51: 58–66. Paris.

Larsen, H.
    1950   Archaeological investigations in southwestern Alaska. A Ant 15: 177–186.

———, and Rainey, F.
    1948   Ipiutak and the arctic whale hunting culture. AMNH-AP 42.

Lartet, E.
    1860   Sur l'ancienneté géologique de l'espèce humaine. Comptes Rendus de l'Acad. des Sciences 50: 790–791. Paris.

Laudermilk, J. D.
    1937   The preservation of textile remains. A Ant 2: 277–281.

Laws, R. M.
    1960   Laminated structure of bones from some marine mammals. Nature 187: 338–339.

Layard, N. F.
    1922   Prehistoric cooking places in Norfolk. PPS of East Anglia 3: 483–498.

Leakey, L. S. B.
    1953   Adam's ancestors (4th ed.). Methuen, London.
    1954   Working stone, bone, and wood. In C. Singer, E. Holmyard, and A. Hall (eds.), A history of technology (Vol. 1, pp. 128–143). Oxford Univ. Press.

———, Simpson, R. D., and Clements, T.
    1968   Archaeological excavations in the Calico Mountains, California: preliminary report. Science 160: 1022–1023.

Leakey, M. D.
    1971   Olduvai Gorge, Vol. 3: Excavations in Beds I and II, 1960–1963. Cambridge Univ. Press.

Lee, R. F.
    1970   The Antiquities Act of 1906. Eastern Service Center, Office of History and Historic Architecture, National Park Service, U.S. Dept. of Interior, Washington, D.C.

Leechman, D.
    1931   Technical methods in the preservation of anthropological museum specimens. Annual Report, 1929, National Mus. of Canada, Bull. 67: 127–158. Ottawa.
    1950   Aboriginal tree-felling. National Mus. of Canada, Bull. 118. Ottawa.

Lehmann, H.
    1957   Ma plus belle découverte. Marco Polo 27: 13–24.

Lehmer, D. J.
    1939   Notes on the field preservation of human bone. SAA-N 1: 30. (Mimeographed.)
    1954   Archaeological investigations in the Oahe Dam area, South Dakota, 1950–51. River Basin Surveys Papers, BAE-B 158.
    1960   A review of Trans-Pecos archaeology. TAS-B 29 (for 1958): 109–144.

Leighton, M. M.
    1931   Some observations on the antiquity of man in Illinois. Trans. of Illinois Acad. of Science 25: 38.
    1936   Geological aspects of the findings of primitive man, near Abilene, Texas. GP-MP 24.
    1937   The significance of profiles of weathering in stratigraphic archaeology. In G. G. MacCurdy (ed.), Early man (pp. 163–172). Lippincott, Philadelphia.

Leone, M. P.
    1971   Review of S. R. Binford and L. R. Binford (eds.), "New perspectives in archeology." A Ant 36(2): 220–222.
    1972a   Contemporary archaeology. Southern Illinois Univ. Press, Carbondale.
    1972b   Issues in anthropological archaeology. In M. P. Leone (ed.), Contemporary archaeology (pp. 14–27). Southern Illinois Univ. Press. Carbondale.

Lerici, C. M.
    1962   New archaeological techniques and international cooperation in Italy. Expedition 4(3): 5–10.

Levi, H.
    1955   Bibliography of radiocarbon dating compiled at the Copenhagen Dating Laboratory. Quaternaria 2: 1–7. Rome.

Lewin, S. Z.
1966   The preservation of natural stone, 1839–1965: an annotated bibliography. Art and Arch., Technical Abstracts 6(1), Suppl.: 185–272.

Lewis, T. M. N., and Kneberg, M. K.
1946   Hiwassee Island. Univ. of Tennessee Press, Knoxville.

Li Lien-chieh
1943   Rate of soil development as indicated by profile studies in Indian mounds. Thesis abstracts, Univ. of Illinois.

Libby, W. F.
1955   Radiocarbon dating (2nd ed.). Univ. of Chicago Press.
1956   Radiocarbon dating. Amer. Scientist 44: 98–112.
1961   Radiocarbon dating. Science 133: 621–629.
1963   Accuracy of radiocarbon dates. Science 140: 278–280.
1970a   The physical science of radiocarbon dating. In R. Berger (ed.), Scientific methods in medieval archaeology (pp. 17–21). Univ. of California Press, Berkeley and Los Angeles.
1970b   Radiocarbon dating. In T. E. Allibone et al., The impact of the natural sciences on archaeology (pp. 1–10). Oxford Univ. Press.

Linder, D. H.
1942   The diatoms. In F. Johnson (ed.), The Boylston Street fishweir (pp. 67–81). Papers of R. S. Peabody Foundation for Arch. 2.

Linington, R. E.
1970   Techniques used in archaeological field surveys. Royal Soc. of London, Philos. Trans., Ser. A, Vol. 269, No. 1193: 89–108.

Linton, R.
1936   The study of man. Appleton, New York.

Lipe, W. D.
1964   Comment on Dempsey and Baumhoff's "The statistical of artifact distributions to establish chronological sequence." AA 30: 103–104.

Lister, R. H.
1955   The present status of the archaeology of western Mexico: a distributional study. Univ. of Colorado Studies, Ser. in Anthro., No. 5.

Livingston, J. L.
1967   Archeological map symbols. Plains Anthropologist 12(38): 363–366.

Lloyd, S.
1963   Mounds of the Near East. Edinburgh Univ. Press.

Logan, W. D.
1952   Graham Cave—an Archaic site in Montgomery County, Missouri, Missouri Arch. Soc., Memoir 2. Columbus.

Longacre, W. A.
1962   Archaeological reconnaissance in eastern Arizona. FMNH-Fieldiana 53: 148–167.
1964   Archaeology as anthropology: a case study. Science 144: 1454–1455.
1970a   Current thinking in American archaeology. In A. Fischer (ed.), Current directions in anthropology (pp. 126–138). AAA-Bull. 3(3), Pt. 2.
1970b   A historical review. In W. A. Longacre (ed.), Reconstructing prehistoric Pueblo societies (pp. 1–10). School of Amer. Research, Albuquerque.

Longin, R.
1971   New method of collagen extraction for radiocarbon dating. Nature 230: 241–243.

Lorch, W.
1939   Methodische Untersuchungen zur Wüstungsforschung. Arbeiten zur Landes- und Volksforschung, Vol. 4. G. Fischer, Jena.

Lorenzo, J. L.
1956   Técnica de exploración arquelógica. Tlatoani, Ser. 2, No. 10: 18–21. Mexico City.

Lothrop, S. K.
1928   The Indians of Tierra del Fuego. MAIHF-Contributions 10.
1937   Coclé: an archaeological study of central Panama. PM-M 7, Pt. 1.
1942   Coclé: an archaeological site of Panama, Part II: Pottery of the Sitio Conte and other archaeological sites. PM-M 8.

Lotspeich, F. B.
1961   Soil science in the service of archaeology. Fort Burgwin Research Center, Publ. 1: 137–144. Univ. of New Mexico Press, Albuquerque.

Loud, L. L., and Harrington, M. R.
1929   Lovelock Cave. UC-PAAE 25: 1–183.

Lougee, R. J.
1953   A chronology of postglacial time in Eastern North America. Scientific Monthly 76: 259–276.

Louis, M.
1946   Méthode des phosphates. Cahiers d'Hist. et d'Arch.: 119–120.

Low, J. W.
1952   Plane table mapping. Harper, New York.

Lowie, R. H.
1915   Oral tradition and history. AA 17: 597–599.
1917   Oral tradition and history. Journal of Amer. Folk-Lore 30: 161–167.

Lucas, A.
1932   Antiques, their care and preservation. E. Arnold, London.
———, and Harris, J. R.
1962   Ancient Egyptian materials and industries (4th ed.). E. Arnold, London.

Luedtke, B.
1974   Characterization of chert sources by neutron activation analysis. Paper presented at 39th annual meeting of Soc. for Amer. Arch., Washington, D.C.

Lutz, B. J., and Slaby, D. L.
1972   A simplified procedure for photographing obsidian. A Ant 37: 262–263.

Lynch, B. D., and Lynch, T. F.
1968   The beginnings of a scientific approach to prehistoric archaeology in 17th and 18th century Britain. SWJA 24: 33–65.

MacClintock, P., et al.
1936   A Pleistocene lake in the White River Valley. Amer. Naturalist 70: 346–360.

McConnell, D.
1962   Dating of fossil bone by the fluorine method. Science 136: 241–244.

McCown, T. D.
1961   Animals, climate, and paleolithic man. Kroeber Anthro. Soc. Papers 25: 221–230.

MacDonald, G. F., and Sanger, D.
1968   Some aspects of microscope analysis and photomicrography of lithic artifacts. A Ant 33: 237–240.

McEwen, J. M.
1946   An experiment with primitive Maori carving tools. Journal of Polynesian Soc. 55: 111–116.

McFadgen, B. G.
1971   An application of stereo-photogrammetry to archaeological recording. Archaeometry 13: 71–81.

McGimsey, C. R., III
1956   Cerro Mangote: a preceramic site in Panama. A Ant 22: 151–161.
1972   Public archaeology. Seminar Press, New York.

McGuire, J. D.
1892   Materials, apparatus and processes of the aboriginal lapidary. AA 5: 165–176.
1896   Study of the primitive methods of drilling. USNM-R for 1894.

MacIver, R.
1921   On the manufacture of Etruscan and other ancient black wares. Man 21: 86–88.

McKern, T. W.
1958   The use of short wave ultra-violet rays for the segregation of commingled skeletal remains. Environmental Protection Research Division, Quartermaster Research and Engineering Command, U.S. Army, Natick, Mass., Technical Report EP-98.

———, and Stewart, T. D.
1957   Skeletal age changes in young American males. Quartermaster Research and Development Center, U.S. Army, Natick, Mass., Technical Report EP-45.

McKern, W. C.
1930   The Kletzien and Nitschke Mound groups. Bull. of Public Mus. of City of Milwaukee 3(4).
1934   Certain culture classification problems in Middle Western archaeology. National Research Council, Circular Ser., No. 17. (Mineographed.)
1939   The Mid-Western taxonomic method as an aid to archaeological culture study. A Ant 4: 301–313.

McKusick, M.
1969   Changing site designations: a reply. A Ant 34(4): 840.

McLaren, I. A.
1958   The biology of the ringed seal (*Phoca hispida* Schreber) in the eastern Canadian Arctic. Fisheries Research Board of Canada, Bull. 118.

McNeil, P. L.
1969   Legal safeguards for preserving the past. TAS-B 40: 263–280.

MacNeish, R. S.
1958   Preliminary archaeological investigations in the Sierra de Tamaulipas, Mexico. Trans. of Amer. Philos. Soc., No. 48, Pt. 6.

——— (assembler)
1973   Early man in America: readings from Scientific American. Freeman, San Francisco.

MacWhite, E.
1956   On the interpretation of archaeological evidence in historical and sociological terms. AA 58: 3–25.

Malan, B. D.
1945   Excavation method in South African prehistoric caves. South African Mus. Assoc. Bull., Dec. 1944: 1–8.

Malde, H. E.
1964   The ecologic significance of some unfamiliar geologic processes. *In* Reconstruction of past environments (pp. 7–15). Fort Burgwin Center Report No. 3.

Mallery, G.
1877   A calendar of the Dakota nation. Bull. of U.S. Geol. and Geog. Survey 3, Art. 1.

Mandelbaum, D. C.
1964   Anthropology as study and as career. *In* J. S. Childers (ed.), Listen to leaders in science (pp. 177–192). Holt, Rinehart and Winston, New York.

Marquina, I.
1951   Arquitectura prehispánica. Memorias del Instituto Nacional de Antropología e Historia 1. Mexico City.

Marshack, A.
1964   Lunar notation on Upper Paleolithic remains. Science 146: 743–745.

Marshall, N. F., and Moriarty, J. R.
1964   Principles of underwater archaeology. Pacific Discovery 17(5): 18–25.

Martin, Paul S. (Chicago Natural History Museum)
1971   The revolution in archaeology. A Ant 36: 1–8.
1974   Early development in Mogollon research. *In* G. R. Willey (ed.), Archaeological researches in retrospect (pp. 3–29). Winthrop, Cambridge, Mass.

———, and Rinaldo, J. B.
1947   The SU site: excavations at a Mogollon village, western New Mexico, third season, 1946. FMNH-PAS 32(3).
1951   The Southwestern co-tradition. SWJA 7: 215–229.

————, Longacre, W. A. and Hill, J. N.
  1967   Chapters in the prehistory of eastern Arizona, III. FMNH-Fieldiana 57.

————, Quimby, G. I., and Collier, D.
  1947   Indians before Columbus. Univ. of Chicago Press.

————, et al.
  1952   Mogollon cultural continuity and change: the stratigraphic analysis of Tularosa and Cordova caves. FMNH-PAS 40.

Martin, Paul S. (University of Arizona)
  1963   The last 10,000 years. Univ. of Arizona Press, Tucson.
  1973   The discovery of America. Science 179: 969–974.

————, and Sharrock, F. W.
  1964   Pollen analysis of prehistoric human feces: a new approach to ethnobotany. A Ant 30: 169–180.

Mason, J. A.
  1942   New excavations at the Sitio Conte, Coclé, Panamá. Proc. of Eighth Amer. Scientific Congress 2: 103–107.
  1961   The ancient civilizations of Peru. Penguin Books, Baltimore.

Mathiassen, T.
  1927   Archaeology of the Central Eskimos. Report of 5th Thule Expedition, 1921–24, Vol. 4, Pt. 1. Glyden Danske Boghandel, Nordisk Forlag. Copenhagen.
  1931   Ancient Eskimo settlements in the Kangamiut area. Medell. om Gronland 91(1).

Matson, F. R. (ed.)
  1956   Ceramics and man. VFPA No. 41.

Matteson, M. R.
  1959   Land snails in archaeological sites. AA 61: 10 1094–1096.
  1960   Reconstruction of prehistoric environments through the analysis of molluscan collections from shell middens. A Ant 26: 117–120.

Mayes, P., et al.
  1961   The firing of a pottery kiln of Romano-British type at Boston, Lincs. Archaeometry 4: 4–30.
  1962   The firing of a second pottery kiln of Romano-British type at Boston, Lincs. Archaeometry 5: 80–107.

Mazess, R. B., and Zimmerman, D. W.
  1966   Pottery dating by thermoluminescence. Science 152: 347–348.

Meggers, B. J., and Evans, C.
  1957   Archeological investigations at the mouth of the Amazon. BAE-B 167.

————, Evans, C., and Estrada, E.
  1965   Early formative periods of coastal Ecuador. Smithsonian Contributions to Anthro 1.

Mehringer, P. J.
  1965   Late Pleistocene vegetation in the Mohave Desert of southern Nevada. Journal of Arizona Acad. of Science 3: 172–188.

Meighan, C. W.
  1950   Observations on the efficiency of shovel archaeology. UCAS-R 7: 15–21.
  1956   Responsibilities of the archaeologist in using the radiocarbon method. Univ. of Utah Anthro. Papers 26: 48–53.
  1961   The archaeologist's note book. Chandler, San Francisco.

————, et al.
  1958   Ecological interpretation in archaeology: Part I. A Ant 24: 1–23.

Mellaart, J.
  1962–64 Excavations at Chatal Huyuk. Anatolian Studies 12, 13, and 14. London.

Meloy, H.
  1968   Mummies of Mammoth Cave. Privately printed, Shelbyville, Ind.

Merrill, R. H.
  1941a   Photo-surveying assists archaeologists. Civil Engineering 11: 233–235.
  1941b   Photographic surveying. A Ant 6: 343–346.

Mewhinney, H.
  1957   Manual for Neanderthals. Univ. of Texas Press, Austin.

Meyers, K.
  1973   The plundered past. Atheneum, New York.

Michael, H. N., and Ralph, E. K.
  1971a   Carbon-14 dating. *In* H. N. Michael and E. K. Ralph (eds.), Dating techniques for the archaeologist (pp. 1–48). Mass. Inst. of Technology Press, Cambridge.
  1971b   Dating techniques for the archaeologist. Mass. Inst. of Technology Press, Cambridge.

Michels, J. W.
  1967   Archeology and dating by hydration of obsidian. Science 158: 211–214.
  1973   Dating methods in archaeology. Seminar Press, New York.

————, and Berbrich, C. A.
  1971   Obsidian hydration dating. *In* H. N. Michael and E. K. Ralph (eds.), Dating techniques for the archaeologist (pp. 164–221). Mass. Inst. of Technology Press, Cambridge.

Michie, J. L.
  1969   A mechanical sifting device. Notebook, Inst. of Arch. and Anthro., Univ. of South Carolina 2(4/5): 15–19.

Middleton, J.
  1844   On flourine in bones, its source and its application to the determination of geological age of fossil bones. Proc. of Geol. Soc. of London 4: 431–433. (Also Geol. Soc. Journal 1 [1845]: 214–216.)

Miller, W. C.
  1957   Uses of aerial photographs in archaeological field work. A Ant 23: 46–62.

Millon, R.
  1964   The Teotihuacan mapping project. A Ant 29: 345–352.

Milne, J.
  1881   The Stone Age in Japan. JRAI 10: 389–423.

Mirambell, S. L.
  1964   Estudio microfotografico de artefactos liticos. Dept. de Prehistoria, Inst. Nacional de Antropología e Historia, 14.

Mitchell, B.
  1967   Growth layers in the dental cement for determining the age of red deer (*Cervus elephus,* L.). Journal of Animal Ecology 36(2): 279–293.

Moberg, C. A.
  1961   Mängder av fornfynd (with English summary: Trends in the present development of quantitative methods in archaeology). Göteborgs Univ. Arsskrift 67(1).

Mohammed Sana Ullah, Khan Bahadur
  1946   Notes on the preservation of antiquities in the field. Ancient India 1: 77–82.

Moir, J. R.
  1926   Experiments in the shaping of wood with flint implements. Nature 117: 655–656.

Mongait, A. L.
  1969   Archaeology in the U.S.S.R. (trans. and ed. by M. W. Thompson). Penguin Books, Baltimore.

Montagu, M. F. A., and Oakley, K. P.
  1949   The antiquity of Galley Hill man. AJPA, n.s., 7: 363–380.

Montgomery, A.
  1963   The source of the fibrolite axes. El Palacio 70: 34–48.

Morgan, C. G.
  1973   Archaeology and exploration. World Archaeology 4(3): 259–276.

Morley, S. G.
  1937–38 The inscriptions of Peten. 5 vols. CIW-P No. 437.

Morris, E. H.
  1939   Archaeological studies in the La Plata district. CIW-P No. 519.

————, and Burgh, R.
1954   Basket Maker II sites near Durango, Colorado. CIW-P No. 604.

————, Charlot, J., and Morris, A. A.
1931   The temple of the warriors at Chichen Itza, Yucatan. 2 vols. CIW-P No. 406.

Morrison, F.
1971   High-sensitivity magnetometers in archaeological exploration. *In* F. H. Stross (ed.), The application of the physical sciences to archaeology (pp. 6-20). UC-CARF 12.

————, Clewlow, C. W., Jr., and Heizer, R. F.
1970   Magnetometer survey of the La Venta Pyramid. UC-CARF 8: 1-20.

————, et al.
1970   Magnetometer evidence of a structure within the La Venta Pyramid. Science 167: 1488-1490.

Morrison, J. P. E.
1942   Preliminary report on mollusks found in the shell mounds of the Pickwick Landing Basin in the Tennessee River Valley. BAE-B 129: 341-392.

Morse, D. F.
1973   Dalton culture in northeast Arkansas. Florida Anthropologist 26(1): 23-38.

Morse, E. S.
1882   Changes in *Mya* and *Lunatia* since the deposition of the New England shell-heaps. Proc. of Amer. Assoc. for Advancement of Science 30: 345. Cincinnati.

Morton, N. E.
1968   Problems and methods in the genetics of primitive groups. AJPA 28: 191-202.

Movius, H. L., Jr.
1944   Early man and Pleistocene stratigraphy in southern and eastern Asia. PM-P 19(3).
1949   Old World Paleolithic archaeology. Bull. of Geol. Soc. of Amer. 60: 1443-1456.
1960   Radiocarbon dates and Upper Paleolithic archaeology in central and western Europe. Current Anthro. 1: 355-392.
1974   The Abri Pataud Program of the French Upper Paleolithic in retrospect. *In* G. R. Willey (ed.), Archaeological researches in retrospect (pp. 87-116). Winthrop, Cambridge, Mass.

————, and Judson, S.
1956   The rock-shelter at La Colombière. Amer. School of Prehist. Research, Peabody Mus., Harvard Univ., Bull. 19.

————, et al.
1968   An analysis of certain major classes of Upper Paleolithic tools. Amer. School of Prehist. Research, Peabody Mus., Harvard Univ., Bull. 26.

Müller-Beck, H.
1965   Seeberg Burgäschsee-Süd: Part 5, Holzgerate und Holzbearbeitung. Acta Bernensi 2, Pt. 5.

Mulloy, W.
1942   The Hagen site. Univ. of Montana Publs. in Social Science, No. 1.

Munro, R.
1897   Prehistoric problems. W. Blackwood, London.

Munsell soil color charts
1954   Munsell Color Co., Baltimore.

Myers, O. H.
1950   Some applications of statistics to archaeology. Service des Antiquités de l'Egypte.

Nance, J. D.
1971   Functional interpretation from microscopic analysis. A Ant 36: 361-366.

Napton, L. K., and Heizer, R. F.
1970   Analysis of human coprolites from archaeological contexts, with primary reference to Lovelock Cave, Nevada. *In* R. F. Heizer and L. K. Napton (eds.), Archaeology and the prehistoric Great Basin lacustrine subsistence regime as seen from Lovelock Cave, Nevada (pp. 87-129). UC-CARF 10.

Naroll, R.
1962   Floor area and settlement pattern. A Ant 27: 587–589.
1965   On ethnic unit classification. Current Anthro. 5(4): 283–312.

Neill, W. T.
1952   The manufacture of fluted points. Florida Anthropologist 5: 9–16.

Nelson, N. C.
1909   Shellmounds of the San Francisco Bay region. UC-PAAE 7: 309–348.
1910   The Ellis Landing shellmound. UC-PAAE 7: 357–426.
1916   Chronology of the Tano Ruins. AA 18: 159–180.
1928   Pseudo-artifacts from the Pliocene of Nebraska. Science 67: 316–317.
1938   Prehistoric archaeology. In F. Boas (ed.), General anthropology (pp. 146–148). Heath, Boston.

Nero, R. W.
1957   A "graver" site in Wisconsin. A Ant 22: 300–304.

Neuman, R. W.
1962   A historical note on tree-ring dating. Pennsylvania Archaeologist 7: 188–189.

Neumann, G. K.
1938   The human remains from Mammoth Cave, Kentucky. A Ant 3: 339–353.
1940   Evidence for the antiquity of scalping from central Illinois. A Ant 5: 287–289.

Newell, P., and Krieger, A. D.
1949   The George C. Davis site, Cherokee County, Texas. SAA-M No. 5.

Newman, H. H., Freeman, F. N., and Holzinger, K. J.
1937   Twins: a study of heredity and environment. Univ. of Chicago Press.

Nichols, D. R., and Wright, N. A.
1971   Preliminary map of historic margins of marshland, San Francisco Bay, California. USGS, San Francisco Bay Environment and Resources Planning Study, Basic Data Contribution No. 9.

Nichols, H. W.
1930   Restoration of ancient bronze and cure of malignant patina. FMNH-Mus. Technique Ser 3.

Nickerson, G. S.
1962a   Considerations of the problems of vandalism and pot-hunting in American archaeology. Montana State Univ., Anthro. and Sociology Papers No. 22. Missoula.
1962b   Professional, amateur and pot-hunter: the archaeological hierarchy in the United States. Washington Archaeologist 6: 8–12. Univ. of Washington, Seattle.

Nietsch, H.
1939   Wald und Siedlung im vorgeschichtlichen Mitteleuropa. Leipzig.

Nishimura, S.
1971   Fission track dating of archaeological materials from Japan. Nature 230: 242–243.

Noble, J. V.
1960   The technique of Attic vase painting. Amer. Jounral of Arch. 64: 307–318.

Noël-Hume, I.
1953   Archaeology in Britain. Foyle, London.
1969   Historical archaeology. Knopf, New York.

Nopitsch, M.
1953   Preventive treatments for textiles and leather. Ciba Review 9: 3606–3609.

Nunley, J. P.
1973   An assessment of the archeological resources of Garza-Little Elm Reservoir. Richland Arch. Soc., Misc. Papers 1. Dallas.

———, and Hester, T. R.
1966   Preliminary archeological investigations in Dimmit County, Texas. Texas Journal of Science 18(3): 233–253.

Oakley, K. P.
1948   Flourine and the relative dating of bones. Advancement of Science 4: 336–337.
1951   The flourine-dating method. Yearbook of Physical Anthro. 5: 44–52 (for 1949).
1953   Dating fossil human remains. In A. L. Kroeber (ed.), Anthropology today (pp. 43–56). Univ. of Chicago Press.
1956   Man the tool-maker (3rd ed.). British Mus., London.
1963a   Analytical methods of dating bones. In D. R. Brothwell and E. S. Higgs (eds.), Science in archaeology (pp. 24–34). Thames and Hudson, London.
1963b   Fluorine, uranium, and nitrogen dating of bone. In E. Pyddoke (ed.), The scientist and archaeology (pp. 111–119). Phoenix House, London.
1964a   Frameworks for dating fossil man. Aldine, Chicago.
1964b   The problem of man's antiquity. Bull. of British Mus. (Nat. Hist.) 9(5).
1965   Man the toolmaker (5th ed.). British Mus., London.

———, and Howells, W. W.
1961   Age of the skeleton from the Lagow Sand Pit, Texas. A Ant 26: 543–545.

O'Bryan, D.
1949   Methods of felling trees and tree-ring dating in the Southwest. A Ant 15: 155–156.

O'Kelly, M. J.
1954   Excavation and experiments in ancient Irish cooking-places. Journal of Royal Soc. of Antiquaries of Ireland 84: 105–155.

Olsen, S. J.
1961   SCUBA as an aid to archaeologists and paleontologists. Curator 4: 317–318.
1971   Zooarchaeology: animal bones in archaeology and their interpretation. Addison-Wesley Module in Anthro. 2. Reading, Mass.

Olson, A. P.
1962   A history of the phase concept in the Southwest. A Ant 27 27: 457–472.

Olson, R. L.
1930   Chumash prehistory. UC-PAAE 28: 1–22.

Orchard, W. C.
1929   Beads and beadwork of the American Indians. MAIHF, Contributions 11.

Ordoñez, E.
1892   La Roca del Calendario Azteca. Soc. Científica "Antonio Alzate," Memorias 6: 327–332. Mexico City.

Organ, R. M.
1953   Use of ion-exchange resins in the treatment of lead objects. Museums Journal 53: 49–52.
1963   Analysis and microscopic study of metals. In E. Pyddoke (ed.), The scientist and archaeology (pp. 141–167). Phoenix House, London.

Orr, K. G.
1951   Change at Kincaid: a study of cultural dynamics. In F. C. Cole, Kincaid, a prehistoric Illinois metropolis (App. II, pp. 293–359). Univ. of Chicago Press.

Orr, P. C.
1942   The Queen of Mescalitan Island, Scientific Monthly 54: 482–484.

Ortner, D. J., Vonendt, D. W., and Robinson, M. C.
1972   The effect of temperature on protein decay in bone: its significance in nitrogen dating of archaeological specimens. A Ant 37: 514–519.

Osborne, D.
1968   Jabber, jargon and long, long words. A Ant 33(3): 382–383.

Outwater, J. O.
1957   Pre-Columbian wood-cutting techniques. A Ant 22: 410–411.

Pallis, S. A.
1956   The antiquity of Iraq. E. Munksgaard, Copenhagen.

Pannella, G.
   1971   Fish otoliths: daily growth layers and periodical patterns. Science 173 (4002): 1124–1127.

———, and MacClintock, C.
   1968   Biological and environmental rhythms reflected in molluscan shell growth. Paleontological Soc., Memoir No. 2: 64–80.

Parker, A. C.
   1924   The great Algonkin flint mines at Coxsackie. Researches and Trans. of New York State Arch. Assoc., L. H. Morgan Chapter, Vol. 4, No. 4.

Parmalee, P. W.
   1965   Food economy of Archaic and Woodland peoples at the Tick Creek Cave site, Missouri. Missouri Archaeologist 27: 1–34.

Parrot, A.
   1953   Archéologie mésopotamienne: II, Technique et problémes. A. Michel, Paris.

Parsons, J. R.
   1971   Prehistoric settlement patterns in the Texcoco region, Mexico. Mus. of Anthro., Univ. of Michigan, Memoirs 3.

Parsons, R. B.
   1962   Indian mounds of northeast Iowa as soil genesis benchmarks. Journal of Iowa Arch. Soc. 12(2). Iowa City.

Patterson, C. C.
   1971   Native copper, silver and gold accessible to early metallurgists. A Ant 36(3): 286–321.

Patterson, T. C.
   1963   Contemporaneity and cross-dating in archaeological interpretation. A Ant 28: 389–392.

Payne, S.
   1972   Partial recovery and sample bias: the results of some sieving experiments. In E. S. Higgs (ed.), Problems in economic prehistory (pp. 49–63). Cambridge Univ. Press.

Peabody, F. E.
   1961   Annual growth zones in living and fossil vertebrates. Journal of Morphology 108(1): 11–62.

Peacock, D. P. S.
   1970   The scientific analysis of ancient ceramics: a review. World Archaeology 1(3): 375–389.

Peake, H. J. E.
   1940   The study of prehistoric times. JRAI 70: 103–146.

Peets, O. H.
   1960   Experiments in the use of atlatl weights. A Ant 26: 108–110.

Pei, W. C.
   1938   Le rôle des animaux et des causes naturelles dans la cassure des os. Paléont. Sinica, n.s. D, No. 7; whole series No. 118. Peiping.

Pelikan, J. B.
   1964   The use of polyphosphate complexes in the preservation of iron and steel objects. Studies in Conservation 9: 59–66.

Pendergast, D. M.
   1971   Excavations at Eduardo Quiroz Cave, British Honduras (Belize). Royal Ontario Mus., Art and Archaeology Occasional Paper 21. Toronto.

Perino, G. H.
   1968   The Pete Klunk Mound group, Calhoun County, Illinois: the Archaic and Hopewell occupations (with an appendix on the Gibson Mound group). In J. A. Brown (ed.), Hopewell and Woodland site archaeology in Illinois. Illinois Arch. Survey, Bull. 6.

Perlman, I., and Asaro, F.
   1969   Pottery analysis by neutron activation analysis. Archaeometry 11: 21–52.
   1970   Deduction of provenience of pottery from trace element analysis. In R. Berger (ed.), Scientific methods in medieval archaeology (pp. 389–408). Univ. of California Press, Berkeley and Los Angeles.

Peterson, M.
1965   History under the sea: a handbook for underwater exploration. SI Publs., No. 4538.

Petrbok, J.
1931   Bedeutung der Mollusken für die prähistorische Archäologie. Archiv für Molluskenkunde 63.

Petrie, W. M. F.
1899   Sequences in prehistoric remains. JRAI 29: 295–301.
1901   Diospolis Parva. Egypt Exploration Fund, Memoir 20.
1904   Methods and aims of archaeology. Macmillan, London.
1930   The building of a pyramid. Ancient Egypt 1930, Pt. 2: 33–39.

Petsche, J. E.
1968   Bibliography of salvage archeology in the United States. SI, River Basin Surveys, Publs. in Salvage Arch. 10.

Péwé, T. L.
1954   The geological approach to dating archaeological sites. A Ant 20: 51–61.

Pfeiffer, J. E.
1969   Experimental archaeology. In The emergence of man (Chap. 17). Holt, Rinehart and Winston, New York.

Phillips, E. W. J.
1948   Identification of softwoods by their microsopic structure. Great Britain Forest Products Research Laboratory Bull. 22. London.

Phillips, P.
1972   Population, economy and society in the Chassey-Cortaillod-Lagozza cultures. World Archaeology 4(1): 41–56.
———, Ford, J. A., and Griffin, J. B.
1951   Archaeological survey in the Lower Mississippi alluvial valley, 1940–47. PM-P 25.

Phleger, F. B., Jr.
1949   The foraminifera [of Boylston Street fishweir]. In F. Johnson (ed.), The Boylston Street fishweir II (pp. 99–108). Papers of R. S. Peabody Foundation for Arch. 4(1).

Piggott, S.
1962   The West Kennett long barrow: excavations 1955–56; App. II: Analysis of cremations. Great Britain Ministry of Works Arch. Reports, No. 4. London.
———, and Hope-Taylor, B.
1965   Archaeological draughtsmanship: principles and practice. Antiquity 39: 165–177.
———, and Murray, M.
1966   A new photographic technique at Croft Moraig. Antiquity 40: 304.

Pittioni, R
1960   Metallurgical analysis of archaeological materials: II. VFPA No. 28: 21–24.

Pitt-Rivers, A. H. Lane-Fox
1876   Excavations in Cissbury camp. Sussex: being a report of the exploration committee of the Anthropological Inst. for the year 1875. JRAI 5: 357–390.
1898   Excavations in Cranborne Chase, Vol. 4. Privately printed, London.

Platz, K. A.
1971   Drawing artifacts for identification purposes. Newsletter, Missouri Arch. Soc. 250: 5–8.

Plenderleith, H. J.
1934   The preservation of antiquities. Mus. Assoc., London.
1952   Fakes and forgeries in museums. Museums Journal 52: 143–148.
1956   The conservation of antiquities and works of art. Oxford Univ. Press.

Polach, H. A., and Golson, J.
1966   Collection of specimens for radiocarbon dating and interpretation of results. Australian Inst. of Aboriginal Studies, Manual No. 2. Canberra.

Pollock, H. E. D.
    1931-40 The architectural survey of Yucatan. CIW-P Yearbook 30: 117-119; 31: 96-97; 34: 124-126; 35: 122-125; 36: 141-143; 39: 265-267.

———, et al.
    1962   Mayapan, Yucatan, Mexico. CIW-P No. 169.

Ponce Sanginés, C.
    1961   Informe de labores. Centro de Investigaciones Arqueológicas en Tiwanaku, Publ. No. 1. La Paz.

———, and Mogrovejo Terrazas, G.
    1970   Acerca de la procedencia del material litico de los monumentos de Tiwanaku. Acad. Nacional de Ciencias de Bolivia, Publ. No. 21. La Paz.

Pond, A.
    1930   Primitive methods of working stone based on experiments by Halvor L. Skavlem. Logan Mus. Bull. 2(1). Beloit College, Beloit, Wisc.

Pope, S. T.
    1923   A study of bows and arrows. UC-PAAE 13(9). (Reprinted by Univ. of California Press, Berkeley, 1962.)

Porter, J. E.
    1965   Archeological applications of aerial photography. Arkansas Archeologist 6(1): 9-11.

Porter, M. N.
    1953   Tlatilco and the pre-Classic cultures of the New World. VFPA No. 19.

Powell, T., and Daniel, G.
    1956   Barclodiad y Gawres, the excavation of a meglalithic chamber tomb in Anglesey 1952-53; App. B: Cremation analysis. Liverpool Univ. Press.

Pratt, P. P.
    1961   Oneida Iroquois glass trade bead sequence, 1585-1745. Fort Stanwix Mus., Indian Glass Trade Beads Color Guide No. 1. Rome, N.Y.

Preston, N. E.
    1973   A test on the use of drills. The Record Dallas Arch. Soc. 29: 1-2.

Price, J. C., Hunter, R. G., and McMichael, E. V.
    1964   Core drilling in an archaeological site. A Ant 30(2): 219-222.

Printup, D.
    1961   A method of pottery reconstruction. Tennessee Archaeologist 17: 10-14. Knoxville.

Protsch, R.
    1970   Osteo-archeology and the dating of bones. Anthropology UCLA 2: 29-38.

———, and Berger, R.
    1973   Earliest radiocarbon dates for domesticated animals. Science 179: 235-239.

Proudfoot, V. B.
    1964   Experimental earthworks in the British Isles. Geog. Review 54: 584-586.
    1967   Experiments in archaeology. Science Journal 3: 59-65.

Provan, D. M. J.
    1971   Soil phosphate analysis as a tool in archeology. Norwegian Arch. Review 4: 37-50.

Puleston, D. E.
    1971   An experimental approach to the function of Classic Maya chultuns. A Ant 36: 322-334.

Purdy, B. A.
    1974   The Key Marco, Florida, Collection: experiment and reflection. A Ant 39(1): 105-109.

———, and Brooks, H. K.
    1971   Thermal alteration of silica minerals: an archaeological approach. Science 173: 322-325.

Pyddoke, E.
    1961   Stratification for the archaeologist. Phoenix House, London.
    1964   What is archaeology? Roy Publishers, New York.

———— (ed.)
1963   The scientist and archaeology. Phoenix House, London.

Quimby, G. I., Jr.
1939   European trade articles as chronological indicators for the archaeology of the historic period in Michigan. Papers of Michigan Acad. of Science, Arts and Letters 24, Pt. 4: 25–31.
1941   Indian trade objects in Michigan and Louisiana. Papers of Michigan Acad. of Science, Arts and Letters 28: 543–551.
1949   A Hopewell tool for decorating pottery. A Ant 14: 344.
1951   The Medora site, West Baton Rouge Parish, Louisiana. FMNH-PAS 24(2).
1960   Indian life in the Upper Great Lakes 11,000 B.C. to A.D. 1800. Univ. of Chicago Press.

Rainey, F. G.
1966   New techniques in archaeology. Proc. of Amer. Philos. Soc. 110: 146–152.

————, and Ralph, E. K.
1966   Archaeology and its new technology. Science 153: 1481–1491.

Raisz, E.
1962   Principles of cartography. McGraw-Hill, New York.

Ralph, E. K.
1969   Archaeological prospecting. Expedition 11(2): 14–21.
1971   Carbon-14 dating. In H. N. Michael and E. K. Ralph (eds.), Dating techniques for the archaeologist (Chap. 1). Mass. Inst. of Technology Press, Cambridge.

————, and Han, M. C.
1966   Dating of pottery by thermoluminescence. Nature 210: 245–247.

————, Morrison, F., and O'Brien, D. P.
1968   Archaeological surveying utilizing a high-sensitivity difference magnetometer. Geoexploration 6: 109–122.

Rapp, G., Cooke, S. R. B., and Henrickson, E.
1973   Pumice from Thera (Santorini) identified from a Greek mainland archeological excavation. Science 179: 471–473.

Rappaport, R. A., and Rappaport, A.
1967   Analysis of coastal deposits for midden content. AMNH-AP 51: 201–205.

Rathgen, F.
1926   Die Konservierung von Altertumsfunden. 2 vols. W. De Gruyter, Leipzig.

Rau, C.
1869   Drilling in stone without metal. SI-AR 1868: 392–400.
1881   Aboriginal stone drilling. Amer. Naturalist 15: 536–542.

Redman, C. L.
1973a   Multistage fieldwork and analytical techniques. A Ant 38(1): 61–79.

———— (ed.)
1973b   Research and theory in current archeology. Wiley-Interscience, New York.
1974   Archeological sampling strategies. Addison-Wesley Module in Anthropology 55. Reading, Mass.

————, and Watson, P. J.
1970   Systematic, intensive surface collection. A Ant 35(3): 279–291.

Reed, C. A.
1961   Osteological evidences for prehistoric domestication in southwestern Asia. Zeitschrift für Tierzüchtung und Züchtungsbiologie 76: 31–38.
1962   Snails on a Persian hillside. Postilla, No. 66. Yale Peabody Mus. of Nat. Hist.

Reed, E. K.
1940   Review of H. S. Colton, "Prehistoric culture units and their relationships in northern Arizona." A Ant 6: 189–192.

Reed, N. A., Bennett, J. W., and Porter, J. W.
1968   Solid core drilling of Monk's Mound: technique and findings. A Ant 33(2): 137–148.

Reed, S. A.
1966   A fortifying preservative for wood and wood fibers. Curator 9: 41–50.

Reichel-Dolmatoff, G., and Reichel-Dolmatoff, A.
1951   Investigaciones arquelógicas en el Depto. del Magdalena, Colombia, 1946–50. Bol. de Arqueología 3.
1956   Momíl, excavaciones en el Sinu. Revista Colombiana de Antropología 5: 109–333. Bogota.

Reid, J. J., Rathje, W. L., and Schiffer, M. B.
1974   Expanding archaeology. A Ant 39(1): 125–126.

Reinhold, R.
1973   The plundered land of the Maya. New York Times, March 26, 27, and 28.

Renaud, E. G.
1936   The archaeological survey of the high western plains, eighth report: pictographs and petroglyphs of the high western plains. Univ. of Denver.

Renfrew, C.
1970   The tree-ring calibration of radiocarbon: an archaeological evaluation. PPS 36: 280–311.
———, and Clark, R. M.
1974   Problems of the radiocarbon calendar and its calibration. Archaeometry 16(1): 5–18.

Renfrew, J. M.
1973   Palaeoethnobotany. Columbia Univ. Press, New York.

Rhoads, D. C., and Pannella, G.
1970   The use of molluscan shell growth patterns in ecology and paleoecology. Lethaia 3: 143–161.

Rich, C.
1819   Second memoir on Babylon. London.

Richards, H. G.
1936   Mollusks associated with early man in the Southwest. Amer. Naturalist 70: 369–371.
1937   Marine Pleistocene mollusks as indicators of time and ecological conditions. In G. G. MacCurdy (ed.), Early man (pp. 75–84). Lippincott, Philadelphia.

Ridgway, J. L.
1938   Scientific illustration. Stanford Univ. Press.

Riegger, H.
1972   Primitive pottery. Van Nostrand, Reinhold, New York.

Riskind, D. H.
1970   Pollen analysis of human coprolites from Parida Cave. In Archeological investigations at Parida Cave, Val Verde County, Texas (pp. 89–101). TASP-P 19.

Ritchie, P. R., and Pugh, J.
1963   Ultra-violet radiation and excavation. Antiquity 37: 259–263.

Ritchie, W. A.
1940   Two prehistoric village sites at Brewerton, New York. Researches and Trans. of New York Arch. Assoc. 9(1). Rochester.
1944   The pre-Iroquoian occupations of New York State. Rochester Mus. of Arts and Science, Memoir 1.
1954   Dutch Hollow, an early historic period Seneca site in Livingston County, New York. Trans. and Researchers of New York State Mus. 13(1).

Rivard, S.-J.
1964   Technical illustrations applied to archaeology. Massachusetts Arch. Soc., Bull 25(2): 44–45.

Robbins, L.
1971   A Woodland "mummy" from Salt Cave, Kentucky. A Ant 36: 200–206.

Robbins, M.
1968   An archaic ceremonial complex at Assawompsett. Massachusetts Arch. Soc., Attleboro.
———, and Irving, M. B.
1965   The amateur archaeologist's handbook. Crowell, New York.

Robertson, M. G.
    1972   Monument thievery in Mesoamerica. A Ant 37(2): 147–155.

Robinson, A. H., and Sale, R. D.
    1969   Elements of cartography. Wiley, New York.

Robinson, E.
    1942   Shell fishhooks of the California coast. Occasional Papers of Bernice P. Bishop Mus. 17(4).

Robinson, W. S.
    1951   A method for chronologically ordering archaeological deposits. A Ant 16: 293–301.

Roder, J.
    1944–49 Bilder zum Megalithentransport. Paideuma 3: 84–87.

Roefer, F., English, M., and Lothson, G.
    1973   The Jeffers petroglyphs: a cultural-ecological study. Minnesota Hist. Soc.

Rogers, M. J.
    1939   Early lithic industries of the lower basin of the Colorado River and adjacent areas. SDM-P 3.

Roney, J. C.
    1959   Paleopathology of a California archaeological site. Bull. of Hist. of Medicine 33: 97–109.

Rootenberg, S.
    1964   Archaeological field sampling. A Ant 30: 181–188.

Rosenfeld, A.
    1971   The examination of use-marks on some Magdalenian end scrapers. Prehistoric and Roman Studies, British Mus. Quarterly 35(1/4): 176–182.

Rouse, I.
    1939   Prehistory in Haiti: a study of method. YU-PA 21.
    1944   On the typological method. A Ant 10: 202–204.
    1954   On the use of the concept of area co-tradition. A Ant 19: 221–225.
    1957   Culture area and co-tradition. SWJA 13: 123–133.
    1960   The classification of artifacts in archaeology. A Ant 25: 313–323.
    1962   Southwestern archaeology today. In A. V. Kidder, Introduction to the study of Southwestern archaeology (pp. 1–53). Yale Paperbounds, Yale Univ. Press, New Haven.
    1965   The place of "peoples" in prehistoric research. JRAI 95: 1–15.
    1970   Classification for what? Norwegian Arch. Review 3: 4–34.
    1972   Introduction to prehistory: a systematic approach. McGraw-Hill, New York.

Roust, N. L.
    1967   Preliminary examination of prehistoric human coprolites from four western Nevada caves. UCAS-R 70: 49–88.

Rowe, J. H.
    1954   Archaeology as a career. Archaeology 7(4): 229–236.
    1959   Archaeological dating and cultural process. SWJA 15: 317–324.
    1962   Stages and periods in archaeological interpretation. SWJA 18: 40–54.
    1965   The Renaissance foundations of anthropology. AA 67: 1–20.
    1971   Site designation in the Americas. A Ant 36(4): 477–481.

Rowlett, R. M.
    1970   A random number generator for field use. A Ant 35(4): 491.

Rubin, M., and Taylor, D. W.
    1963   Radiocarbon activity of shells from living clams and snails. Science 141: 637.

Ruppe, R. J.
    1966   The archaeological survey: a defense. A Ant 31: 313–333.

Ryan, E. J., and Bass, G. F.
    1962   Underwater surveying and draughting—a technique. Antiquity 36: 252–261.

Ryder, M. L.
1966   Can one cook in a skin? Antiquity 40: 225–227.
1969   Paunch cooking. Antiquity 43: 218–220.

Sabloff, J. A., Beale, T. W., and Kurland, A. M., Jr.
1973   Recent developments in archaeology. Annals of Amer. Acad. of Political and Social Science 408: 103–118.

Sachs, A.
1970   Absolute dating from Mesopotamian records. In T. E. Allibone et al., The impact of the natural sciences on archaeology (pp. 19–22). Oxford Univ. Press.

Sackett, J. R.
1966   Quantitative analysis of Upper Paleolithic stone tools. AA 68(2), Pt. 2: 356–394.

Sadek-Kooros, H.
1972   Primitive bone fracturing: a method of research. A Ant 37(3): 369–382.

St. Joseph, J. K. S.
1966   The uses of air photography. J. Baker, London.

Salwen, B.
1962   Sea levels and archaeology in the Long Island Sound area. A Ant 28(1): 46–55.

Samolin, W.
1965   Technical studies of Chinese and Eurasian archaeological objects. Technology and Culture 6: 249–255.

Sankalia, H. D.
1969   Problems in Indian archaeology, and methods and techniques adopted to tackle them. World Archaeology 1(1): 29–40.

Sapir, E.
1916   Time perspective in aboriginal American culture, a study in method. Canadian Geol. Survey, Memoir 90. (Reprinted in D. Mandelbaum [ed.], Selected writings of Edward Sapir [pp. 389–462], Univ. of California Press, Berkeley, 1949.)

Saraydar, S. C., and Shimada, I.
1973   Experimental archaeology: a new outlook. A Ant 38: 344–350.

Satterthwaite, L.
1965   Calendrics of the lowland Maya. In G. R. Willey (ed.), Handbook of Middle American Indians (Vol. 3, pp. 603–631), Univ. of Texas Press, Austin.

Saucier, R. T.
1966   Soil-survey reports and archaeological investigations. A Ant 31: 419–422.

Saxon, A., and Higham, C.
1969   A new research method for economic prehistorians. A Ant 34(3): 303–311.

Sayles, E. B.
1935   An archaeological survey of Texas. GP-MP 17.
1937   Disposal of the dead. GP-MP 25: 91–100.

Sayre, E. V., Murrenhoff, A., and Weick, C. F.
1958   The non-destructive analysis of ancient potsherds through neutron activation. Brookhaven National Laboratory, BNL 508 (T-122).

Schaafsma, P.
1963   Rock art in the Navajo Reservoir district. Mus. of New Mexico Papers in Anthro., No. 7. Santa Fe.
1972   Rock art in New Mexico. State Planning Office, Santa Fe.

Schaber, G. G., and Gumerman, G. J.
1969   Infrared scanning images: an archaeological application. Science 164: 712–713.

Schenck, W. E.
1926   The Emeryville shellmound. UC-PAAE 23: 147–282.

Schmalz, R. F.
1960   Flint and the patination of flint artifacts. PPS 26: 44–49.

Schmid, E.
1972   Atlas of animal bones, "Tierknochenatlas." Elsevier, New York.

Schmidt, E. F.
    1927   A stratigraphic study in the Gila Salt region, Arizona. Proc. of National Acad. of Science 13: 291-298.
    1928   Time-relations of prehistoric pottery types in southern Arizona. AMNH-AP 30, Pt. 5.

Schneider, K. A., and Noakes, J. E.
    1970   Site analysis with a mobile archaeological laboratory: microsample extraction and radiocarbon dating. Southeastern Arch. Conference Bull. 13: 82-87.

Schock, J. M.
    1971   Indoor water flotation—a technique for the recovery of archaeological materials. Plains Anthropologist 16(53): 228-231.

Scholtz, J. A.
    1962   What about sifting? Arkansas Archeologist 3(1): 11-13.

Schoute-Vanneck, C. A.
    1960   A chemical method for the relative dating of coastal shell middens. South African Journal of Science 56: 67-70.

Schroeder, D. L., and Ruhl, K. C.
    1968   Metallurgical characteristics of North American prehistoric copper work. A Ant 33: 162-169.

Schulman, E.
    1940   A bibliography of tree-ring analysis. Tree-Ring Bull. 6: 1-12.
    1941   Some propositions in tree-ring analysis. Ecology 22: 193-195.
    1958   Bristlecone pine, oldest known living thing. National Geog. Magazine 113: 353-372.

Schultz, C. B.
    1938   The first Americans. Nat. Hist. 42: 346-356, 378.
———, and Frankfurter, W. D.
    1948   Preliminary report on the Lime Creek sites: new evidence of early man in southwestern Nebraska. Bull. of Univ. of Nebraska State Mus. 3(4), Pt. 2.

Schuyler, R. L.
    1971   The history of American archaeology: an examination of procedure. A Ant 36: 383-409.

Schwarz, G. T.
    1964   Stereoscopic views taken with an ordinary single camera—a new technique for archaelogists. Archaeometry 7: 36-42.
    1967   A simplified chemical test for archaeological field work. Archaeometry 10: 57-63.
———, and Junghans, G.
    1967   A new method for three-dimensional recording of archaeological finds. Archaeometry 10: 64-69.

Scollar, I.
    1962   Electromagnetic prospecting methods in archaeology. Archaeometry 5: 146-153.
    1969   Some techniques for the evaluation of archaeological surveys. World Archaeology 1(1): 77-89.
    1970   Magnetic methods of archeological prospecting—advances in instrumentation and evaluation techniques. Royal Soc. of London, Philos. Trans., Ser. A, 269(1193): 109-119.

Sears, P. B.
    1932   The archaeology of environment in eastern North America. AA 34: 610-622.
    1937   Pollen analysis as an aid in dating cultural deposits in the United States. In G. G. MacCurdy (ed.), Early man (pp. 61-66). Lippincott, Philadelphia.
    1952   Palynology in southern North America, I: Archaeological horizons in the basins of Mexico. Bull. of Geol. Soc. of America 63: 241-246.
———, and Roosma, A.
    1961   A climatic sequence from two Nevada caves. Amer. Journal of Science 259: 669-678.

Sears, W. H.
    1960   Ceramic systems and Eastern archaeology. A Ant 25: 324-329.
    1961   The study of social and religious systems in North American archaeology. Current Anthro. 2: 223-246.

Seborg, R. M., and Inverarity, R. B.
    1962   Conservation of 200-year-old water-logged boats with polyethylene glycol. Studies in Conservation 7: 11-12. (Also in Science 136: 649-650.)

Sellstedt, H., Engstrand, L., and Gejvall, N. G.
    1967   Radiocarbon dating of bone. Nature 213: 415.

Semenov, S. A.
    1964   Prehistoric technology (trans. by M. W. Thompson). Cory, Adams and MacKay, London.

Sense, R. G.
    1973   The use of water and water pumps in archaeological excavations. A Ant 38(2): 218–220.

Service, E.
    1941   Lithic patina as an age criterion. Papers of Michigan Acad. of Science 27, Pt. 4: 553–557.

Setzler, F. M., and Jennings, J. D.
    1941   Peachtree mound and village site. Cherokee County, North Carolina. BAE-B 131.

Shaeffer, J. B.
    1960   The county grid system of site designation. Plains Anthropologist 5: 29–31.

Shafer, H. J.
    1971a   An archaeological reconnaissance of Sanderson Canyon watershed, Texas. TASP-Survey Reports 7.
    1971b   Investigations into south plains prehistory, west central Texas. TASP-P 20.

Shapley, H. (ed.)
    1953   Climatic change: evidence, causes and effects. Harvard Univ. Press, Cambridge.

Shawcross, W.
    1967   An investigation of prehistoric diet and economy on a coastal site at Galatea Bay, New Zealand. PPS 33: 107–131.

Sheets, P. D.
    1973   The pillage of prehistory. A Ant 38(3): 317–320.

Shepard, A. O.
    1956   Ceramics for the archaeologist. CIW-P No. 609.
    1971   Ceramic analysis: the interrelations of methods; the relations of analysts and archaeologist. In R. H. Brill (ed.), Science and archaeology (pp. 165–177). Massachusetts Inst. of Technology Press, Cambridge.

Shepard, F. P.
    1964   Sea level changes in the past 6000 years: possible archaeological significance. Science 143: 574–576.

Shetrone, H. C.
    1930   The mound-builders. Appleton, New York.

Shook, E. M., and Kidder, A. V.
    1952   Mound E-III-3, Kaminalijuyu, Guatemala. CIW-P 596.

Shorer, P.
    1964   A method for the transfer of archaeological soil sections on to a flexible rubber backing. Studies in Conservation 9.

Shutler, R.
    1961   Lost city. Nevada State Mus., Anthro. Papers, No. 5.

———— (ed.)
    1971   Papers from a symposium on Early Man in North America, new developments: 1960–1970. Arctic Anthro. 8(2): 1–91. Madison.

Sierts, W.
    1968   How were rock engravings made? South African Journal of Science 64: 281–285.

Sieveking, G. de, et al.
    1972   Prehistoric flint mines and their identification as sources of raw material. Archaeometry 14: 151–176.

Sigstad, J. S.
    1970   A field test for catlinite. A Ant 35(3): 377–382.

Silverberg, R.
    1963   Sunken history: the story of underwater archaeology. Chilton, Philadelphia.

Simonson, R. W.
    1954   Identification and interpretation of buried soils. Amer. Journal of Science 252: 705–32.

Simmons, H. C.
    1969   Archaeological photography. New York Univ. Press.

Simpson, G. G., Roe, A., and Lewontin, R. C.
    1960   Quantitative zoology. Harcourt, Brace, New York.

Sinex, F. M., and Faris, B.
    1959   Isolation of gelatin from ancient bones. Science 129: 969.

Singer, C., Holmyard, E. J., and Hall, A. R. (eds.)
    1954   A history of technology, Vol. 1. Oxford Univ. Press.

Siniaguin, J. J.
    1943   A method for determining the absolute age of soils. Comptes Rendus de l'Acad. des Sciences de l'URSS
            40: 335–336.

Sisson, E. B.
    1973   First annual report of the Coxcatlan project. Phillips Acad., Andover.

Skinner, S. A.
    1971   Prehistoric settlement of the DeCordova Bend Reservoir, central Texas. TAS-B 42: 149–269.

———, and Bousman, C. B.
    1973   Prehistoric archaeology in the Three-Mile and Sulphur Draw watershed. Arch. Research Program,
            Southern Methodist Univ., Dallas.

Slonim, M. J.
    1960   Sampling in a nutshell. Simon and Schuster, New York.

Smiley, T. L.
    1951   A summary of tree-ring dates from some Southwestern archaeological sites. Univ. of Arizona Bull. 22(4).

———, (ed.)
    1955   Geochronology. Univ. of Arizona Bull. 26(2): 177–195.

Smith, A. L.
    1950   Uaxactun, Guatemala: excavations of 1931–1937. CIW-P No. 588.
    1972   Excavations at Altar de Sacrificios. PM-P 62(2).

———, and Kidder, A. V.
    1943   Explorations in the Motagua Valley, Guatemala. CIW-P No. 546, Contribution 41.

Smith, C. E., et al.
    1966   Bibliography of American archaeological plant remains. Economic Botany 20: 446–460.

Smith, C. S.
    1953   Digging up the Plains Indian's past. Univ. of Kansas Alumni Magazine 52: 4–5. (Reprinted in R. F. Heizer
            [ed.], The archaeologist at work [pp. 131–133], Harper, New York, 1959.)

Smith, F. H., and Gannon, B. L.
    1972   Sectioning of charcoals and dry ancient woods. A Ant 38(4): 468–472.

Smith, G. V.
    1893   The use of flint blades to work pine wood. SI-AR 1893: 601–605

Smith, H. G.
    1948   Two historical archaeological periods in Florida. A Ant 13: 313–319.

Smith, R. E.
    1955   Ceramic sequence at Uaxactun, Guatemala. 2 vols. Middle Amer. Research Inst., Tulane Univ., Publ.
            No. 20.

———, and Gifford, J. C.
    1965   Pottery of the Maya lowlands. In G. R. Willey (ed.), Handbook of Middle American Indians (Vol. 2,
            pp. 498–534). Univ. of Texas Press, Austin.

———, Willey, G. R., and Gifford, J. C.
    1960   The type-variety concept as a basis for the analysis of Maya pottery. A Ant 25: 330–340.

Smith, R. H.
    1970   An approach to the drawing of pottery and small finds for excavation reports. World Archaeology 2(2): 212–228.

Smith, W.
    1952   Kiva mural decorations at Awatovi and Kawaika-a. PM-P 37.

Snow, C. E.
    1948   Indian Knoll skeletons of site Oh-2, Ohio County, Kentucky. Univ. of Kentucky Reports in Anthro. 4(3), Pt. 2.

Sokoloff, V. P., and Carter, G. F.
    1952   Time and trace metals in archaeological sites. Science 116: 1–5.

———, and Lorenzo, J. L.
    1953   Modern and ancient soils at some archaeological sites in the Valley of Mexico. A Ant 19: 50–55.

Solecki, R. S.
    1949   The trinomial classification system (for sites) for West Virginia. West Virginia Archaeologist 1: 5–6.
    1951   Notes on soil analysis and archaeology. A Ant 16: 254–256.
    1957   Practical aerial photography for archaeologists. A Ant 22: 337–351.
    1963   Prehistory in Shanidar Valley, northern Iraq. Science 139: 179–193.

Solheim, G. W., II
    1960   The use of sherd weights and counts in the handling of archaeological data. Current Anthro. 1: 325–329.

Sollberger, J. B.
    1969   The basic tool kit required to make and notch arrow shafts for stone points. TAS-B 40: 232–240.

———, and Hester, T. R.
    1972   Some additional data on the thermal alteration of siliceous stone. Bull., Oklahoma Anthro. Soc. 21: 181–185.

Sonnenfeld, J.
    1962a   Interpreting the function of primitive implements: the celt and the hoe. A Ant 28: 56–65.
    1962b   Prehistoric technology: functional interpretations and geographic implications. Professional Geographer 14: 4–8.

South, S. A.
    1962   A method of cleaning iron artifacts. Southeastern Arch. Conference Newsletter 9: 17–18. Cambridge, Mass.

Spaulding, A. C.
    1951   Recent advances in surveying techniques and their application to archaeology. Univ. of Michigan Anthro. Papers, No. 8: 2–16.
    1953   Statistical techniques for the discovery of artifact types. A Ant 18: 305–313.
    1958   The significance of differences between radiocarbon dates. A Ant 23: 309–311.
    1960   Statistical description and comparison of artifact types. VFPA No. 28: 60–92.
    1973   The concept of artifact type in archaeology. Plateau 45(3): 149–163.

Spence, M. W., and Parsons, J. R.
    1972   Prehispanic obsidian exploitation in central Mexico: a preliminary synthesis. Mus. of Anthro., Univ. of Michigan, Anthro. Papers 45: 1–44.

Spencer, L.
    1974   Replicative experiments in the manufacture and use of a Great Basin atlatl. Ballena Press Publs. in Arch., Ethnology, and Hist., Ramona, Calif. No. 2: 37–82.

Sperry, J. E.
    1968   The Shermer site, 32EM10. Plains Anthropologist, Memoir 5.

Spier, L.
    1916   New data on the Trenton Argillite culture. AA 18: 181–189.
    1917   Outline of chronology of the Zuni ruins. AMNH-AP 18: 209–331.
    1931   N. C. Nelson's stratigraphic technique in the reconstruction of prehistoric sequences in Southwestern America. In S. A. Rice (ed.), Methods in social science (pp. 275–283). Chicago Univ. Press.
    1955   Mohave culture items. Mus. of Northern Arizona, Bull. No. 28. Flagstaff.

Spier, R. F.
    1970   Surveying and mapping: a manual of simplified techniques. Holt, Rinehart and Winston, New York

Spuhler, J. N., and Kluckhohn, C.
    1953   Inbreeding coefficients of the Ramah Navaho population. Human Biology 25: 295–317.

Squier, R. J.
    1953   The manufacture of flint implements by the Indians of northern and central California. UCAS-R 19: 15–44.

Stallings, W. S., Jr.
    1939   Dating prehistoric ruins by tree rings. Laboratory of Anthro., Mus. of New Mexico, General Ser., Bull. 8. Santa Fe.

Staniland, L. N.
    1953   The principles of line illustration with emphasis on the requirements of biological and other scientific workers. Harvard Univ. Press, Cambridge.

Stanislawski, M. B.
    1969   The ethno-archaeology of Hopi pottery making. Plateau 42(1): 27–33.

Stanton, W.
    1965   The scientific approach to the study of man in America. Journal of World Hist. 8: 768–788. UNESCO, New York.

Steele, R. H.
    1930   Experiments in Kaitaho (Ngai-Tahu) methods in drilling. Journal of the Polynesian Soc. 39: 181–188.

Steensberg, A.
    1943   Ancient harvesting implements: a study in archaeology and human geography. Nationalmuseets Skrifter, Arkeologisk-Historisk Raekke 1. Copenhagen.
    1964   A Bronze Age and type from Hama, Syria, intended for rope traction. Berytus 15: 111–139. Copenhagen.

Steggerda, M.
    1941   Maya Indians of Yucatan. CIW-P No. 531.

Stelcl, J., and Malina, J.
    1970   Anwendung der Petrographie in der Archäologie. Folia Facultatis Scientiarum Naturalium, Universitatis Purkynianae Brunensis 11(5). Brno.

Stephenson, R. I.
    1954   Salvage archaeology. Bible Arch. Digest 9(2): 2–11.

Stern, C.
    1960   Principles of human genetics (2nd ed.). Freeman, San Francisco.

Stetson, H. C., and Parker, F. L.
    1942   Mechanical analysis of the sediments and the identification of the foraminifera from the building excavation. In F. Johnson (ed.), The Boylston Street fishweir (pp. 41–44). Papers of R. S. Peabody Foundation for Arch. 2.

Stevenson, D. P., Stross, F. H., and Heizer, R. F.
    1971   An evaluation of x-ray fluorescence analysis as a method for correlating obsidian artifacts with source location. Archaeometry 13: 17–26.

Steward, J. H.
    1929   Petroglyphs of California and adjoining states. UC-PAAE 24: 47–238.
    1937   Ancient caves of the Great Salt Lake region. BAE-B 116: 9–10, 91–93, 107.
    1941   Archaeological reconnaissance of southern Utah. BAE-B 128: 277–356.
    1942   The direct-historical approach to archaeology. A Ant 7: 337–343.
    1944   Re archaeological tools and jobs. A Ant 10: 99–100.
    1949   Cultural causality and law: a trial formulation of the development of early civilizations. A Ant 51: 2–27.
    1954   Types of types. AA 56: 54–57.

————, et al.
    1955   Irrigation civilizations: a comparative study. Pan Amer. Union, Social Science Monographs, 1. Washington, D.C.

Stewart, O. C.
1947a   Objectives and methods for an archaeological survey. Southwestern Lore 12: 62–75.
1947b   Field manual for an archaeological survey. Southwestern Lore 13: 1–11.
Stewart, T. D.
1934   Sequence of epiphyseal union, third molar eruption, and suture closure in Eskimos and American Indians. AJPA 19: 433–452.
1954   Sex determination of the skeleton by guess and by measurement. AJPA 12: 385–392.
———, and Trotter, M.
1954   Basic readings on the identification of human skeletons: estimation of age. Wenner-Gren Foundation for Anthro. Research, New York.
Stirling, M. W., Rainey, F., and Stirling, M. W., Jr.
1960   Electronics and archaeology. Expedition 2(4): 19–29.
Stock, C.
1936   The succession of mammalian forms within the period in which human remains are known to occur in America. Amer. Naturalist 70: 324–331.
Stone, E. H.
1924   Stones of Stonehenge. Scott, London.
Story, D. A.
1968   Archaeological investigations at two central Texas Gulf Coast sites. State Building Commission, Arch. Program, Report 13.
Straffin, D.
1971   A device for vertical archaeological photography. Plains Anthropologist 16(53): 232–243.
Strandberg, C. H., and Tomlinson, R.
1969   Photoarchaeological analysis of Potomac River fish traps. A Ant 34(3): 312–319.
Strong, W. D.
1935   An introduction to Nebraska archaeology. SI-MC 93(10).
1940a   From history to prehistory in the northern Great Plains. SI-MC 100: 353–394.
1940b   What is a Pre-Amerindian? Science 91: 594–596.
1948   Cultural epochs and refuse stratigraphy in Peruvian archaeology. In W. C. Bennett (assembler), Re-appraisal of Peruvian archaeology (pp. 93–102). SAA-M 4.
———, and Corbett, J. M.
1943   A ceramic sequence at Pachacamac. Columbia Studies in Arch. and Ethnology 1(2).
———, and Evans, C.
1952   Cultural stratigraphy in the Virú Valley, northern Peru; the formative and florescent epochs. Columbia Studies in Arch. and Ethnology 4.
Stross, F. H.
1960   Authentication of antique stone objects by physical and chemical means. Analytical Chemistry 32: 17A–24A.
1973   Chemistry digs the past. The Vortex 34(5): 110–112. Berkeley.
——— (ed.)
1971   The application of the physical sciences to archaeology. UC-CARF 12.
———, et al.
in
press   Chemical and archaeological studies of Mesoamerican obsidian. In R. E. Taylor (ed.), Advances in obsidian glass studies: archaeological and geochemical perspectives. Noyes Press, Park Ridge, N.J.
Struever, S.
1968a   Flotation techniques for the recovery of small-scale archaeological remains. A Ant 33(3): 353–362.
1968b   Problems, methods and organization: a disparity in the growth of archeology. In B. Meggers (ed.), Anthropological archeology in the Americas (pp. 131–151). Anthro. Soc. of Washington, Washington, D.C.
1968c   Woodland subsistence-settlement systems in the Lower Illinois Valley. In S. R. Binford and L. R. Binford (eds.), New perspectives in archeology (pp. 285–312). Aldine, Chicago.
1971   Comments on archaeological data requirements and research strategy. A Ant 36: 9–19.

Stuckenrath, R.
1965   On the care and feeding of radiocarbon dates. Archaeology 18: 277–281.

Stuiver, M., and Suess, H.
1966   On the relationship between radiocarbon dates and true sample ages. Radiocarbon 8: 534–540.

Sturtevant, W. C.
1958   Anthropology as a career. SI Publ. 4343.

Suess, H.
1967   Bristlecone pine calibration of the radiocarbon time scale from 4100 B.C. to 1500 B.C. Proc. of Symposium on Radioactive Dating and Methods of Low-Level Counting. Monaco (IAEA, Vienna).
1970   Bristlecone pine calibration of the radiocarbon time scale 5400 B.C. to present. In I. U. Olsson (ed.), Radiocarbon variations and absolute chronology (pp. 303–312). Proc., Twelfth Nobel Symposium, Uppsala, 1969. Wiley, New York.

Suhm, D. A., Krieger, A. D., and Jelks, E. B.
1954   An introductory handbook of Texas archaeology. TAS-B 25.

Sutcliffe, A.
1970   Spotted hyena: crusher, gnawer, digester, and collector of bones. Nature 227: 1110–1113.

Suzuki, H.
1935   Chronological study of prehistoric shell-mounds around the bay of Tokyo based upon the changes in the form of clam shells. Shizengaku Zasshi 7: 51–94. (In Japanese.)

Suzuki, M., and Watanabe, N.
1968   Fission tract dating of archaeological materials from Japan. Proc., 8th International Congress of Anthro. and Ethnological Sciences 3: 169–171.

Swadesh, M.
1953   Archaeological and linguistic chronology of Indo-European. AA 55: 349–352.
1959   Linguistics as an instrument of prehistory. SWJA 15: 20–35.
1960   Estudios sobre lengua y cultura. Acta Antropológica, la Epoca 2(2). Mexico City.
1962   Linguistic relations across Bering Strait. AA 64: 1262–1291.

Swanson, E. H., Jr.
1963   Reconnaissance and the archaeological survey system of the University Museum. Occasional Papers of Idaho State Univ. Mus., No. 12.

Swanton, J. R.
1939   Final report of the United States De Soto Expedition Commission. 76th Congress, 1st Sess., House Doc. No. 71.

Swartz, B. K., Jr.
1963   Aluminum powder: a technique for photographically recording petroglyphs. A Ant 28: 400–401.
n.d.   Archaeological field manual. (Mimeographed; refers to Indiana archaeology.)

Swauger, J. L., and Wallace, B. L.
1964   An experiment in skinning with Egyptian Paleolithic and Neolithic stone implements. Pennsylvania Archaeologist 34: 1–7.

Switsur, V. R.
1973   The radiocarbon calendar recalibrated. Antiquity 47 (186): 131–137.

Tamers, N., and Pearson, F.
1965   The validity of radiocarbon dates on bone. Nature 208: 1053–1056.

Tanner, J. M.
1964   Human growth and constitution. In G. A. Harrison et al., Human biology (pp. 299–397). Oxford Univ. Press.

Tappen, N. C., and Peske, G. R.
1970   Weathering cracks and split-line patterns in archaeological bone. A Ant 35: 383–386.

Taylor, D., and Rouse, I.
1955   Linguistic and archaeological time depth in the West Indies. International Journal of Amer. Linguistics 21: 105–115.

Taylor, J.
1965   Marine archaeology: developments during sixty years in the Mediterranean. Crowell, New York.

Taylor, R. E., and Berger, R.
1967   Radiocarbon content of marine shells from the Pacific coasts of Central and South America. Science 158: 1180–1182.

Taylor, W. W.
1948   A study of archaeology. AAA-M 69.
1961   Archaeology and language in western North America. A Ant 27: 71–81.
1966   Archaic cultures adjacent to the northeastern frontiers of Mesoamerica. In G. F. Ekholm and G. R. Willey (eds.), Handbook of Middle American Indians (Vol. 4, pp. 59–94). Univ. of Texas Press, Austin.
1972   Old wine and new skins: a contemporary parable. In M. Leone (ed.), Contemporary archaeology (pp. 28–33). Southern Illinois Univ. Press, Carbondale.

——— (ed.)
1957   The identification of non-artifactual archaeological materials. National Acad. of Sciences, National Research Council, Publ. 565.

———, and Gonzales Rul, F.
1961   An archaeological reconnaissance behind the Diablo Dam, Coahuila, Mexico. TAS-B 31: 153–165.

Tellefsen, O.
1970   A new theory of pyramid building. Nat. Hist. 79: 10–14.

Tello, J. C.
1942   Origen y dessarrollo de las civilizaciones prehistoricas andinas. Actas y Trabajo Científicos, Lima.

Thellier, E., and Thellier, O.
1959   Sur l'intensité du champ magnétique terrestre dans le passé historique et géologique. Annales Géophysiques 15: 285–376.

Thieme, F., and Schull, W. J.
1957   Sex determination from the skeleton. Human Biology 29: 242–273.

Thomas, D. H.
1969a   Great Basin hunting patterns: a quantitative method for treating faunal remains. A Ant 34: 392–401.
1969b   Regional sampling in archaeology: a pilot Great Basin research design. Annual Report, UCLA Arch. Survey for 1969: 87–100.
1971   On distinguishing natural from cultural bone in archaeological sites. A Ant 36: 366–371.
1974   Predicting the past: an introduction to anthropological archaeology. Holt, Rinehart and Winston, New York.

Thomas, H. H.
1923   The source of the stones of Stonehenge. Antiquaries Journal 3: 239–260.

Thompson, J. E. S.
1941   A coordination of the history of Chichen Itza with ceramic sequences in central Mexico. Revista Mexicana de Estudios Antropologicos 5: 97–111.
1950   Maya hieroglyphic writing. CIW-P No. 589.

Thomsen, R. H. G.
1954   A note on Stonehenge. In C. Singer, E. J. Holmyard, and A. R. Hall (eds.), A history of technology (Vol. 1, pp. 490–494). Oxford Univ. Press.

Thorneycroft, W.
1933   Observations on hut circles near the eastern border of Perthshire, north of Blaigowrie. Proc. of Soc. of Antiquaries of Scotland 67: 187–208.

Thorp, J.
1949   Interrelations of Pleistocene geology and soil science. Bull. of Geol. Soc. of America 60: 1517–1526.

Throckmorton, P., and Bullitt, J. M.
1963   Underwater surveys in Greece: 1962. Expedition 5: 17–23.

Tilton, G. R., and Hart, S. R.
1963   Geochronology. Science 140: 357–366.

Tite, M. S.
    1972   Methods of physical examination in archaeology. Seminar Press, London and New York.

Todd, T. W.
    1920–21   Age changes in the pubic bone. AJPA 3: 285–334; 4: 1–70, 407–424.

———, and Lyon, D. W.
    1925   Ectocranial suture closure. AJPA 8: 23–47, 149–168.

Tolstoy, P.
    1958   Surface survey of the northern Valley of Mexico: the Classic and post-Classic periods. Amer. Philos.
              Soc., Trans. 48, Pt. 5.

Toulmin, S., and Goodfield, J.
    1965   The discovery of time. Harper and Row, New York.

Treganza, A. E.
    1959   Salvage archaeology in the Trinity Reservoir area, northern California: field season, 1958. UCAS-R 46.

———, and Cook, S. F.
    1948   The quantitative investigation of aboriginal sites: complete excavation with physical and archaeological
              analysis of a single mound. A Ant 13: 287–297.

Trigger, B. G.
    1970   Aims in prehistoric archaeology. Antiquity 44: 26–37.

Troike, R. C.
    1957   Time and types in archaeological analysis: the Brainerd-Robinson technique. TAS-B 28: 269–284.

Trotter, M., and Gleser, G. C.
    1958   A re-evaluation of estimation of stature based on measurements of stature taken during life and of long
              bones after death. AJPA 16: 79–123.

Tugby, D. J.
    1958   A typological analysis of axes and choppers from southeast Australia. A Ant 24: 24–33.
    1965   Archaeological objectives and statistical methods: a frontier in archaeology. A Ant 31(1): 1–16.

Tuggle, H. D.
    1972   Review of P. J. Watson, S. A. LeBlanc, and C. L. Redman, "Explanation in archeology: an explicitly
              scientific approach." Philosophy of Science 39(4): 564–566.

Tuohy, D.
    1963   Archaeological survey in southwestern Idaho and northern Nevada. Nevada State Mus. Anthro. Papers,
              No. 8.

Turner, C. G.
    1963   Petrographs of the Glen Canyon region. Mus. of Northern Arizona, Bull. 38. Flagstaff.

———, and Lofgren, L.
    1966   Household size of prehistoric Western Pueblo Indians. SWJA 22: 117–132.

Tuthill, C., and Allanson, A. A.
    1954   Ocean-bottom artifacts. SM-M 28: 222–232.

Ucko, P. J., Tringham, R., and Dimbleby, G. W. (eds.)
    1972   Man, settlement and urbanism. Duckworth, London.

Uerpmann, H.-P.
    1973   Animal bone finds and economic archaeology: a critical study of "osteo-archaeological" method. World
              Archaeology 4(3): 307–322.

Uhle, M.
    1903   Pachacamac. Dept. of Arch., Univ. of Pennsylvania.
    1907   The Emeryville shellmound. UC-PAAE 7: 1–106.

U.N. Economic Commission for Asia and the Far East
    1961   Earthmoving by manual labour and machines. ST/ECAFE/SER. F/17. Bangkok.

Valliant, G. C.
    1935   Excavations at El Arbolillo. AMNH-AP 35, Pt. 2.
    1938   Correlation of archaeological and historical sequence in the Valley of Mexico. AA 40: 535–578.

Vallois, H. V.
1960   Vital statistics in prehistoric populations as determined from archaeological data. VFPA No. 28: 181–222.

van der Merwe, N. J., and Stein, P. H.
1972   Soil chemistry of post molds and rodent burrows: identification without excavation. A Ant 37: 245–254.

Van Riet Lowe, C.
1954   Notes on the drawing of stone implements. South African Arch. Bull. 9(33): 30–33.

Vansina, J.
1961   Oral tradition: a study in historical methodology. Aldine, Chicago.

Van Stone, J. W.
1968   Tikchik village, a nineteenth century riverine community in southwestern Alaska. FMNH-Fieldiana 56(3).

———, and Townsend, J. B.
1970   Kijik, an historic Tanaina settlement. FMNH-Fieldiana 59.

Varner, D. M.
1968   The nature of non-buried archeological data: problems in northeastern Mexico. TAS-B 38: 51–65.

Vértes, L.
1965   "Lunar calendar" from the Hungarian Upper Paleolithic. Science 149: 855–856.

Vescelius, G.
1960   Archaeological sampling: a problem in statistical inference. In G. E. Dole and R. L. Carneiro (eds.), Essays in the science of culture (pp. 457–470). Crowell, New York.

Vinnicombe, P.
1963   Proposed scheme for standard representation of color in black-and-white illustrations for publication. South African Arch. Bull. 18(70): 49–50.

Vinton, K. W.
1962   Carbon-dated ocean level changes offer a new system of correlating archaeological data. Atken des 34. Internationalen Amerikanistenkongresses, Wien, 1960: 390–395.

Voce, E.
1951   Bronze casting in ancient molds. Pitt Rivers Mus., Oxford Univ., Occasional Papers in Technology, No. 4.

Wainwright, F. T.
1962   Archaeology and place-names and history: an essay on problems of co-ordination. Routledge and Kegan Paul, London.

Wakeling, A. F.
1912   Forged Egyptian antiquities. A. and C. Black, London.

Walker, E. F.
1947   Excavation of a Yokuts Indian cemetery. Kern County Hist. Soc., Bakersfield, Calif.

Wallace, B., and Dobzhansky, T.
1967   Genes in Mendelian populations. In N. Korn and F. Thompson (eds.), Human evolution (pp. 21–33). Holt, Rinehart and Winston, New York.

Wallace, W., and Taylor, E. S.
1952   Excavation of Sis-13, a rock-shelter in Siskiyou County, California. UCAS-R 15: 13–39.

Wallis, F. S.
1955   Petrology as an aid to prehistoric and medieval archaeology. Endeavor 14: 146–151.

Wallis, W. D.
1945   Inference of relative age of culture traits from magnitude of distribution. SWJA 1: 142–160.

Ward, G. K.
1974   A systematic approach to the definition of sources of raw material. Archaeometry 16: 41–53.

Warren, S. H.
1914   The experimental investigation of flint fracture and its application to problems of human implements. JRAI 44: 412–450.
1923   Sub-soil pressure flaking. Proc., Geol. Assoc. 34: 153–175.

Washburn, S. L.
    1948   Sex differences in the pubic bone. AJPA, n.s., 6: 199–207.
    1951   The new physical anthropology. Trans., New York Acad. of Science 13(7): 298–304.

Wasley, W. W.
    1957   The archaeological survey of the Arizona State Museum. Arizona State Mus., Univ. of Arizona, Tucson.

Watanabe, H.
    1949   Natural fracture of pebbles from the fossil-bearing Pleistocene deposits near Akashi. Zinruigaku Zassi 60: 121–142. Tokyo.
    1959   The direction of remanent magnetism of baked earth and its application for chronology for anthropology and archaeology in Japan: an introduction to geomagnetochronology. Journal of Faculty of Science, Univ. of Tokyo, Section 5, Anthro. 2, Pt. 1.
    1964   The Ainu: a study of ecology and the system of social solidarity between man and nature in relation to group structure. Journal of Faculty of Science, Univ. of Tokyo, Section 5, Anthro. 2, Pt. 6.

Watanabe, N., and Suzuki, M.
    1969   Fission track dating of archaeological glass materials from Japan. Nature 222: 1057–1058.

Waterbolk, H. T.
    1971   Working with radiocarbon dates. PPS 37, Pt. 2: 15–33.

Waters, J. H.
    1962   Animals used as food by Late Archaic and Woodland cultural groups in New England. Science 137: 283–284.

Watson, J. P. N.
    1972   Fragmentation analysis of animal bone samples from archaeological sites. Archaeometry 14: 221–228.

Watson, P. J., LeBlanc, S. A., and Redman, C. L.
    1971   Explanation in archeology: an explicitly scientific approach. Columbia Univ. Press, New York.

Watson, W.
    1950   Flint implements, an account of Stone Age techniques and cultures. British Mus., London.

Wauchope, R.
    1950   A tentative sequence of pre-Classic ceramics in Middle America. Middle Amer. Research Inst., Tulane Univ., Publ. 15: 211–250.

———— (ed.)
    1956   Seminars in archaeology: 1955. A Ant, Memoir 2.

Weaver, J., and Stross, F.
    1965   Analysis by x-ray fluorescence of some American obsidians. UC-CARF 1: 89–93.

Webb, C. H.
    1959   The Belcher Mound, a stratified Caddoan site in Caddo Parish, Louisiana. SAA-M 16.

Webb, W. S.
    1939   An archaeological survey of Wheeler Basin on the Tennessee River in northern Alabama. BAE-B 122.
    1946   The Indian Knoll: site Oh-2, Ohio County, Kentucky. Reports in Arch. and Anthro., Univ. of Kentucky 4: 115–365.

————, and De Jarnette, D. L.
    1942   Archaeological survey of Pickwick Basin in the adjacent portions of the states of Alabama, Mississippi and Tennessee. BAE-B 129.

————, and Funkhouser, W. D.
    1932   Archaeological survey of Kentucky. Reports in Arch. and Anthro., Univ. of Kentucky 2.

————, and Haag, W. G.
    1939   The Chiggerville site. Reports in Arch. and Anthro., Univ. of Kentucky 4: 5–62.

Weber, J. N., and La Rocque, A.
    1963   Isotope ratios in marine mollusk shells after prolonged contact with flowing fresh water. Science 142: 1666.

Webster, G.
    1963   Practical archaeology. Adam and Black, London.

Webster, W. J. E.
  1962   Techniques of field photography for archaeological purposes. Oceania 33: 139–142.
  1966   Ultra-violet photography of Australian rock paintings. Antiquity 40: 144.
Wedel, W. R.
  1936   An introduction to Pawnee archaeology. BAE-B 112.
  1938   The direct historical approach to Pawnee archaeology. SI-MC 97, No. 7.
  1941   Archaeological investigations at Buena Vista Lake, Kern County, California. BAE-B 130.
  1951   The use of earth-moving machinery in archaeological investigations. Univ. of Michigan Papers 8: 17–28.
  1959   An introduction to Kansas archaeology. BAE-B 174.
  1961   Prehistoric man on the Great Plains. Univ. of Oklahoma Press, Norman.
Weide, D. L., and Webster, G. D.
  1967   Ammonium chloride powder used in the photography of artifacts. A Ant 32: 104–105.
Weigand, P. C.
  1970   Huichol ceremonial reuse of a fluted point. A Ant 35(3): 365–367.
Weiner, J. S.
  1955   The Piltdown forgery. Oxford Univ. Press.
Wells, C.
  1960   A study of cremation. Antiquity 34: 29–37.
  1964   Bones, bodies and disease. Thames and Hudson, London.
Wells, P. V.
  1966   Late Pleistocene vegetation and degree of pluvial climatic change in the Chihuahuan Desert. Science 153: 970–976.
———, and Jorgensen, C.
  1964   Pleistocene wood rat middens and climatic change in the Mohave Desert: a record of juniper wood-lands. Science 143: 1171–1173.
Wendorf, F. (ed.)
  1961   Paleoecology of the Llano Estacado. Fort Burgwin Research Center, Publ. No. 1. Univ. of New Mexico Press. Albuquerque.
  1962   A guide for salvage archaeology. Mus. of New Mexico Press, Santa Fe.
  1968   The prehistory of Nubia. Southern Methodist Univ., Contributions in Anthro. 2.
Werlhof, J. C. von
  1965   Rock art of Owens Valley, UCAS-R 65.
Werner, S. B.
  1974   Coccidioidomycosis among archaeology students: recommendations for prevention. A Ant 39: 367–370.
———, et al.
  1972   An epidemic of Coccidioidomycosis among archeology students in northern California. New England Journal of Medicine 286: 507–512.
Wertime, T. A.
  1973   The beginnings of metallurgy: a new look. Science 182: 875–877.
Wesolowsky, A. B.
  1973   The skeletons of Lerna Hollow. Hesperia 42(3): 340–351.
Western, A. C.
  1963   Wood and charcoal in antiquity. In D. R. Brothwell and E. S. Higgs (eds.), Science in archaeology (pp. 150–158). Thames and Hudson, London.
Weymouth, J. W.
  1973   X-ray diffraction of prehistoric pottery. A Ant 38(3): 339–344.
Whallon, R.
  1972   A new approach to pottery typology. A Ant 37(1): 13–33.
Wheat, J. B.
  1965   Keeping the record straight. Southwestern Lore 22: 3–5.
  1972   The Olsen Chubbuck site, a Paleo-Indian bison kill. SAA-M No. 26.

Wheeler, R. E. M.
 1950   What matters in archaeology? Antiquity 24: 122–130.
 1953   An Early Iron Age "beach head" at Lulworth, Dorset. Antiquaries Journal 33: 1–13.
 1954   Archaeology from the earth. Oxford, Clarendon Press.

White, J. P.
 1967   Ethno-archaeology in New Guinea: two examples. Mankind 6(9): 409–414.

White, T. E.
 1953   Observations on the butchering technique of some aboriginal peoples: 2. A Ant 19: 160–164.

Whitney, M. I., and Dietrich, R. V.
 1973   Ventifact sculpture by windblown dust. Geol. Soc. of America, Bull. 84: 2561–2582.

Whittlesey, J.
 1966   Photogrammetry for the excavator. Archaeology 19: 273–276.
 1967   Balloon over Sardis. Archaeology 20: 67–68.

Wiertelak, J., and Czarnecki, J.
 1935   Paraffin-impregnated wood. Industrial and Engineering Chemistry 27: 543–547.

Wilcox, R. C.
 1965   Volcanic-ash chronology. In H. E. Wright and D. G. Frey (eds.), The Quaternary of the United States (pp. 809–816). Princeton Univ. Press.

Wilford, L. A.
 1954   Archaeological method in the Eastern United States. In R. F. Spencer (ed.), Method and perspective in anthropology (pp. 171–191). Univ. of Minnesota Press, Minneapolis.

Wilkinson, K.
 1968   A method of preparing translucent artifacts for photography. Reporter, Nevada Arch. Survey 2(2): 10–11.

Will, G. F., and Spinden, H. J.
 1906   The Mandans, a study of their culture, archaeology and language. PM-P 3(4).

Willey, G. R.
 1939   Ceramic stratigraphy in a Georgia village site. A Ant 5: 140–147.
 1945   Horizon styles and pottery traditions in Peruvian archaeology. A Ant 11: 49–56.
 1948   A functional analysis of "Horizon styles" in Peruvian archaeology. In W. C. Bennett (assembler), A reappraisal of Peruvian archaeology (pp. 8–15). SAA-M No. 4.
 1949   Archaeology of the Florida Gulf Coast. SI-MC 113.
 1953   Prehistoric settlement patterns in the Viru Valley, Peru. BAF-B 153.
 1961   Volume in pottery and the selection of samples. A Ant 27: 230–231.
 1966   An introduction to American archaeology, Vol. 1. Prentice-Hall, Englewood Cliffs, N.J.
 1968   One hundred years of American archaeology. In J. O. Brew (ed.), One hundred years of anthropology (pp. 29–53). Harvard Univ. Press, Cambridge.

———— (ed.)
 1974   Archaeological researches in retrospect. Winthrop, Cambridge, Mass.

————, and Corbett, J. M.
 1954   Early Ancon and early Supe culture. Columbia Studies in Arch. and Ethnology 3. Columbia Univ.

————, and McGimsey, C. R.
 1954   The Monagrillo culture of Panama. PM-P 49(2).

————, and Phillips, P.
 1955   Method and theory in American archaeology II: historical development interpretation. AA 57: 723–819.
 1958   Method and theory in American archaeology. Univ. of Chicago Press.

————, and Sabloff, J. A.
 1974   A history of American archaeology. Freeman, San Francisco.

Williams, D.
 1973   Flotation at Siraf. Antiquity 47(188): 288–292.

Williams, H.
 1952   Geologic observations on the ancient human footprints near Managua, Nicaragua. CIW-P 596 (Contributions to Amer. Anthro. and Hist. No. 52).

1956   Petrographic notes on tempers of pottery from Chupicuaro Cerro del Tepalcate and Ticomán, Mexico. *In* M. N. Porter, Excavations at Chupicuaro, Guanajuato, Mexico (pp. 576-580). Amer. Philos. Soc. Trans. 46, Pt. 5.

————, and Heizer, R. F.
1965a   Sources of rocks used in Olmec monuments. UC-CARF 1: 1-40.
1965b   Geological notes on the ruins of Mitla and other Oaxacan sites. UC-CARF 1: 41-54.

Williams, R. B. G.
1973   Frost and the works of man. Antiquity 47: 19-31.

Williams, S.
1972   Ripping off the past. Saturday Review 55(40): 44-53.

Willis, E. H.
1963   Radiocarbon dating. *In* D. R. Brothwell and E. S. Higgs (eds.), Science in archaeology (pp. 35-56). Thames and Hudson, London.

Wilmsen, E. N.
1965   An outline of early man studies in the United States. A Ant 31: 172-192.
1968   Functional analysis of flaked stone artifacts. A Ant 33(2): 156-161.

Wilson, G. L.
1917   Agriculture of the Hidatsa Indians: an Indian interpretation. Univ. of Minnesota, Studies in Social Sciences, No. 9.

Wilson, J. A.
1942   Archaeology as a tool in humanistic and social studies. Journal of Near Eastern Studies 1: 3-9.

Wilson, L. R.
1949   A microfossil analysis of the lower peat and associated sediments at the John Hancock fishweir site. *In* F. Johnson (ed.), The Boylston Street fishweir II (pp. 84-98). Papers of R. S. Peabody Foundation for Arch. 4(1).

Wilson, R. L.
1972   Elementary forest surveying and mapping. Oregon State Univ. Bookstores, Corvallis.

Winter, J.
1971   Thermoluminescent dating of pottery. *In* H. N. Michael and E. K. Ralph (eds.), Dating techniques for the archaeologist (pp. 118-151). Mass. Inst. of Technology Press, Cambridge.

Wise, E. N.
1955   The C-14 age determination method. *In* T. L. Smiley (ed.), Geochronology (pp. 170-176). Univ. of Arizona Bull. Ser., No. 26.

Wissler, C.
1916   The application of statistical methods to the data on the Trenton Argillite culture. AA 18: 190-197.
1923   State archaeological surveys: suggestions in method and technique. National Research Council.

Witthoft, J.
1955   Worn stone tools from southeastern Pennsylvania. Pennsylvania Archaeologist 25(1): 16-31.

Wolff, E. G.
1960   Pottery restoration. Curator 3: 75-87.

Wood, F. D.
1945   Color photography applied to stratigraphy. Connecticut Acad. of Arts and Science, Trans. 36: 879-882.

Wood, W. R.
1971   Biesterfeldt: a post-contact coalescent site on the northeastern plains. Smithsonian Contributions to Anthro. 15.

———— (ed.)
1969   Two house sites in the central plains: an experiment in archaeology. Plains Anthropologist, Memoir 6.

Woodall, J. N.
1968   The uses of statistics in archaeology: a bibliography. TAS-B 38: 25-38.

Woodbury, R. B.
    1954   Prehistoric stone implements from northeastern Arizona. PM-P 34.
    1960   Nels C. Nelson and chronological archaeology. A Ant 25: 400–401.

Woodward, A.
    1965   Indian trade goods. Oregon Arch. Soc., Publ. No. 2. Portland.

Wooley, L.
    1954   Digging up the past. Benn, London.

Word, J. H., and Douglas, C. L.
    1970   Excavations at Baker Cave, Val Verde County, Texas. Texas Memorial Mus. Bull. 16.

Wormington, H. M.
    1957   Ancient man in North America (4th ed.). Denver Mus. of Natural History.

Wright, G. A.
    1969   Obsidian analyses and prehistoric Near Eastern trade: 7500–3500 B.C. Mus. of Anthro., Univ. of Michigan, Anthro. Papers, No. 37.
    1974   Archaeology and trade. Addison-Wesley Module in Anthro. 49. Reading, Mass.

Wright, H. E., and Frey, D. G. (eds.)
    1965   The Quaternary of the United States. Princeton Univ. Press.

Wright, R. H.
    1971   Map showing location of samples dated by radiocarbon methods in the San Francisco Bay region. USGS, San Francisco Bay Region Environment and Resources Planning Study, Misc. Field Studies Map MF-317, Basic Data Contribution 33.

Wylie, H. G.
    1974   Promontory pegs as elements of Great Basin subsistence technology. Tebiwa 16: 46–67.

Wynne, E. J., and Tylecote, R. F.
    1958   An experimental investigation into primitive iron smelting techniques. Journal of Iron and Steel Inst. 191: 339–348.

Yao, T. C., and Stross, F. H.
    1965   The use of analysis by x-ray fluorescence in the study of coins. Amer. Journal of Arch. 69: 154–155.

Yarnell, R. A.
    1964   Aboriginal relationships between culture and plant life in the Upper Great Lakes region. Mus., of Anthro., Univ. of Michigan, Anthro. Papers, No. 23.
    1965   Implications of distinctive flora on Pueblo ruins. AA 67: 662–674.

Young, K. S.
    1970   A technique for illustrating pottery designs. A Ant 35(4): 488–491.

Zeuner, F. E.
    1948   Recent work on chronology. Advancement of science 4: 333–335.
    1950   Archaeology and geology. Southeastern Naturalist and Antiquarian 55: 5–16.
    1958   Dating the past (4th ed., rev.). Hutchinson, London.

Ziegler, A. C.
    1963   Unmodified mammal and bird remains from Deer Creek Cave, Elko County, Nevada. In M. E. Shutler and R. Shutler, Jr. (eds.), Deer Creek Cave (pp. 15–24). Nevada State Mus. Anthro. Papers, No. 11.
    1973   Inference from prehistoric faunal remains. Addison-Wesley Module in Anthro. 43. Reading, Mass.

Zimmerman, D. W.
    1971   Thermoluminescent dating using fine grains from pottery. Archaeometry 13: 29–52.

——, and Huxtable, J.
    1971   Thermoluminescent dating of Upper Paleolithic fried clay from Dolni Vestonice. Archaeometry 13: 53–57.

Zingg, R. M.
    1940   Report on archaeology of southern Chihuahua. Contributions, Univ. of Denver Center of Latin Amer. Studies, No. 1.

Zubrow, E. B. W.
    1971   Carrying capacity and dynamic equilibrium in the prehistoric Southwest. A Ant 36(2): 127–138.

INDEX OF AUTHORS CITED

SUBJECT INDEX

References to illustrations are printed in **boldface** type.